THE
P...ECT
W...OUT

FT Prentice Hall
FINANCIAL TIMES

In an increasingly competitive world, we believe it's quality of thinking that will give you the edge – an idea that opens new doors, a technique that solves a problem, or an insight that simply makes sense of it all. The more you know, the smarter and faster you can go.

That's why we work with the best minds in business and finance to bring cutting-edge thinking and best learning practice to a global market.

Under a range of leading imprints, including *Financial Times Prentice Hall*, we create world-class print publications and electronic products bringing our readers knowledge, skills and understanding which can be applied whether studying or at work.

To find out more about Pearson Education publications, or tell us about the books you'd like to find, you can visit us at **www.pearsoned.co.uk**

THE
PROJECT
WORKOUT

FOURTH EDITION

The ultimate handbook of project and programme management

ROBERT BUTTRICK

FT Prentice Hall
FINANCIAL TIMES

An imprint of **Pearson Education**
Harlow, England • London • New York • Boston • San Francisco • Toronto
Sydney • Tokyo • Singapore • Hong Kong • Seoul • Taipei • New Delhi
Cape Town • Madrid • Mexico City • Amsterdam • Munich • Paris • Milan

Pearson Education Limited
Edinburgh Gate
Harlow CM20 2JE
Tel: +44 (0)1279 623623
Fax: +44 (0)1279 431059
Website: www.pearsoned.co.uk

First published in Great Britain in 1997
Second edition published 2000
Third edition published 2005
This fourth edition published 2009

© Robert Buttrick 1997, 2009

The right of Robert Buttrick to be identified as author
of this work has been asserted by him in accordance
with the Copyright, Designs and Patents Act 1988.

ISBN: 978-0-273-72389-9

British Library Cataloguing in Publication Data
A CIP catalogue record for this book is available from the British Library.

Library of Congress Cataloging in Publication Data
A catalog record for this book is available from the Library of Congress.

10 9 8 7 6 5 4 3 2 1
13 12 11 10 09

Typeset by 30
Printed and bound in Great Britain by Ashford Colour Press Ltd, Gosport, Hants

The Publisher's policy is to use paper manufactured from sustainable forests.

About the Author

Robert Buttrick has worked in a number of the world's most turbulent industrial sectors including telecommunications and systems engineering. He was accountable for creating and running a project-based framework for managing change within Cable and Wireless, enabling it to plan for, and develop, new systems, products, services and capabilities to meet the ever growing needs of its customers. Prior to this he was a member of the management team which was accountable for managing the company's UK residential sector, acting as coach to sponsors and project managers, enabling them to succeed in a wide range of business projects. More recently he has been engaged on a £1bn programme to implement health systems in the UK.

Before taking up his corporate career in 1993, Robert was with PA Consulting Group, a management and technology consultancy. There, he specialised in business-led project management, advising clients such as Lloyds TSB Bank, National Rivers Authority, Property Services Agency, Avon Industrial Polymers, National Westminster Bank and RHM.

His early career was as a civil engineer. After graduating from the University of Liverpool with a first class honours degree, he joined Gibb Ltd, who provide consulting, design and management services for infra-structure projects worldwide. He has lived and worked in countries as diverse as Kenya, Mauritius, Yemen, Senegal and Sudan on the evalua-tion, design and supervision of a number of marine and water resource projects. He has also worked with the World Bank in Washington DC on investment appraisals for major development projects. Following this, he became Gibb's manager for marketing strategy and analysis.

Robert is a Master of Business Administration (Henley Management College), a Member of the Chartered Institute of Marketing and a Member of the Institution of Civil Engineers.

His main pastime is watercolour painting. His one, unknown, claim to fame is that he once stopped a column of Russian tanks dead in its tracks.

Robert can be contacted via his website, projectworkout.com.

FOR RHODRI,
my son, who, when he was six years old said,
'Dad, if you have too much work, do it in sections
and then you'll have time to play with me.'

Contents

Part Three: Dealing With Many Projects

Part Five: Implementing the Framework

List of Project Workouts

Foreword

The forward progress of organisations has always depended heavily on the management of projects. New plants, new products, new organisations, new methods, new ventures – all required dedicated teams working to strict timetables and separate budgets. But today there's a vital difference. The project management mode has broadened and evolved to the point where managers may spend as much time in interdisciplinary, cross-functional, interdepartmental project teams as they do in their normal posts.

Many factors have contributed to this unstoppable development – among them the increased complexity of all businesses, the closer inter-relationships within organisations and with customers and suppliers outside, and the mounting pressure for speed. The latter demands synchronous working. Organisations can no longer afford to play pass-the-parcel, with each department or function waiting for the others to finish. There simply isn't enough time to waste.

That pressure demands not only speed but effective delivery, on time, on specification and on budget. That will not happen by accident – and Robert Buttrick's book, based on his extensive corporate experience, is an invaluable, lucid and practical guide to a crucial area of management which has been crying out for the treatment it receives in these pages. Unlike management in general, project management is self-contained and dedicated to clearly defined ends. The organisations and the managers who best master the methods and maxims in this book will not only achieve their specific objectives, they will win the whole game.

Robert Heller

Acknowledgments

This book is built on the experience and knowledge of many people I have worked with over the years. If I named them all, the list would be as long as the credits at the end of an epic film! Here are a few mentions for those who have gone the extra mile with me.

I would like to thank my former colleagues at Gibb Ltd who took me on as a graduate and turned me into an engineer. Thanks, too, to those at PA Consulting Group who took on an engineer and gave me my grounding in business-led project management. Also I thank their clients with whom I worked and who presented me with such valuable challenges. Nick Warrillow, of Lloyds TSB Bank, is just one I want to mention.

Unlike many books, this one was written by one of the 'infantry': I am not an academic. I would like to thank Jim Reynolds, formerly the Products and Services Director at Cable and Wireless, for giving me the opportunity to write the book and to share my experiences with you. My thanks also to Grant Holdom at BT, for creating an environment in which the methods described in this book could thrive, and to Alan Fowler, of Isochron, for his stunning insights into benefits management, to Dr Eddie Obeng for introducing me to his frameworks and concepts relating to project types, to Oded Cohen of the Goldratt Institute who opened my eyes to the Theory of Constraints, to Chris Worseley at CITI for his work on project manager profiling, to Alan Crean of Process Master for his ground breaking process design tool and to John Anderson for his insights into portfolio management.

Thank you also to the companies who took part in the benchmarking.

Putting a business-led project framework in place is a challenging and difficult task. Having the ideas is not enough – it is what you do with them that counts. During 1995, I worked with Anatoli Kaminov from Bain & Company. He looked at what I was doing and added his own spark of intelligence and practicality. He also said to me, 'Robert, you've done the ground-work; why don't you write the book?' So, thanks Anatoli, for giving me a push to produce the first edition . . . and now here is the fourth edition.

Most important of all, I would like to thank my wife, Sandra, for hours of proof-reading and the solid support she has given me to ensure this venture succeeds.

And after all this, am I satisfied with what has been achieved? No – there's always more to do!

Robert Buttrick, June 2009
projectworkout.com

Preface to the Fourth Edition

Programme and project management have been with us for a long time. Yet we continue to see many businesses not using these essential tools adequately and the effects this has on their performance. These include a lack of discipline, focus and rigour in the execution of project work, an inability to measure project performance and outcomes, the use of non-standard ways of working (which breed confusion) and a break-down of handoffs at organisational boundaries. All of these problem areas can be helped through the effective use of programme and project management, creating a step-change in delivery performance within any organisation.

Over recent years, many organisations, across all sectors (private and public) have started to grasp programme and project management as the key to creating beneficial change. It is as relevant in times of expansion, as in times of recession, when survival itself is crucial. Both situations generate opportunities and threats and therefore benefit from a business-led management approach. I regard projects as the core vehicles for directing and managing change and believe that those who do not grasp their significance will find success very elusive.

Having competent project managers is only one aspect of the solution. Effective business-led project management starts at the very top of an organisation, where the leadership sets the direction, provides a context for project selection and, through the right behaviours, sets the tone for how change will be directed and managed. This is one area of business where the senior team is very much on the field of play, as project sponsors, taking an active role, rather then handing off to middle management.

The Project Workout is about *all* these issues. It is about the tough choices leaders need to make and the new roles and behaviours people (at all levels in the organisation) need to adopt. The book introduces ways of thinking and working which deal with uncertainty and risk by providing a practical, top-to-bottom guide to making business-led project management work for you and for your organisation. As such, I recommend it to all business leaders who really seek to make a positive difference.

Ian Livingston
CEO, BT Group PLC

Introduction

This book is about driving change in your organisation by selecting the right projects and managing them in the right way. The approach is to keep to some basic principles supported by only a few formal 'rules.' In this way the likelihood of success is increased dramatically and you, as an executive, director, or manager, will have the freedom to manage.

Sir Ian Gibson, President - Nissan Europe, said in the mid 1990s:

> *'As organisations we must become increasingly able to change quickly and easily. This means building on and around people's abilities rather than limiting them for the convenience of recognisable roles.'*

All those years ago, he recognised the need for a new way of managing our businesses; one that is flexible and not tied to specific departments; one where people can be used to the best effect; where what they do counts more than the department or function they come from. In his company, the structures are flat, there are no job titles and most personnel moves are sideways. This applies from top to bottom and no one can ever say, 'I won't do that, it's not my job!' Change is built into the way they work.

Today, some organisations have attained this vision, but many have not. This book looks at one aspect of this, the part which relates to implementing change in your organisation. A 'new way' of doing this has been with us for a long time, buried within the bowels of our technical and engineering departments, but it is now being recognised by business and governments alike. It is **programme and project management**.

In fact, since the first edition was published in 1997 there has been strong evidence of many more organisations taking deliberate steps to use business-led project methods. However, in some the support and training given to those sponsoring or managing projects is pitifully small. Managers are often given a project because it is 'good for their development'. True, but not if they have to think it all out for themselves with no grounding whatsoever. I have never heard of an accountant who was expected to do his or her job 'from first principles'. Such newcomers to project management are often termed 'accidental' project managers or project sponsors. Billions of dollars rest on the shoulders of these 'accidental project sponsors' and yet it is still a cause for concern that many major organisations do not provide the training, method or tool kit for these people. If I can help them perform and deliver more effectively, the time spent on this book will have been worthwhile.

Unfortunately, the discipline of project management is generally made to look too complicated, is frequently misunderstood and often poorly practised at a business level. Consequently, it does not always deliver the promised rewards. Whether you are a senior executive, manager, project manager or 'one of the infantry', I aim to make the 'art of project management' clearer to you in this book by:

- explaining the challenges faced by many organisations;
- outlining some lessons and advice from leading organisations;
- proposing a staged framework for managing individual projects;
- explaining the key roles which need to be fulfilled;
- showing how business leaders can manage and track all their projects as a portfolio through their life cycles;
- providing best practice for directing and managing projects.

Reading this book will benefit you as:

- having read it, you can really start doing it!
- the 'mystique' of projects is exposed, making it simple to understand and accessible to finance, sales, marketing, customer services, administrators and technologists alike;
- it gives practical, immediately usable methods for directing and managing complete portfolios of projects as well as individual projects;
- the content is not tied to any formally published 'methods' but is positioned as 'common sense' which overrides them all.

Part One of the book covers the challenges and lessons. Part Two looks at a typical project life cycle. Part Three looks at dealing with the many projects you have in your organisation. Part Four proposes a control framework for your projects. Part Five contains some thoughts on how you can implement a projects approach in your organisation.

Many of the key points will be restated in different sections throughout the book. This is intentional, both as reinforcement and to enable you to dip into separate sections without the need to follow up multiple cross-references simply to understand the basic message. Successful project management is a complete system and to describe elements of it in isolation would be deficient.

If much of the book seems to you to be 'mere common sense' then I have succeeded in relaying an important message. It is common sense; however, while it is obvious common sense to state it, the common sense of doing it is rare.

If much of the book seems simple, I have succeeded in relaying it to you in a form that can be understood by anyone in your organisation. Everyone involved in a project, be he/she a top executive or a line worker, needs to be able to understand the basic principles. If they don't, you shouldn't be surprised if things go wrong.

Project management is an 'art'. To be effective it requires both powerful interpersonal skills (soft skills) and structured management (hard skills). I have concentrated on the latter as this is where the myth of project management most needs exploding. I do, however, refer throughout to the soft skills needed, but this book is not aimed at being a handbook on motivation, leadership, enrolment or management style. If you want a good book which does cover the softer aspects, try Dr Eddie Obeng's *All Change! The Project Leader's Secret Handbook* (London: Financial Times Series, 1995).

> *Project management is an 'art'. To be effective it requires both powerful interpersonal skills (soft skills) and structured management (hard skills).*

THE PROJECT WORKOUTS

The book contains a number of exercises, problem posers and techniques to help you put the 'book work' into practice. They will be both a stimulant and a practical help.

Case studies

The case studies are derived from real-life incidents, but some have been amended to make them more concise to convey the particular message being illustrated.

> *'Change the name and it's about you, that story.'*
>
> HORACE 65–8 BC

POINTS OF INTEREST

Throughout the book I have included a number of points of interest which relate to the core theme of each chapter. These may be passed over on first reading so that you are not diverted from the main message. They may, however, provide you with some greater understanding of the subject. If this book were a presentation, these would be the questions which interrupt the presenter or the anecdotes the presenter may use to help bring the story to life.

Definitions

The way we use words is important. In the field of project management there is a converging consensus on what words mean but there are still instances where people have differing opinions. You will find a number of words which may be new to you or have been used in a new way. Appendix A comprises a jargon-busting glossary. So, if you come across a new word, look it up.

'How often misused words generate misleading thoughts.'
HUBERT SPENCER

Principles

These are the basic principles you need to apply if your projects are to succeed. You should ensure that any 'rules' or procedures you develop and use within your organisation are compatible with these.

Key points

Key points are short checklists which will keep you on the right track.

Cartoons

In many of the chapters I have used cartoons to emphasise a point. The cartoons are all set 2,000 years ago in the Roman Empire and show how, if the Romans had run their affairs as many modern organisations do, they would have failed miserably. This drives home the point that project management is essentially no more than applying the common sense that has been with us for thousands of years.

The question 'why' is very powerful

Copyright © 1997 Robert Buttrick

CD-ROM, website and 'Live'

The CD-ROM

You are probably a very busy person and the last thing you want to do is struggle with a photocopier, trying to produce a clean copy of a useful page for a project workshop you are running. The CD-ROM enclosed with this book contains all the Workouts, ready for you to print out and use with your team. You can find them either by reference number (as given in the book) or through a context sensitive framework which collects together all the workouts relevant to a particular stage or point in your project.

We have also included a number of the templates described in Part Four of the book including the Health Check, MS Project views and project logs. These can be downloaded to your desktop ready for use.

Finally, when you come to Part Five and you want to put enterprise-wide project management in place in your organisation, the content of this CD may give you an idea or two about the design of your own project management website.

To use the software included, please refer to readme.txt on the CD.

The website – projectworkout.com

The CD-ROM also has a hotlink to the author's website, **projectworkout. com**, where you can find:

- a 'contact' form so that you may contact the author;
- an outline of the services that are available to you, including consulting support and seminars;
- articles and cartoons;
- frequently asked questions;
- references and useful links.

e:PSO demonstration system

Chapter 17 covers project management information systems. In order to give readers a feel for this, I have provided access to a demonstration version of the system that I use in this chapter. The e:PSO tool is a means of making the status of all projects, portfolios and programmes visible. It is web based to enable entry and analysis from multiple project sites. The project manager enters project data, which is then used to create high level status indicators and graphical interpretations of the project progress. Users are given access to the information which is relevant for their role in the project team, ensuring that everyone is kept up to date without the need to share confidential project information.

Every owner of *The Project Workout* can try out e:PSO online. For more details see **live.projectworkout.com**.

ProcessPad evaluation system

Throughout this book I have made use of flow charts to demonstrate the sequence of activities you need to go through to undertake some aspects of project management. Nowadays, processes are becoming a way of life in many organisations, particularly those moving up the maturity level and adopting models such as SEI's CMMI for Development. Unfortunately there are very few 'easy to use' process tools on the market but one I have come across and use very effectively in my day to day corporate life is ProcessPad. All the flow charts in this book were created using it.

Every owner of *The Project Workout* can obtain an evaluation copy free, and for university lecturers there is a set of accompanying lecture notes. For more details see **process.projectworkout.com**.

CHALLENGES TO BE FACED

'Minds are like parachutes; they only work when open.'
LORD DEWAR

In this part of the book I set out the challenges many organisations are facing in driving through the changes they need to make in pursuit of their strategic objectives. This is followed by a review of good practice being used by many of the world's leading companies.

How to use Part One

Part One is for you to read and learn from. When first reading it, you should forget about your own situation and the problems in your organisation. Open your mind to what others are saying and doing. If you find yourself saying '…but we don't do it like that, we are different!', pull yourself back – LISTEN. You are different. So is everyone else. Other people's experience may give you a clue to dealing with issues confronting you.

The project workouts in Part One are designed to help you think about 'projects' in your organisation, and to prompt action or discussion on the parts you feel will benefit you.

You can share your own experience with the author on **projectworkout.com**.

Challenges We Need to Face

Problems, more problems

Initiatives fail, are cancelled, or never get started – why?

In our new world of the twenty-first century no organisation is immune from 'shut down' if it fails to perform.

'Facts do not cease to exist because they are ignored.'
ALDOUS HUXLEY

Problems, more problems

All organisations have problems with the way they undertake their work and tackle change. Problems may be related to any aspect, be it technology, people, processes, systems or structure. Theme is always something, somewhere that needs to be created or improved. Since the later part of the twentieth century a variety of techniques and offerings has been available to business leaders to enable them to do this, including:

- O&M;
- Total Quality Management;
- Six Sigma;
- Business Process Reengineering.

All these have contributed greatly to the performance of a significant number of organisations but it is a sad fact that many organisations have failed (and continue to fail) to secure the enduring benefits which were initially promised. Something has gone wrong. It would seem that we are not all as good as we should be at managing and controlling change in order to achieve sustained benefits from such initiatives.

'Grand' initiatives of the kind just mentioned are not the only ones that can fail; organisations must continually strive to solve particular problems or achieve specific objectives. For example:

- new products and services are developed, old ones are enhanced or withdrawn;
- supply chains are changed;
- manufacturing processes are altered to take account of new methods and technologies;
- sales channels are developed;
- new plant and offices are opened, old ones are closed;
- key business functions are out-sourced;
- businesses are disposed of;
- acquisitions are integrated into the mainstream business;
- computer systems are built to give greater efficiency and add to the overall effectiveness of the operation.

Again, many of these initiatives fail. Either they:

- cost too much;
- take too long;
- are inadequately defined and specified;
- or simply don't realise the expected benefits.

> **Something has gone wrong. It would seem that we are not all as good as we should be at managing and controlling change in order to achieve sustained benefits from such initiatives.**

This amounts to failure on a scale which costs billions every year and for some organisations results in their demise. It happens in both private and public sectors, small undertakings and major multinational enterprises. In our new world of the twenty-first century no organisation is immune from 'shut down' if it fails to perform.

Initiatives fail, are cancelled or never get started – why?

> **A review of a representative cross-section of large companies reveals a common pattern of cause and effect.**

A review of a representative cross-section of large companies reveals a common pattern of cause and effect. Figure 1.1 shows that the fundamental reasons are twofold:

- Organisations don't know HOW to control change. There is no 'organisation-wide' way of undertaking business change initiatives.
- Organisations don't know WHAT they should be doing. There is no clear strategy driving requirements and decision making.

This book concentrates on how you can solve the first of these root causes (how to do it) but, as Figure 1.1 shows, successful projects rely heavily on the latter (what to do) being in place. You will, therefore, see frequent references to business strategy throughout the book. For a practical approach to developing your strategy, read and use Cyril Levicki's *The Interactive Strategy Workout: Analyze and Develop the Fitness of Your Business* (Financial Times Prentice Hall, 2003).

If any of the problems identified in this chapter or drawn out from Figure 1.1 are familiar to you and recognisable in your organisation, there is clearly scope for improving your performance:

- The solution to issues relating to single initiatives in isolation I refer to as **project management**.
- The solution to issues relating to groups of connected projects I refer to as **programme management**.
- The solution to issues relating to the undertaking of a large number of programmes and projects I refer to as **portfolio management** or **business programme management**.

If an organisation is to reap the full benefits, it must be competent at all three.

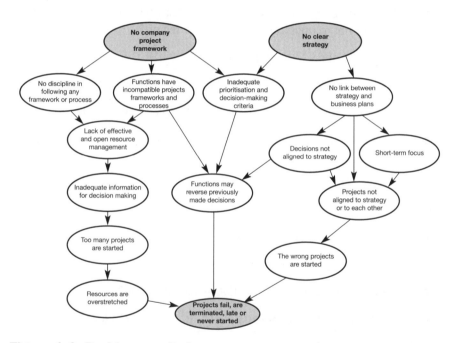

Figure 1.1 Problem analysis
A cause and effect analysis of the reasons for the failure of business change projects shows two fundamental reasons: (i) a lack of clear strategy, (ii) a lack of a rational way of managing the required changes. If your projects fail, then ultimately so will your business.

SELF-DIAGNOSIS

1.1

This Workout is best done with a group of executives, directors or managers.

1 Use the following questions as prompts to help you establish the areas of competence you may need to address.

- Can you establish a clear link between your current strategy and business plan and all the initiatives you have underway?

- Is it always clear what you should be doing and why?

- Do you find middle management passes on communications and instructions accurately?

- Do you find it easy to get decisions made?

- Do you have any documented criteria against which decisions on whether or not to undertake initiatives are tested?

- If so, do they apply to all your initiatives?

- Is there a disciplined way of managing initiatives across your organisation?

- Is there always enough time to do those things which must be done?

- Do your managers and employees commit themselves to and meet the targets set for them?

Do you really KNOW:

- What your resources are working on?

- When you will have spare resources to start new initiatives?

- Who is managing each initiative?

- Who wants the benefits each initiative should realise?

- The sum total of the costs and benefits from all your initiatives?

- Who makes the decisions on each initiative?

- Who makes the decisions when initiatives are competing for resource?

2 Build a cause and effect diagram similar to Figure 1.1 for your organisation. Start with 'Projects fail, are terminated, late or never started' written on a Post-it Note at the bottom of a flip chart. Ask yourself why this happens. Write each possible reason on a Post-It Note and place these on the flip chart. Again, for each Post-It Note, ask the reason why, writing these on more Post-It Notes. Eventually, if you are honest, you will discover a core reason(s), picking up many symptoms on the way.

Advice the Best Organisations Give Us

The advice in this chapter is based on a benchmarking exercise undertaken by the author, coupled with his own experience of working within a number of major organisations.

'Example moves the world more than doctrine.'

HENRY MILLER

The study

The problems outlined in the previous chapter are significant and far reaching. Finding solutions you can trust and have confidence in, is itself difficult. The advice in this chapter is based on a benchmarking study undertaken by the author, coupled with his own experience of working within several major organisations across a number of industries.

The benchmarking questions were not directly related to project management but to 'product development'. In a business context, a project is a project, regardless of whether it is technology based, for cultural change, complex change, or whatever. As the development and launching of new products and services touches almost every part of an organisation, projects in this field are an excellent medium for learning about complex, cross-functional projects and how organisations address them. If an organisation cannot develop new products and services efficiently, it is probable that it cannot tackle any other form of cross-functional project effectively either. The full set of questions is on the CD-ROM. The study had the following characteristics:

> *In a business context, a project is a project, regardless of whether it is technology based, for cultural change, complex change, or whatever.*

- It covered a wide range of industries.
- It was predominantly qualitative with only a few quantitative questions added to obtain such 'hard data' as were available. It was considered more important to find out how people worked rather than collect statistics. Even today, obtaining statistics which are truly comparable across different organisations and sectors is very difficult.

The objective was to 'learn from the best', hence the inclusion of a number of industries, both rich and poor, in the study:

- aerospace;
- construction;
- computer hardware;
- telecommunications;

- manufacturing;
- systems integrators.

The organisations chosen for the study were those which had clearly demonstrated success in their own fields and markets. Despite the diverse industries, we found a marked similarity in approach taken by all those organisations interviewed. They are all using or currently implementing a 'staged', 'cross-functional' framework within which to manage their product development projects (Figure 2.1). The number of stages may differ from organisation to organisation, but all have the characteristic of investing a certain amount of the organisation's resources to obtain more information across the full range of activities which impact a project and its outcome, namely:

> *Despite the diverse industries, we found a marked similarity in approach taken by all those organisations interviewed. They are all using or currently implementing a 'staged', 'cross-functional' framework within which to manage their product development projects.*

- market;
- operational;
- technical;
- commercial and financial.

The additional finding was that some of the organisations did not confine their approach to product development only, but applied it to business change projects generally, i.e. to everything they did that created change in the organisation. In other words, they had a common business-led project framework for managing change generally.

> *The organisations did not confine their approach to product development only, but applied it to business change projects generally, i.e. to everything they did that created change in the organisation.*

There, however, the similarities between organisations end as the individual culture and the nature of the different industries take over. Figure 2.2 illustrates that any process (including project management) sits within a context of culture, systems and organisation structure; alter any one and it will affect the others.

This single observation means that although project management processes in many organisations may be similar in principle, the culture

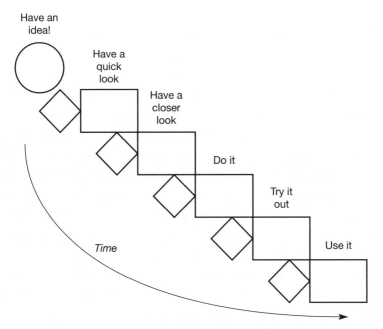

Figure 2.1 A typical staged project process framework

A staged approach to projects starts with a preliminary look at the objectives and possible solutions and results, via a more detailed investigation, development and trial, and the release of the outputs into the business' operational environment. You should not start any stage without meeting the prescribed criteria at the preceding gate. This includes checks on strategic fit and 'do-ability' as well as financial considerations.

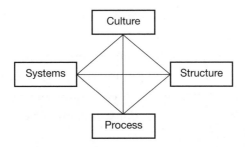

Figure 2.2 The organisational context for project management and other processes

No process sits in isolation. How you are organised, the systems you use to support the process and the prevailing culture of the organisation, all affect how well any process works.

and behaviours which makes them work are different. Logically, if an already proven process appears to break down, the fault may lie outside the process itself in one of the other aspects of the organisation. One CEO told me, 'We know our process is logical; if it isn't working we look first at the people trying to make it work rather than at the process itself.' This company had a well-established project management process in which it had a very high degree of confidence. However, it still maintained the good practice of continually improving its processes by promoting feed-back and having quarterly performance reviews. Another organisation had a very effective gating process (see Chapter 3), which totally failed when a new management team took over the programme. This observation also means that a process which works fine in one organisation will not necessarily work in every organisation.

Also notable was that certain industries were excellent in particular aspects of managing projects as a result of the nature of their business. Often, they took this for granted. For example:

'Concentrate on the early stages' was a message which came across loud and clear, but it was the organisations that relied on bids or tenders for their business which really put the effort in up front as the effect of failure was immediately obvious – they lost business or won unprofitable business. In organisations where 'bidding' is not the rule, the effects of poor upfront work are not so immediately obvious and may take a long time to become apparent. Too long.

'Manage risks' was another message. The only company to tell me, unprompted, that it was excellent in risk management was in avionics, where the consequences of failure can be painfully obvious – aircraft fall out of the sky. Interestingly enough, the company does not claim to use very sophisticated risk-management techniques, but rather has designed its whole approach with a risk-management bias. It cites its staged process as a key part of this.

'Measure everything you do.' Organisations which need to keep a track of man hours in order to bill their customers (e.g. consultants, system development houses) also have the most comprehensive cost and resource planning and monitoring systems. These provide not only a view of each individual project, but also enable them to collate and summarise the current status for all their projects, giving them a quantum leap in management information which most other organisations do not have.

The lessons and their implications

The lessons are summarised below and are described more fully on the following pages. The quotations are taken from the study notes.

The first seven lessons apply throughout the life of a project:

1 Make sure your projects are driven by benefits which support your strategy.
2 Use the same, simple and well-defined framework, with a staged approach, for all projects in all circumstances.
3 Address and revalidate the marketing, commercial, operational and technical viability of the project throughout its life.
4 Incorporate stakeholders into the project to understand their current and future needs.
5 Build excellence in project management techniques and controls across the organisation.
6 Break down functional boundaries by using cross-functional teams.
7 Use dedicated resources for each category of development and prioritise within each category.

The next three lessons apply to particular stages in the project:

8 THE START
   Place high emphasis on the early stages of the project.
9 THE MIDDLE
   Build the business case into the company's forward plan as soon as the project has been formally approved.
10 THE END
   Close the project formally to build a bridge to the future, to learn any lessons and to ensure a clean handover.

1   Make sure your projects are driven by benefits which support your strategy

'If you don't know why you want to do a project, don't do it!'

All the organisations were able to demonstrate explicitly how each project they undertook fitted their business strategy. The screening out of unwanted projects as soon as possible was key. At the start, there is usually insufficient information of a financial nature to make a decision regarding the viability of the project. However, strategic fit should be assessable from the beginning. Not surprisingly, those organisations which had clear strategies were able to screen more effectively than those which didn't. Strategic fit was often assessed by using simple questions such as:

- Will this product ensure we maintain our leadership position?
- Will the results promote a long-term relationship with our customers?

> **The less clear the strategy, the more likely projects are to pass the initial screening: resulting in the organisation losing focus.**

The less clear the strategy, the more likely projects are to pass the initial screening: so there will be more projects competing for scarce resources resulting in the company losing focus and jeopardising its overall performance.

2 Use the same, simple and well-defined framework, with a staged approach, for all projects in all circumstances

'Our usual process is our fast-track process.'

As discussed earlier, use of a staged framework was found to be well established. Rarely is it possible to plan a project in its entirety from start to finish; there are simply too many unknowns. By using defined project stages, it is possible to plan the next stage in detail, with the remaining stages planned in summary. As you progress through the project from stage to stage, your end-point becomes clearer and your confidence in delivery increases. It was apparent that organisations were striving to make their project frameworks as simple as possible, minimising the number of stages and cutting down the weight of supporting documentation. Further, the same generic stages were used for all types of project (e.g. for a new plastic bottle and for a new manufacturing line; for a project of £1,000 cost to one of £10m cost).

This makes the use and understanding of the framework very much easier and avoids the need for learning different frameworks and processes for different types of project. This is particularly important for those sponsoring projects or who are infrequently involved in projects. By having one basic framework they are able to understand their role within it and do not have to learn a new language and approach for each situation.

What differs is the work content of each project, the level of activity, the nature of the activity, the degree of risk, the resources required, and the stakeholders and decision makers needed.

A common criticism is that a staged approach slows projects down. This was explored in the interviews and found not to be the case. In contrast, a staged approach was believed to speed up desirable projects. One relevant point is the nature of the gates. Some organisations used them as 'entry' points to the next stage rather than the more traditionally accepted 'exit' point from a previous stage. This simple principle has the effect of allowing a stage to start before the previous stage has been completed. In this way stages can overlap without increasing the risk to the business, provided the gate criteria are met.

The existence of so-called 'fast-track' processes to speed up projects was also investigated. In all cases, the organisations said that their 'usual process' was the fast track. Doing anything else, such as skipping stages or going ahead without fully preparing for each stage, increases the risk of the project failing. The message from the more mature organisations was that 'going fast' by missing essential work actually slowed the project down; the amount of rework required was nearly always much greater than the effort saved. When people talk of fast tracking, what they usually mean is raising the priority of a project so it is not slowed down by lack of resources.

> *A common criticism is that a staged approach slows projects down. This was explored in the interviews and found not to be the case. In contrast, a staged approach was believed to speed up desirable projects.*

What's the point of speeding if you're on the wrong road?

3 Address and revalidate the marketing, commercial, operational and technical viability of the project throughout its life

'We are very good at slamming on the brakes very quickly if we see we cannot achieve our goals.'

All the organisations address all aspects throughout the life of a project. No single facet is allowed to proceed at a greater pace than the others as, for example, there is little point in:

- having an excellent technological product which has no adequate market rationale relating to it and cannot be economically produced;
- developing a superb new staff appraisal system if there are no processes to administer it and make it happen.

As the project moves forward, the level of knowledge increases and hence the level of risk should decrease. The only exception is where there is a particularly large area of risk and this work may be brought forward in order to understand the problems and manage the consequences as part of a planned risk-management strategy.

Coupled with this, the ability of organisations to stop (terminate) projects was seen to be important. Some expressed themselves to be experts at this. A problem in any one aspect of the project (e.g. market, operations, technology, finance) can lead to termination. For example, one company, which has a product leadership strategy, killed a new product just prior to launch as a competitor had just released a superior product. It was better to abort the launch and work on the next generation product, than to proceed with releasing a new product which could be seen, by the market, as inferior. If the company had done so, its strategy of product leadership would have been compromised, with the technical press rubbing their hands with glee!

Naturally, the gates prior to each stage are the key checkpoints for revalidating a project. The best organisations also monitor the validity of the project between gates and are prepared to stop it if their business objectives are not likely to be met. At all times, the project schedule, cost, scope and benefits must be kept in balance (Figure 2.3).

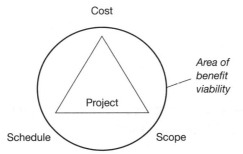

Figure 2.3 The project balance
A project comprises a defined scope (deliverables), to be delivered in an agreed timescale, at an agreed cost. These must be combined in such a way to ensure that the project is always viable and will realise the expected benefits. If any one of these falls outside the area of benefit viability, the others should be changed to bring the project back on target. If this cannot be done the project should be terminated.

4   Incorporate stakeholders into the project to understand their current and future needs

> *'The front line customer interface has been and is our primary focus.'*

The involvement of stakeholders, such as users and customers, in projects was seen to add considerable value in all stages of a project. Usually, the earlier they are involved, the better the result.

The more 'consultancy-oriented' organisations must, by the nature of the work they do, talk to customers to ascertain their needs. But even these organisations said they often misinterpreted the real needs of the customer despite great efforts to avoid this. Where project teams are more removed from their users or customers, there is even greater scope for error.

Many innovative ways have been used to obtain this involvement including:

- focus groups;
- facilitated workshops;
- early prototyping;
- simulations.

Involving the stakeholders is a powerful mover for change, while ignoring them can lead to failure. When viewed from a stakeholder's perspective, your project may be just one more that the stakeholder has to cope with as well as fulfilling his or her usual duties; it may even appear irrelevant or regressive. If the stakeholders' consent is required to make things happen, you ignore them at your peril!

5 Build excellence in project management techniques and controls across the organisation

'Never see project management as an overhead.'

All the organisations I interviewed see good project management techniques and controls as prerequisites to effecting change. Project management skills are still most obvious in the engineering-based organisations, particularly those which have a project/line matrix management structure. However, other organisations had taken, or were taking, active steps to improve this discipline across all parts of the business.

There must be project management guidance, training and support for all staff related to projects, including senior managers who sponsor projects or make project-related decisions. Core control techniques identified in the organisations included planning and managing risk, issues, scope changes, schedule, costs and reviews.

Planning as a discipline is seen as essential. If you have no definition of the project and no plan, you are unlikely to be successful. It is virtually impossible to communicate your intentions to the project team and stakeholders. Further, if there is no plan, phrases such as 'early', 'late' and 'within budget' have no real meaning. Planning should be seen to be holistic, encompassing schedule, cost, scope and benefits refined in light of resource constraints and business risk (Figure 2.4).

Risk was particularly mentioned: using a staged approach is itself a risk-management technique with the gates acting as formal review points where risk is put in the context of the business benefits and cost of delivery. Projects are risky and it is essential to analyse the project, determine which are the inherently risky parts and take action to reduce, avoid or, in some cases, insure against those risks.

Despite good planning things will not always go smoothly. Unforeseen issues do arise which, if not resolved, threaten the success of the project. Monitoring and forecasting against the agreed plan is a discipline which

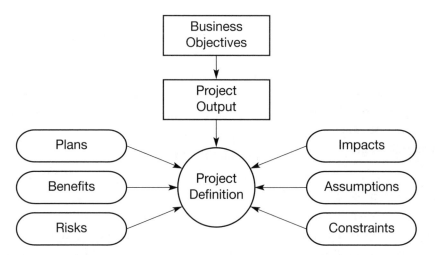

Figure 2.4 Planning
Planning should be seen to be holistic, encompassing schedule, cost, scope and
benefits refined in light of resource constraints and business risk.

ensures events do not take those involved in the project by surprise. This is
illustrated by the 'project control cycle' in Figure 2.5. The appropriate frequency for the cycle depends on the project, its stage of development and
inherent risk. Monthly is considered the most appropriate by many of the
organisations although in certain circumstances this is increased to weekly.

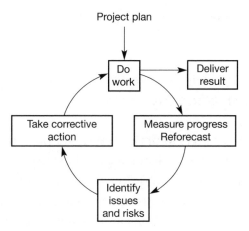

Figure 2.5 Project control cycle
The project control cycle comprises doing the work as set out in your plan, measuring
progress against that plan, identifying any risks, opportunities or issues and taking
corrective action to keep the project on track. From time to time, results, in the form of
deliverables, are generated. (Copyright © PA Consulting Group, London)

Such monitoring should focus more on future benefits and performance than on what has actually been completed. Completion of activities is evidence of progress but not sufficient to predict that milestones will continue to be met. The project manager should be continually checking to see that the plan is still fit for its purpose and likely to realise the business benefits on time. Here, the future is more important than the past.

Completion of activities is evidence of progress but not sufficient to predict that milestones will continue to be met.

It is a sad fact that many projects are late, or never reach completion. One of the reasons for this is 'scope creep'. More and more ideas are incorporated into the project scope resulting in higher costs and late delivery. Controlling change is critical to ensuring that benefits are achieved and that the project is not derailed by 'good ideas' or 'good intentions'. Changes are a fact of life and cannot be avoided. Good planning and a staged approach reduce the potential for major change but cannot prevent it. Changes, even beneficial ones, must be controlled to ensure that only those which enable the project benefits to be realised are accepted. Contracting industries are particularly good at controlling change as their income is directly derived from projects – doing 'that bit more' without checking its impact on their contractual obligations is not good business. Why should it be any less so when dealing with 'internal projects?'

6 Break down functional boundaries by using cross-functional teams

'No one in this company can consider themselves outside the scope and influence of projects.'

The need for many projects to draw on people from a range of functions means that a cross-functional team approach is essential. Running 'projects' in functional parts with coordination between them always slows down progress, produces less satisfactory results and increases the likelihood of errors. All the organisations in the study recognise this and have working practices which encourage lateral cooperation and communication rather than hierarchical (Figure 2.6). In some cases this goes as far as removing staff from their own departmental locations and grouping them in project team work spaces. In others, departments which frequently work together are located as close as practical in the company's premises. Generally, the closer people work, the better they perform. Although this is not always practical, closeness can be compensated for by frequent meetings and good communication.

Cross-functional team working, however, is not the only facet. It was also seen that decision making has to be on a cross-functional basis. Decision making and the associated processes was an area where some of the organisations were less than satisfied with their current position. Either decision makers took too narrow a view or insufficient information was available.

Another requirement of cross-functional working is to ensure that both corporate and individual objectives are not placed in conflict. For example, one company found that team members on the same project received different levels of bonuses merely because they belonged to different departments.

The more functionally structured an organisation is, the more difficult it is to implement effective project management. This is because project management, by its nature, crosses functional boundaries. To make projects suc-

> *The more functionally structured an organisation is, the more difficult it is to implement effective project management.*

ceed, the balance of power usually needs to be tipped toward the project and away from line management (see Figure 2.11). For a 'traditional', functionally led company, this is often a sacrifice its leaders refuse to make … at the expense of overall business performance.

THE FULL PROJECT ENVIRONMENT

Lesson 5 says use 'good project management tools and techniques', BUT it is only one of ten findings which provide the full environment for projects to work. Is this why some organisations say 'we do project management, but it doesn't work for us'?

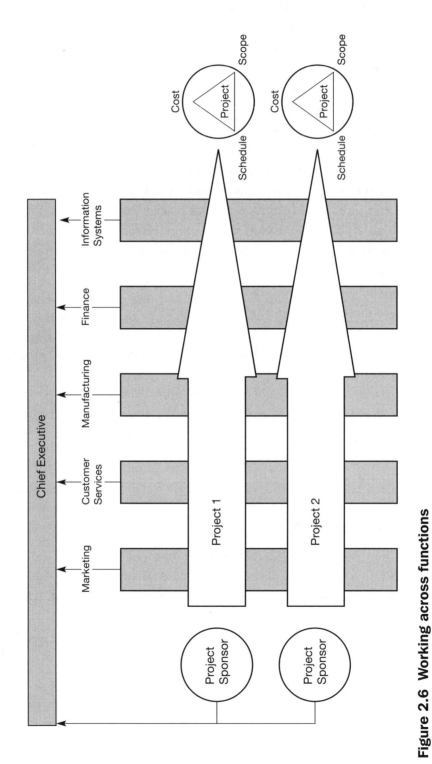

Figure 2.6 Working across functions

A project is a set of activities aligned to achieve a defined result. It draws in people from across the organisation who provide their particular expertise and knowledge.

7 Use dedicated resources for each category of development and prioritise within each category

'We thought long and hard about ring fencing (dedicating) resources and decided, for us, it was the best way to minimise internal conflict.'

The management and allocation of resources was acknowledged by many organisations to be a problem. There is often continual competition for scarce resources between projects. One company said that at one time this had reached such a level that it was proving destructive. The impact was often that too many projects were started and few were finished.

I discovered that this problem was dealt with in two separate ways, both of which have their merits.

The first (Figure 2.7) is to apply dedicated (separate) resources for each category of project (say, aligned around a business unit) and take this principle as deep as possible into the organisation. In this way the potential conflicts are limited and the decisions and choices are more localised. In fact, the more separate and dedicated you make your resources, the

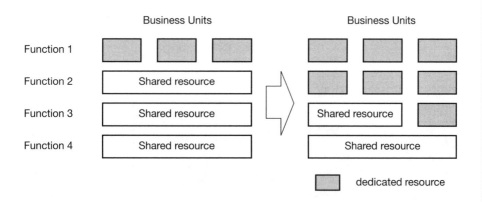

Figure 2.7 Apply dedicated resource to each project portfolio (e.g. by strategic business unit, market sector) as deeply as possible
Some organisations, as a result of their organisational structure, share most of their resources across a number of categories. This allows them to deploy the most appropriate people to any project regardless of where they are in the organisation. It also ensures that there is little duplication of functions within the organisation. Other organisations separate their resources to a greater extent and confine them to working on a single business unit's projects. This allows quicker and more localised resource management but can lead to duplication of functional capabilities.

more local your decision making can be, providing a project only needs to draw resource from that single pool. The down side of such an approach is that you will have to continually reorganise and resize your resource pools to meet demand. In a fast-moving industry this can mean you may have the right number of people but they may be deployed in the wrong places. It can lead to continual, expensive reorganisations. Most traditional, functionally based organisations follow this approach.

The second extreme is to have all staff in a single pool (shared) and to use effective matrix management support tools for resource allocation and forecasting (Figure 2.8). This method was adopted by the consulting and engineering organisations. In one case a person may work on up to ten projects in a week and there may be 300 projects in progress at any one time. It is very effective, conceptually simple and totally flexible. Major reorganisations are less frequent but it is also the most difficult to implement in a company which has a strong functional management bias.

In practice, a hybrid between the two extremes will provide the simplicity of purely functionally based organisations with the flexibility of full matrix-managed organisations. The implication is, however, that the resource management and accounting systems must be able to view the company in a consistent way from both perspectives.

Figure 2.8 Resources from all functions are applied anywhere, to best effect
In this model anyone from any function can work on any project. It is the most flexible way of organising but, without good control systems, is the most complex.

8   Place high emphasis on the early stages of the project

'Skipping the first stage is a driver for failure.'

All organisations see the early stages of a project as fundamental to success. Some could not stress this enough. High emphasis for some meant that between 30 and 50 per cent of the project life is spent on the investigative stages before any final deliverable is physically built. One American company had research data explic-itly stating that this emphasis significantly decreased time to completion. Good inves-tigative work means clearer objectives and plans; work spent on this is rarely wasted.

> **All organisations see the early stages of a project as fundamental to success.**

Decisions taken in the early stages of a project have a far reaching effect and set the tone for the remainder of the project. In the early stages, creative solutions can slash delivery times in half and cut costs dramatically. However, once development is under way, it is rarely possible to effect savings of anything other than a few per cent. Good upfront work also reduces the likelihood of change later, as most changes on projects are actually reactive to misunderstandings over requirements and approach rather than proactive decisions to change the project for the better. The further you are into the project the more costly change becomes.

Despite this, there is often pressure, for what appear to be all the right commercial reasons, to skip the investigative stages and 'get on with the real work' as soon as possible (so-called fast tracking, see Lesson 2). Two organisations interviewed had found through bitter experience that you can't go any faster by missing out essential work. One told me that 'skipping the investigative stages led to failure'; the other: 'Whenever we've tried to leave a bit out for the sake of speed, we've always failed and had to do more extensive rework later which cost us far in excess of anything we might have saved.'

> **Two organisations interviewed had found through bitter experience that you can't go any faster by missing out essential work.**

9 Build the business case into the organisation's forward plan as soon as the project has been formally approved

'Once it is authorised, pin it down!'

Projects are the vehicles for implementing future strategic change and revenue generation for a company. The best organisations are always sure that the projects they are undertaking will produce what they need and that they fit the company's wider objectives. In all cases, organisations had far more proposals for projects than they could handle. It is, therefore, essential to know what future resources (cash, manpower, etc.) have already been committed and what benefits (revenues, cost savings, etc.) are expected. Unless this is done the 'gap' between where the company is now and where it wants to be is not known and so the choice of projects to fill the gap is made more difficult (Figure 2.9).

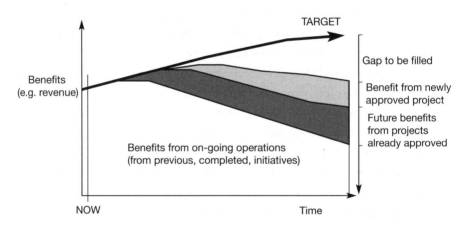

Figure 2.9 Build the project into your business plan as soon as it is authorised

The figure shows the revenue which will be generated by the organisation if no new projects are started. It then shows the revenue which will be generated by projects which are currently in progress. The gap between the sum of these and the target revenue needs to be filled. This can be by starting off new projects which will cause this to be generated or/and by starting initiatives in the line which will deliver the extra revenue to fill the gap.

Organisations handle this by having set points in the project life cycle at which cost and benefit streams are built into the business plan usually at the Development Gate (see Figures 3.6 and 3.7).

Clearly, financial planning and resource systems must be able to be updated at any time as projects do not recognise fiscal periods as relevant to start or finish dates. Also, any such project systems must be seen as a part of the business and not be seen as an 'add-on' outside the usual pattern of planning, forecasting and accounting.

10 Close the project formally to build a bridge to the future, to learn any lessons and to ensure a clean handover

'We close projects quickly to prevent any left-over budget from being wasted.'

Closing projects formally is for some organisations essential. For example, low margin organisations must close the project accounts down to ensure that no more time is spent working on projects which are finished, no matter how interesting! Their tight profit margins simply won't allow this luxury. Similarly, component products in an aircraft can be in service long after the project team has dispersed or even well after some team members have retired! Not to have full records (resurrection documents) on these critical components for times of need is unthinkable.

All the organisations interviewed either have a formal closure procedure or were actively implementing one. This usually takes the form of a closure report which highlights any outstanding issues, ensures explicit handover of accountabilities and makes it clear to those who need to know that the project is finished.

Another key reason given for formal closure was that it provides an opportunity for learning lessons and improving the processes and workings of the company. One company left 'closure' out of its process in the original design, but soon realised it was vital and added it in. It simply found that if it did not close projects, the list of projects it was doing was just growing by the day.

2.1

REVIEW OF THE TEN LESSONS

1 As a management team for the business, review the ten lessons given in this chapter and ask yourself how well you apply them in your organisation at present. Agree a mark out of 10 and mark the relevant column in the table on p. 33 with an 'X.'

10 = we currently apply this lesson fully across our organisation and can demonstrate this with ease.

0 = this is not applied at all.

2 Ask the project managers of, say, five of your projects to answer the same questions. Plot their answers with 'P'.

3 Ask the line managers of a number of your functions to answer the same questions. Plot their answers with 'L'.

4 Discuss, as a management team, the responses. Compare the answers you receive from the different stakeholder groups. Are there differences? If so, why do you think this is? Which lessons are not being applied? Why not?

5 What do you propose to do about this?

Lesson	POOR										EXCELLENT
	0	1	2	3	4	5	6	7	8	9	10
1 Make sure your projects are driven by benefits which support your strategy.											
2 Use the same, simple and well-defined framework, with a staged approach, for all projects in all circumstances.											
3 Address and revalidate the marketing, commercial, operational and technical viability of the project throughout its life.											
4 Incorporate stakeholders into the project to understand their current and future needs.											
5 Build excellence in project management techniques and controls across the organisation.											
6 Break down functional boundaries by using cross-functional teams.											
7 Use dedicated resources for each category of development and prioritise within each category.											
8 Place high emphasis on the early stages of the project.											
9 Build the business case into the organisation's forward plan as soon as the project has been formally approved.											
10 Close the project formally to build a bridge to the future, to learn any lessons and to ensure a clean handover.											

But we're different! – organisational context

Project processes only work if they are supported by compatible accountabilities, culture and systems (Figure 2.10). The previous sections in this
chapter described how many organisations use or are moving toward a
staged project framework, but that the environments in which they operate are entirely different. So, when you hear the plaintive cry of 'this
won't work here, we're different!', you can confidently answer 'yes, we
are different but we can make it work if we really want to.'

The following sections describe some of the wide range of approaches
taken by different organisations.

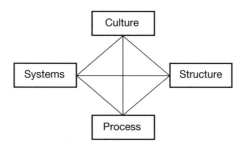

Figure 2.10 The organisational context for project management and other processes
Ensure all your bases are covered. Culture sets out how we behave toward each other, top
to bottom and side to side. Structure sets the accountabilities and relationships. Process
provides consistency where consistency adds value. Systems make what we do easier,
quicker, more reliable and cheaper. Change any one of these and it will impact the others.

Structure and accountabilities

Organisation structures vary from pure project to pure functional; this
impacts the ease of cross-functional working and project management.
Figure 2.11 shows the range of organisation shapes and the effect they tend
to have on project management. In heavily functionally driven organisations, project managers are generally very weak, disempowered and at the
mercy of the functional heads of department. They are often called 'project
coordinators', which is very apt. In full project organisations, the project
managers have greater power and influence over and above heads of
department. In the middle is matrix management. This is a much maligned
structure but one that can be very effective in organisations which require

a relatively stable functional structure but still need to have the advantages of a cross-functional project approach. It has often been said 'matrices don't work, they just confuse'. Yes, that's probably true if they are attempted in an environment with no suitable controls and incompatible line and project accountabilities and processes. Generally, those organisations which have moved the balance of power away from the line and towards the project, have found project management and cross-functional working more effective and reap greater rewards.

The acceptance of clear definitions of roles, accountabilities and relationships for the key players are most apparent with those organisations which are comfortable with their processes. Further, the separation of 'role' from job description is seen as crucial to maintaining simplicity, as in cross-functional, project environments, the role a person takes (e.g. as project sponsor or project manager) is more important than the job title or position in the functional hierarchy.

Some organisations set up cross-functional groups to undertake particular tasks on an on-going basis. The most obvious are those groups which undertake the screening of proposals prior to entry to the project process. In

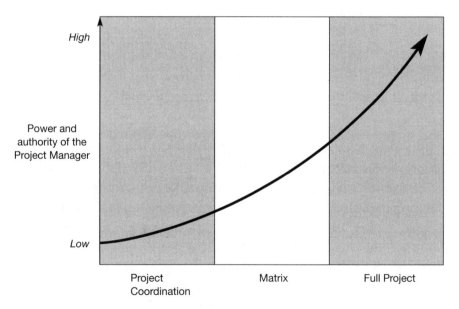

Figure 2.11 Project organisations
Organisations can structure themselves with differing emphasis on line and project management authority. When the most power is invested in line management, project managers are reduced to a 'coordination' role. In full project structures, the project manager has greater power than the line manager.

this way the structures created match the process (rather than leading or following the process). This must also apply to any review or decision-making bodies which are created. The one most commonly found to be adrift is that relating to financial authorisations. Many organisations have almost parallel financial processes shadowing their project processes, demanding similar but different justifications and descriptions of projects. This is usually found where finance functions have disproportionate power and act as controllers rather than in an assurance or business partner mode. The better organisations ensured that there was little divergence between decisions required for finance and those relating to strategy. They make certain that financial expertise is built into the project in the same way as any other discipline, with finance people being included on the project team.

Projects are 'temporary' and cease to exist once completed. Clear accountability for on-going management of the outputs in the line ensures that the right people are involved in the project and that the handover is clean and explicit. Career progression and continuity of employment for people involved in projects must be a top consideration. Projects are about change and about the future of your organisation. Good organisations ensure that the people who create these changes are retained and that projects are not seen as career limiting and the fast track to redundancy. You need your best people to create your future organisation, not the 'leftovers' from running yesterday's organisation.

> *You need your best people to create your future organisation, not the 'leftovers' from running yesterday's organisation.*

A large, global company was having difficulty ensuring its people worked cooperatively across department and functional boundaries (typical silo behaviour). This had been raised on a number of occasions at senior team level. One day, the chief executive officer told me he had fixed the problem. 'How?' I asked. 'I've put all problem functions under Andy,' he replied. 'How does an extra management tier and the creation of an even bigger silo solve the problem?' I asked. There was silence lasting for a full minute. 'Well, that's what I've done,' he eventually said.

Clearly, this chief executive officer had not fully understood the problem and was merely offloading it onto someone else. Further, he was using a structural solution in an attempt to solve a cultural problem. (You will recall Figure 2.10.)

Culture

Culture is probably the least reproducible facet of an organisation and the most intangible. It does, however, have a very significant impact on how projects are carried out and how project management is implemented.

For example, the corporate attitude to risk and the way an organisation behaves if high-risk projects have to be stopped will have far reaching effects on the quality of the outputs produced. In avionics the 'least risk' approach is generally preferred to the 'least cost' despite being within an industry in which accepting the lowest tender is a primary driver.

One company interviewed explicitly strives to make its own products obsolete as it clearly sees itself as a product leader. It is forever initiating new projects to build better products quicker and more frequently than the competition. This same company focuses its rewards on teams, not individuals, and takes great care to ensure its performance measurement systems avoid internal conflict. Another company admitted that its bonus schemes were all based on functional performance and not team performance despite 60 per cent of the staff working cross-functionally. An example was given of a staff member who received no bonus for his year's work, but all his colleagues on the the same project (in a different department!) had large bonuses. This was not seen as 'fair', and was the result of basing bonuses on something that could be counted easily rather than on something that actually counted!

Another company has no bonus scheme below senior management level but provides 'Well Done' awards (financial) for individuals whom they consider merit them. These are given almost immediately after the event which prompted the award and are well appreciated. This same company also has 100 per cent employee ownership and salesmen who are not commissioned.

Most of the organisations interviewed encouraged direct access to decision makers as it improves the quality of decisions. Project roles, rather than 'job descriptions', promote this. Functional hierarchies tend to have a greater 'power distance' and decision makers become remote from the effects of their actions or the issues involved.

As a paradox, those organisations which have the most comprehensive control systems (project accounting, resource management, time sheeting, etc.) are able to delegate decision making lower in the organisation. Senior management does not lose sight of what is happening and always knows who is accountable.

A major producer of project scheduling software confided in me that when it came to managing its own internal business projects, all the good practice and advice the company advocated as essential to its customers was ignored. The culture of the company's management simply does not fit the product it sells. Organisations can be very successful without any rational approach to business projects but are unlikely to remain successful for long.

WHAT HAPPENS TO PROJECT MANAGERS IN YOUR ORGANISATION WHEN THE PROJECT IS FINISHED?

2.2

(a) They are kept on the payroll and assigned to a manager for 'pay and rations' until a new project or suitable alternative work is found.

(b) They are put on a redeployment list and then made redundant if no suitable opening is found for them within x months.

(c) They leave the organisation straightaway if no suitable opening is found for them.

(d) They leave the organisation.

(e) I don't have this problem as they are all contracted in when needed.

If you answered (b) to (d) you are probably very functionally driven and projects tend to be difficult to undertake.

If you answered (e) you may be in a very fortunate position to be able to source such key people OR you are in the same situation as (b) to (d).

If you answered (a) you are probably in a good position to reap the rewards of project working or are already doing so!

Debate with your colleagues: what motivates your staff to work on projects?

If you answered (b) to (d), do you really expect to have your best people volunteering to work on projects?

Systems and tools

A number of organisations stated that the accounting systems must serve to integrate process, project and line management. Projects must not be seen as an 'add-on'.

Resource management and allocation was found to be a problem for many organisations. Those which found least difficulty centrally managed their entire resource across all their departments so that the departments and the projects used the same core system; only the reporting emphasis was different.

Other organisations had developed systems to cope with what they saw as their particular needs; for example, risk management or action tracking.

The American organisations had acquired the practice of constantly validating their processes and systems through benchmarking.

Conclusion

The benchmarking study confirmed that:

- The staged framework is widely used for business change projects and is delivering better value than more traditional functionally based processes. This is discussed further in Part Two of the book.
- A cross-functional, project management-based approach is essential. This is discussed further in Part Four of the book.

What is apparent is that the infrastructure which makes projects work varies considerably, in particular the level of information that decision makers have to support them. For example, it is usually relatively easy to decide if a project in isolation is viable or not. However, if you are to decide which of a number of projects should go ahead based on relative benefits, answers to the following questions are needed:

- What overall business objectives is the project driving toward?
- On what other projects does this project depend?
- What other projects depend on this project?
- When will we have the capacity to undertake the project (in terms of people and other resources)?
- Can the business accept this change together with all the other changes being imposed? If so, when?

- Do we have enough cash to carry out the project?
- After what length of time will the project cease to be viable?
- How big is the overall risk of the full project portfolio with/without this project?

The challenge lies in having processes, systems, accountabilities and a culture which address these, both at a working level and at the decision-making level. If this is not addressed it will result in:

- the wrong projects being undertaken;
- late delivery;
- failure to realise the expected benefits.

This will be in spite of having excellent processes and tools at an individual project level. These questions are addressed in Part Three of this book.

In one company, it was not unusual to find directors reporting to graduates on projects. The directors are on the project teams to add their particular knowledge and skills and not to lead the project. This company saw nothing strange about this arrangement. The most appropriate people were being used in the most appropriate way.

Reorganising isn't always the answer!

Copyright © 1997 Robert Buttrick

Quotation from Gaius Petronius Arbiter, AD66

ENEMIES WITHIN

Running a project is difficult enough, but we often make it more arduous than it need be by creating problems for ourselves. Here are a few examples:

Reorganising – either the company or a part of it. Tinkering with your structure is usually NOT the solution to your problems, it just confuses people. The Romans realised this 2,000 years ago (see cartoon). If you are a senior executive, however, this is a great way to hide non-delivery!

Functional thinking – not taking the helicopter, the organisation-wide view. This often happens when executives' or individuals' bonuses are based on targets which are at odds with the organisation's needs, e.g. sales bonus rewarded on revenue, regardless of profit or contribution.

Having too many rules – the more rules you have, the more sinners you create and the less happy your people become. Have you ever met a happy bureaucrat?

Disappearing and changing sponsors – without a sponsor there should be no project. Continual changing of the 'driver' will cause you to lose focus and forget WHY you are undertaking the project. Consider terminating such a project to see who really wants it!

Ignoring the risks – risks don't go away, so acknowledge them and manage them. If I said that a certain aeroplane is likely to crash, would you fly on it? And yet, every day executives approve projects when a simple risk analysis shows they are highly likely to fail.

Dash in and get on with it! – if a project is that important, you haven't the time NOT to plan your way ahead. High activity levels do not necessarily mean action or progress.

Analysis paralysis – you need to investigate, but only enough to gain the confidence to move on. This is the opposite to dash in and ignore the risks. It is also a ploy used to delay projects: '. . . I haven't quite enough information to make a decision, just do some more study work.'

Untested assumptions – all assumptions are risks; treat them as such.

Forgetting what the project is for – if this happens, terminate the project. If it is that useful, someone will scream and remember why it is being done.

Executive's 'pet projects' – have no exceptions. If an executive's idea is really so good, it should stand up to the scrutiny that all the others go through. He or she may have a helicopter view, but might also have their head in the clouds.

Part Two

A WALK THROUGH A PROJECT

'How narrow is the line which separates an adventure from an ordeal.'

HAROLD NICHOLSON

In this part I will explain the management framework for a single project, taking it from being an idea through the various life cycle stages until benefits start being realised in your organisation:

- Make sure that your projects are driven by benefits which support your strategy.
- Manage your projects within a staged framework.
- Place high emphasis on the early stages.
- Treat gates as 'entry' points to stages, not 'exit' points.
- Address and revalidate the business aspects of the project through-out its life.

How to use Part Two

Chapters 3 and 4 are for you to read and understand. The workouts are designed to help you place the project framework in the context of the projects you undertake in your organisation.

Chapters 5 to 11 comprise a skeleton project management framework. In these chapters, I explain what happens during each stage of a project and who is accountable. You can use these directly or adopt and adapt them to meet the particular needs and language for your organisation. Each chapter describes a set of 'control documents' for that stage: the content for these is given on the CD-ROM. Each chapter concludes with a project workout in order to review any projects you currently have: choose the workout which matches most closely the life cycle stage of your project. Appendix B contains some ideas of how to construct your processes in practice.

In the final chapters (12 and 13) I take this basic framework and show how you can apply the principles of the staged approach to match diverse business situations.

The Project Framework:
An Overview of its Gates and Stages

Project management is still seen as a specialist discipline requiring special people who are difficult to find and to retain. While this is to a certain extent true, a scarcity of 'project managers' should not be a barrier to any organisation starting to develop a 'projects' approach to managing its own future.

'The Golden Rule is that there is no golden rule.'

GEORGE BERNARD SHAW

Projects as vehicles of change

'Projects' are rapidly becoming the way organisations should manage change and this applies not only to traditional activities such as large construction projects, but also to any change initiative aimed at putting a part of your business strategy into action. Projects, in the modern sense, are strategic management tools and you ignore the newly reborn discipline of enterprise-wide project management at your peril. It is fast becoming a core competence which many organisations require their employees and leaders to have. It is no longer the preserve of specialists and the engineering sector, but an activity for everyone. The problem is that most people simply do not have the right skills. Project management is still seen as a specialist discipline requiring special people who are difficult to find and to retain. While this is to a certain extent true, a scarcity of 'project managers' should not be a barrier to any organisation starting to develop a 'projects' approach to managing its future. Project management is simply applied common sense. All organisations say that their most important asset is their people (although the shareholders may be more interested in profit), but no organisation, however excellent, has a monopoly on 'good people'; they are simply much better at getting 'ordinary' people to perform in an extraordinary way and their few

> **Projects, in the modern sense, are strategic management tools and you ignore the newly reborn discipline of project management at your peril. It is fast becoming a core competence which many organisations require their employees and leaders to have. It is no longer the preserve of specialists and the engineering sector, but an activity for everyone.**

'extraordinary' people to perform beyond expectations. These organisations provide an environment which enables this to happen. Add to this a few, well-chosen project experts and you have a sound foundation for generating successful projects. Well-managed projects will enable you to react and adapt speedily to meet the challenges of your competitive environment, ensuring you drive toward an attainable, visible, corporate goal.

Most organisations are never short of good ideas for improvement and your own is probably no exception. Ideas can come from anywhere within the organisation or even outside it: from competitors, customers or suppliers. However, deciding which of all these good ideas you should actually spend time and money on is not easy. You must take care in choosing which projects you do, as:

● you probably don't have enough money, manpower, or management energy to pursue all of your ideas;
● undertaking projects which you cannot easily reconcile with your organisation's strategy will, almost certainly, create internal conflicts between projects, confuse the direction of the business and, ultimately, reduce the return on your company's investment.

You should consider for selection only those projects which:

● have a firm root in your strategy (see p. 17).
● will realise real benefits;
● meet defined business needs;
● are derived from gaps identified in business plans;

Having created a shortlist of 'possible projects' it is important you work on them in the right order, recognising interdependencies, sharing scarce resources and bringing the benefits forward whenever possible.

Figure 3.1 shows this in a diagram. Selecting the right projects will help you achieve your business objectives by realising benefits which support your strategy. Two key roles are associated with projects:

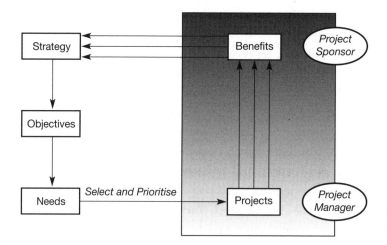

Figure 3.1 Select the right projects to support your strategy
Selecting the right projects will help you achieve your objectives by realising benefits which support your strategy.
(Copyright © PA Consulting Group, London. Adapted with kind permission)

The project sponsor is the person who wants the benefits the project will provide.

The project manager is the person who manages the project on a day-to-day basis, ensuring that its deliverables are presented on time, at the right quality and to budget.

A simple illustration of these key project roles is that you may want to build an extension to your house that will give you a fully equipped den and/or home office. You want the benefits that will accrue. You and your family do not want all the dust, debris and inconvenience that construction will entail, but you accept this is the price (together with the monetary cost) you are willing to pay in order to obtain the benefits you seek. By the same token, the architect is more interested in designing and seeing constructed an elegant and appropriate solution that will meet your needs. As project manager, he/she is not fundamentally interested in the benefits you seek, but rather in the benefits received for carrying out the work (the fee). He/she must, however, understand your needs fully so that an appropriate solution can be delivered. In a good partnership, sponsorship and management are mutually compatible. Thus:

- the **project sponsor** is 'benefits focused';
- the **project manager** is 'action and delivery focused.'

The framework for managing business-led projects is aimed at making the results of projects more predictable by:

- being benefits focused;
- building in quality;
- managing risks and exposure;
- exploiting the skill base of your organisation.

As a project proceeds over time, the amount of money invested in it increases. If none of this money is spent on reducing the risks associated with the project then it is poorly spent. Your objective is to ensure that risks are driven down as the project moves from being an idea to becoming a reality (see also pp. 18, 29).

Figure 3.2 demonstrates this. The investigative stages are crucial and you should hold back any development work until your investigations show you know what you are doing and have proved that the risks are acceptable.

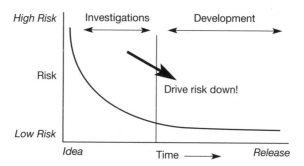

Figure 3.2 Managing the risk
The investigative stages are crucial and you should hold back any development work until your investigations show you know what you are doing and have proved that the risks are acceptable.

You do this by using a staged approach where each stage serves as a launch pad for the subsequent stage. In this book I have used five stages, but other models are equally acceptable if they suit the environment and culture of your organisation.

Internal and customer-facing projects

Regardless of the organisational context, projects may be undertaken:

- **Internally**, to fulfil a need within an organisation, where the organisation undertakes a project for itself in order to achieve its business objectives and realise certain benefits. For example, a manufacturer may wish to build a new production plant to produce certain product lines efficiently.
- **For customers**, where an organisation (or supplier) undertakes a project, for payment. For example a civil engineering contractor would undertake a project for the construction of a bridge, but may have no interest in the bridge once it is handed over.

There are primarily two type of organisation commonly engaged on projects:

- **Promoting** organisations, which identify a business, strategic or political need, translate this into a set of objectives and, through project management, produce the outputs and changes to ensure those objectives are met. A promoting organisation may let out part of the project to a contracting organisation or supplier.

- **Contracting** organisations, which identify a project through an invitation to tender or similar sales channel, prepare a response and then, if successful, undertake the contracted work.

Note that a promoting organisation's sublet 'project' may be a contracting organisation's 'customer project'. In both cases, the project has two distinct phases:

- The investigative stages, where the promoter determines how best to meet the objectives and the contractor determines the 'bid design', cost and price.
- The implementing stages, where the promoter and contractor undertake their planned work.

The distinction between promoting and contracting organisations is not always obvious, especially in the case where a contractor undertakes the operation of any outputs from the projects as part of an extended project life cycle. In more complex situations the distinctions should be clear within the contractual arrangements and formal authorities agreed between the parties.

Stages and gates

Stages

Stages are specific periods during which work on the project takes place. These are when information is collected and outputs created.

For each stage in the project, you should carry out the full range of work covering the entire scope of functional inputs required (Figure 3.3). These functions should not work on the project in isolation but in a continuous dialogue with each other, thus enabling the best overall solution to be developed. In this way your knowledge develops and increases on all fronts at a similar pace and solutions are designed, built and tested in an integrated way. No one area of work should advance ahead of the others. Your solution will not be what is merely optimal for one function alone but will be a pragmatic solution which is best for your organisation as a whole. This has the benefit of shortcutting the functional hierarchies, enabling the flat, lean structures we all

> *Your solution will not be what is merely optimal for one function alone but will be a pragmatic solution which is best for your organisation as a whole.*

seek to attain to work in practice as it forces people with different perspectives to work together, rather than apart. The business of the future, that is created and built using a cross-functional team, will find it much easier to run the all-encompassing cross-functional processes that business process re-engineers and the Theory of Constraints (see Chapter 21) tell us is the way forward. Further, you should limit the work undertaken in any stage to that which is needed at the next gate: there is little point in spending effort and money until you need to.

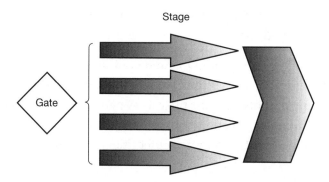

Figure 3.3 Address all aspects of the project in parallel
For each stage in the project, you should carry out the full range of work covering the entire scope of functional inputs required. In this way your knowledge develops and increases on all fronts at a similar pace and solutions are designed, built and tested in an integrated way.

RUNAWAY HORSES AND CATTLE DRIVES

A project is not a horse race, where the individual departments and functions are horses, each competing to see who can finish first. Projects are more like a cattle drive where all of the cattle must complete the run to market in tip top condition. Some cattle will be faster and stronger (better resourced), other cattle are yoked together (by process and functional hierarchy). As drivers, we must ensure that some cattle do not get too far ahead and that others do not lag behind. We must also ensure that they aren't distracted by wolves (other projects) and scattered. But please don't take the analogy too far and treat your people like cattle!

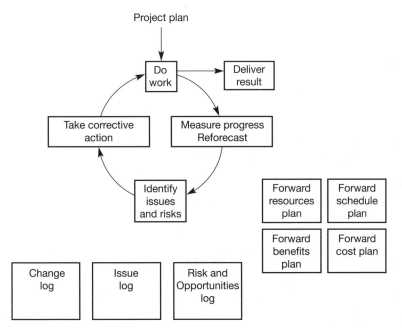

Figure 3.4 A typical stage
A stage may be represented by the project control cycle together with the key control tools you need to manage it (these are described in Part Four).

During each stage it is essential for the project manager to continuously forecast and reforecast the benefits, resources and costs needed to complete the project. He/she should always keep the relevant functions informed and check on behalf of the sponsor that the project still makes sound business sense. This is illustrated by the 'project control cycle' in Figure 3.4.

Before you start work on any stage, you should always know what you are going to do next in order to increase your confidence and decrease risks; you should have a project plan for at least the next stage in detail and for the full project in summary.

> *Before you start work on any stage, you should always know what you are going to do next in order to increase your confidence and decrease risks.*

> *'An unwatched pot boils immediately.'*

> H F ELLIS

Gates

Gates are the decision points which precede every stage. Unless specific criteria have been met, as evidenced by certain approved deliverables, the subsequent stage should not be started (see also p. 18). Gates serve as points to:

- check that the project is still required and the risks are acceptable;
- confirm its priority relative to other projects;
- agree the plans for the remainder of the project;
- make a go/no go decision regarding continuing the project.

You should not regard gates as 'end of term exams', but rather the culmination of a period of continual assessment with the gates acting as formal review points.

Gate criteria are often repeated in consecutive gates to ensure that the same strands of the project are followed through as the project progresses. You should expect a greater level of confidence in the responses to the criteria, the further into the project you move.

At each gate you will need to answer three distinct questions (Figure 3.5):

- Is there a real need for this project and, in its own right, is it viable?
- What is its priority relative to other projects?
- Do you have the funding to continue the project?

It is convenient to think in terms of these questions because, in many organisations, discrete people or groups are needed to address each of them.

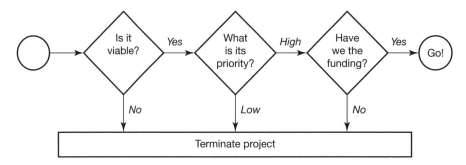

Figure 3.5 The three decisions required at each gate

The first question concerns the viability of the project assuming no other constraints. Does it fit your strategy? Does it make business sense? Are the risks acceptable? You will see later on that this question is addressed by the 'project sponsor'.

The second question (priority) concerns the project in its context. It may be a very worthy project *but* how does it measure against all the other projects you want to do or are currently doing? Are there more worthwhile projects to address? Is it just 'one more risk too far,' bearing in mind what you are already committed to? This question is dealt with in Part Three where I will propose a basic method of managing such decisions.

The third question involves funding. Traditionally, businesses have discrete and very formal rules concerning the allocation of funds and which are generally managed by a finance function. So, you might have a viable project, it may be the best of those proposed BUT have you the working capital to finance it? This question is also dealt with in Part Three. If your finance function is less dominant, the funding question(s) come before the question of priority.

Gates – an end or a beginning?

Gates have traditionally been defined as end-points to the preceding stage. The logic is that the work in the stage culminates in a review (viz. end of stage assessment) where a check is done to ensure everything is complete before starting the next stage.

However, due to time pressures, it is often necessary to start the next stage before everything in the previous stage has been fully finalised. For example, in the typical framework in Figure 3.6, we see that it is sound sense to undertake a trial operation of our new output before all the process, training and communication work is completed. What is essential is that we have sufficient work done to enable us to start the next stage with confidence. We are, therefore, left with the difficulty of having a traditional 'rule' that common sense encourages us to break.

The solution to this dilemma is to treat gates as entry points to the next stage. In this way you can start the next stage (provided relevant criteria and checks have been done) as soon as you are ready, regardless of whether or not the full work scope of the previous stage has been completed.

> *Treat gates as entry points to the next stage. In this way you can start as soon as you are ready, regardless of whether or not the previous stage has been completed.*

In this way, stages can overlap, reducing timescales, without increasing the risk associated with the project.

This approach also opens another powerful characteristic of the staged framework. Gates are compulsory, stages are not. In other words, provided you have done the work needed to pass into a stage, how you arrived there is immaterial. This allows you to follow the strict principles of the staged approach even if a stage is omitted. In Chapter 12, I will introduce the concept of 'simple' projects and show how this principle enables them to be accommodated.

The project framework

As we have learned, projects draw on many resources from a wide range of functions within an organisation. Ensuring these are focused on achieving specific, identified benefits for the organisation is your key management challenge. You can increase the likelihood of success for your projects, and hence of your business, by following a project framework which:

- is benefit driven;
- is user and customer focused;
- capitalises on the skills and resources in the organisation;
- builds 'quality' into the project deliverables;
- helps manage risk;
- allows many activities to proceed in parallel (hence greater velocity);
- is used by people across your whole organisation.

As we have already seen in Part One (p. 18), sound approaches to tackling projects achieve all these objectives by breaking each project into a series of generic stages and gates which form a framework within which every project in the organisation can be aligned.

This enables you to gain control of two key aspects of your business:

1 You know that each project is being undertaken in a rational way with the correct level of checks and balances at key points in its life.
2 You are able to view your entire portfolio of projects at a summary level and, by using the generic stage descriptions, know where each project is and the implication this has on risk and commitment.

The remainder of this part of the book concentrates on the 'single' project (point 1) and takes you step by step through a framework you can use on your projects. Part Three will describe the management of portfolios of projects (point 2).

The project framework is shown in Figure 3.6 as a bar chart and in Figure 3.7 as a diagrammatic overview. The stages are, briefly, as follows:

Identify the need – Proposal: a need is first formally recognised by describing it (i.e. say why you want to initiate a project). If known, you should also describe what you believe the project will produce (i.e. its output) but don't jump to conclusions too soon.

Have a quick look – Initial Investigation Stage: the first stage in the project – a quick study of the proposal, to outline the scope and make a rough assessment of the possible ways of meeting the need, benefits, resources and costs needed to complete it. At the end of this stage you should be sure of why you are doing it. You may also know what you are doing, although this may comprise a range of defined options. You will know how to go about at least the next stage, if not the full project.

Have a closer look – Detailed Investigation Stage: a feasibility study, definition and a full investment appraisal culminating in a decision to proceed with development work. At the end of this stage you will have high confidence in all aspects of the project and 'What you wanted to do' becomes 'What you are going to do!'

Do it! – Develop and Test Stage: the actual development and implementation work.

Try it – Trial Stage: a trial of all aspects of the development in the users' or customers' operational and working environment. What has been created may work very well under 'test conditions', but does it work under normal operational conditions?

Use it – Release Stage: the last stage in the project, when you unleash your creation on the world. This is when products are launched, new computer systems used, new manufacturing plant goes into production, new organisation units start operating to the 'new rules', new processes are invoked, acquisitions sealed and disposals shed. The on-going operational aspects are embedded in the organisation and the project is formally recognised as complete.

About three to six months after completion, a check, known as a **Post-Implementation Review**, is done to see if the project is achieving its business objectives and its outputs are performing to the standards expected.

Figure 3.6 The project framework as a bar chart

The project framework is shown here in 'bar chart format' at the top, with the document deliverables for each stage shown below. These are described more fully in Chapters 5 to 11; see also the CD-ROM for more details on each document.

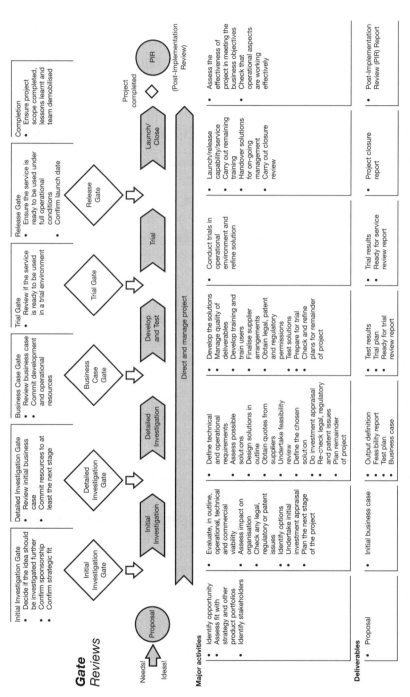

Figure 3.7 The project framework in diagrammatic form

The project framework is shown here in a format which clearly distinguishes between the gates and the stages. It also shows the activities and deliverables which relate to each stage.

PORTFOLIOS, PROGRAMMES, PHASES, STAGES and GATES

In this book I refer to STAGES and GATES as convenient descriptions for the periods when work is done and for the points in time when a check is made on the project prior to starting the next stage. Terminology often found in practice also includes:

For stage: Phase

For gate: Tollgate; Gateway; Quality Gate; Checkpoint; Assessment; Review

In this book, I reserve the use of the word '**phase**' to describe a programme that is to be introduced or built with benefits designed to arrive in different time frames. For example, major roads projects are frequently introduced in phases so motorists can benefit from the first 20 miles built and do not have to wait for the full 80-mile stretch to be completed. Each phase is in fact a project in its own right and comprises a number of stages.

The word '**programme**' is also problematic, much used and abused to the extent that it is often meaningless. For example I had a job title of 'programme manager', but I did not use it on my business cards as it did not tell anyone what I did; indeed it might even have misled them. Programmes are discussed more fully in Chapter 13 as a tightly aligned and tightly coupled set of projects. Note this does not conflict with the emerging view that programmes include the period of benefits realisation, as in the Project Workout, where all projects are business and benefit led.

The word 'programme' is frequently used to bundle any projects together for the convenience of reporting, planning, or other management purpose. In this book I refer to these as a '**portfolio**'. This is discussed further in Chapter 14 in relation to what I term 'business programmes'. Just to keep you on your toes, 'portfolio' can also refer to bundles of programmes as well as projects.

In hierarchical terms the relationship is:

- the organisation's portfolio(s) of programmes and projects;
- programme;
- project;
- stage.

The above terms can look confusing, mainly because there is no universal definition for them. Each organisation (or standards body) will choose its own definitions. The point therefore is for you, in your organisation, to choose what suits, visibly define the terms and use them consistently.

Some key questions

How many stages should I have?

Consider the types of project you undertake in your organisation. Do they fit the generic stages described earlier? Are there some modifications you would like to make? Some organisations have only four stages, others six or more. Generally, the fewer the better, but they must be meaningful to you and fit every project you are likely to do. My experience is that three is too few and five will fit most purposes, so if in doubt try five. Of the five stages used in this book, it is the Trial Stage which is often either left out (see 'Is a trial really needed' later in this chapter) or merged in with the Develop and Test Stage. I prefer to have the trial as a distinct stage to differentiate it from testing. Testing is very much an internal, 'private' activity. A trial on the other hand is 'public' involving real users and customers. You are therefore open to poor press comment and to hostile reactions from employees. By making the trial a distinct stage you force people to focus on whether they really are ready. There have been enough high profile cases of beta test failures of software and of premium automobiles receiving very poor press due to a poor state of market readiness to act as a warning to us all.

How do I decide what work is done in the investigative stages?

The investigative stages exist in order to reduce risk (see Figure 3.2). Therefore everything you do should have that aim. If any proposed activity does not reduce risk, you should consider postponing it to a later stage.

Avoiding looking foolish

A 'wife' is a 'wife' and a 'husband' is a 'husband'. It would be ludicrous to call one a 'husband-wife' and the other a 'wife-husband'! Similarly, a 'stage' is a 'stage' and a 'gate' is a 'gate'; they are fundamentally different, so don't make a fool of yourself and confuse others by using the nonsense term, 'stage-gate'.

What should I call the stages and gates?

The stage and gate names I have chosen and used throughout this book have evolved over a number of years and are based on my experience of working in several organisations on different business projects. What you choose to call them is up to you but that decision is not trivial. Words are emotive and hence can be both very powerful movers for change or inhibitors of change. In all organisations there are words which:

- mean something particular to everyone;
- mean different things to different people.

You can build on the former by exploiting them in your project framework, provided the meaning is compatible with what you wish to achieve when using the words.

You should avoid the latter and choose different words, even making up new words if the dictionary cannot help you. For example, working in one company I found the word 'concept' problematic, despite its being very well defined and in the dictionary. 'Concept' to some people was a high level statement of an idea (the meaning I wanted to convey), but to others it meant a detailed assessment of what has been decided should be done (this was not what I wanted). Rather than try to re-educate people in their everyday language, I found a word (proposal) which had no strong linkages to current use of language. There were similar problems with the word 'implement': it has so many preconceived meanings that it is better not to use it at all! If you look at the list of possible names, you will notice that certain words appear in more than one place: this is a sure sign that they might be misunderstood.

The same issues apply to the naming of the gates. For these, however, it is better to name each one according to the stage it precedes. This emphasises the 'gate as an entry point' concept. An alternative approach is to name the gate after the document which is used as the control on the gate. You will see I have mixed these. Again this is your choice, but make the same terminology apply across the whole organisation.

I do, however, strongly suggest you do not refer to the stages and gates by a number or letter. It will cause difficulties later (including significant cost) if you need to revise your framework. You will not believe the number of times a 'Gate 0' or 'Stage 0' has had to be added to the front of a framework! Using proper names is simpler, more obvious and will not box you in for the future.

Stage names used in this book	Possible alternatives
Proposal 'Identify the need'	Concept Start up Initiation Ideation Idea generation
Initial Investigation 'Have a quick look'	Pre-feasibility Initial assessment Preliminary investigation Evaluation Research
Detailed Investigation 'Have a closer look'	Feasibility Appraisal Definition Scope Specify Design Business case Evaluation Authorisation
Develop and Test 'Do it'	Implementation Execution Realisation Develop Production Construction Build
Trial 'Try it'	Beta test Validation Commissioning
Release 'Use it'	Finalisation Launch Completion Implementation Handover Acceptance Closure/closedown
Post-Implementation Review	Business review Project audit Post-project review

Gate names used in this book	Possible alternatives
Initial Investigation Gate	Concept gate Proposal gate Initiation gate
Detailed Investigation Gate	Feasibility gate Evaluation gate Design gate
Development Gate	Business case gate Authorisation gate Implementation gate Execution gate
Trial Gate	Beta gate Validation gate Commissioning gate
Release Gate	Ready for service gate Operation gate Implementation gate Handover gate
Project completed	Closure gate Project end gate

Where do people go wrong?

In designing their frameworks, I have found people make mistakes in two key areas, the front end and the back end.

All too often, I see frameworks with minimal start-up activity, immediately followed by the Develop and Test Stage. They have in effect gone from 'idea' to 'do it' in one small step. In all but the simplest projects such a leap is naive and may account for why so many projects are ill-defined and doomed to failure. By all means make it easy to start the project off (i.e. pass through the Intial Investigation Gate), but do ensure there is rigour in the actual investigations themselves. A project comprises both investigation and execution.

> **I have found people make mistakes in two key areas, the front end and the back end.**

At the back end, people often confuse Project Closure with Post-Implementation Review. The former looks at project efficiency and delivery, whilst the latter looks at benefits realisation and operational effectiveness. These two views cannot be combined as the measurement points are entirely separated by time. Also note that 'Proposal' and 'Post-Implementation Review' are not stages of the project. They are activities which happen *before* and *after* the project, respectively; that is why they are shown as a circle and not an arrow in Figures 3.6 and 3.7.

Is a trial really needed?

'I have already tested this rigorously. Surely I don't really need to trial it all as well? Won't this just delay the benefits?'

This is a very valid question. The answer, as always, is 'yes and no'. Assume you have a choice of strategy from:

- product leadership;
- operational efficiency;
- customer intimacy.

1 Under 'product leadership' you are developing and delivering innovative, new products and services; you must be sure they really work as intended. You are aiming to be first and best in your market.
2 Under 'operational efficiency' you deliver what others deliver but more efficiently and at lower cost.
3 Under 'customer intimacy' you provide an experience for your customers such that they want to do business with you.

Thus, if your strategy is to have any practical meaning you must be sure that anything you do does not compromise it. The choice of 'to trial or not to trial' comes down to risk. What is the likely impact on your business if this goes wrong? How confident are you that it won't go wrong? With this in mind, you may choose to subject certain aspects to a trial more rigorously than others – balancing the speed to benefits realisation with the risks.

Always assume that you need a trial. Omit it only if you have proved to yourself and your stakeholders that it will not add any value to your project. Never skip the trial because you are in a hurry! If in doubt, try it out.

> **Always assume that you need a trial. Omit it only if you have proved to yourself and your stakeholders that it will not add any value to your project.**

If in doubt, try it out

Copyright © 1997 Robert Buttrick

How can I apply the framework?

The staged approach is the framework for the management of any type of project, for any purpose. As such, it is flexible and provides project managers with the opportunity to tailor it to suit the requirements of their individual projects. This ensures an optimum path through the generic project framework rather than one which is tied by bureaucracy. Any such tailoring of the project must, however, be recorded as part of the project definition (see p. 298).

Particular types of project require their own methodologies and steps but, provided you know how they match the overall high level framework, they can be used with confidence and in an environment where the business also knows what is happening. A common project framework will ensure alignment between different parts of the organisation with clearer communication and understanding. The table opposite shows how a range of different projects can fit into the framework.

Chapters 5 to 11 of this book describe the key actions, deliverables and decisions for each stage and gate of the framework. Chapter 12 looks at how you can apply the framework to simple, complex, phased, rapid and other types of project.

	Initial Investigation Stage	*Detailed Investigation Stage*	*Develop and Test Stage*	*Trial Stage*	*Release Stage*
Product development	Concept	Alternatives and feasibility	Develop and test	Market validation	Launch
Product withdrawal	Initial investigation	Detailed investigation	Develop and test	Pilot withdrawal	Close operations
Information systems	Analysis	Logical and outline physical design	Detailed design, build and test	Pilot	Cutover
Bid or tender	Receive request and evaluate	Prepare detailed tender tender	Develop, build, internal test	Commissioning trials	Handover
Construction	Inception study	Feasibility study, tender design	Detailed design and construction	Commissioning trials	Handover
Publishing	Proposal	Prepare manuscript	Edit, typeset	Final proof	Launch
IT	Requirements review	Analysis and design	Build	Beta test	Cutover

3.1

TAILOR YOUR OWN FRAMEWORK

Consider the above list of different types of project. Do you recognise any from your own organisation? Can you add to the list? If so, reproduce Figure 3.7 with modified activities, deliverables and gate review criteria. You'll find a blank template for this on the CD-ROM.

3.2

YOUR CURRENT BUSINESS PROJECTS

List the business projects you are undertaking at present in your organisation. Based on the simple descriptions just given, state which stage of the project life cycle each project is at. If you have completed Project Workout 3.1, use your own stage names; if not, use those in Figure 3.7.

Talking the stages

A product marketing manager is accosted in the corridor by an engineer:

Engineer: I just heard that you've got plans to muck about with my installation. You ignore me as usual. Why on earth wasn't I told? It looks like a really big change!

Product Manager: But, Leigh, we only decided to start the initial investigation two days ago. I've told no one yet: the proposal goes out tomorrow.

Engineer: Sorry Bill. From what I heard, I assumed it was more advanced than that. I look forward to getting the proposal.

In this scenario, an interdepartmental conflict was diffused because, despite having totally different business backgrounds, they both understood the project framework for the organisation they worked in. If they had each talked in their own jargon (e.g. marketing concepts, pre-feasibility studies, inception reports) they would as likely as not have been none the wiser and continued their argument.

Who Does What?

The players

In simple terms a project needs a person: who comes up with the idea (the originator), who wants the project benefits (project sponsor), who manages the project (project manager) and who undertakes the work (the project team).

'Even emperors can't do it all by themselves.'

BERTOLT BRECHT

Chapter 2 showed that a process is nothing without the culture, systems and organisation that support it (see pp. 14, 34). Project processes are no exception. Hence, to understand 'projects' you need to have a firm grasp of who the players are and what is expected of them. The roles described here are relevant to a single project (see Figure 4.1). Roles required for running a portfolio of projects are described in Part Three.

In simple terms a project needs a person:

● who comes up with the idea – the originator;
● who wants the project benefits – project sponsor and project board;
● who manages the project – the project manager;
● who undertakes the work – the team managers and members.

Appendix B shows, in diagrammatic form, how these different account-abilities interact.

Figure 4.1 A typical project organisation structure
The project sponsor who requires the benefits is supported either by a project board, management team or business programme board. The project manager reports to the project sponsor and is accountable for the day-to-day running of the project. A project coach supports these key roles. All team members report to the project manager.

The players

The originator

He/she is the person who identifies the 'need' for a project and publishes it in the form of a proposal. This person can come from any function or level inside or outside the organisation. Ideally, if the idea comes directly from the strategy, the orginator will become the sponsor.

The project sponsor

The project sponsor is accountable for realising the benefits to the organisation. This is an active role and includes ensuring the project always makes sound business sense, involving all benefiting units (and using a **project board** if appropriate), owning the business case and making decisions or recommendations at critical points in the project's life. The project sponsor is usually a director, executive, or senior manager.[1]

Project sponsor

The project sponsor is accountable for realising the benefits for the organisation. He/she will:

- ensure a real business need is being addressed by the project;
- define and communicate the business objectives in a concise and unambiguous way (see Chapter 20);
- ensure the project remains a viable business proposition;
- initiate project reviews (see Chapter 26);
- ensure the delivered solution matches the needs of the business;
- represent the business in key project decisions;
- approve key project deliverables and project closure;
- resolve project issues that are outside the control of the project manager;
- chair the project board (if one is required);
- appoint the project manager and facilitate the appointment of team members;
- engage and manage key stakeholders.

---

[1] The Financial Times Executive Briefing, *The Role of the Executive Project Sponsor*, by Robert Buttrick (Financial Times Prentice Hall, 2002), looks at projects from the perspective of this senior role. See the 'Publications' section of projectworkout.com for more details.

The project sponsor is ultimately accountable to the chief executive/president via a project board (where required) or to an intermediate management team or board.

An underlying principle of project management is that of 'single point accountability'. This is meant to stop things 'falling down the cracks' and applies not only to the management of projects and the constituent work packages, but also to the direction of a project; there should be only one project sponsor per project. In this respect, the term 'sponsorship' should not be used in the same sense as 'sponsoring Tom to run a marathon', where the objective is to have as many sponsors as possible. If a project sponsor is to be effective, rather than just someone who gives some money, he/she will need to be:

- a business leader;
- a change agent; and
- a decision maker.

The project sponsor as a business leader

Project sponsorship is not merely a 'figurehead' role. A sponsor is fundamentally accountable for ensuring 'why' the organisation is spending time and resources on a particular project. He/she must ensure that the business objectives are clearly articulated, that whatever is being created is really needed and that this need is fulfilled in a viable way. The project team will have their **heads down**, developing whatever outputs and deliverables are needed. The sponsor has to keep his/her **head up**, making sure the need still exists and the capabilities being produced fit the need. This cannot be over-emphasised; current research indicates that a prime cause of project failure is the lack of effective sponsorship and stakeholder engagement (we will come to stakeholders later, in Chapter 19).

The project sponsor as a change agent

Some may see the role of change agent and leader as synonymous. If so, that is good. For others, I have separated these out so it can be related to what many consultants and academics often refer to as 'the management of change'. Every project will create some change in the organisation, otherwise

> **Every project will create some change in the organisation, otherwise there is no point in undertaking it!**

there is no point in undertaking it! However, some changes are 'easier' to effect than others as they align with the status quo and do not cross any politically sensitive boundaries. In essence, most of the people carry on as they always have done. Other changes, however, are fundamental and will result in shifts in power bases internal to the organisation or even external, such as in unions, suppliers or customers.

All organisations are 'political' to some extent and the greater a project's scope to change the status quo, the more those involved will need to be tuned in. Whilst projects create change, that change may not necessarily be beneficial to everyone it touches, and this will trigger a political dimension to the sponsor's role. People's attitudes to 'corporate politics' differ, ranging from believing it is unnecessary through to seeing it as an opportunity. Suffice to say, you must acknowledge the political aspects, understand the sources and motivations of the key players and then develop an appropriate approach to them.

The project sponsor as a decision maker

The decisions a sponsor will need to make fall into two broad types:

- decisions which steer the project in a certain direction;
- approval of certain deliverables.

The first type relates to go/no go decisions at the gates, decisions regarding how to react to issues and changes, and decisions on when to close the project. The second type relates to particular outputs from the project.

If a person is unable to make decisions, the project sponsor is not likely to be a role they will be comfortable with. Most of the decisions which have to be made will be predictable (in terms of timing, if not outcome!) and backed up by evidence. The project documentation, such as business cases and closure reports, are designed to provide the sponsor with the information he/she needs.

THE PROJECT SPONSOR'S TROOPER – THE PROJECT CHAMPION

Quite often a project requires high level sponsorship from either a vice president or even from the company president himself/herself. Unfortunately, senior ranks do not always have the time to carry out all the duties that being a project sponsor entails. Here, it is best if they delegate the role and name someone else as sponsor. Half-hearted sponsorship can be very demotivating for the team and may even lead to the failure of the project. Alternatively, another manager may be assigned to act on their behalf. This person is often a 'project champion' who is as committed to the benefits as the sponsor him/herself. In all practical terms, the project champion acts on a day-to-day basis as the project sponsor, only referring decisions upwards as required.

The project board

A project board is usually required for projects which span a number of processes or functional boundaries and/or where the benefits are directed to more than one market segment or function. If no project board is required, the role can be undertaken by a programme board or management team. A programme board has accountability for a set of closely aligned projects. Programmes are illustrated more fully in Chapter 14. Unfortunately, bodies such as project boards are often ineffective, adding little value to the project. It is the project sponsor's responsibility, as chair of the group, to keep board members focused on the key aspects of the project where their experience can be used to best effect.

The project board

The role of the project board (if required) is to support the project sponsor in realising the project benefits and in particular:

- to monitor the project progress and ensure that the interests of your organisation are best served;
- to provide a forum for taking strategic, cross-functional decisions, removing obstacles and for resolving issues.

A project board is often called a steering group, or steering board.

WHO'S RUNNING THIS ORGANISATION?

Do you often find people in your organisation hunting around for someone to 'sponsor their project'? If so, who do you think is running the organisation? Surely, it is the accountability of the business leaders (i.e. sponsors) to set the direction and identify the needs that must be met. They should be the ones looking for people to manage **their** projects, not the other way round. Is your organisation led by its generals or by its troops? Is your project framework going to be a vehicle for change or merely an elaborate suggestion scheme?

The project manager

He/she is accountable to the project sponsor for the day-to-day management of the project involving the project team across all necessary functions. Thus all project managers will need to be familiar with Parts Two and Four of this book. Depending on the size of the project, the project manager may be supported by a project administrator, or office support team (see Chapter 27).

Project manager

The project manager is accountable for managing the project on a day-to-day basis. He/she will:

- assemble the project team, with the agreement of appropriate line managers;
- prepare the business case, project definition and detailed plans;
- define the accountabilities, work scope and targets for each team member;
- monitor and manage project progress;
- monitor and manage risk and opportunities;
- manage the resolution of project issues;
- manage the scope of the project and control changes;
- forecast likely business benefits;
- deliver the project deliverables on time, to budget, at agreed quality;
- monitor and manage supplier performance;
- communicate with stakeholders;
- manage the closure of the project.

The bodies of knowledge of various associations, such as the Association for Project Management or the Project Management Institute, seek to define the attributes of project managers. They are, however, not so easy to apply in practice. To put them in context, consider three levels of project manager competence.

- **Intuitive** project managers are capable of managing a small or simple project very effectively with a small team. They rely on their own acquired common sense, much of which is inherent good practice in project management. They intuitively engage stakeholders, seek solutions, plan ahead, allocate work and check progress. Many 'accidental' project managers fall into this category.
- **Methodical** project managers are capable of managing larger, more complex projects where it is not possible to keep the whole venture on track using simple tools and memory. Formal methods, procedures and practices are put in place to ensure the project is managed effectively.
- **Judgmental** project managers can cope with highly complex and often difficult projects. They can apply methods creatively to build a project approach and plan which is both flexible and effective, whilst keeping true to all the principles of good project management.

Performance in a role can be looked at as a combination of four factors: knowledge, experience, skill and behaviours.

- **Knowledge** comprises learning a set of tools and techniques which are unique to project management.
- **Skills** are the application of tools and techniques.
- **Behaviours** represent the attitude and style used by the project manager toward team members, sponsor, board and stakeholders.
- **Experience** measures the depth to which any knowledge, skills or behaviours have been applied.

Figure 4.2 gives a summary of these.

The preceding paragraphs should give the dimensions to look for when selecting a project manager and are sufficient for you to discuss a brief either with other managers or your Human Resources department. However, when it comes down to it, how would you distinguish between people who have similar skill sets? What should you look for or avoid?

Knowledge	Skills
Project definition Project planning Benefits management Schedule management Financial management Risk and opportunity management Issues management Change control	Team building Facilitation and coaching Conflict resolution Analytical thinking and problem solving Organisation Administration Technical expertise Communication (verbal, written and active listening)
Behaviours	**Experience factors**
Integrity Self-motivated – proactive Comfortable with ambiguity Open Even-handed Approachable	Evidence of delivery Evidence of problem solving Size and complexity of teams managed Number of projects managed Complexity of projects managed Evidence of effective leadership

Figure 4.2 Attributes of a good project manager
The figure shows those attributes which have been shown to be essential to good project manager performance. The extent to which a person complies very much depends on their level of attainment. You would expect an intuitive project manager to have far less project experience than a judgmental one.
Source: CITI Limited.

Good reasons for selecting a particular project manager include the following:

- **Inherent enthusiasm.** They need to understand the role and what it entails or be willing to learn and have the aptitude to cope. Look for the spark that tells you they really want this to succeed.
- **High tolerance of uncertainty.** They need to be able to work effectively across the organisation, without formal line authority or rank authority. They need to be able, especially in the investigative stages, to deal with the many potentially conflicting needs and signals as the project hunts its way toward a solution.
- **Excellent coalition and team-building skills.** People are at the heart of projects, both as team members and stakeholders. If the project manager hasn't the necessary 'people' skills, the project is unlikely to be a success.
- **Client orientation.** This means they need to understand the expectations and differing success criteria of the various stakeholders, especially the project sponsor.

Poor reasons for selecting a project manager, if taken in isolation, include the following:

- **Availability.** The worst reason to appoint a person is simply because he or she is available. Why are they available? What aptitude do they have? This tends to happen in organisations with a low level of maturity in project management, as 'project staff' are often not seen as part of the normal work of the organisation and having them 'do something', rather than 'nothing' is seen as more important.
- **Technical skill.** This can be useful on a project but not essential. The project manager can draw on technical experts as part of the core team. The danger when the project manager is also the technical expert is that he/she will concentrate on the technical area of interest to the exclusion of everything else. For example, a good systems programmer may ignore the roll out, training and usability of a new system as they are more interested in the technical architectures and features.
- **Toughness.** The 'macho' project manager who closely supervises every aspect of the project, placing demand upon demand upon the team (or else!), is the way to demoralise a team. Add to this the likelihood that many of the team may be working part time it may be a fast way of losing the very people who are vital to a successful outcome. Yes, a project manager needs to be emotionally tough and resilient but this should not translate into being a bully.
- **Age.** Grey hairs do not necessarily indicate a better project manager (although there are very many excellent older project managers). Maturity in project management comes from exposure to a wide range of different situations and projects. Managing a single project over five years is quite different to managing ten projects each of six-month duration. Length of time alone is not an indicator of experience.

The team managers and members

The team managers and members are the 'doers' who report to the project manager and are accountable for prescribed work packages and deliverables. This may range from a complete subproject to a single deliverable. It is essential that the full experience of the team be brought to bear on any problems or solutions from the start. In the case of large projects, the project manager may choose to have a small core team, each member of which manages his or her own subsidiary teams either on work packages or subprojects. Project teams often comprise two parts:

- The **core team** – those members who are full time on the project and report directly to the project manager. A core team size of six to ten people is about right.
- The **extended team** – those members who report to the core team (team managers) and who may be part or full time.

It is essential that each member of staff working on your project has a clearly defined:

- role and reporting line to the project manager when working on the project (he/she may maintain their normal reporting line for other activities);
- scope of work and list of deliverables (both final and intermediate deliverables);
- level of authority (i.e. directions on what decisions he/she can and cannot take on behalf of his/her line function).

All groups of individuals associated with the project and which make up the team should be identified and listed with their role, scope and accountabilities.

The team managers and members

Team managers and members are accountable to the project manager. The role of team members is to:

- be accountable for such deliverables as are delegated to them by the project manager, ensuring they are completed on time and to budget;
- liaise and work with other team managers and members in the carrying out of their work;
- contribute to and review key project documentation;
- monitor and manage progress on their delegated work scope;
- manage the resolution of issues, escalating any which they can not deal with to the project manager;
- monitor changes to their work scope, informing the project manager of any which require approval;
- monitor risk associated with their work scope;
- be responsible for advising the appropriate team managers and/or project manager of potential issues, risks or opportunities they have noticed.

In addition, a team manager is accountable for directing and supervising the individual members of the team.

Project coach/facilitator

The project coach or facilitator is accountable for supporting the project manager, project sponsor and project board. This may be by pure coaching or by giving advice, facilitation and guidance on project management. Both approaches will help project teams, both experienced and inexperienced, to perform beyond their own expectations. It is a role which is found infrequently but one which can prove extremely effective.

Remember, in many business-oriented projects the participants are likely not to be fully trained and capable project managers. They may need to have someone who can give them the confidence to work in a way which may be alien to them.

Remember, in business-oriented projects the participants are likely not to be fully trained and capable project managers. They need to have someone who can give them the confidence to work in a way which may be alien to them.

The power of coaching and facilitation

A cross-functional team was put together with the aim of reducing the delivery time for a telecommunications product from ten days to less than two hours. The team comprised people drawn from line, operational roles who had little project management experience. A project coach was employed to facilitate the initiation of the project and to provide on-going guidance throughout the execution. Setup was hard work and many of the team complained that it was wasting valuable time which could be better spent doing 'real work'. Perseverance and a commitment on behalf of the coach to seeing the team succeed got the team through the early stages and, once the development stage was underway, all of them understood the project fully. At the end, a marketing manager on the project commented to the coach, 'I wondered what you were doing to us; I now see it was key to have the hassle at the start if we were to actually achieve our objectives.' Things did go wrong on the project but as all the core team members knew their own role and that of the others, changes could be more easily, speedily and effectively implemented so that the overall objective was met. In fact the delivery time was reduced to an average of 20 minutes.

Project support

Project support provides support and administrative services to the project manager on activities such as filing, planning, project monitoring and control.

The provision of project support on a formal basis is optional. Tasks need to be done by the project manager or delegated to a separate body/person and this will be driven by the needs of the individual project and project manager. Project support could be in the form of advice on project management tools, guidance, administrative services such as filing and the collection of actuals, to one or more related projects. Where set up as an official body, project support can act as a repository for lessons learned and a central source of expertise in specialist support tools.

Project support

Specific responsibilities may include the following:

- set up and maintain project files;
- establish document control procedures on the project;
- compile, copy and distribute all project management deliverables;
- collect actuals data and forecasts;
- update plans;
- assist with the compilation of reports;
- administer the document review process;
- administer project meetings;
- monitor and administer risks, issues, changes and defects;
- provide specialist knowledge (for example estimating, risk management);
- provide specialist tool expertise (for example planning and control tools, risk analysis).

ROLES AND ACCOUNTABILITIES

This workout is best done with the project team, but may be done by the project manager or sponsor as an exercise in isolation.

4.1

1 Take any one of your key projects from Project Workout 3.2 and identify who (both individuals and teams) is involved in it. List them, one per Post-It Note. Place these on a flip chart.

2 Against each name, write in your own words what that person's needs or accountabilities are regarding the project.

3 On the left hand side of a separate flip chart, list the roles described in Chapter 4.

4 Match, as best you can, the names from step 2 to the key project roles described above.

5 For those names listed against 'team member', divide them into 'core team member' and 'extended team member'.

6 If you cannot allocate a person to one of the defined roles, put him/her in a separate cluster called 'stakeholders'.

Look at the role descriptions described in the chapter again. Do the individuals have the knowledge, skills and competences to perform the roles?

You should have only one name against project sponsor and one against project manager. If not, your roles and accountabilities are likely to be confused. Further, it is not good practice if the sponsor and manager is the same person.

Project sponsor

☐ Can this person articulate the benefits the project will provide?

Project board

☐ As a group, does it have all the facets of the project covered?

☐ Have its members ever met as a group?

☐ Could they all describe the project objectives and its current status consistently?

Core team members

☐ Do the core team members cover the required work between them?

☐ Are they supported with adequate resources and expertise?

☐ Do they ever meet with the project manager as a group?

☐ Could they all describe the project and its current status consistently?

Extended team members

☐ Do the extended team members know who they are accountable to on the project and what they have to deliver?

☐ Could they all describe the project and its current status consistently?

Stakeholders

☐ Your list of stakeholders may be extensive. They will be at all levels in the organisation, in diverse departments, they may be suppliers, they may be shareholders, the bank or even ... customers! Keep this list for use in Project Workout 19.5. (Stakeholders are discussed further on p. 317.)

ACTION

1 Review the roles and accountabilities on all key projects in your organisation.

2 Build on the project list from Project Workout 3.2 and add the names of the project sponsor, project manager and project board.

3 Ask each project manager and project sponsor to agree a list of stakeholders.

4 Ask each project manager to list the team members and their role on the project.

The Proposal:
Identify the Need!

Overview

Key deliverable

Process steps

The gate prior to the initial investigation is the first decision point when resources are committed to working on the proposal; it is also the point at which the potential project is first formally recognised. This gate is unique in that it is the only one in the project life cycle which does not require you to have a plan for how you undertake the work which follows.

'One of the greatest pains to human nature is the pain of a new idea.'

WALTER BAGEHOT, 1826

Overview

The proposal describes the business need (i.e. it focuses on **why** you want a project) and, if known, what you want to do. You should document it formally and have it reviewed by potential stakeholders prior to a go/no go decision for starting an initial investigation. The proposal document is used as the key deliverable at the Initial Investigation Gate. This gate, just prior to the initial investigation stage, is the first decision point when resources are committed to working on the proposal; it is also the point at which the potential project is first formally recognised. The gate is unique in that it is the only one in the project life cycle which does not require you to have a plan for how you undertake the work which follows.

> *The proposal describes the business need (i.e. it focuses on why you want a project).*

It is important for you to document the proposal as:

- it acts as the brief for the Initial Investigation Stage;
- the mere fact of writing the proposal down serves to clarify thinking and ensure clear communication of your intentions;
- if you can't be bothered to write it down, why should you expect anyone to work on it?

Key deliverable

The Proposal is a very brief document (one to five pages) which outlines the need the project will meet, what it is intended to produce (if known), its benefits, and how it fits with current strategy. If known, the impact on the organisation (market, technology and operational), broad estimates of benefits and cost, and required time to completion are also included. The CD-ROM contains a template.

Deliverable	Prepared by	Reviewed by	Approved by
Proposal	Originator	Functions or business units likely to be impacted by or to benefit from the proposal	Sponsor

Process steps

1 The need (or idea!) for a project should result directly from your business strategies and plans. This is not always the case as, for example, commercial opportunities may be spotted as the result of technical innovation, operational experience or from feedback from suppliers or customers.

2 The originator of the 'idea' should identify a senior executive in the company who is likely to benefit most from the project. (If the project comes directly from the business plan, that person will be obvious, or may even be the originator!)

3 The senior executive first checks that a similar idea has not been proposed before. If it has, the 'idea' should not be pursued further unless different circumstances now exist (market, technology, etc.). He/she should determine who else in the company has a stake in the idea in terms of benefit, impact and/or contribution, and then appoint a potential project sponsor. In the case of large projects or small companies, the senior executive may become the project sponsor.

4 The potential project sponsor should write up the idea in the form of a proposal. The draft proposal is reviewed with any other stakeholders identified in point 3. If necessary, it is amended. This review should look not only at the proposal in question but also at any other related proposals and projects. It is essential to screen out any duplicate proposals and those which do not form part of a coherent programme of change related to the business strategy and plan.

5 The potential project sponsor should identify a project manager who will be accountable for managing the Initial Investigation Stage, complete the registration of the proposal and file a reference copy.

The proposal is submitted for gate authorisation.

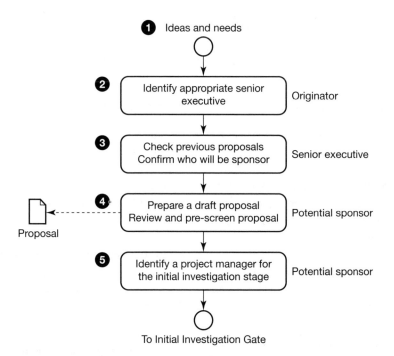

Figure 5.1 Steps prior to the Initial Investigation Stage

5.1

CHECKLIST FOR STARTING THE
INITIAL INVESTIGATION STAGE

Business need and strategic fit

☐ Is it clear that the project fits the strategy?

☐ Is the opportunity attractive (size, share, cost saving, contribution, etc.) relative to alternative proposals?

☐ Is the proposal likely to be acceptable to the customers and users?

☐ Do any competitors have capabilities similar to this? If so, will this proposal provide you with any competitive advantage?

Health check!

☐ Has a project 'health check' been done to identify areas which need to be covered (see p. 456)?

Accountabilities

☐ Has a project sponsor been identified?

☐ Has a project manager been identified for the Initial Investigation Stage?

☐ Can resources be committed to do the initial investigation?

Operational and technical

☐ Is the organisation likely to be able to develop or acquire the required capabilities to support this proposal, if they don't yet exist?

☐ Is it technically feasible with current technology?

☐ Has the organisation the operational capability to support it? If not, can it acquire this?

Health check scores

P	R	O	J	E	C	T	Total
☐	☐	☐	☐	☐	☐	☐	☐

Risk

☐ Low   ☐ Medium   ☐ High   ☐ Impossible

Issues

Risk

Executive action

The Initial Investigation Stage:

Have a Quick Look at It!

Overview

Key deliverables

Process steps

The goal of the Initial Investigation Stage is for you to examine the proposal as quickly as possible (say, within one to six weeks), and to evaluate it against the existing business plans of the company to determine if what is intended is likely to be viable in financial, operational, technical and customer terms.

'To have begun is half the job: be bold and be sensible.'

HORACE, 65–8 BC

Overview

The goal of the Initial Investigation Stage is for you to examine the proposal, as quickly as possible, (say, within one to six weeks), and to evaluate it against the existing business plans of the company. You need to determine if what is intended is likely to be viable in financial, operational, technical and customer terms.

You will need to:

- make a preliminary assessment of the business opportunity, benefits, possible solutions, costs, technology needs and the likely impact on the operational platforms and groups, infrastructure and capabilities;
- check for overlap, synergy or conflict with other projects in progress or capabilities in use;
- plan the work content for the remaining stages of the project.

Remember, this is only an initial assessment; do not run ahead of yourself by working to too high a degree of accuracy. Think in ranges, rather than absolutes. For example, 'this project will cost between $75,000 and $200,000 and take four to eight months, with cost savings of the order of $100,000–200,000 per year.'

Key deliverables

The Initial Business Case document contains the business rationale for the project. It is the document which outlines WHY you need the project, WHAT options you intend to work on, HOW you will do it, and WHO is needed to make it happen. It also answers the question HOW MUCH? and hence is used to authorise the funding for at least the next stage of the project. The Initial Business Case does not comprise a full analysis, but only sufficient to enable you to decide if it is worthwhile continuing the project. The full Business Case will provide the definitive appraisal for the project.

The Initial Business Case includes:

- a preliminary assessment of the financial aspects of the proposed development;
- an outline of the requirement in terms of customer/user 'feel,' technology, commercial, and market needs;
- a definition of the project which would be required to meet these (in detail for the next stage and in outline for the whole project).

It also evaluates the project against the existing strategies and goals of the company to confirm its fit and to determine if it is likely to be viable in both business, technical, operational, and customer terms. See the CD-ROM and p. 293 for more detail.

The Project Plan is a key appendix to the initial business case and defines the schedule, cost, and resource requirements for the project. This is defined in summary to completion of the project and in detail for the Detailed Investigation Stage.

Deliverable	Prepared by	Review by	Approved, prior to gate, by
Initial Business Case	Project manager	Impacted or benefiting functions and business units	Project sponsor
Project Plan	Project manager	Impacted or benefiting functions and business units	Project sponsor

Note: These are minimum roles and deliverables only. Each project manager should define the full set prior to the start of the stage. At the discretion of the project manager, a separate initial investigation report and/or output definition may also be produced.

Process steps

Initial Investigation Gate. This gate is the point at which a decision is made as to whether an initial investigation (business, technical, marketing and operational) should be undertaken and whether there are resources to do it. If the Proposal is authorised, the Initial Investigation Stage is started. See checklist on p. 92.

1 The appointed project manager engages the study team, registers the project, ensures a project account has been opened, and informs all relevant stakeholders of stage entry (see Chapter 19).

2 The team, led by the project manager, undertakes the initial investigation, confirming the need for the project, objectives and strategic fit. They will also derive possible solutions for further investigation. The project manager agrees the outcome and recommendations with the project sponsor.

3 The team defines the project and prepares the project plan, in detail for the next stage and in outline beyond. The potential resource needs should be discussed and agreed with the relevant functions.

4 The project manager, with the team members, prepares and agrees the initial business case document.

5 The Initial Business Case, including the project plan, is reviewed by the project sponsor and any other relevant stakeholders. It is then either accepted, rejected, deferred or amendments are requested.

The Initial Business Case is submitted for gate authorisation.

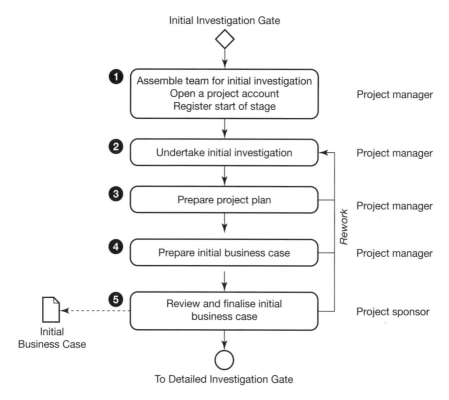

Figure 6.1 Steps in the Initial Investigation Stage

CHECKLIST FOR STARTING THE DETAILED INVESTIGATION STAGE

6.1

Business need and strategic fit

☐ Does the project fit the strategy?

☐ Is the business opportunity attractive?

☐ Are the risks acceptable?

Deliverables

☐ Is the Initial Business Case and investment appraisal acceptable?

☐ Is there a detailed schedule, resource and cost plan for the Detailed Investigation Stage?

☐ Is there an outline schedule, resource and cost plan for the full project?

☐ Have all the relevant business units and functions been involved in creating and reviewing the deliverables?

Health check!

☐ Has a project 'health check' been done and been found acceptable (see p. 456)?

Accountabilities

☐ Has a project sponsor been identified for the project?

☐ Has a project manager been identified for the project?

☐ Do you have the resources to undertake the Detailed Investigation Stage?

Operational and technical

☐ On current knowledge, is it technically feasible with current technology or is there a possible technical development path to provide the capability or service?

☐ Does the organisation currently have the operational capability to support it? If not is it likely this can be put in place within the current/proposed process architecture?

Health check scores

P	R	O	J	E	C	T	Total
☐	☐	☐	☐	☐	☐	☐	☐

Risk

☐ Low ☐ Medium ☐ High ☐ Impossible

Issues

Risk

Executive action

The Detailed Investigation Stage:

Promising ... Let's Have a Closer Look

Overview

Key deliverables

Process steps

During the Detailed investigation Stage you will identify and define the optimum solution and commercial proposition.

'Understanding is the beginning of approving.'

ANDRÉ GIDE, 1902

Overview

During the Detailed Investigation Stage you will identify and define the optimum solution and commercial proposition.

You will need to:

- evaluate possible options and identify a preferred solution;
- ensure the preferred solution will meet the defined needs;
- define process, technical, and operational requirements where appropriate;
- test/research the concept with the target users and/or customers.
- check any legal or regulatory issues;
- evaluate possible suppliers and partners.

The next gate, for which this stage prepares you, is critical as it is the last point at which you can stop the project before substantial financial commitments are made.

The next gate, for which this stage prepares you, is critical as it is the last point at which you can stop the project before substantial financial commitments are made.

Key deliverables

The Output Definition is the fundamental document set describing the output of the project in terms of process, organisation, systems, technology and culture. It is the document which integrates all the individual system, process and platform requirements. It also specifies how they will work together. The document set will continue to develop as the project proceeds and will be handed over to the manager(s) of any operational parts before the project is completed.

The Feasibility Report builds on the Initial Business Case. It includes the recommendation for which option should be adopted as the solution (including processes), and compares it against rejected solutions in financial and non-financial terms (see the CD-ROM for a template).

The Business Case contains the business rationale. It is the document on which the decision is made to authorise funding for the remainder of the project and the building in of costs and benefits to the business plan. The document is 'live' and under strict version control for the remainder of the project (see the CD-ROM for a template).

The Project Plan includes the detailed schedule, resource and cost plans for the Develop and Test Stage with the remaining stages in summary.

The Test Plan documents the tests required to verify performance of any outputs from the project both in isolation and working as a complete system (see the CD-ROM for a template).

Deliverable	Prepared by	Review by	Approved, prior to gate, by
Output definition	Project manager	Team members and experts	Project sponsor
Feasibility Report	Project manager	Team members and experts	Project sponsor
Business Case	Project manager	Team members and key functional managers	Project sponsor
Project Plan	Project manager	as above	Project sponsor
Test Plan	Project manager	as above	Proposed owners of deliverable

Note: These are minimum review roles and deliverables only. Each project manager should define the full set prior to the start of the stage.

Process steps

Detailed Investigation Gate. This gate determines whether further effort and resources should be invested in undertaking a detailed investigation. If the Initial Business Case is authorised, the Detailed Investigation Stage is started. See checklist on p. 98.

The Initial Business Case and project plans now come under formal version control.

1 The project manager informs the stakeholders and key team members that authority to start the stage has been given.
2 The project manager ensures the start of the stage has been registered and assembles the team and briefs them on the scope for this stage (see Chapter 19).
3 The detailed investigation work is carried out (within the project control cycle, see pp. 23, 55) to assess the possible solutions and a preferred option is recommended, bearing in mind the risks and the benefits. A feasibility report is prepared.
4 The feasibility report is reviewed, amended if necessary, and agreed by the project sponsor who decides which option should be chosen and refined further.
5 Work on defining the chosen option is carried out. This may involve refining the output definition, the operational aspects, training plans, business processes, market plans and system designs.

The Output Definition now comes under formal version control.

6 The project manager, with the team, prepares the detailed plan for the Develop and Test stage and finalises the business case document. These are reviewed with the team and stakeholders and, if necessary, are amended.
7 The detailed plan and business case are reviewed by the project sponsor and any other relevant stakeholders. It is then either accepted, rejected, deferred or amendments are requested.

The Business Case is submitted for gate authorisation.

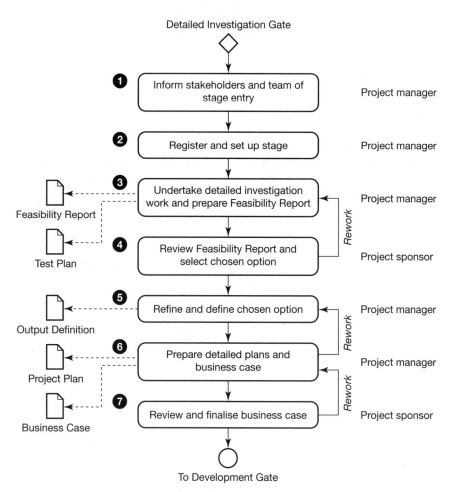

Figure 7.1 Steps in the Detailed Investigation Stage

CHECKLIST FOR STARTING THE DEVELOP AND TEST STAGE

7.1

Business need and strategic fit

☐ Does the project still fit the strategy?

☐ Have the development concepts (e.g. marketing) been researched and tested on target segments and the need reaffirmed?

☐ Is the business case acceptable and compelling?

☐ Have the key sensitivities and scenarios for the recommended option been checked and confirmed as acceptable?

☐ Is the Business Case ready to be built into the overall business plan?

Project plan

☐ Is there a detailed schedule, resource and cost plan for the develop and test stage?

☐ Is there an outline schedule, resource and cost plan for the full project?

☐ Are there sufficient review points in the plan (see Chapter 26)?

☐ Has the project been designed to eliminate known high risks (see Chapter 23)?

Accountabilities

☐ Are there resources to undertake the Develop and Test Stage?

☐ Have formal commitments been made by the relevant line managers?

Operational and technical

☐ Is it technically feasible with current technology?

☐ Does the organisation have the operational capability to support it?

Deliverables

☐ Is the output definition complete?

☐ Is it clear how the output will be tested?

Health check!

☐ Has a project health check been done and been found acceptable (see p. 456)?

Health check scores

P	R	O	J	E	C	T	Total
☐	☐	☐	☐	☐	☐	☐	☐

Risk

☐ Low ☐ Medium ☐ High ☐ Impossible

Issues

Risk

Executive action

The Develop and Test Stage:
Do It!

Overview

Key deliverables

Process steps

The Develop and Test Stage is when you spend the bulk of the costs relating to the project.

'The world can only be grasped by action, not contemplation.'
JACOB BRONOWSKI

Overview

The Develop and Test Stage is when you usually spend the bulk of the costs relating to the project. It comprises the outstanding design, development, creation and building of the chosen solution and its supporting systems, manuals, business processes, organisation and training. It concludes with a full test in a controlled environment to verify that the deliverables have been 'built right'. If this stage is of long duration (more than four months), it is essential that review points are built into the plan to ensure its on-going viability is assessed (see 'Reviews during a project', Chapter 26). It is also wise to have additional review points just prior to letting any major contracts relating to the project.

During this stage you will need to make a decision to start the Trial Stage, when you you validate, with customers and users, that what you have produced is the 'right thing'. This decision can be taken prior to completion of the full work scope for the stage, as only activities required for the trial need be completed.

Key deliverables

The Test Results verify that any testing has been completed in accordance with the test plans and acceptance criteria, prior to doing the ready for trial review. Any outstanding issues are noted (see the CD-ROM for a template).

The Trial Plan documents the way in which the output will be piloted and the criteria for determining whether it was successful (see the CD-ROM for a template).

The Ready for Trial Review Report is a short report which confirms that all deliverables, resources, and prerequisites across all functions required for starting the trial are in place (see the CD-ROM for a template).

The Project Plan: the schedule, resource and cost plan for the Trial Stage should be fully detailed with the remainder of the project in outline.

Deliverable	Prepared by	Review by	Approval, prior to gate, by
Test Results	Project manager	Team members and experts	Project sponsor
Trial plan	Project manager	Team members Operational staff	Project sponsor
Ready for Trial Review Report	Project manager	Team members Operational staff	Project sponsor
The Project Plan	Project manager	Team members	Project sponsor

Note: These are minimum review roles and deliverables only. Each project should define its full set prior to the start of the stage.

Process steps

Development Gate. This gate determines whether the development and testing work should start. If the Business Case is authorised, the Develop and Test stage is started and the benefits, revenues and costs are built into the Business Plan. See checklist on p. 106.

1 The project manager informs the stakeholders and key team members that authorisation to start development has been given.
2 The project manager assembles the team (including suppliers) and confirms the project controls, roles and accountabilities for each individual. The plan (as produced at the end of the previous stage) should be reviewed to ensure it is still valid.
3 The work, as defined in the business case and laid out in the project plan, is carried out within the project control cycle (see p. 23). Work is done, progress is measured, issues and variances noted and corrections made. As deliverables are produced they are reviewed, amended and finally accepted. These comprise those which are required prior to:
   - starting testing;
   - starting the Trial Stage (if one is required);
   - the Release Gate.

4 The tests are carried out, the results are reviewed, and any modification and retesting done. Some deliverables and the output definition may need to be amended in light of the tests.

5 A review is done to check that all activities have been done and deliverables are ready for the following stage(s) to start. All project documentation (including the project plan, output definition and business case) is updated.

If a Trial Stage is required, submit the Ready for Trial Report for gate authorisation. If a trial is not required, submit the Ready for Service Report for gate authorisation.

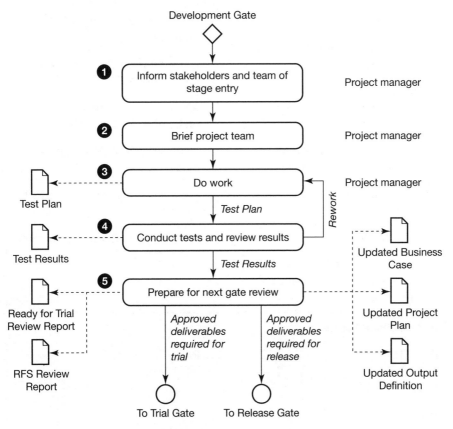

Figure 8.1 Steps in the Develop and Test Stage

CHECKLIST FOR STARTING THE TRIAL STAGE

8.1

Business need and strategic fit

☐ Is the project still a good business proposition?

☐ Is the project still correctly reflected in the overall business plan?

☐ Have all high risks been eliminated?

Project plan

☐ Is the project plan up to date, full and complete?

☐ Is there a detailed schedule, resource and cost plan for the Trial Stage?

☐ Is there an outline plan for the remainder of the project?

☐ Do we have sufficient resources to undertake the trial?

Health check!

☐ Has a project 'health check' been done and been found acceptable (see p. 456)?

For the trial

☐ Have the tests been finished and the results accepted?

☐ Has the trial plan been prepared?

☐ Have checklists been prepared for the customers and users?

☐ Have customers/users been identified and trial agreements drafted?

☐ Have the business processes been finalised?

☐ Are all relevant functions and units ready for the trial?

☐ Is the communications material ready?

☐ Are results monitoring systems in place?

☐ Have the trial acceptance criteria been agreed?

Health check scores

P	R	O	J	E	C	T	Total
☐	☐	☐	☐	☐	☐	☐	☐

Risk

☐ Low   ☐ Medium   ☐ High   ☐ Impossible

Issues

Risk

Executive action

The Trial Stage:
Try It Out

Overview

Key deliverables

Process steps

The solution must be acceptable to the users, functionally correct and highly likely to meet the organisation's business objectives.

'The full area of ignorance is not yet mapped. We are at present only exploring the fringes.'

J D BERNARL

Overview

During this stage, your partially proven solution is validated in the operational environment with live users and/or customers. The purpose is to validate whether:

- the solution is acceptable to the users and customers;
- all the capabilities work in a live environment, including all the business processes and supporting infrastructure;
- the business objective is likely to be met.

In this respect, the solution must be acceptable to the users, functionally correct and highly likely to meet the organisation's business objectives (see also p. 67 if you are not sure if you need a trial). The trial confirms that you have 'built the right thing'.

Key deliverables

The Trial Results is a summary document which confirms that the trials have been completed in accordance with the plan and acceptance criteria, and the developed solution is now ready to move to the Release Stage. Any outstanding issues are also noted (see the CD-ROM for a template).

The Ready For Service (RFS) Review Report is a short report which confirms that all deliverables and prerequisite activities required before starting the Release Stage have been completed (see the CD-ROM for a template).

The Project Plan: the schedule, resource and cost plan for the Release Stage should be fully detailed.

Deliverable	Prepared by	Review by	Approved, prior to gate, by
Trial results	Project manager	Team members	Project sponsor
RFS review report	Project manager	Team members	Project sponsor
The project plan	Project manager	Team members	Project sponsor

Note: These above are minimum review roles and deliverables only. Each project manager should define the full set prior to the start of the stage.

Process steps

Trial Gate. This gate determines whether you can start a trial of the proposed solution using real users or customers. If the Ready for Trial Report is authorised, the Trial Stage is started. See checklist on p. 112.

1 The project manager informs the relevant stakeholders and key team members that approval to start the Trial Stage has been given.
2 The project manager assembles the team and confirms the project controls, roles and accountabilities for each individual. The plan (as produced at the end of the previous stage) should be reviewed to ensure it is still valid.
3 The final preparations for the trial are carried out, as laid out in the project plan.
4 The trial is carried out, the results are reviewed and any modification and retrials done.

While the trial is being carried out, other activities and deliverables (such as training) are being delivered from the Develop and Test Stage.

5 A review is done to check the trial was acceptable, all activities have been done and deliverables are ready for the Release Stage to start. All project documentation (including the project plan, output definition and business case) is updated.

The Ready for Service Review Report is submitted for gate authorisation.

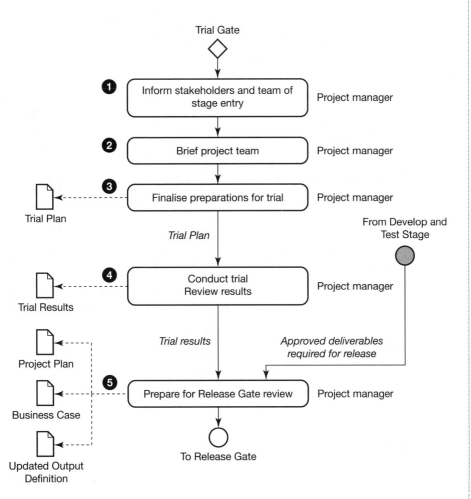

Figure 9.1 Steps in the Trial Stage

CHECKLIST FOR STARTING THE
RELEASE STAGE

9.1

Business need and strategic fit

- [ ] Is the project still a good business proposition?

- [ ] Have all high and medium risks been eliminated from the project?

Ready for service

- [ ] Are you absolutely sure, beyond reasonable doubt, that it will work? (Your reputation is at stake!)

- [ ] Have process designs across the organisation (and to third parties if needed) been accepted and is all training completed?

- [ ] Are benefits/results monitoring systems in place?

- [ ] Have the costs and benefits been reforecast against the business plan?

Project plan

- [ ] Is the project plan updated, full and complete?

- [ ] Is there a detailed schedule, resource and cost plan for the release stage?

- [ ] Do we have the resources to undertake the release stage?

Health check!

- [ ] Has a project 'health check' been done and been found acceptable (see p. 456)?

Health check scores

P	R	O	J	E	C	T	Total
[ ]	[ ]	[ ]	[ ]	[ ]	[ ]	[ ]	[ ]

Risk

[ ] Low   [ ] Medium   [ ] High   [ ] Impossible

_____

Issues
_____

Risk
_____

Executive action

The Release Stage:
Let's Get Going!

Overview

Key deliverable

Process steps

This is the stage when the 'rubber hits the road'.

'What we call the beginning is often the end. And to make an end is to make a beginning.'

T S ELIOT

Overview

This is the stage when 'the rubber hits the road', you unleash your creation on the world and start to reap the benefits your project was set up to realise. It involves:

- releasing the validated solution into its operational environment;
- the start of all operational support;
- the handover of the solution from the project manager to the functions and business units for on-going operation and assurance.

In addition, work is carried out post-release to ensure the environment left by the project is 'clean.'

It finishes with a project closure review, at which the project is formally shut down. The review takes the form of a 'lessons learned' session. What worked well on the project? What didn't? Were all the controls effective and useful? What would we use again? What would we do differently next time? Closure is discussed in more detail in Chapter 27.

Key deliverable

The Project Closure Report contains the notes of solution handover and project closure, including 'lessons learned' from the project in terms of how the processes, organisation, systems and team worked (i.e. the efficiency of the project). A terms of reference for the Post-Implementation Review is also included (see the CD-ROM for a template).

Deliverable	Review by	Approval, prior to gate, by
Project Closure Report	Involved key team members	Project sponsor

Note: These are minimum review roles and deliverables only. Each project should define its full set prior to the start of the stage.

Process steps

Release Gate. This gate determines whether you can start using the proposed solution in a full operational environment. If the ready for service report is authorised, the Release Stage is started. See checklist on p. 118.

1 The project manager informs the stakeholders and key team members that approval to start the Release Stage has been given.
2 The project manager assembles the team and confirms the project controls, roles and accountabilities for each individual. The plan (as produced at the end of the previous stage) should be reviewed to ensure it is still valid.
3 Final release activities and preparations are carried out (e.g. major print runs, manufacturing, final training).
4 The decision on the launch date is confirmed and communicated to all who need to know. If there are any snags then release may be put 'on hold' until they are sorted out.
5 The launch/release takes place.
6 Preparations for project closure are made.
7 Any outstanding work to complete the scope of the project is carried out. This may include removing redundant data from systems, withdrawing old manuals or literature, and shutting down redundant capabilities.
8 The project closure review is held and the project sponsor declares the project formally completed:
   - the project accounts are closed;
   - the development(s) (with output definition(s)) is handed over to the line for on-going management;
   - the terms of reference, accountabilities and timing for the Post-Implementation Review are agreed (see p. 127);
   - lessons on the efficacy of the project process are recorded and fed back to the process owner.

The project is now completed and closed.

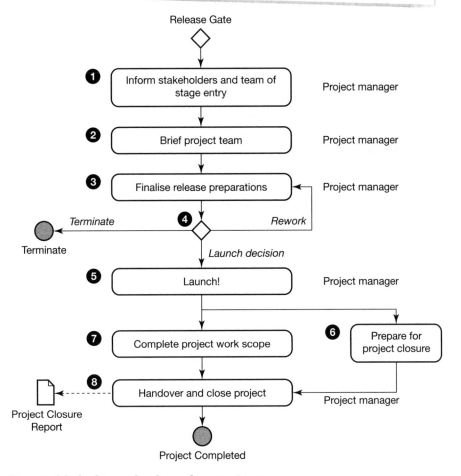

Figure 10.1 Steps in the release stage

CHECKLIST AT PROJECT CLOSURE

Business need and strategic fit

☐ Has the business forecast been updated to take into account the benefits arising from the project?

☐ Has someone agreed to be accountable for monitoring the benefits?

☐ Have review points and metrics for measuring the benefits been defined?

☐ Has the project account been closed so that no more costs can be incurred?

Risks and issues

☐ Have all issues been resolved?

☐ Has ownership of each outstanding risk and issue been accepted by a NAMED person in the line or in another project?

Post-Implementation Review (PIR)

☐ Have the timing, accountabilities, and terms of reference for the PIR been agreed?

Team/stakeholders

☐ Have all who need to know about the closure of the project been informed?

☐ Have team appraisals relating to the project been completed?

☐ Have those who deserve special thanks been acknowledged?

Lessons learned

☐ Have all lessons learned been recorded and communicated to the relevant process and documentation owners?

Handed over risks, issues and actions
Lessons learned
Executive action

The Post-Implementation Review:

How Did We Do?

Overview

Key deliverable

To be effective, the review must not be used as a 'witch hunt'. If you use it in this way, you'll never have the truth presented to you again!

'You can do anything in this world if you are prepared to take the consequences.'

W SOMERSET MAUGHAM

Overview

You should carry out a Post-Implementation Review after sufficient time has elapsed for the benefits of the project to be assessable. The review cannot cover every aspect but it should establish whether:

- the predicted benefits were delivered;
- the most effective operational processes were designed;
- the solution really met the business needs, both for users and customers.

As the project sponsor is the one who wants the benefits and for whom the project is undertaken, it is in his/her interest to initiate the review. This review should result in action plans for improvement where necessary and hence help in the achievement of the benefits. For major projects this review may be carried out by an 'audit' function, but in all cases it is better (although not essential) if it is conducted by someone independent from the project team. To be effective, the review must not be used as a 'witch hunt'. If you use it in this way, you'll never have the truth presented to you again! (See also Chapter 26.)

Key deliverable

The Post-Implementation Review (PIR) report assesses the success of the project against predefined criteria given in the business case and confirmed in the terms of reference for the PIR. It assesses how effective the project was in meeting its objectives and includes recommendations for improvements (see the CD-ROM for a template).

Deliverable	Review by	Approved by
Post-Implementation Review report	Independent reviewer or internal audit	Project sponsor

Note: Minimum review and approval criteria: the terms of reference should define all those who need to be involved.

CHECKLIST AT POST-IMPLEMENTATION REVIEW

11.1

Business need

☐ Are the benefits being realised as expected?

Operational aspects

☐ Are all aspects of the solution working as envisaged?

Action

☐ Has a corrective action plan been put in place to address any shortfall in expected benefits?

☐ Has a corrective action plan been put in place to address any shortfall in operational aspects?

☐ Have all lessons learned been recorded and communicated to the relevant stakeholders?

Applying the Staged Framework

Four types of project

Fitting into the staged framework

Small stuff, or 'simple' projects

Agile or rapid projects

'Just do it' projects – loose cannons

Big stuff, or projects and subprojects

Work packages

The extended project life cycle

*The staged framework requires that, by the time you reach the Development Gate, you know, with a reasonable level of confidence, **what** you are going to do, **how** you are going to do it and **who** is accountable for seeing it is done.*

'Through the unknown remembered gate.'

T S ELIOT

The previous chapters have taken you through a project management framework you can use for each of your projects. This framework leads the project sponsor and project manager on a course which, if followed, will ensure that quality and purpose are built into your projects from the start and developed as you proceed to your end-point. It also ensures all projects undertaken in your organisation can be referenced to the same, defined and known set of stages. How can this simple set of stages be applied to the different types of projects you have to do?

> **This framework leads the project sponsor and project manager on a course which, if followed, will ensure that quality and purpose are built into your projects from the start and developed as you proceed to your end-point.**

Four types of project

In his book, *All Change! The Project Leader's Secret Handbook*, Eddie Obeng describes four types of projects, each of which deals with a different kind of change. I have shown these in Figure 12.1.

Figure 12.1 Different types of change project
If you know what you are doing and how you are going to do it, you have a 'painting by numbers' project. If you know how but not what, you have a 'movie'. A 'quest' is when you know what you want, but not how you will achieve it. Finally a 'fog' is when you don't know what you want, nor how to achieve it.

Painting by numbers

Traditional projects tend to be of this kind. These projects have clear goals and a clearly defined set of activities to be carried out. You know *what* you want to achieve and *how* you will achieve it.

This project is often formally called a *closed project*.

Going on a quest

You are clear on *what* is to be done but clueless as to the means (*how*) to achieve it. It is named after the famous quest for the Holy Grail. The secret of this type of project is get your 'knights' fired up to seek for solutions in different places at the same time and ensure that they all return to report progress and share their findings on a fixed date. You can then continue to send them out, again and again, until you have sufficient information on how you can achieve your objectives.

Quests are invaluable as they give 'permission' for your people to explore 'out of the box' possibilities. However, they are notorious for overspending, being very late, or simply delivering nothing of benefit. You must keep very strict control over costs and timescales while allowing the scope free range.

This project is formally called a *semi-closed project*.

Making movies

In this type of project you are very sure of *how* you will do something but have no idea *what* to do. Typically your organisation has built up significant expertise and capability and you are looking for ways to apply it. There must be several people committed to the methods you will use.

This project is formally called a *semi-open project*.

Walking in the fog

This type of project is one where you have no idea *what* to do nor *how* to do it. It is often prompted as a reaction to a change in circumstances (e.g. political, competitive, social), although it can be set off proactively. You know you have to change and do something different; you simply can't stay still. You also may need to act with awesome velocity. This project needs, in some ways, to be managed like a quest. You need to have very tight control over costs and timescale; you need to investigate many options and possible solutions in parallel. Like a quest, these projects can end up in delivering nothing of benefit unless firmly controlled.

This project is formally called an *open project*.

Each of these project types has different characteristics and requires different leadership styles. They are also suited for different purposes.

Project type	Type of change it helps create or manage	Application
Painting by numbers	Evolutionary	Improving your continuing business operations
Going on a quest	Revolutionary outside current	Proactively exploring operations and ways of working (recipe)
Making a movie	Evolutionary	Leveraging existing capabilities
Lost in a fog	Revolutionary	Solving problem or exploring area outside your current operations and ways of working (recipe)

Source: Eddie Obeng, *Putting Strategy to Work* (London: Pitman Publishing, 1996)

Fitting into the staged framework

The staged framework requires that, by the time you reach the Development Gate, you know, with a reasonable level of confidence, *what* you are going to do and *how* you are going to do it. That is to say, at the Development Gate you will have a painting by numbers project (see Figure 12.2). The investigative stages are there to give you the time, resources and money to discover a solution to your problem. The Proposal will have settled *why* you need the project. However, your level of background knowledge will differ for each proposal you want to do. This will have a considerable impact on the way you undertake the investigative stages and the level of risk associated with the project at the start. Painting by numbers projects tend to be less risky than others, but not always. Figure 12.3 shows this in a different way: a 'normal' project (if there is such a thing!) can change from being a quest, movie, or fog to painting by numbers as it moves through the project life cycle. The clarity of your scope, timescale, costs and benefits will improve as you gain more knowledge. In addition, as we learned earlier (p. 52), the level of risk should decrease as you progress through the project.

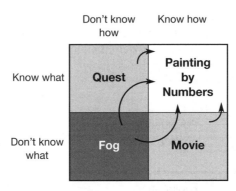

Figure 12.2 Creating a project you can implement

The staged framework requires, by the time you reach the Development Gate, that you know what you are going to do and how. That is to say, at the Development Gate, you will have a painting by numbers project. You may, however, start off as any of the project types – the investigative stages are the means by which you create the final project.

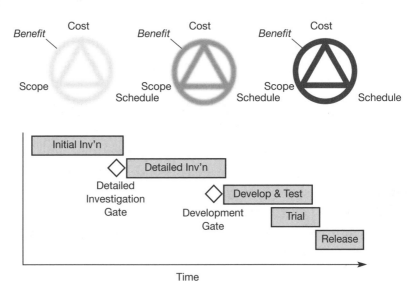

Figure 12.3 Getting to paint by numbers

A 'normal' project can change from being a 'quest', 'movie' or 'fog' to 'painting by numbers' as it moves through the project life cycle. The clarity of your scope, timescale, costs and benefits will improve as you gain more knowledge.

However, just to make your day, there are circumstances when you would allow a project to continue past the Development Gate as a fog, movie or quest. The level of risk would be higher than under normal circumstances but that is your choice. The 'game' of projects has principles but few rules. Directors have to direct and managers have to manage; that is your role. If an action makes common sense, do it and do it openly.

RULES AND EXCEPTIONS

Some companies tie themselves up in process rules bound neatly in files with quality assurance labels. These rules often go to great levels of detail covering every conceivable scenario.

I would argue that this is a fruitless exercise. It is far better to have a few basic principles and make sure your people understand why you need them and how they help them do their jobs. You can then handle the odd 'exception' using 'exception management', dealing with it on its own merits within the principles you have laid out. In other words, give the managers and supervisors the freedom to do their jobs and exercise the very skills you are paying them for.

If you write rules at a microlevel:

- you may get them wrong;
- you will spend a long time writing them thus diverting you from the real issues;
- people will look for 'legitimate' ways round them;
- you will cause people to break them (perhaps through ignorance) and then risk making them feel bad about it;
- you risk employing an army of police to check that the rules are being adhered to.

Small stuff, or 'simple' projects

'I understand stages and gates,' you may say, 'but isn't it all a bit too much for smaller simple projects?' Let us take the example of how what I would term a 'simple' project differs from the type of project normally associated with staged processes and how you can deal with them using the same management framework.

A normal project may start off as painting by numbers, a fog, a quest or a movie. The investigative stages are worked through until you are confident (say, around 90–95 per cent certain) that the required benefits can be achieved. At the Detailed Investigation Gate you will have narrowed your options down and have approval and funding to complete the Detailed Investigation Stage. At the Development Gate you would have approval to complete the project as a whole – it has become a painting by numbers project.

With a simple project, you usually know a great deal about it before you even start. By the time you finish the Initial Investigation Stage you may have fully defined the project outputs and plan and your confidence level will be as high as it is normally for a larger project at the Development Gate (Figure 12.4).

In these circumstances, the Detailed Investigation Stage may either be:

- reduced in scope and time to become very small;
- or dispensed with altogether.

In these circumstances, full authorisation to complete the project can be given at the Detailed Investigation Gate (see Figure 12.5). This doesn't mean you can bypass the remaining gates, you still need to have reviews and checks to ensure on-going viability. So if you omit the Detailed Investigation Stage you must meet the full criteria of the Development Gate before you continue.

In this way, you have used the principles of the framework, checking at every gate but you have avoided doing any unnecessary work. Making the key control documents, Initial Business Case and Business Case identical enables this to happen without the need to duplicate any documentation. (See also p. 194 for a discussion of simple projects in relation to decision making.)

Figure 12.4 Simple project

A simple project can be defined very closely, in the Initial Investigation Stage.

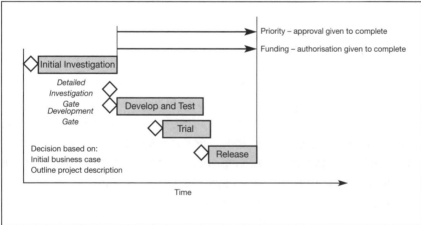

Figure 12.5 The stages for a simple project

The top diagram represents a project where some detailed investigation work still needs to be done. Nevertheless, the level of confidence is high enough to authorise and fund the project to completion.

The lower diagram represents an even simpler case where no further investigative work needs to be done. The project is checked against the criteria for the Development Gate and, if acceptable, moves straight into the Develop and Test Stage.

Agile or rapid projects

Consider also the concept of 'agile', 'rapid' and 'dynamic system development' projects. These are particular development techniques or methods where a project is defined with a fixed budget and timescale but where the scope is varied to suit (see Figure 12.6). If the team runs out of time or money, the scope is reduced in order to meet the time/cost targets. Provided a predefined, minimum scope is delivered, the project will remain within its area of benefit viability. In many ways, it is like a 'simple' project except that the scope is variable within known limits. You are, therefore, able to assign resources to it with confidence, knowing when they will become available for other projects.

Agile techniques usually involve iterative requirements definition, design and delivery using either a prototype platform or the actual operational platform. Thus the Detailed Investigation Stage is often merged with the Develop and Test Stage. Having two stages running in parallel on closely knit work such as this can confuse people. The usual point made is 'What stage do I book my time to on the time sheet?' This can be dealt with by dispensing with the detailed investigation altogether and moving straight from the Initial Investigation Stage to the Develop and Test Stage (similar to Figure 12.5, lower diagram).

RAPID OR RABID?

The lessons from Chapter 2 have taught us that there is no 'fast track' process. If there were, it would become the usual process (see p. 18). 'Agile', 'Rapid' or 'DSDM' are software development methods or techniques which enable you to develop your deliverables faster within the overall project framework. A correctly designed and applied staged framework should not slow any projects down unless they need to be.

> *The lessons have taught us that there is no 'fast track' process. If there were, it would become the usual process.*

Agile techniques are used when they suit the particular circumstances of the project. If you use them merely because you are 'in a hurry', you risk reducing your project to chaos, i.e. it will become 'rabid' rather than rapid!

Figure 12.6 Rapid project
A project using rapid techniques has fixed timescale, cost and minimum benefits. The scope varies to suit these constraints.

'Just do it' projects – loose cannons

There are cases when senior management will issue an edict to finish a project by a certain time whatever the cost. In certain circumstances this is a valid thing to do, especially when the survival of the organisation requires it. Such projects must be treated with extreme caution as often they come about as an executive's 'pet project' and may have little proven foundation in business strategy. I would argue that there are very few instances in companies where something needs to be done regardless of the costs and consequences. These projects invariably start off being optimistic and end up bouncing around the organisation with the demand that more and more resources are assigned to it without delay. Consequently, there can be considerable impact on day-to-day operations as well as significant delays to other projects, remembering delayed projects equate to delayed benefits. They also tend to be very stressful for those associated with them. The damage left in the wake of such projects can be awesome even if they appear to succeed!

Most organisations can cope with one of these kinds of projects – occasionally. Most organisations cope better if there aren't any. However, if you believe one is needed it should still be aligned into the project framework as closely as possible and managed as an 'exception'.

But before starting, consider the following questions:

- Why am I doing this?
- Is it really far more important than everything else?
- Am I really sure what I am doing?

There must be very compelling reasons to allow a loose cannon project to start. Responding to a problem by panicking is not usually a good enough reason! Using the issue breakthrough technique is a better starting point (see Chapter 24).

You must be absolutely clear what other activities and projects it can be allowed to disrupt. You can create more problems, for yourself and for others, than you will solve. You must consider the real 'cost/benefit' and take into consideration the inefficiencies and lost or delayed benefits from the disrupted projects. After all that, if you really must do it then:

1 Undertake an initial investigation first so you can make an informed decision;
2 Keep the project as short as possible (say, three months maximum). If you need longer, break the project up into smaller pieces.

- **No matter what project you want to undertake, always carry out an initial investigation so that you can decide, on an informed basis, the most appropriate way to take the project forward (e.g. normal, simple, rapid).**
- **Having decided your approach, record it in your initial business case in Section 2.10 on project approach (see p. 302).**

Big stuff, or projects and subprojects

Defining the scope and boundaries of a project is often problematic. The term 'project', like its cousin 'programme', is often used so loosely that it has very little meaning. In some cases, what one person calls a project, another will call a programme. Similarly 'subproject' and 'project' can cause confusion. The relative structural relationship is identical:

Programme		Project
Project	*is equivalent to*	Subproject

Nine times out of ten it doesn't really matter what you call things but, if you are to understand business projects fully, you need to be able to see the distinction. It may be that the way your project support systems are configured will determine the terminology for you.

If you are to have clarity of communication in your business, you must decide on the definitions which suit you best and stick to them (see p. 62).

A project, in a business environment, is:

- a finite piece of work (it has a beginning and an end) undertaken in stages;
- within defined cost and time constraints;
- *directed at achieving a stated business benefit.*

In other words, the key elements of benefit, scope, time and cost are all present. The only place where all this is recorded is in the Business Case, which serves as the key document for approving and authorising the project in initial form at the Detailed Investigation Gate and in full at the Development Gate. As a working assumption, therefore, we can say a project is only a project if it has a Business Case. Business Cases are attached to business projects!

It, therefore, follows that . . . any piece of work which is finite, and time and cost constrained, but does not realise business benefit, is not in fact a business project. It may be managed using project techniques or it may be a subproject or work package within a project. On its own, however, it has no direct value. Only when combined with other elements of work does it have any value. It is for this reason that you need to carefully consider how you handle what are often called 'enabling projects'. Enabling projects are undertaken in order to create a capability or platform which later projects will use as part of the solution. Enabling projects do not create any value on their own. For this reason, enabling projects cannot be 'standalone' but must be considered as part of a wider programme, under a single programme-wide business case.

> *Any piece of work which is finite, and time and cost constrained, but does not realise business benefit, is not in fact a business project. It may be managed using project techniques or it may be a subproject or work package within a project.*

Work packages

In any project, the project manager delegates accountability for parts of the work to members of the core team. This is done by breaking the project into work packages, usually centred around deliverables. Each work package has a person accountable for it. This work package can be decomposed again and again until you reach activity or task level. This structure is called a 'work breakdown structure' (WBS) and is a fundamental control tool for a project.

The first level of breakdown is the project itself. The second level of breakdown comprises the life cycle stages (initial investigation, detailed investigation, etc.). Below this are the more detailed work packages.

The top diagram in Figure 12.7 shows this: the Develop and Test Stage comprises three work packages (XX, YY and ZZ). Of these, package YY is divided into three more (Y1, Y2 and Y3). The whole structure of the pro-

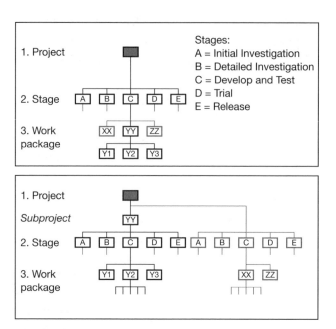

Figure 12.7 Explaining work packages and subprojects
The top diagram shows a project divided into the five stages of the project framework. Each stage can then be divided into a number of work packages (e.g. C is divided into XX, YY and ZZ). In the bottom diagram the same project has been restructured to have YY managed as a subproject.

ject flows logically from project to stage to work package. Each work package has its own defined time, cost, scope and person accountable. It will *not* have its own discrete benefit. All things being equal, this is the way you should structure your projects. It provides good control as no part of the project can proceed into the next stage without all preconditions being present.

The bottom diagram in Figure 12.7 shows an alternative structure for exactly the same project. In this case, however, the project manager has chosen to treat work YY as a subproject. In other words, it has a single identifiable work package, which is itself divided into stages and then into the lower level work packages (Y1, Y2 and Y3). The remainder of the project is dealt with in the preferred way. There are risks in using this structure:

- You may have a timing misalignment between subproject YY and the rest of the project as there are two separate life cycle stage sets.
- It is a more complex structure for the same work scope.

Both these require greater coordination by the project manager.

From this we are able to define subprojects more exactly:

Subprojects are tightly coupled and tightly aligned parts of a project which are undertaken in stages.

The conditions under which you would choose to set up subprojects depend on the degree of delegation you want to effect – it is akin to sub-contracting the work. You also find this type of structure happens as a result of systems and process limitations or reporting requirements. It may be more convenient to represent and report a completely delegated piece of work as a subproject as it may relate to work which has been let externally, under a contract or internally. Many companies treat their internal software development in this way.

The extended project life cycle

Many projects are undertaken to not only create products, services or capabilities but also to operate the outcomes of the project. For example, a contractor may not only build a road, but also maintain it throughout its useful life. In such situations the traditional project life cycle, described in Chapter 3, is extended to cover the full operation of the ser-vice (sometimes this is referred to as a product life cycle). In such situations, the stages of the project may cover:

- **Development stages** a new capability is developed using a project as the delivery vehicle, taking into account the 'whole life' needs of the organisation, with respect to the use of the outputs, cost of creation and cost of operation. The last stage of the project (Release Stage) typi-cally overlaps the early operation of the new capability, in order to facilitate knowledge transfer and to be able to react to any operational issues uncovered. In a contracting situation, this is often defined in the contract (for example in construction's 'Maintenance Period').
- **Operational stages** the capability is used and minor upgrades are done as 'business as usual'.
- **Upgrade stages** more significant upgrades are undertaken to extend the product life, often using a project as the delivery vehicle.
- **Retirement or withdrawal stages** the capability is withdrawn, retired or decommissioned when it is no longer needed. This is often complex and also requires a project approach.

Whilst the 'extended' or 'product life cycle' is being seen more frequently, particularly in government work, except in the simplest cases, it is taking the project concept too far to treat all the above as a 'single project'. It is better to treat such situations as programmes and thereby provide a greater degree of flexibility in how they are directed, managed and structured. Figure 12.8 shows a typical extended project life cycle.

Figure 12.8 The extended project life cycle
The project framework in Chapter 3 can be extended to include the operational stages of the outputs; however, such situations are usually better treated as a programme.

A Few Related Projects:
Simple Programmes

Simple programmes

Sharing projects – interdependencies

Some projects are simply too large to manage as a single entity.

'Adventure is the result of poor planning.'

COL. BLASHFORD SNELL

Simple programmes

We have seen that the staged project framework can be applied to any type of project for any purpose. It is a tool that you can adopt and adapt to suit your needs. Nevertheless, a simple string of activities, passing through five defined stages, may not give you the full flexibility you require. We saw in Figure 12.7 how we can manage the subparts of a project using the work break-down structure. This is how the project manager delegates work to the managers within the core team.

Programmes

Some projects, however, are simply too large to manage as a single entity. It is often more convenient and effective to define the work in a series of closely related and linked projects, each of which is managed by a project manager, reporting to a programme manager (Figure 13.1). The role of the programme manager in this respect is similar to that of a project manager (as described in Chapter 4) except that detailed management of parts of the project is delegated, as is the associated administration. He/she will have a core team of project managers, rather than team managers.

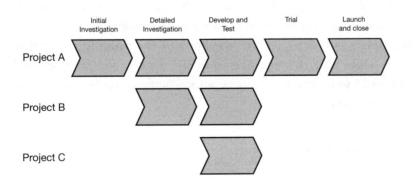

Figure 13.1 A simple programme
A programme where each constituent project is used to manage a substantial work scope.

Phased programmes

Other projects are so extended in time it is beneficial to phase the development and delivery of the solutions. This ensures that the organisation starts benefiting as early as possible and also increases the likelihood of success (Figure 13.2). It also gives the organisation a 'get-out' if the need the programme was set up to fill either evaporates or if the chosen solution is not meeting it. The start-point for each new phase (or tranche) acts as just such a review point.

Figure 13.2 A phased programme
A programme comprising a number (in this case three) of phased deliverables, each managed as a project, with its own life cycle.

The permutations beyond this are endless. For example, you may have a phased programme where each phase is itself a programme such as that described in Figure 13.1. There are no rules, you just have to make it very clear what you are doing. The staged framework is very useful in this respect as it can give an overview of the programme in terms of known stages such that any person in the organisation can understand it. You should treat any programme which is not described in this way as very suspicious.

Programme organisations

Organisation structures for simple programmes are many and varied. In principle, however, they are very similar to those described in Chapter 4. The key difference is that instead of the structure comprising a project manager supported by team managers and members, it comprises a programme manager supported by project managers, all of whom have their own teams. This is shown in Figure 13.3. The accountabilities of a programme manager in other respects are the same as that for a project manager. However, the scale of most programmes is such that the experience and skill set required to carry out the accountabilities are quite different. Note, in this structure, the programme manager would take on the 'project sponsor' role for each project within the programme. It is, however, perfectly acceptable for the sponsorship role to be undertaken directly by the programme sponsor or another person appointed by him/her.

Figure 13.3 A typical simple programme structure
A programme structure comprises a programme manager supported by project managers. In addition, there is often a programme support group to undertake the essential coordination and administration, and to implement common standards. The project sponsor role for each project may be undertaken by the programme manager or assigned by the programme sponsor to others.

Sharing projects – interdependencies

A project comprises all the work required to ensure you put the changes in place to enable the benefits to be realised. On occasions, however, the deliverable you require may be produced by another project, often within the same programme, but not necessarily so. In this case your project is said to be *dependent* on the other project. Such interdependencies are noted in the business case in the 'scope, impacts and interdependencies' section (see also pp. 299, 353). Sharing of work between projects:

- adds to the efficient use of resources on your projects;
- ensures consistency between developments;
- reduces costs of projects for your business.

In all, it sounds like a 'good thing'. With most companies relying heavily on information systems to enable them to run the business, software development, whether in-house or out-sourced, is frequently required as part of business change and is 'shared' between projects. From the point of view of the systems developer, it is preferable to batch requirements from new projects and deliver them as a new software release. It makes life easier for the development team, for configuration management, for implementation and for training. In many cases, this is in fact sound practice but it does need to be considered more widely than that. If you take this approach, a number of projects, serving different needs and under different programmes, may be bundled together. If this one software delivery is delayed by just a single problematic part of the development, relating to one project only, the whole bundle slips. In other words, the full set of interdependent projects is tied to the one with the greatest risk. In fact, the slippage may be caused by the features required by the lowest priority project in the bundle. It is hardly surprising that software delivery is invariably 'blamed' for making projects late. (While I have made an example of software, the same principle applies to any deliverable which is shared between projects.)

> *If this one software delivery is delayed by just a single problematic part of the development, relating to one project only, the whole bundle slips. In other words, the full set of interdependent projects is tied to the one with the greatest risk.*

From a risk-management viewpoint it is often preferable to separate out the discrete high-priority developments and carry them out in separate releases. Don't build in risk from the start by bundling things that need not be bundled. The loss of efficiency may be paid for many times over by the benefits flowing from having projects deliver on time.

> *Don't build in risk from the start by bundling things that need not be bundled.*

PROGRAMMES

As discussed in Chapter 3, words such as 'programme' can be used in many different ways. Although some standards organisations and methodology writers are trying to create global definitions, in my experience, it will take a long time for these to become fully accepted, if at all. Three different uses of the term 'programme' are given below, which show the range of possible interpretations:

- **Portfolio**: a set of related projects aimed at meeting the business plan needs (or part of). These are dealt with in Part Three of this book as 'business programmes'.
- **Goal directed**: a set of closely related projects aimed at creating a new capability (as described in this chapter). This is typically outside the usual routine of the organisation. They are a way of effecting one-off, major change. in this book, I simply call them 'programmes' or 'big projects'.
- **Heartbeat**: a set of activities managed around service delivery, e.g. regular releases for a large IT system. This is a very 'functional' view and not really much to do with business-led project management, although its work content may represent work packages.

These are shown below:

	Portfolio	Goal directed	Heartbeat
Programme's control of projects	Coordinate to extract synergy benefits	Definition and direction of all projects within the programme	Integration of identified changes into a cohesive programme
Planning organisation	Programme overlays project roles: project and project manager retain strong relationship	Programme acts as sponsor client for all projects	Programme arbitrates between multiple client needs
Planning horizon	Indeterminate: as long as it adds value	Until the goal is achieved	Until the 'system' is withdrawn
Programme relationship the line	Draws on line resources and complements line management with business leadership	Draws resources from line management	Takes on traditional line management role of functions (e.g. operational performance)

Source: Pellegrinelli, S. (1997) 'Programme management: organising project-based change', *International Journal of Project Management*, vol. 15, no. 3 (June 1997), pp. 141–149.

QUESTIONING YOUR PROGRAMMES

13.1

1 Choose any programme in your organisation and identify the component projects.

2 Split each project into the five project stages, one stage per Post-It Note, using a different colour for each project.

3 Prepare a large sheet of paper or a white board, indicating a timescale on the horizontal axis sufficient to include the entire programme timescale. Draw a vertical 'time now' line.

4 Place each project onto the board, with each stage aligned to the appropriate date. Can you actually do this? If not, question how you really know what is going on and how you can direct the programme with any degree of confidence or knowledge.

5 Identify any interdependencies and mark them with a down arrow from the delivering project to the receiving project. Check for multiple two-way dependencies – this could indicate poor project definition. Remember, interdependencies are potential weak points which can be forgotten or where accountability is abdicated. Good programme definition minimises dependencies!

6 Look for any very long stages – can you shorten these? Be very wary of any prolonged investigative stages.

7 Look for when benefits start to flow – can you redesign the programme to achieve any benefits earlier than this?

8 Look at where your key review and decision points are (they should map onto your gates) – have you sufficient of these to ensure control? Be very wary if it has all been authorised in one lump.

DEALING WITH MANY PROJECTS

'The certainties of one age are the problems of the next.'

R H TAWNEY, 1926

In Part Two we looked at the framework for managing a single project, taking it from being an idea, through various life cycle stages until benefits are being realised. We also examined how the staged approach could be used as a management framework for any type of project you might choose and/or bundles of related projects (programmes).

In Part Three I will explain how you can keep track of all the projects and programmes which together make up the set of initiatives aimed at changing your business to suit its future strategic direction. The different ways in which organisations control the full portfolio of projects they are undertaking are as diverse and numerous as the organisations themselves. It is here that the aspects of culture, structure and systems come to the fore to influence what you actually do. There is no one 'right' way, but there are many 'wrong' ways!

- **Balance the risks across your project portfolio.**
- **Build the business case into your business plan as soon as the project has been approved.**
- **Make *informed* decisions on which projects you allow to continue.**
- **Prioritise *benefits*, not projects.**
- **Ensure that you have the freedom to change by having 'white space' resources.**
- **Keep a list of the projects you are undertaking.**

How to use Part Three

Read Part Three with an open mind. Understand the principles. Note what needs to be taken into account. Consider how you can deal with these in your organisation with the particular constraints you have. Do not be too quick to discard the approaches given. Adapt them to meet your needs, within the constraints you have, but stick to the basic principles.

Portfolios of Projects

The Business Programme

What's different about Business Programme management?

Managing the portfolio

Prerequisites for effective portfolio management

Directing a 'portfolio' of projects is a key senior management task, as it is this 'bundle' of projects that will take you from where you are now to your, hopefully, better future.

'What shall become of us without the barbarians? Those people were a kind of solution.'

CONSTANTINE CAVAFY, 1863–1933

The Business Programme

In Chapters 12 and 13 we considered the following definitions:
A **project**, in a business environment, is:

- a piece of work with a beginning and end;
- undertaken within defined cost and time constraints;
- *directed at achieving a stated business benefit.*

Subprojects are tightly coupled and tightly aligned parts of a project.
Programmes are a tightly coupled and tightly aligned grouping of projects.

We also saw how a project moves from being 'undefined' to being 'defined'. This was then put into the context of four project types:

- painting by numbers;
- going on a quest;
- making movies;
- walking in a fog.

Once this is understood, you should be able to define a single project in terms of its life cycle stages. However, business is rarely so simple that a single project or even programme can achieve all that is needed. The next step is to understand how bundles (or portfolios) of programmes and standalone projects are used together with other business activities to further your aims. We will call these 'Business Programmes'.

Business Programmes comprise current benefit generating business activities together with a loosely coupled but tightly aligned portfolio of projects and programmes, aimed at realising the benefits of part of a business plan or strategy.

They are best explained by using a simplified example.

You may have a business objective to increase your revenue from $10m to $15m in two years. You've chosen to do this by increasing your share of an under-exploited segment of your market. The alternative is to withdraw from that segment, milking whatever cash you can from it on the way. In order to achieve the required target revenue, you have found that you need to:

- Enhance your current product to include some new features. (Project 1 – enhance old product.)
- Develop a new product to exploit an unfulfilled need identified in the market. To do this quickly, you have decided to launch a basic version of the new product, as soon as practical, to start engaging the market. This would use existing manufacturing capability. (Project 2 – the basic new product.) The launch would be followed up four months later with an enhanced product which meets the full needs. (Project 2A – the enhanced new product.)
- Speed of delivery is a buying factor for your target market and current delivery channels are too slow. You need to decrease delivery time to protect revenues. If the speed of delivery can be greatly increased it will enhance revenues enabling you to win business off competitors. (Project 2B – decrease delivery time.)
- You also know there is a quality problem in manufacturing the current product. While the levels of faults have been acceptable to the target market in the past, this is not the case for the future. You need to reduce manufacturing faults and hence protect revenue. If faults stay at present levels, customers will choose alternative products. (Project 3 – reduce faults.)

You can see that the five projects are aligned to your overall strategy and that each provides a discrete business benefit. Most are independent. (Only Project 2A depends on Project 2 as you cannot enhance a product until you know what it is.)

> **Traditionally, organisations make their projects too big. Dividing projects into smaller pieces makes success more likely and implementation easier.**

Notice that the approach has been to split the new product development into two phases (Projects 2 and 2A). This benefits you by gaining early revenue and having a foothold in the market. Traditionally, organisations make their projects too big. Dividing projects into smaller pieces (chunks of change) makes success more likely and implementation easier.

Finally, you need to take account of the benefits you are expecting from the product as it currently is in the market. Your aim is to obtain a $15m revenue. The benefits from your current product and future projects and initiatives need to be sufficiently high to meet that target.

As a business manager, you are not particularly concerned with the individual performance of each project and product. Of more interest is the total benefit. Thus, if your current product starts to perform better than expected, a delay in a project may not be too significant. Only *you* can decide the relative importance of the projects within the business programme.

How did the projects within the business programme come about?

Keeping to the example, how did the managers derive their approach and end up with the five projects I described? The starting point was a problem for the directors of the organisation: they needed more revenue. They needed to look at their complete mix of products and markets and decide the most likely areas for gaining the additional, profitable revenue. (Perhaps they needed a new product and a new market!) One option identified by the review was that they either take a minimum prescribed market share of a particular segment or they withdraw from it completely. It was considered untenable to keep the status quo. This would lead to a decline in revenue to about $7m per year. This conversation is firmly within the domain of business strategy and planning. What is needed now is to take it to action.

The five projects could not, in fact, have come about directly as the result of a strategic review. The organisation simply would not have known enough to make that jump. At most, a required timescale and overall affordable budget annual cash flow could have been set (i.e. constraints applied by the business). However, a project could have been initiated to look at various options – a quest! The Initial Investigation Stage would spawn a set of possible projects. These may just have been:

- enhance the existing product (Project 1);
- develop a new product (Project 2);
- reduce faults (Project 3).

Each fulfils the definition of a business project by realising discrete benefits. Each will further the aims of the organisation to attain more revenue.

However, the investigative stages of Project 2 came up with a constraint on manufacturing the new product. It was not possible to do it in the time available and hence a decision was made to create the product in two phases. We now have:

- enhance the existing product (Project 1);
- develop a new product (Project 2);
- enhance the new product (Project 2A);
- reduce faults (Project 3).

Again, the Detailed Investigation Stage of Project 2 found, as part of the market research, that delivery time was a more important buying factor than realised. If amendments to Project 2 were made to incorporate this, it would have slipped and the revenue targets would have been missed. Consequently, a separate project was started off to take this aspect into account (Project 2B) (see Figure 14.1).

Notice what has happened. Projects spawn projects! A simple business objective of 'Get $15m revenue' has been translated into action in the form of five projects. When combined, these realise the benefit that the business requires.

Note that each project is defined such that it delivers a slice of that benefit, either independently or, as in the case of Projects 2 and 3, in series. Also notice that the business solution has been broken into discrete pieces. This has the effect of making them easier to implement and also allows benefits to be realised earlier than if the full scope were undertaken in a single project. You can also proceed with parts of the business programme as soon as you're ready, while other parts are still in the fog.

Look at the projects that have resulted. Did they start off as fogs, quests, movies or painting by numbers? Probably the mix is as follows:

Project 1 – enhance old product: Painting by numbers
Project 2 – the basic new product: Movie
Project 2A – the enhanced new product: Quest or fog
Project 2B – decrease delivery time: Quest
Project 3 – reduce faults: Quest

Project 2 has to use existing manufacturing plant for producing the new product. Project 2A needs to be converted to a painting by numbers project if it is to succeed. Projects 2B and 3 are more open ended. You may spend a fortune looking at possibilities but still not achieve a breakthrough. This, on its own, gives you a feel for the risk you are facing. You are not likely to have too much confidence in the benefits for those projects which finish more than a year from now. So, to make sure that your business programme is robust, you will need continually to reforecast your benefits. With a business programme like that shown, a related business planning and forecasting cycle of three months would probably be about right.

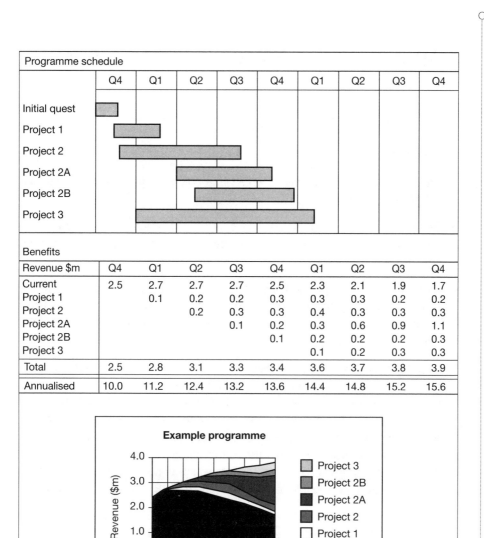

Programme schedule	Q4	Q1	Q2	Q3	Q4	Q1	Q2	Q3	Q4
Initial quest									
Project 1									
Project 2									
Project 2A									
Project 2B									
Project 3									

Benefits									
Revenue $m	Q4	Q1	Q2	Q3	Q4	Q1	Q2	Q3	Q4
Current	2.5	2.7	2.7	2.7	2.5	2.3	2.1	1.9	1.7
Project 1		0.1	0.2	0.2	0.3	0.3	0.3	0.2	0.2
Project 2			0.2	0.3	0.3	0.4	0.3	0.3	0.3
Project 2A				0.1	0.2	0.3	0.6	0.9	1.1
Project 2B					0.1	0.2	0.2	0.2	0.3
Project 3						0.1	0.2	0.3	0.3
Total	2.5	2.8	3.1	3.3	3.4	3.6	3.7	3.8	3.9
Annualised	10.0	11.2	12.4	13.2	13.6	14.4	14.8	15.2	15.6

Figure 14.1 Business Programme schedule and expected revenue

The schedule for the projects within the Business Programme is shown at the top; each bar represents a project. The middle part of the figure shows the slices of revenue expected as a result of each project coming to fruition layered on the revenues you expect from the current product. This is shown graphically below.

The example is necessarily simpler than most situations you will find in practice as most Business Programmes comprise many more projects; nevertheless, it does demonstrate the key aspects of Business Programmes.

STARTING TO BUILD YOUR BUSINESS PROGRAMME

14.1

1 List the primary business objectives of your organisation.

2 Take the list of projects from Project Workout 3.2.

3 Write each one on a Post-It Note.

4 Start placing them on a wall or large white board in approximate chronological order.

5 Group together in bands across the board those which you believe are targeted at fulfilling the primary business objective, selected from your list from step 1.

6 Identify any interdependencies between projects (i.e. where one project relies on the deliverable(s) from another in order to meet its objective). Draw an arrow from the project creating the deliverable to the one requiring the deliverable.

7 You may have a very complex picture by now! Try to simplify it. Projects with arrows going both ways between them are probably the same project even if you've defined them as separate. To test this, ask yourself if either one of the projects on its own produces any benefit to the business. If both projects are needed, they are the same project. Look for clusters of linked projects which have no arrows between them and other clusters. They may be your business programmes. Look for projects which don't have significant benefits: mark them for possible termination (see p. 448).

8 Look at the complexity of the interdependencies. The more complex and interwoven, the more risky the portfolio becomes. Think of ways of rescoping projects to create a set of programmes and projects which are relatively independent and will realise benefits early. Rescoping entails moving the accountability for producing a deliverable from one project to another.

CHANGES TO PROJECTS

In some cases, it is necessary to include new scope in an on-going project. Proper control of changes to the project scope are required to ensure that only beneficial changes are made. Chapter 25 explains this more fully.

What's different about Business Programme management?

Business Programmes support business plans

Business Programme management provides a framework and practical tool for managing multiple programmes and projects in pursuit of defined strategic objectives. Business Programme management complements project and programme management but it takes a much broader, enterprise-wide view as it also includes benefits from current operations. Benefits from projects usually start after the project has been completed and the project team has been stood down. However, benefits from Business Programmes start to flow as soon as the first project within the business programme has been completed and its outputs incorporated into 'normal business'. The key focus for Business Programme management is ensuring that current activities plus the programmes and projects as a whole provide the benefit required overall, regardless of the performance of individual components. Other differences are highlighted in the table that follows.

> *The advantages of taking a 'Business Programme approach' is that you are able, as we have seen from the simple example, to break up the required changes into achievable pieces and manage the implementation in a coordinated way.*

The advantages of taking a 'Business Programme approach' is that you are able, as we have seen from the simple example, to break up the required changes into achievable pieces and manage the implementation in a coordinated way. The change is therefore less likely to appear chaotic to the recipients (be they your own employees, your suppliers or your customers). You are also able to maintain a focus on the true business objectives of the Business Programme rather than be lost in the minutiae of delivery. This enables you to spot future gaps in benefits (either due to late projects or under-performance in benefit terms from ones already delivered) and take the necessary corrective action. You are also able to take a balanced view of the risks associated with a Business Programme.

Business Programme management	Programme and project management
Broadly spread activity, concerned with overall strategic objectives as part of a business plan. It's a continuous activity, with no defined end-point	Intense, and focused activity aimed at realising a 'slice' of benefit to the business programme as defined in a business case. It is a discrete activity, with a defined end-point
Is suited to managing and balancing a large number of constituent programmes and projects with complex and often changing interdependencies	Best suited to realising achievable benefits directly related to deliverables and outputs
Is suited to managing the impact of and benefits from a number of aligned programmes and projects in such a way as to ensure a smooth transition from the present to the new order	Is suited to delivering defined benefits within a given environment or scope
Includes benefits from current operations and from the outcomes of current and future projects	Includes future benefits of the project or programme itself
Is governed and constrained by organisation cash flow often seen as an annual budget	Is governed and constrained by a discrete programme or project budget

BUSINESS PROGRAMMES IN SMALL AND LARGE ORGANISATIONS

I have already mentioned the difficulties that certain words can create; 'programme' is just such a problematic word (see pp. 62, 151). No matter how hard you try there will always be someone, somewhere who takes a different view. Accept it and don't fight it. I expect there are many readers who say my definition of Business Programme is their definition of 'portfolio' – neither of us is wrong, but the key point is that, in your organisation, you must make sure you use words consistently in all your written documents, especially management reports. If you use the language consistently, people will gradually pick it up. In this book I distinguish business programme from programme from project. In a small organisation the business programme may represent the entire organisation, in which case the term becomes redundant – the organisation *is* the Business Programme. In larger organisations, the business plan will need to be divided into a number of Business Programmes each of which represents a part of the overall business plan.

To test if your 'programme' and mine are similar, look at Figure 14.2. Business Programmes are above the 'authorisation process'; they are the entities from which programmes and projects are initiated. They are governed by business plans, which usually give no authority for actual work to take place. Projects are below the 'authorisation process', being governed by business cases, which are used as the basis for authorising funding and resources to start work.

Business Programme accountabilities

If a Business Programme is a chunk of the business plan, who is accountable for it and what are those accountabilities? For small organisations, we have seen from the Point of Interest above that 'Business Programme' may be a meaningless term – the organisation *is* the Business Programme. It therefore follows that the role of the CEO or President and that of the senior team is relevant. These roles are primarily about the leadership of change and this requires both sponsorship (benefit/needs) and management (making it happen). For Business Programmes, I will call these roles 'Business Programme Sponsor' and 'Business Programme Manager', respectively.

If you are to have Business Programmes in your organisation, you will have a number of them and therefore you will need some body or individual accountable for directing them. There is no accepted term for such a body; for convenience I will call this the 'Business Strategy and Planning Board'. Together, these business programme accountabilities form a key part in the governance of the organisation. The other aspect of governance is authorisation, where 'permission' is required before any work is started or funds spent. I deal with this in Chapter 15.

ROLE PROCESS CONTROLLING
DELIVERABLE

GOVERNANCE ROLES AND PROCESSES

**Business Strategy
and Planning Board**

Direct and review
Business Programmes

Business Strategy
Business Plan

• *Approve of Business
  Programme Plan*
• *Direction, targets
  and decisions*

• *Draft Business
  Programme Plan*
• *Request for approval
  and direction*

**Business Programme
Sponsor**
**Business Programme
Manager**

Direct and manage
a Business Programme

Business Programme
Plan

• *Request to
  initiate project*

• *Direction and
  decisions on
  authorised
  projects*

• *Requests for direction
  and decisions*
• *Progress Reports*
• *Slippage Reports*
• *RFS and Closure Report*
• *PIR Report*

**Programme Review Group
(or as delegated)**

*Authorise
projects*

Project Sponsor
Project Manager

*Direct and manage
a programme/project*

Business Case

Figure 14.2 Business Programme accountabilities

The Business Strategy and Planning Board sets policy and direction for the whole
organisation which are set out in the Business Strategy and Business Plan documents.
They approve the plans for each Business Programme, each of which is directed by a
Business Programme Sponsor and managed by a Business Programme Manager.
Projects are initiated from the business programmes, through the authorisation process.
Each project is directed by a Project Sponsor and managed by a Project Manager.

REARRANGING THE DECK CHAIRS

Naming roles and bodies can be very difficult. Each needs to be as self-
explanatory as possible so that people can intuitively understand what each
role is for. This can be doubly difficult in a project environment where the
words 'project' and 'programme' take on so many different meanings. I have
chosen a set of role names which are consistently applied throughout the
book and which draw on associated terminology. I tend to use 'sponsor'

where the role is 'directing' and 'manager' where the role is 'managing'. You may call them what you want but I advise that:

- you make sure role names are distinct;
- you don't choose names which will date;
- you keep the roles separate from job titles;
- if referring to 'boards', you keep the roles separated from the Board titles;
- having chosen your role names, you don't change them.

Keeping roles and titles separate enables you to have a number of roles undertaken by a single person or body, thereby saving you from having to rewrite all your processes simply because of a minor change in personnel. For example, the CEO's Leadership Team may take on the role of the Business Strategy and Planning Board and the Project Review Group. Changing role names is a common ploy by 'new directors' to show they 'have arrived' but all it usually does is confuse people. A colleague of mine once referred to this as 'rearranging the deck chairs on the Titanic'.

The Business Strategy and Planning Board is accountable to the Chief Executive Officer for setting business strategy, directing corporate change and ensuring the business programmes realise the benefits required.

> **Business Strategy and Planning Board**
> - Sets strategic direction, policy and priorities.
> - Sets business and benefits realisation objectives and constraints for the organisation as a whole and for key elements of each Business Programme, to ensure maximum benefits and progress toward the strategic vision.
> - Allocates funding and resources to each Business Programme and function, through the approval of the business plan and each Business Programme Plan within it.
> - Monitors and reviews benefits realisation, delivery and costs from all Business Programmes, directing corrective action where appropriate.

The Business Programme Sponsor is accountable to the Business Strategy and Planning Board for directing the Business Programme, ensuring that the portfolio of projects and activities (Business Programme) within his/her scope realises the required benefits.

Business Programme Sponsor

- Provides business direction to the Business Programme in terms of making decisions, initiating new projects, terminating unwanted projects and resolving issues.
- Approves the Business Programme Plan prior to authorisation by higher authority.
- Ensures that the combined benefits for the Business Programme are realised.
- Ensures that the scope of the Business Programme covers the needs of the business.
- Directs priorities between contending projects and activities within the Business Programme.

The Business Programme Manager is accountable to the Business Programme Sponsor for day-to-day management of the Business Programme, ensuring that the portfolio is planned and managed to ensure maximum focus and speed of benefit realisation.

Business Programme Manager

- Prepares and maintains a plan of scope, timescale, benefits and costs for the Business Programme, including reserve for as yet unidentified projects and activities.
- Selects and manages the portfolio of projects within the Business Programme to realise the required benefits and to ensure that the contributions of all parts of the organisation are taken into account.
- Approves and authorises projects as delegated.
- Monitors performance against the Business Programme Plan, initiating corrective action and ensuring the integrity of the plan (including interdependencies).
- Provides regular progress reports to the Business Programme Sponsor and senior management.
- Ensures use of best practice methods and organisation procedures.
- Assigns the project sponsor role for each project within the Business Programme.
- Approves and authorises projects as delegated.
- Ensures the projects are progressed, by the project sponsor, through the authorisation process.

A **Business Programme Board**, if required, would support the Business Programme Sponsor in carrying out his/her accountabilities, particularly in respect of senior management alignment and engagement.

A **Business Programme Office** would provide the Business Programme Sponsor and Manager with the necessary administration, expertise, knowledge and resources to ensure that the above accountabilities are undertaken effectively. See Chapter 17 for more on this.

BUSINESS PROGRAMMES AND CROSS-ORGANISATION LEADERSHIP

Test the business programme roles. Replace the words **Business Programme Sponsor** by **CEO** and the business by shareholder. Notice the fit? The implication is that the role is truly one of leadership and not one of functional management. Business Programme Sponsors may be top directors or executives who have some functional accountability but, in the world of projects, they need to take on a cross-organisation role as we know any single function can achieve very little on its own. You will see a similar correlation between COO (or deputy CEO) and Business Programme Manager.

CHUNKS OF CHANGE

Look at any one of your longer running projects, say over a six-month duration. Critically review it to decide if you could have implemented it in smaller pieces. What was the minimum that was needed to be done?

14.2

Look at projects you are starting off now. Can these be divided into more digestible pieces?

Forecasting cycles

How often do you do your business forecasting? Annually? Quarterly? Monthly? If you do it only annually, consider how you can have confidence in the forecasts. Do you really know so much about the future that you could forecast a year in advance? Is your organisation really in such a slow-moving competitive environment?

Note: Forecasting is predicting what your management accounts and information systems will tell you in the future. Setting a target is not forecasting.

Managing the portfolio

In Chapter 1 we identified a number of commonly found deficiencies in how projects are managed. A key factor in the success of your organisation is the speed and effectiveness with which you can stay ahead of, or respond to, changing circumstances. Unless deficiencies in implementing the necessary changes are addressed, you will always be losing time and energy in fighting internal conflicts rather than addressing real external opportunities and threats.

No organisation, however, has just a single project, there are always several on the go and (as we have seen from the example on p. 163) 'projects spawn projects' there will always be more to come, either as part of a programme or as stand-alone initiatives. Directing this 'portfolio' of projects is a senior management task, as it is this 'bundle' of projects that will take you from where you are now to your, hopefully, better future.

A portfolio is a range of investments held by a person or organisation. A business programme is a very special type of portfolio.

I also use the word portfolio to represent any bundle or grouping of projects which we may choose to select for the convenience of management, reporting or analysis. After all, projects are investments of time and resources made by organisations to achieve benefits. Thus, the full set of projects undertaken within a organisation is its organisation portfolio. The set of projects held by a project sponsor is a sponsorship portfolio. The set of projects project managed by a person or function is a management portfolio.

At an organisation portfolio level, the actual performance of individual projects (or even programmes) becomes less critical. You can accept some being terminated, some being late, some costing too much or simply delivering the wrong thing. What is more critical is that the whole portfolio performs well enough to move your business forward as effectively and efficiently as possible. Like investments in the stock market, your portfolio of projects should be balanced with respect to risk. You should have some (but not too many!) projects which are risky, which will create a step change if they work or which are pushing forward the boundaries of your thinking and capability. Without these, you will be too rooted in today's paradigms and not reaching for new horizons.

> *Like investments in the stock market, your portfolio of projects should be balanced with respect to risk. You should have some (but not too many!) projects which are risky, which will create a step change if they work or which are pushing forward the boundaries of your corporate thinking and capability.*

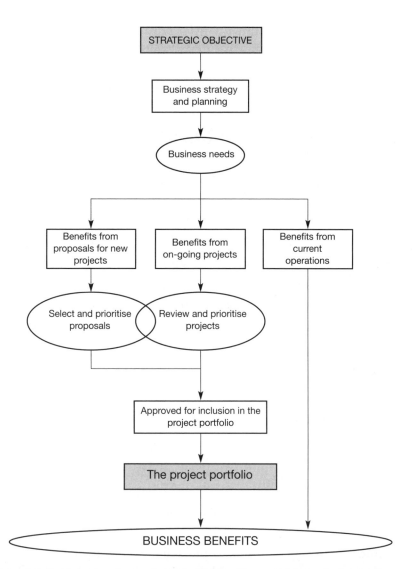

Figure 14.3 Proposals and projects in the context of strategy

Any change project you have starts as a proposal, becomes part of the project portfolio and eventually its output is subsumed into 'business as usual'. The speed and reliability with which you can do this is a critical success factor for your organisation. Compare the build-up of benefits in Figure 14.1 with this diagram to see how each part fits.

Figure 14.3 illustrates the framework. Future benefits come from three sources in your organisation:

- the operation of the organisation as currently set up;
- the changes created by projects you already have under way;
- proposals you have identified which are yet to be started (or not even thought of!).

Any change starts as a proposal, becomes part of the project portfolio and eventually its output is subsumed into 'business as usual'. The speed and reliability with which you can do this is a critical success factor for your organisation.

Prerequisites for effective portfolio management

So what are the prerequisites for managing a portfolio on a organisation-wide basis? The central 'plank' to managing a portfolio is reliable management of the individual projects:

- **A staged approach**: you should use a simple staged framework for the management of your projects to enable key decisions to be made at known points (gates).
- **Good project control techniques**: you should ensure that a basic foundation knowledge of project management techniques is understood and practised.

To make these work, you must have a organisation-wide environment (Figure 14.4) for:

- **Strategic alignment**: ensuring you choose the 'right' projects to turn your strategy into action.
- **Decision making**: you must make decisions which are respected, are the right ones and are made in the best interest of your organisation.
- **Resource management**: you must ensure that you have visibility of the availability and consumption of resources you need to undertake your projects and operate the outcomes.
- **Business planning**: you should make the management of your portfolio of projects a part of your business – it is not an optional extra. Projects **are** 'business as usual'.
- **Project register management**: you need to know what projects you are doing, when, why, who for and who's impacted.
- **Fund management**: you should ensure funding follows the projects you want to undertake.

The lack of any of these capabilities has implications on your organisation:

- **Poor strategic alignment**: you may end up doing the wrong projects.
- **Poor decision making**: decisions made in one part of the organisation may be overturned by another part, decisions may take too long or too many projects may be initiated.

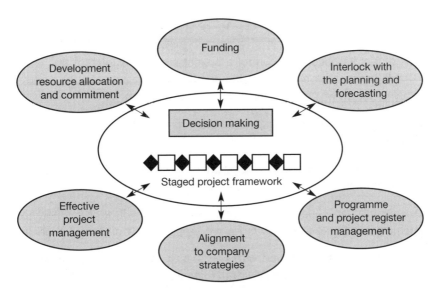

Figure 14.4 The environment for managing your portfolio of projects
The staged project framework is the central 'plank' around which the key aspects of
managing the portfolio revolve. While shown as separate 'items' they in fact have a large
degree of interdependence.

- **Poor resource management**: you don't know if you have sufficient
  resources to finish what you've started, let alone start anything new.
- **Poor business planning**: if you do not integrate the 'future' as created
  by your projects into your business plan, how will the plan make any
  sense and how will you know if you have anyone to use the outcomes?
- **Poor project register management**: if you have no list of or method for
  tracking your projects, they won't be visible and people are unlikely to
  know what has been authorised and what has not. You will not know
  which projects are interdependent. You risk overloading your organisation with change.
- **Poor fund management**: you won't know if you have the funds to
  complete the projects you have started or be able to fund new ones.
  You will spend your money on the wrong things.

Business programmes are a vehicle which enable you to tackle these
needs. Business programmes are chunks of your strategy and your business plan. They are the link between what you do now and what you will
do in the future. They therefore also form the most appropriate vehicle
for dividing up your organisation's spending, with the highest priority
business programmes attracting the greatest investment. Finally, they are
the control environment for ensuring you do not overload your organisation with 'too much change'.

THE PROJECT PROCESS ENVIRONMENT

14.3

The list of factors needed to control a project portfolio is long. In this workout you should assess your current 'health' and use that as a prompt for discussion to help you decide which you need to concentrate on first.

Take each in turn and, with respect to projects and change initiatives in your organisation:

1 Assess, without any in-depth analysis, the effectiveness of each competence – 0 = no capability, 5 = excellent in your organisation.

2 Discuss the implications on your organisation of any lack of competence in each area and note them down. Do not expect to be excellent in every area.

3 If you are basically satisfied with your assessment, consider whether the competencies you have actually work together as whole.

Competence	Score	Implications
Strategic alignment		
Decision making		
Resource management		
Business planning		
Register management		
Fund management		
Project management		

15

There are Too Many Projects to Do!

Principles for selecting projects

Project authorisation

Selecting the right projects

Far too many projects!

Putting the brakes on

By having a staged approach you do not need to make all the decisions at the same time. A staged framework enables you to make the necessary choices when you have adequate information to hand, rather than being forced into premature and ill-conceived choices.

'When you choose anything, you reject everything else.'
G K CHESTERTON

Principles for selecting projects

There are always far more ideas for projects to change a business than resources or money can support. To make matters worse, the less clear your strategy is, the more ideas there will be, thus compounding the problem.

How can you:

- make sure you undertake the projects you need to?
- limit the number of projects without stifling the good ideas?
- kill off the projects which have no place in your organisation?
- ensure that speed through the project stages is sustained?

The staged framework within which each project is managed, coupled with effective decision making and business planning, is the key to ensuring you can do all of this. By having a staged approach you do not need to make all the decisions at the same time. A staged framework enables you to make the necessary choices when you have adequate information to hand, rather than being forced into premature and ill-conceived choices. Keeping to three basic principles will help you do this:

1 **Do not put a lid on the creation of new ideas for projects.**
2 **As soon as you can, make an informed decision on which projects to continue.**
3 **Having decided to do a project, do it, but stop if circumstances change.**

1 Do not put a lid on the creation of new ideas for projects

In Part Two you saw that a project should not be started unless a person stands up as needing the benefits (the project sponsor). You should encourage the creation of as many ideas as possible, letting them originate in any part of the organisation (see p. 89). Stifle creativity and you risk stifling the future growth of your organisation. The use of a targeted proposal template, such as that given on the CD-ROM should ensure that enough information is collected about an idea (or need) to enable the organisation to review and approve or reject it on the grounds of strategic fit.

The decision to start a project is taken at the Initial Investigation Gate and is only concerned with the first of the three gate questions: 'Is there a real need for this project and, in its own right, is it likely to be viable?' (see p. 56). Once the go ahead is given, the initial investigation should start.

A REMINDER OF THE KEY QUESTIONS

The decision points prior to the start of each stage are called gates and answer three distinct questions:

1 Is there a real need for this project and, in its own right, is it viable?
2 What is its priority relative to other competing projects?
3 Do I have the funding to undertake the project?

If you are uncertain of your strategy, you will create more proposals than if you really understand the direction the organisation is to take. However, if a proposal passes this first gate, you know that at least one person (the project sponsor) believes the proposal does fit the strategy and should be evaluated. In this way you will benefit from knowing how your senior managers are converting their understanding of strategy into action. The aim of portfolio management is to make projects visible: the 'outing of projects'. If a manager is undertaking projects his/her colleagues consider to be outside the needs of the business or of low priority, this will be exposed. Consider also what else such a manager may be doing which may be contrary to the direction of the business but which is invisible!

I cannot over-emphasise the impact that a clearly *communicated* strategy and business plan has on the effectiveness of selecting and managing your project portfolio. Part of this relates to the number of projects started and terminated.

2 As soon as you can, make an informed decision on which projects to continue

The first gate enables you to start investigating the unknowns on the project. You should know *why* you are undertaking the project but, on some projects, you may not know *what* exactly you are going to have as an output or *how* you will go about it. For relatively simple projects you may know both these things. The objective of the initial investigation is to reduce this uncertainty. The output of the initial investigation should provide sufficient knowledge to:

- confirm strategic fit;
- understand the possible scope and implications;
- know what you are going to do next.

In other words, you will have the information to hand which will enable you to make an *informed* decision on whether the project should continue, rather than one based on your own 'feel' and limited knowledge.

If you have only one project to do, its priority is easy to assess. It is PRIORITY ONE. If you have more than one project to review, the question of priority has no significance if you have the resources and funding to do them all when they are required. Priority only becomes an issue if you have insufficient resources to do everything you want to do, when you want to do them.

> *Priority only becomes an issue if you have insufficient resources to do everything you want to do, when you want to do it.*

Assessing relative priority should be done on an informed basis and so cannot happen until you reach the Detailed Investigation Gate, after the output from the Initial Investigation Stage is available. Once the project sponsors have confirmed that they still need the benefits their projects will produce, you will need to concentrate on:

- the 'doability' of the projects;
- their fit within the overall project portfolio.

Doability takes for granted the project sponsors' assessment of strategic fit and the soundness of each project on a stand-alone basis. It concentrates mainly on whether you have the resources and funding to undertake all the projects. If you do, a portfolio assessment is done.

The **portfolio assessment** looks at the balance of risk and opportunity for the proposed projects together with the current project portfolio. The aim is to assess whether this mix is in fact moving the organisation in the desired direction.

If you are unable to undertake all the desired new projects, you will need to make comparisons between them and choose which should continue. This implies that you need to *batch* your projects at the Detailed

> **It is more powerful, from a decision-making viewpoint, to prioritise the benefits the projects produce rather than the activities the project comprises.**

Investigation Gate to make this decision. In practice you will be deciding which projects should proceed, as it is projects which lead to action, but it is more powerful, from a decision-making viewpoint, to prioritise the *benefits* the projects produce rather than the activities the project comprises. After all, the benefits are what you need, not the projects. By prioritising benefits you will:

- stay focused on *why* you are doing the project;
- trap the projects which actually have no real benefit!

It is best if the prioritisation decision coincides with a review and reforecast of your business plan as a whole. You will be able to build whichever projects and benefits you need into the plan, while ensuring the totality of future benefits from 'business as usual' and projects adds up to the figures you need (Figure 15.1).

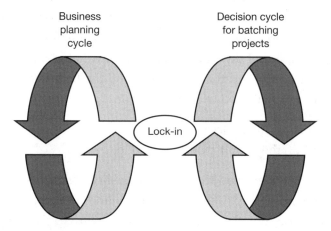

Business planning cycle

Decision cycle for batching projects

Lock-in

Figure 15.1 Matching the batching time frame to your business planning cycle
If the decision as to which projects should continue coincides with a review and reforecast of your business plan as a whole, you will be able to build whichever projects you need into the plan, while ensuring the totality of future benefits from 'business as usual' and projects adds up to the figures you need.

ENOUGH INFORMATION?

You can always avoid making decisions by saying you haven't got enough information. It's a very effective tactic for blocking anything you don't want done. You will never have enough information for decision making. You need to make an assessment of what you have at stake if your decision is wrong and balance this against what you stand to gain if your decision is right. If you have a staged approach to projects, coupled with good control techniques, you will be able to 'de-risk' your decision making to the extent that you are answering the question, 'Can I confidently continue with the next stage of this project?' You very rarely find you are making life and death choices.

3 Having decided to do a project, do it – but stop it if circumstances change

Having decided to carry on with a project after the review at the Detailed Investigation Gate it is useful to presume it will continue. You, therefore, need only assess the relative merits of the new projects you wish to introduce to your project portfolio. This avoids going back over previous decisions and puts an end to the 'stop–go' mentality that ineffective staged processes can result in. It is a strange phenomenon that today's 'good ideas' tend to look more attractive than yesterday's! Consequently, the temptation is to ditch yesterday's partially completed projects in favour of new ones. The result is that nothing is actually finished!

> *It is a strange phenomenon that today's 'good ideas' tend to look more attractive than yesterday's! Consequently, the temptation is to ditch yesterday's partially completed projects in favour of new ones. The result is that nothing is actually finished!*

A presumption that on-going projects will continue does not mean that you should never stop a project that a project sponsor is relying on. For example, assume you have sufficient resources to do all except one new project, and this cannot be done because a key, scarce resource is already occupied on an on-going project. In such circumstances you would usually presume the ongoing project continues and the new project is delayed. The new project, however, may have considerably more lever-age, resulting in greater benefit, in a shorter time, at less risk than the existing one. Hence you may take the view that it serves the overall inter-est of the organisation better to terminate the existing project and start the new one. Such decisions should be very rare, as, if they are not:

- your portfolio will be unstable and you will run the risk of delivering nothing of value;
- it may be symptomatic of poor business planning and a lack of clearly understood strategy.

Ability to change – decision making

To what extent does the ability to devolve decision making influence how fast you can implement change? In the planning stages of a complex change programme, the project managers identified each point which required either a board decision or the decision of one of the directors. In all, about 200 decisions were identified spanning nine change projects. Figure 15.2 shows this. This begs some questions:

- Were the board members in fact capable of making that number of deci-sions in the timescales required, on top of all their 'business as usual' decisions?
- Were there any decisions which could have been delegated to relieve them of the burden? If not, what impact would the decision overload have had on the programme?

Notice the shapes of the two graphs. The board as a group has most of its decisions toward the front. As the projects get under way and alignment has been achieved, the bulk of the decisions is made by individual directors. The shape of the curve for the directors has both a front-end peak and peaks toward the back. This is because they not only approve the initial work, but also completion of the key final deliverables toward the end of each project. This does, however, also highlight a common failing of many boards: they lose interest once they have made their initial decisions!

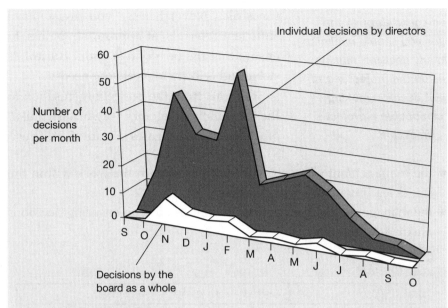

Figure 15.2 **Decisions**

In the planning stages of a complex change programme, the project managers identified each point which required either a board decision or the decision of one of the directors. In all, about 200 decisions were identified, spanning nine key change projects.

Beware of trying to do too much

Copyright © 1997 Robert Buttrick

Project authorisation

Harnessing the staged framework

The management of the full portfolio of projects relies on a basic staged project framework being in place. To ensure speed through the project stages you should minimise referral to any decision-making bodies outside the project team. Inefficient decision making at gates can double a project's

> *To ensure speed through the project stages you should minimise referral to any decision-making bodies outside the project team. Inefficient decision making at gates can double a project's timescale.*

timescale. Nevertheless, you must have sufficient referrals, at appropriate points, to ensure that the portfolio is under control, is stable and is likely to meet your needs.

Referrals from the project organisation to the portfolio management organisation usually happens at the gates (Figure 15.3). Thus:

- the management of a project is concerned with the work within the stages leading up to a gate decision;
- the management of the portfolio is concerned with ensuring decisions are made at the gates.

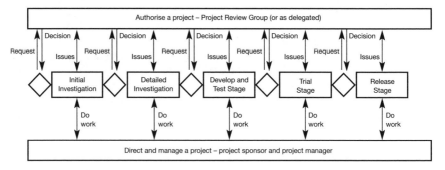

Figure 15.3 Interaction between managing a project and managing the portfolio

Referrals from the project to the 'authorisation process' happen primarily at the gates. Where a problem (issue) on a project requires a change, a referral may be made during the course of a stage. In this diagram, the project review group is shown as the authorising body; for large organisations, there is likely to be some delegation, say to the Business Programme Manager.

Where an issue on a project requires a change, a referral may be made from project management to portfolio management during the course of a stage.

The choice of who contributes to the decisions is crucial. Earlier (pp. 56, 180) we saw that the decision is the culmination of three distinct questions. The roles relating to these are as follows:

- **The project sponsor** answers the gate question 1 – is there a real need for this project and, in its own right, is it viable? The project sponsor is the person who requires the benefits the project will realise and who assesses its fit to strategy.
- **The project review group** answers the gate question 2 – what is the priority? It assesses the 'doability' and integrity of the portfolio as a whole. (The typical activities which this group undertake are given on p. 188.)
- **The investment review group** answers gate question 3 – do we have the funding? It ensures that the financial 'rules' are applied, that the project makes sound business sense and that funds are available to do it.

I have shown the roles of the investment review group and the project review group separately. In practice it is better, but not essential, if the roles are combined into a single body. Note that both these titles are used to illustrate a role required in the governance of projects; what you choose to call them is your choice – there are no commonly accepted terms. Also, you may choose to combine a number of roles in a single body.

Gate decisions

Assuming that the project, on its own, makes sound business sense, what else does the project review group need to know about a project or investment before it can commit the organisation to it?

- What are the project's overall business objectives?
- On what projects does this project depend?
- What projects depend on this project?
- When will we have the resources to carry out the project (people and facilities)?
- Do we have enough cash to fund the project?
- Can the organisation accept this change on top of everything else we are doing?
- After what time will the project cease to be viable?
- How big is the overall risk of the portfolio with and without this project?

1 ROLE OF PROJECT REVIEW GROUP

A cross-functional (or cross-process) group of decision makers for authorisation, prioritisation, issues escalation and resource allocation. Its primary aim is to keep the pipeline of projects flowing. As such the project review group is the gate keeper for all the project framework gates and accountable as owner of the authorisation process.

2 AIM OF PROJECT REVIEW GROUP

The project review group exists to manage and communicate the authorisation, prioritisation, planning and pre-launch implementation planning for business change projects.

This includes ensuring that fully resourced and committed plans for projects are created and aligned within the organisation's rolling forecast and each has a viable business case.

3 ACCOUNTABILITIES

The accountabilities of the group are:

- to authorise projects and oversee any delegation of such authority;
- to ensure that the portfolio can be delivered within existing funding allocations by ensuring the organisation's business plan reflects the projects within the portfolio;
- to ensure each project is locked in and committed to by those required to develop it and operate the outputs post-release;
- to identify options for resolution of issues involving resources and escalate for resolution if appropriate;
- to ensure that functions have planned in 'white space' resources to undertake initial investigations (see Chapter 16);
- to communicate/publish the current status of the organisation's portfolio;
- to act as the change control point for the organisation's portfolio;
- to be the owner of the authorisation process.

Each gate in the project framework is described, from the perspective of decision making, in the following sections.

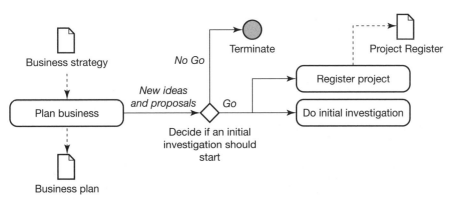

Figure 15.4 Decision process at the Initial Investigation Gate
Any idea that the business programme sponsor wishes to study further should be
investigated without delay.

Initial Investigation Gate

While all gates are held by the project review group, this first one is often delegated to a Business Programme Sponsor or Manager. Any proposal which they believe is worthy of further study should pass into the Initial Investigation Stage without undue delay

> *Any proposal which the business programme sponsor believes is worthy of further study should pass into the Initial Investigation Stage without undue delay.*

(Figure 15.4). Some organisations have a special group to review proposals and take decisions on which should proceed. However, an effective business planning process should make such a group unnecessary. In most cases, except for extreme reactions to market or business conditions, the business plan should spawn the proposals, hence they will have effectively already been 'approved', at least in outline.

Detailed Investigation Gate

Assuming each project has been approved by the project sponsor, the candidate projects are batched and an informed choice is made as to which should be authorised to proceed into detailed investigation (Figure 15.5). Two basic questions need to be asked by the project review group:

- Is it likely that all these projects can be completed?
- If we include them all, is the portfolio balanced?

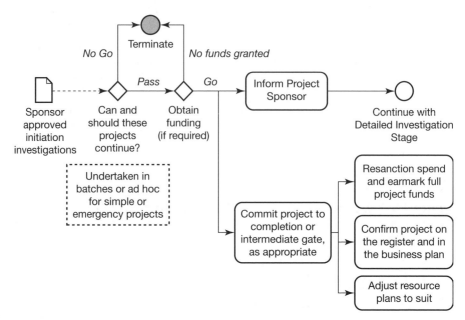

Figure 15.5 Decision process at the Detailed Investigation Gate
Decide which out of a number of projects can, and should, continue to the next stage.

If the answer to both these questions is 'yes', and there is sufficient funding, the full batch of projects proceeds into the Detailed Investigation Stage. If, however, all the projects cannot be done, then those in contention are compared and a decision is made as to which of them should proceed. Alternatively the constraint may be identified and, if possible, released (e.g. by delaying a project or applying new resources).

It should be your intention that any project which is allowed past this gate is going to move to completion *unless it loses its viability or becomes unacceptably risky.* For this reason you can think of this as the NO gate, i.e. where the business says 'No, we will not consider that project further'.

A project in which confidence to complete it is relatively high and which is committed to completion need not be referred back to the project review group unless it hits an issue which requires a reassessment of the project viability and resourcing. The 'simple' projects referred to in Chapter 12 are an example of this. In other instances, however, the project review group will not have sufficient information to commit a project to completion. In which case, the project will be committed only as far as the Development Gate, when another assessment is done.

Once agreed by the project review group, the investment review group should provide funding to complete either the project or at least the Detailed

Investigation Stage and the project costs, benefits and resource needs should be locked into the business plan. In some organisations the project review group and investment review group may be one and the same.

THE CAPACITY OF THE TOTAL SYSTEM IS THE CAPACITY OF THE BOTTLENECK

When the project review group assesses whether a project can be done, it must satisfy itself that ALL aspects can be done: operational, technical, marketing, process, etc. If one part is missing, then there is little point in doing any of the other work. Your ability to complete projects is, therefore, constrained by the bottlenecks imposed by scarce resources for a particular aspect of work. By undertaking a formal 'doability' check, you will quickly identify any constraints and also be able to assess the cost to the organisation of missing or insufficient resource. This cost is the sum of the benefits from the projects you could not do because that resource was not available. This simple concept is the basis for what is called Critical Chain in Eli Goldratt's Theory of Constraints.[1]

Development Gate

At the Development Gate, the project review group is only concerned with those projects it could not previously commit to completion. Again, the same questions are asked at the Detailed Investigation Gate. In principle, any project which has reached this gate is one which the organisation wants to continue. Forward planning should have earmarked the resources required to complete the project. As the presumption is to continue the project unless circumstances dictate otherwise, what is looked for here is confirmation that the project can continue. For this reason, the Development Gate should be considered as the YES gate. The investment review group provides funding to complete the project if this had not been given earlier. The business plan is amended to incorporate changes to costs, benefits and resource needs resulting from the detailed investigation. The process is shown in Figure 15.6.

[1] See Goldratt, E.M., *Critical Chain* (North River Press, 1997).

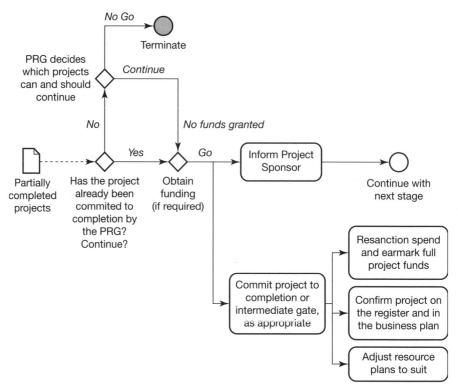

Figure 15.6 Decision process after the Detailed Investigation Gate
If the project has already been committed for completion and is still within the scope, timescale and cost approved at the detailed Investigation Gate, no referral to the project review group is needed. The project just continues, obtaining extra funding, if not already allocated. For all other projects, the project review group needs to confirm it within the project portfolio.

Trial Gate

The project sponsor is often delegated accountability for approving the move into trial. This is based on advice given by the project manager and team and is based on a ready for trial report. The project sponsor holds the decision as it is he/she who requires the benefits. Trials are often the first time a change is presented to the outside world and it is in the interests of the sponsor to ensure that a premature presentation does not compromise downstream benefits. The project review group needs to be consulted only if there are any prioritisation issues. In such cases, the process in Figure 15.6 is followed.

Release Gate

Again, this is primarily a project sponsor decision. As with a trial, the sponsor does not want the benefits jeopardised by releasing the project output before everything is ready. Alternatively, depending on the scale of impact of the change, this decision could be made by a business programme board, project board, or even a management board. The project review group only needs to be consulted if there are any prioritisation or resource issues or if this gate decision has been explicitly retained by them. In such cases, the process in Figure 15.6 is followed.

Summary of decision-making roles at each gate

The following table summarises the decisions at the gates and who is involved. In the case of this table, a business programme board may delegate the decision to a project board or to the project sponsor. Consider this table as a starting point for you to assess the appropriate decision-making bodies and levels in your organisation. Remember, as the project definition document contains a list of deliverables and who has approval accountability (see p. 300), you are able to choose the most appropriate people or groups for each project on a case-by-case basis if your 'usual rules' are not appropriate.

	Initial Investigation Gate	Detailed Investigation Gate	Development Gate	Trial Gate	Release Gate
Business programme board	Decides if an initial investigation should start	Confirms the project should continue	Confirms the project should continue	Confirms the project should continue	Confirms the output should be released
Project review group	Not usually required	Decides if the detailed investigation should start	Decides if the peoject should be completed	No referral needed	No referral needed
Investment review group	Not usually required	Provides funding for the detailed investigation	Provides funding to complete the remainder of the project	No referral	No referral
Document on which gate decision is based	Proposal	Initial business case	Business case	Ready for trial report report	Ready for service report
NOTES	Projects start as soon as practical	Projects batched for a comparative decision	Stage starts as soon as practical	Stage starts as soon as practical	Stage starts as soon as practical

Batching projects

Earlier (p. 181) I said that you would need to batch potential projects at the Detailed Investigation Gate so that you can make an informed decision regarding which should continue. If you do not have batching, prioritisation can become meaningless. Projects are likely to be allocated resources on a first come, first served basis rather than on a 'biggest win for the organisation' basis. Batching, however, begs two questions:

- How frequently should I do the batching?
- Won't this slow down the projects by introducing a pause?

As far as frequency is concerned, you need to select a time period which enables a reasonable number of initial business cases to be drawn up and to be compared with one another while not introducing too long a delay:

- Annual batching would be too infrequent. The business environment would have changed so much in that time that the exercise would be futile.
- Weekly may be too frequent. There would be an insufficient number of projects to allow meaningful decisions to be made.
- Between a month and a quarter is probably about right.

As for slowing projects down, the answer is no. Batching should not usually slow anything down. Unless there is spare resource available to undertake the project immediately, nothing can happen. Consider also that there is no point in rushing ahead with a project if it is the wrong one! Nevertheless, there will be cases where delaying a project to allow batching to occur is not in the best business interests. These cases are for:

- 'simple' projects;
- emergencies;
- exceptions.

Simple projects were discussed in Part Two (p. 136). They are projects where you can see clearly to the end by the time you have completed the initial investigation. They also tend to consume few resources and little money. In such cases, the project review group allows the project to proceed into detailed investigation without delay, as the chances of the project compromising future 'better projects' are very slim. A project may be thought of as 'simple' by the project manager, but it is the project review group who actually decides this. I would also argue that defining, in quantitative terms, what constitutes 'simple' may be a time-consuming and difficult exercise. Further, once you have defined it, you may find that project sponsors and managers massage their initial business cases to fall within your defined threshold and thus ensure their projects go through without delay. This is not the behaviour you should encourage. It is more pragmatic to phrase the definition of 'simple' in terms of principles and allow the project review group to exercise its own discretion. After all, it should be made up of responsible managers and not merely administrators of predefined 'rules'.

Emergencies are another exception to batching. I define an emergency as a project which, if delayed, would severely damage the organisation. An emergency is not a 'panic' as a result of poor management in a particular part of the organisation. Unlike simple projects, emergencies may need to displace resources from on-going projects, thereby causing earlier commitments to be broken. If they aren't true emergencies, you will simply be moving the problem from one part of the organisation to another. As these projects can have a disruptive effect, the approval for them at the Detailed Investigation Gate should rest with top management (e.g. board), following a detailed impact assessment by the project review group.

GIVING UP SOME PERSONAL POWER?

Who has the authority to commit resources:

- in a department in your organisation?
- in a function within your organisation?
- anywhere within your organisation?
- in another, supplier organisation?

Treat the word 'organisation' as independent operating division if you are in a global organisation. The answers to these questions will probably be, respectively, the head of department, the head of function (often a director or vice president title), the CEO or chief operating officer, and someone in that other organisation. In other words, the power to apply and commit resources usually lies within the functional or line management hierarchy. If this is the case and organisations need to draw on resources from anywhere to undertake projects, there is only one person (maybe two people) in the organisation empowered to do this: the CEO and COO (if you have one). No person, no matter what their title is, has the authority to commit resources which are outside their domains. Unless an organisation has alternative structures to make cross-functional commitments, the top people will become overloaded with operational issues. Hence the need for a cross-organisation decision-making body such as a project review group. In effect, the owners of the resources are giving up part of their power to a cross-functional decision-making body and it therefore also holds that they should respect the decisions of that group and not unilaterally withdraw resources for their own departmental or functional needs. If the lines of communication work and their person on the group plays their part, this should pose no problems.

Exceptions are any other type of project, other than emergency or simple project, that you wish to continue without going through a batching process. In other words, a pragmatic, but open and deliberate, decision, within the principles of business-led project management, which you deem to be in the organisation's interest. It is pointless to dream up possible scenarios and rules for these. It's a waste of time. Just deal with them as they arise. By definition, exceptions are 'exceptional' and rare.

Beyond batching

The whole reason for batching is for you to decide, from among many contenders, which projects are the 'right' ones to take on. By insisting on a named project sponsor, you are obtaining an unequivocal statement that at least one senior manager believes the project is the right project. By having a project review group, you are making a decision body accountable for ensuring the resource is available and that the mix of projects within the portfolio is the right mix. Poor business planning will make the jobs of the project sponsor and project review group more difficult. Conversely, good business planning will make it far easier. Add good information on the current and future commitment of resources and expected benefits and the project review group's task simplifies further. Good business planning will spawn the right proposals, which in turn spawn the right projects. This being the case, batching may become less necessary. If you

> *The whole reason for batching is for you to decide, from among many contenders, which projects are the 'right' ones to take on*

have a view of what is in the project pipeline, ready to arrive at the Detailed Investigation Gate, you will be able to allow more projects to proceed between batches without compromising future projects. Consultants and contractors do this all the time; can they wait and batch up which bids they would like to respond to? No, they have to take a view on their workload, assess the likelihood of success, the availability of resources and the impact on them if they succeed. They then make a choice either to bid or not bid. (Remember which organisations were found to have the best resource management systems? See Part One.)

Issues requiring a high level decision

Not all projects will go according to plan. There will be instances when changes to a project as defined and approved are desirable. Unless this is managed, scope, timescales and costs will creep and the project 'pipeline' will become blocked. There will be too much work to do and not enough people or cash to do it. Small changes can be dealt with either by the project manager or project sponsor. However, where a proposed change has an impact on other commitments the impact must be assessed and the approval of the project review group obtained. Chapter 25 describes the change process fully from a project manager's and sponsor's viewpoint. The process for handling escalated changes is very similar to that for the gate decisions described earlier. It is just that the need for the decision is driven by unexpected events rather than by reaching a predictable milestone (Figure 15.7).

The proposed change is reviewed by the project review group and, if it can be accommodated within the portfolio, approval is given to proceed. Authorisation for any extra funding should also be given, if required. In some cases, the project review group may choose to alter the relative priorities of projects if there are resources or funding constraints. See Chapter 25 for a full treatment of 'change control'.

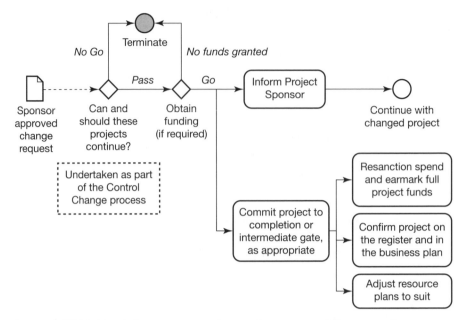

Figure 15.7 Decision process for an issue requiring a major change

The proposed change is reviewed by the project review group and, if it can be accommodated within the portfolio, approval is given to proceed. Authorisation for any extra funding should also be given, if required.

Selecting the right projects

Project selection and business planning

Why do so many enterprises:

- waste scarce funds and resources on worthless projects;
- have little understanding of what benefits will accrue from their project portfolios;
- struggle interminably with the annual budget setting and decision process?

Research by the GenSight Group[2] suggests between 35 and 50 per cent of all investment is directed to unsuccessful projects and that about 30 per cent of project investment by FTSE 100 organisations in 2000 actually destroyed shareholder value!

[2] Munt, D. and Menard, M., *Capital Project Prioritisation and Portfolio Optimisation* (Gen Sight, 2002), available at www.gensight.com.

The demand for improved returns from project investment is now pervasive, from public and private sectors alike, yet most organisations still struggle with the process of deciding what projects to do as well as when to do them. Portfolio management is a discipline that can increase significantly the value derived from project investments. The concepts have been established for 50 years in the financial investment community and are now starting to be applied to planning portfolios of projects.

Portfolio management is an activity that aligns a portfolio of projects to the strategy of the organisation. As such, it is an integral part of business planning. It should enable an organisation to select those projects which will create the greatest value, whilst at the same time:

- ensure strategic balance;
- handle risk explicitly;
- keep within resource and funding constraints;
- respect any dependencies between the selected projects.

In demanding times, this is something all enterprises should be seeking to do, yet it is rarely applied effectively, despite reliable methods now being available.

> 'The cancellation rate of [IT] projects exceeds the default rate of the worst junk bonds – yet bonds have lots of portfolio management applied to them. [IT] investments are huge and risky. It's time we do this.'
> DOUGLAS HUBBARD, HUBBARD DECISION RESEARCH

When creating the next year's business plan, most organisations extrapolate from the previous year's expenditure, adjusting it for changed circumstances, with some superficial analysis of priorities. This is usually done within the organisation's functional 'silos'. The focus is generally upon keeping within a top-down defined budget, often with capital and operational (revenue) expenditure dealt with in different, unrelated streams. Sometimes, consideration is given to resource constraints and the level of change the organisation can cope with. This approach may work, to a limited extent, for steady-state bureaucracies but not for organisations undergoing substantial change. For these, the results are dubious, with little objective attention to:

- the relationship between capital and operational expenditure, which may be unknown or ignored;
- the impact budget cuts can have on benefit realisation, which is usually not understood;
- priorities, which are often contentious;
- the point at which projects must be rejected, which can be nearly impossible to determine;
- resource constraints and project relationships, which are often seen as too complex.

This scepticism regarding the value of some organisation's business planning methods can also apply to outside observers. An analyst at Prudential-Bache said of a FTSE 100 organisation in which top-down cuts had been imposed: *'Our provisional conclusion is that the current management have finally prescribed strong medicine. It remains to be seen how much life remains in the patient.'* Not very comforting!

Choosing how to decide between competing projects can cause a great deal of concern. Five methods I have seen used are outlined below:

- Executive decision;
- Financial return (discounted cash flow);
- Scoring;
- Visualisation;
- Optimisation.

I would, however, point out that none of the methods are foolproof; you cannot make a process of decision making, you can only make a process for the flow of the information required to make decisions. At the end of the day, decisions come down to a choice made by a person or group and not by a process or a clever business model. Nevertheless, there are approaches which can help significantly to improve the quality, objectivity and transparency of the decisions.

Executive decision

Just choose, based on the information and opinions you have to hand. This is a simple and often effective method, especially if you do not have to justify your decisions! Sometimes, decisions are so marginal, it doesn't really matter what you decide as long as you make a decision!

Financial return

Investment appraisal methods based on discounted cash flow are now commonly used in many organisations to justify projects. In these they seek to either maximise the net present value and/or increase the internal rate of return (IRR). In addition, the 'pay-back period' can also have an influence. For example, some organisations will insist that a project returns at least 15 per cent IRR and has a pay-back period of less than two years. The IRR hurdle rate is set to capture projects with returns greater than that required by the market and the pay-back period is set to control cash flow and ensure the benefits stream is not too distant. Different organisations will set different hurdle rates. Those which have very short product life cycles tend to set short pay-back periods and higher IRR targets. You will find more on this in Chapter 22, Managing the Finances.

Making the numbers up?

In one organisation I worked with we noticed that all the projects coming up for either authorisation or selection into the business plan had internal rates of return in the hundreds or even thousands; this organisation should be enormously profitable! Unfortunately, that was not our experience. Despite these 'excellent projects' and more than adequate operational performance, the organisation lost money. We found two things were happening:

- the investment appraisals were 'doctored' so that they gave a far better impression than was the case. Optimism was rife, with 'making the numbers up' being the acceptable approach.
- different projects claimed the same chunk of benefit, resulting in that benefit being double counted (or sometimes counted up to seven times!).

These symptoms are classic in organisations which have poor business planning capabilities and where project selection and portfolio management are divorced from whatever business plan does exist. They are often unduly influenced by the finance function, with project selection and authorisation being perceived by the business leaders as 'bureaucracy getting in the way of what I want to do'.

Scoring techniques

Scoring techniques seek to maximise the value of a portfolio of projects. They build on the discounted cash flow method described above, taking into account factors such as net present value, probability of technical success, probability of commercial success, the project cost and the ongoing cost of operating whatever the outputs from the project are. From these, you can calculate the expected commercial value and then rank the projects according to those with the highest value, ultimately selecting all those that were possible, within the limited budget. Figure 15.8a is a simple example for nine projects (in reality you may have tens or hundreds of projects). If you had a Year 1 annual constraint of a £20m spend, you would select the five projects with the highest commercial value: C, A, I, D and H. This would use £17.7m of the available budget.

The use of the 'strategic importance score' demonstrates how you can use scoring to favour projects with particular characteristics (in this case, link to strategy). Some organisations use a scoring model to take into account a wide number of factors, each of which may be weighted. It can become very complex and subjective and for this reason alone some senior managers can become sceptical!

A modification of the above is to determine the ranking, by dividing the expected commercial value by the constraining factor. In this way you can favour those projects, which give the greatest return for whatever your limited resource is. Hence this is often referred to as the 'most bangs for the bucks' approach! Once the projects have been ranked, keep selecting projects, in rank order, until your constraining resource is exhausted. In the example in Figure 15.8b, I have used the development cost as the constraining resource.

This approach favours projects with certain characteristics: those that are closer to launch, those which have relatively little left to be spent on them, those with a higher likelihood of success and those which use less of the scarce or constraining resource. It also requires financial or other quantitative data. This can be particularly problematic in the early stages of a project. Probabilities can be somewhat difficult to determine. None of the scoring techniques take account of portfolio balance.

Project	NPV (m)	Strategic importance (SI)	Income PV (m)	Likelihood of success Commercial	Technical	Project cost PV (m)	Project cost MOT Yr 1	Yr 2	On-going cost PV (m)	ECV (m)	Rank
Project A	£5.30	2	£11.5	80%	80%	£2.7	£3.0	£0.0	£3.4	£9.2	2
Project B	£3.79	1	£9.3	80%	70%	£2.7	£3.0	£0.0	£2.8	£0.5	9
Project C	£3.92	3	£9.3	70%	75%	£2.6	£2.0	£0.9	£2.8	£9.9	1
Project D	£9.64	1	£22.9	85%	90%	£6.4	£7.0	£0.0	£6.9	£5.0	4
Project E	£1.94	2	£13.2	75%	60%	£7.3	£8.0	£0.0	£3.9	£2.2	6
Project F	£5.28	1	£17.0	80%	85%	£6.6	£7.3	£0.0	£5.1	£0.6	8
Project G	£5.09	1	£9.7	70%	70%	£1.7	£1.0	£1.0	£2.9	£1.0	7
Project H	£3.21	2	£6.1	75%	80%	£1.1	£1.2	£0.0	£1.8	£4.8	5
Project I	£0.64	2	£6.8	90%	90%	£4.1	£4.5	£0.0	£2.0	£5.0	3

Figure 15.8a – Scoring – maximising economic value

$ECV = (I \times SI \times Cp - OC) \times Tp - C$

ECV = Expected commercial value   I = Present value of income stream

SI = Strategic importance score   Cp = Likelihood of commercial success

OC = Present value of on-going costs

Tp = Likelihood of technical success   C = Present value of project costs.

Project name	ECV (m)	Project cost PV (m)	ECV/ Project cost PV Analyses	Rank
Project A	£9.2	£2.7	£3.37	3
Project B	£0.5	£2.7	£0.20	8
Project C	£9.9	£2.6	£3.88	2
Project D	£5.0	£6.4	£0.78	5
Project E	£2.2	£7.3	£0.30	7
Project F	£0.6	£6.6	£0.09	9
Project G	£1.0	£1.7	£0.57	6
Project H	£4.8	£1.1	£4.41	1
Project I	£5.0	£4.1	£1.23	4

Figure 15.8b 'More bangs for the bucks' selection

Divide the Expected commercial value by the limiting resource, in this case Project cost, to determine which projects make best use of that resource. Then select those which make greatest use until the constraint is met. This results in the selection of six projects: H, C, A, I, D, and G, slightly more than the pure 'economic value' method in Figure 15.8a, and using £18.7m of the £20m budget.

Visualisation techniques

Visualisation techniques build on scoring methods but present the output in such a way that the decision maker can gain a better understanding of the non-financial factors. This is done by plotting each project on a matrix with axes representing key decision influencing factors (for example, benefit versus risk) and choosing those which are in the 'less risky, most beneficial' quartile (Figure 15.9). They are called 'bubble diagrams'. The limitations of this method are that you can only have two dimensions, one represented by each axis. A third dimension is often added by using the size of the 'bubble' to indicate a factor such as project size. To use more dimensions you have to invent creative formulae for weighting a collection of factors into a single one. It is, however, relatively simple and can help you analyse a potentially complex set of projects. It also gives a very concise view of portfolio balance. Its output can, on the other hand, be very misleading and, as a minimum, basic management sense should be used to verify the model. In addition, it may tend to favour supposedly strategic projects over those which will yield a real financial return or vice versa, and this can lead to an unbalanced portfolio.

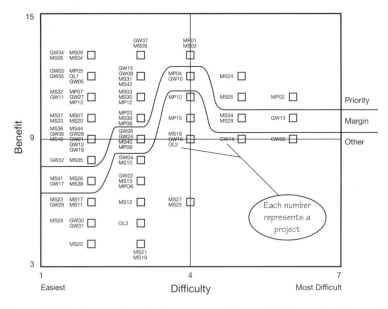

Figure 15.9 Example of using a matrix to aid the selection of projects

Each project is plotted on a matrix with axes representing key decision-influencing factors; in the example shown, this is benefit versus risk. Those projects which are in the 'less risky, most benefit' quartile (top left) were chosen for priority review.

Balanced optimisation

Some organisations now use portfolio optimisation concepts, with computerised models applied if the analysis becomes complex. In these, the business objectives are stated in quantitative terms, usually a mix between financial figures and quality of service indicators. The candidate projects are fed into the model together with constraints, such as capital and resources, and the computer application derives an 'optimum' project mix to meet whatever targets are prescribed. This becomes effectively a scenario, as the objectives, funding or resource amounts can be easily changed to generate further possible mixes. In addition 'essential projects' and dependencies can also be incorporated (Figure 15.10).

Such approaches have the valuable added advantage that the timing of the projects can be considered. Hence a project may be chosen to start in one or two periods to fit within any of the constraints, without it actually being rejected outright because it cannot be scheduled in immediately.

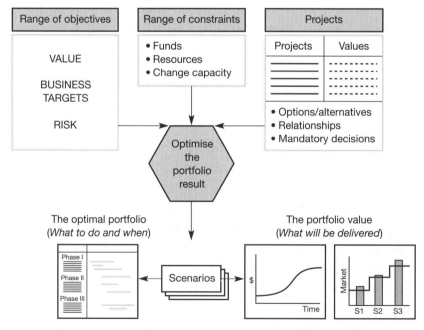

Figure 15.10 Balanced optimisation

A range of business objectives, constraints and a set of candidate projects are used as the data to create a number of scenarios. The objective is to use optimisation to help identify which group of projects and timings takes you closest to your objectives, whilst taking into account other factors, such as risk.

The output from such models can be very enlightening and can stimulate some extremely productive discussion. This, on its own, can improve the quality of the final decision. Of interest, the model I saw also had a constraint called 'chief executive's project'. This allowed any project to be forced into the programme. An alternative scenario could then be to have the same project excluded, with judgment then made as to the effect of doing this project on the whole portfolio. Portfolio optimisation is more informative than the previous methods but does require specialised knowledge to construct – there are some commercial offerings which do not result in the right outputs, so beware! Senior management also need to have faith in the comparative business cases and performance indicators between the constituent projects. Mind you, if they do not trust the basic data, no rational method will satisfy them!

An organisation found that its pipeline of development projects was blocked. There were too many projects (about 120) being undertaken and very few were actually being completed. The organisation set up an exercise to get these on-going projects under control. First, each project was aligned to a staged framework (similar to that in Part Two) and then ranked on a matrix, based on difficulty versus benefit (Figure 15.9). The objective was to include the least difficult projects which gave the most benefit and which were almost complete into the portfolio. The remainder would be stopped. The exercise was not without difficulties but it did result in a smaller and more focused portfolio of projects. The matrix selection method used was known to be imperfect as it favoured short-term revenue-generating projects over longer term strategic projects. However, it was considered adequate for the task required but something better would be needed later, when they would be adding new projects to the portfolio. They agonised over the type of tool they would use when the next batch of projects needed to be prioritised. As it turned out, they did not need to prioritise for six months. The project managers, during the initial investigations, had already identified potential blockages and changed the approach and scope of their projects to circumvent them. The project review group was able to let all new projects continue. Twelve months on and no tool had yet been devised. However, the portfolio was still under control and projects were being completed at the rate of two to three a week.

Is portfolio management worth doing better?

Of course it is! Returning to Figure 1.1, there is no point in becoming really great at the art of project management and then doing all the wrong projects. Business-led project management is about both aspects and they should be indivisible. In the sections above I have very much drawn out the pitfalls relating to the different techniques. Don't let that put you off; just use this as knowledge so you can approach the problem with your eyes 'wide open'. Even a technically or academically poor selection process is more value than none, simply because of the debate it will create amongst the senior team. If they are talking about this topic, you are half way there.

If in doubt, think of the improvements that others have realised:

- in one organisation the overall return through optimising a project portfolio was a massive 15 per cent increase in the total estimated return;
- research has shown a potential advantage of 19 per cent in average growth and 67 per cent in profit for those achieving excellence in portfolio management (see Chapter 28 for more on this).

Benefits on this scale can never be attained by a finance-led slash and burn, cost cutting approach to business planning. It would seem the rewards are there for those organisations which rise to the challenge.

Perhaps what remains is an issue of credibility. How can senior executives become confident that some approaches are practical and can be used to turn what they perceive as 'theoretical benefits' into bottom line results? Some areas of management practice are now evolving, which if combined, can lead to a far more effective result. These include:

- benefits estimation;
- balanced optimisation;
- decision support.

Estimating benefits can be made more accurate

It is now common for organisations to require an estimate of benefits to justify any project investments. Major economic crisis such as the credit crunch in 2008 and the collapse of the dot-com bubble in 2000 have emphasised this trend. No longer is it acceptable to state simplistically that the latest technology or general improvements in service quality are reason enough for investment. We must now quantify the business benefit from the technology or the actual level of service quality that will result and if customers will want to pay for it.

Improved market intelligence, combined with benchmarking and multi-discipline team working, can support much better estimates of benefits. If the enterprise itself makes the effort to lay out this intelligence, with clear analysis of current performance, the sponsors of projects can prepare better estimates and save time whilst doing so.

Balanced optimisation will be more effective

The scorecard prioritisation approach outlined earlier in this chapter is often accepted as the only form of analysis available. Yet this is not the case. Balanced optimisation, using mathematical techniques, can perform the analysis more comprehensively, faster and with a closer representation of real-world complexities.

Experience now shows that not only is such analysis possible, it can also be trusted. It does not replace management judgment but rather supports it by enabling the complex factors of benefits, risks, relationships and constraints to be analysed and drawn together, enabling senior executives to apply their judgment from a far better starting point than other methods yield.

Executive decision making can be better supported

The meetings when project selection decisions are made can be better managed, to take advantage of improved data and analysis. Strategy setting sessions are often carefully orchestrated, with extensive intelligence provided to assess current performance and evolving business trends. Scenario analyses are usually built in. A similar approach can and should be taken for portfolio decision making.

Portfolio management is moving more to a process repeated at regular intervals, rather than an annual budgeting and lobbying round. To support this, those who facilitate the function can design the sequence in which performance, supply and demand are considered to lead to more rational decisions. Technology can be introduced to enable the evaluation of scenarios and options.

In summary

Business planning is serious; without it you have very little basis on which to select your projects. Project selection is the primary influence on the future direction of your business. The projects represent the changes in direction, without which tomorrow will merely be a poorer version of today and, as such, are integral to the business plan and not an 'added extra'.

The popular finance based tools tend to give poorer results on their own than when combined with other tools. The other tools bring the strategic imperative to the fore and help achieve balance and take into account risk. When embarking on this, the scoring methods are an easy entry point, but, in my opinion, balanced optimisation is where we should be aiming; it uses the same data as scoring models but gives far richer and more useful results.

The commercial director of an engineering organisation interrupted the chief executive asking him what colour the new chauffeur cars should be. The chief executive picked up the phone and asked his personal assistant to come in.

'What colour should our new cars be?' he asked.

'Red,' the personal assistant replied.

'There, you have your answer,' the commercial director was told. After the commercial director had left the room, the chief executive commented, 'I like easy decisions which I can make quickly – it makes me feel good. But that was ridiculous!'

The cars were delivered in bright red, BUT the organisation's brand colours were blue and white!

15.1

DECISION-MAKING BODIES

This workout is for you to investigate who contributes to and makes decisions regarding your business projects and when.

1 Identify all the individuals or groups in your organisation that contribute to and make decisions regarding your organisation's projects. List them on the left of a flip chart or white board.

2 Show what decisions these each make, e.g. I have shown the decision-making bodies proposed in this chapter.

3 Consider and discuss:

- Are all three questions (p. 180) represented in your organisation?

- Are the accountabilities on p. 188 covered?

- Has each individual or body the authority to make the decisions?

- Is sufficient information available to those involved?

- Is question 2 considered 'cross-functionally'? If not, consider what effect this has on projects which require resources from a number of different functions.

4 Finally, decide who is accountable. Remember, accountability cannot be shared (see p. 286).

Individual or group	Question 1: Soundness of individual project	Question 2: Priority versus other projects	Question 3: Funding	Remit
Project sponsor				Ensures project is viable
Business programmes sponsor	×	× in own portfolio	Ensure business programme is viable	
Project review group		× across the organisation		Ensures organisation portfolio is viable and resources are available
Investment review group			×	Ensures investment criteria are met

Far too many projects!

So far I have concentrated on decision making on projects where the resources are the limiting factor. This is not always the case. It may be that decision making itself becomes more critical. I have already explained how a project review group can work to ensure that you commit to undertaking only those projects you have the capacity and capability to implement. There may, however, be too many of these for a single group to deal with, so, while you may have the capacity to implement them, you may lack the capacity to decide! The first case study (see p. 184) in this chapter is an example of this.

In the benchmarking study we noted that organisations have some resources which are shared and some which are separate (see p. 27). The former led to greater flexibility, while the latter led to easier, more discrete decision making. If you have separate resources, you can have a dedicated project review group. You will need to rely on business planning to check that the level of resource applied is in line with strategy as it will not be easy to reallocate these people. Where there is shared resource, you have greater difficulty. How can you divide the project review group into a number of subsidiary parts, capable of handling the volume of projects you have? The options for this include:

- by business area (function);
- by target market plus 'corporate';
- by driver.

If you choose to make decisions based on function, you will fall straight back into the trap of encouraging function-based projects, working in isolation. This is not a rational choice if you want a benefits-driven, cross-functional approach. Reject this option!

You could choose to have the project review groups based on your target markets. This has the advantage that you align projects to your customers' needs. Further, if there is little sharing of projects between segments, a logical division would be apparent. You would need to have a 'corporate' project review group to deal with those projects which did not sit within any particular segment.

Another way is by driver. You categorise your projects by those which are directly related to:

- the service or products you offer;
- increasing your capacity to offer more of the same service or product;
- increasing the efficiency of your operations;
- building new overall capability or infrastructures.

This has the advantage that you are quite clear as to what the reason is for the project being undertaken.

Regardless of which way you choose to cut up your project review group, you will find that:

- decisions from two or more groups will come into conflict at some time. It is vital that you have an escalation route to settle these;
- it will sometimes be difficult to categorise a project. This does not really matter, as all projects should be following the same staged framework, which itself leads to more informed decision making regardless of how you label the project.

Finally, when it comes down to making choices between projects, you will need to make sure that the number of projects proposed and undertaken is in line with corporate strategy. You can encourage this by linking the funding of projects to decision making. Two examples of this are provided below.

Example 1

If project review groups are based on market segments you could decide, based on your strategy, which is the most critical and which the least important and ration project funds accordingly. Thus, if the strategy in segment A is to 'milk cash and withdraw' you would have no funding for new capabilities or operational improvements unless they can also be applied to other segments. You would allocate the major share of the development funds to the most important emerging segment.

Example 2

If project review groups are based on drivers, you decide, from your strategy, what relative importance you need to put to each driver. For example, if you see a need to increase operation efficiency, you would have more funds for the 'efficiency' budget than for the others.

Putting the brakes on

This chapter has dealt with the approach to deciding what to continue, however, business-led projects do not always work out as we expect. In some cases, the development of the outputs proves too difficult, lengthy or expensive. In other cases, the opportunity which was identified has either diminished or disappeared altogether. In both cases, the project may no longer be viable. If you follow the approach in this book, such circumstances would lead to an issue being raised (see Chapter 24) which would be escalated to the project sponsor or higher for resolution. Remember that it is the project sponsor who is accountable for the business outcome, and therefore it is not in his/her interest to continue with an unviable project.

The approach to take is shown in Figure 15.11 and is as follows:

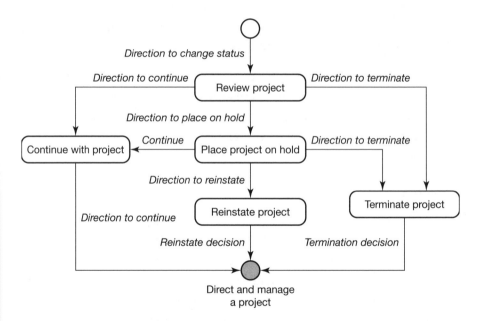

Figure 15.11 Terminating a project
Once the need to terminate a project is recognised, the project should be reviewed to verify this. The review may result in the project continuing, being placed on hold or being terminated. If on hold, the project may later be reinstated or terminated.

Review the project and find out the facts. Exactly what has gone wrong? What possible solution may there be? (Project Workout 24.1 explains a good approach for this). Do not take a knee-jerk decision in the absence of the facts and implications. Undertake the review as quickly as possible; there will be an opportunity later for a deeper investigation, if needed. Following the review you have three possible courses of action:

- **continue** the project. This may be in an altered form and therefore you may need to apply change control to approve any changes to the business case (see Chapter 25);
- **terminate** the project, if the project is never likely to be viable (see Chapter 27);
- **place the project on hold**, pending further investigations.

Placing the project on hold is a 'half way house' between continuing and terminating. When a project is on hold, you should not take on any further commitments or start new stages. You should minimise the amount of work undertaken, balancing the need to reduce costs, if it is terminated and maintaining momentum, should it continue. On a practical basis, the 'on hold' status ensures you can retain your core project team and facilities in case you restart the project. In addition, there will be cases where health and safety issues require some work to continue (for example, in civil engineering, ensuring tunnels are kept drained). The 'on hold' period is useful if the organisation undertaking the project is not able to make a termination decision in isolation, but still needs to protect its interests. Thus a contractor may place a project on hold, pending the client formally terminating it or issuing a change request. Another organisation may need to wait for funding decisions from its banks or other fund providers.

Have I Got the Resources?

Conditions for total resource planning

White space – the freedom to change

How can I meet the three conditions?

How detailed does resource forecasting need to be?

Obtaining resources and holding on to them can be very problematic, especially in functionally oriented organisations, where the balance of power is firmly held by line management. In these circumstances, resources are often committed to projects on the basis of good intention, rather than on good information.

'You've got a goal, I've got a goal. Now all we need is a football team.'

GROUCHO MARX

Conditions for total resource planning

In 1993 the University of Southern California analysed 165 teams in a number of successful organisations to assess the effectiveness of teamwork. Two reasons for teams failing to deliver were found:

- Project objectives were unclear.
- The right people were not working on the project at the right time.

In looking for solutions to these two issues, they found that using a 'projects approach' gave significant benefits in clarifying objectives (which is just as well or it would conflict with the message in this book!). On the question of resources, they found that having visibility of available resources and obtaining commitment of the required resources was key. In other words, if you haven't got the right people you can't expect to complete your project.

Obtaining resources and holding on to them can be very problematic, especially in functionally oriented organisations, where the balance of power is firmly held by line management. In these circumstances, resources are often committed to projects on the basis of good intention, rather than on good information. Consequently, they can be withdrawn, at whim, by the owning department if it believes that its own need is greater than that of the project. The result is that resource and skill shortages do not become apparent until they are a problem. An effective method of resource allocation and commitment is needed, therefore, which meets three conditions:

- **Condition 1** – you have a clear view of how resources are being consumed on a project by project basis.
- **Condition 2** – you have visibility of the resources available, or soon to be available, within the forecasting horizon of your organisation.
- **Condition 3** – commitment of resources should be based on clear information and forms the basis of an 'agreement' between the departments providing the resources and the projects consuming the resource.

Meeting these conditions will enable you to anticipate potential resource conflicts before they become a problem.

Many of the problems that organisations face in trying to allocate their resources efficiently come about as a result of some misconceptions regarding projects and resources. These misconceptions are:

- people work only on projects and do nothing else;
- resources are allocated to projects;
- project managers can choose whoever they want to work for them.

In practice you will find that:

- In most organisations, much of the work is not done on projects, but as part of running the business on a day-to-day basis (for example, when I worked on product management, 25 per cent of time was spent on development projects, 15 per cent on general management and administration, 40 per cent on product management and 20 per cent being sick, trained and on paid leave).
- Work is given to people. Your core employees are there all the time and being paid. You pay them regardless of whether they are working or on paid leave. There are some people you can turn on and off like a tap (temporary or agency staff), but I doubt if these are your key people.
- A project manager will state what he/she needs for the project and the line manager will allocate the most appropriate (or convenient) people. The line managers should know their people and their capabilities. They should be competent in the field of work they are accountable for and hence be best placed to decide who will fit a given role on a project.

The organisations who were best at managing and committing their resources were the consultancies. Their systems and processes were well tuned for this. Tight margins require that they have their staff on fee-paying work for as much of the working year as possible. They also need to continually form and reform teams from across the organisation to address the assignments.

In the benchmarking study, I found that the organisations that were best at managing and committing their resources were the consultancies. Their systems and processes were well tuned for this. Tight margins require that they have their staff on fee-paying work for as much of the working year as possible. They also need continually to form and reform teams from across the organisation to address the assignments. Further, they are never quite sure when a client is going to require their services but when a client does, they have to respond fast. They, therefore, have a conflict that:

- their employees should be gainfully engaged on fee-paying work, i.e. they need to drive staff utilisation up;
- they need to have enough slack in the allocation of resources to enable them to respond to new requests quickly, i.e. don't drive utilisation up too high.

(Compare this with the need on business projects to do an initial investigation of a proposal as soon as possible while trying to do as many of the required projects – it's very similar.) Rather than talk theoretically, I will explain a basic, but very effective resource management method from one of these types of organisations.

The organisation is an engineering consultancy with about 1,200 employees in various locations worldwide. In the past, margins in these organisations were very high and, as long as the people were working on assignments (projects), good profits were made. Management systems did not need to be sophisticated. However, the organisation did have a time-recording capability for all its employees so that time could be booked to assignment accounts and charged on to clients. Time for non-assignment work was also captured, either as process activities (marketing, sales, etc.) or as overheads (training, paid leave, sickness), i.e. the organisation met **condition 1** for resource management.

The competitive environment changed and the organisation found itself very rapidly being drawn into a lower margin industry. It was essential to 'commercialise' the management systems of the organisation fast if they were to retain control. The first attempt was to collect three sets of data from assignment managers, each required by different central functions:

- The invoicing department wanted a forecast of the invoices which would be sent out so that they could ensure they were staffed up to despatch the invoices quickly.
- The financial controller wanted a forecast of cash due, so that he could manage the working capital required and manage the payment of bills.
- The operations director wanted to know who was allocated to assignments and who was coming free so he knew what work he could accept (resource management).

Needless to say, the assignment managers did not look on these three separate sets of 'new demands' kindly. Nevertheless, they did their best.

THE FUTURE ROLE OF FUNCTIONS

If what people do counts more than the function or department they belong to and if you are to use people to best effect anywhere in your organisation, what is the role of the functions? You now know that few changes can be made within a single function in your organisation. You generally require people from a number of areas contributing to the processes, activities and projects you are undertaking.

In the traditional hierarchy, each head of function decides not only the strategic direction of their function, but also what each and every one of his/her employees will do and how it will be done. The danger, if functions are too dominant, is that they will drive the business as they see fit from their own perspective. This may not be in line with the drivers that the organisation leadership wants to effect. The outcome is that the organisation becomes out of balance. For example, efficiency is often seen as a good goal. So also is responsiveness to customer needs. However, the latter may require you to carry excess capacity in order to meet customer needs at short notice. If one function is driving 'efficiency' up by reducing capacity while another is creating a proposition around responsiveness there is likely to be a mismatch and dissatisfied customers.

The projects approach, like the current move toward cross-business processes, aligns all the required skills and capabilities around the attainment of a business objective. In the case of a process, the objective is better operations. In the case of a project, the objective is change for the better. Thus, the functions are not leaders in driving the business, but rather suppliers of people and expertise to projects and processes. The accountability of a head of function is to ensure that the right people are available in the right numbers to service the business needs. They will be accountable for pay, employee satisfaction and personal development. Other key roles will start to become apparent. There will need to be those, expert at particular disciplines, who will create strategy, develop and maintain technical architecture, manage projects, or manage people. However, they will not do this just in the context of a single function, but rather in the context of the complete organisation, working wherever needed across functional boundaries to achieve the business objectives.

When looked at together, however, the three discrete sets of information proved very interesting. The forecast of work, in hours, could be multiplied by a factor to give a good approximation of the invoice values. The cash received should be the same as that invoiced (forgetting bad debts). The only difference between the three sets of figures should be timing:

- the time from doing the work to invoicing represents work-in-progress days;
- the time between invoicing and cash received represents debtor days.

However, even taking account of the timing difference, the three sets of figures could not be reconciled. The forecast was unreliable and inconsistent.

The solution they implemented to deal with this divergence was very simple. They asked for the same data, but had them collected at the same time on two linked data sheets:

- a manpower sheet;
- a financial sheet.

The **manpower sheet**: each assignment manager listed the people (by name, or by grade/discipline) required on the project. Against each, he forecast the number of hours each would book in a given month. There was a cap on the maximum hours each month to provide for unexpected work and 'down time'. (Look ahead to Figure 16.2 for an example.)

The **financial sheet**: the hours from the manpower sheet were then costed at actual pay-roll rates and entered into a second financial sheet as time costs (cost of labour). To this sheet, the assignment manager added the forecast of non-labour costs. He also added, at the top of the sheet, the forecast of invoices required to be sent out, with a line below showing when the cash would be received. In short, they ensured that all necessary data were collected at the same time, using the same form. The whole forecast was input to a computer, added and sorted so that summary reports and analyses could be obtained. The result was consistent data giving consistent forecast reports. No matter who needed the information, they knew it was compatible with that used by others for different purposes. It was so good that the marketing department was able to provide a full analysis of the business on a segmented basis every month, both historic and future. Previously, such an analysis used to take three months to complete.

One of the reports produced from this system was for the heads of function: they each received a listing of all the people within their department, together with a list of which assignments they were committed to and for how many hours each month. The organisation, therefore, had visibility of its future resource needs, i.e. the organisation met **condition 2**, visibility, for resource management. (Look ahead to Figure 16.3 for an example.)

The first few months of operation were problematic as people adjusted the forecasts to take account of what they had learned. However, after a short time it stabilised and became a reliable source of management information. From thereon, whenever the organisation had a request for work from a client or was invited to tender for work, it could assess whether it was likely to have the resources available to meet the need and/or design the bid to fit around its known commitments. Also, as the requesting project completed the resource forecast, this became the 'agreement' between the project manager and the supplying department. i.e. they fulfilled **condition 3** for resource management.

In practice they all chose to do a monthly forecast as it was easier to maintain and amend on this more frequent basis rather than start at a lower level of knowledge on a quarterly basis.

The frequency of reforecasting was set at quarterly intervals as it was expected that the effort of constructing the forecast would be too onerous on a monthly basis. The assignment managers were given the option to do it monthly if they wanted to. In practice they all chose to do a monthly forecast as it was easier to maintain and amend on this more frequent basis rather than start at a lower level of knowledge on a quarterly basis.

This organisation:

- knew what each project and activity in the organisation consumed by way of resources (condition 1);
- had clear visibility, at a high level, of its resource availability (condition 2);
- made future commitments on the basis of knowing what was currently committed and who was available without compromising previously made commitments (condition 3).

In short, it had achieved a level of knowledge about the application of company resources that many organisations can only dream of. Did this process provide reasonable figures? The financial controller predicted the year-end results, six months in advance, to within an accuracy of 2 per cent, excepting extraordinary accounting items, and the company was able to successfully arrange finace well in advance, based on reliable figures. While individual assignments within the portfolio exhibited a fair degree of instability in forecasting, the population, as a whole, was very stable.

This example dealt with a consultancy organisation, where it is crucial to have a tight hold on resources. When one moves into the manufacturing or the service sector, the management of resources becomes less visible and is often hidden within functional hierarchies. Certain parts may be exceptionally well managed (such as individual manufacturing units, warehousing, telephone call centres) but these are usually contained within a given function and deal with day-to-day business rather than change. Business projects frequently draw on resources from across an organisation, not just from one function. If just one part is unable to deliver its contribution to a project, the entire venture is at risk. Few organisations have, or yet see the need for, the capability to manage their entire employee workforce as a block of resources that can be used anywhere, at any time, just as in a consultancy organisation. However, as in consultancy organisations, managers should make sure that their people are being applied to productive work, rather than merely playing a numbers game with head count and departmental budgets – this just leads to suboptimisation, which may be of no benefit at all (see Chapter 20).

> *Managers should make sure that their people are being applied to productive work, rather than merely playing a numbers game with head count and departmental budgets.*

You need all your resources in place to succeed

Copyright © 1997 Robert Buttrick

White space – the freedom to change

The gap between what your resources are committed to and the total resource you have available is what I term 'white space'. It is the resources that you have not yet committed to a given activity or project. If you fulfil conditions 2 and 3, you will know your white space:

White space = resources available – resources already committed

In the very short term this should be small. It will grow as you look further into the future.

White space is fundamental to a organisation's on-going health. If you haven't any in the short to medium term, you are paralysed. You have no one available to change the business to meet new threats or exploit new opportunities unless you withdraw them from previously committed work. White space gives you the resources to effect change in the future. 'We are in a fast moving environment' is the common cry nowadays. If this is truly the case, then you need to ensure that you have 'white space' resources ready to meet future needs. You know the people will be required but you are not yet sure exactly what for. If you have no people to change things, things won't change.

White space must cater for two distinct needs:

- First, it must cover the need to undertake initial investigations resulting from new proposals. These people must be available at very short notice and must be highly knowledgeable if the investigations are to have any value.
- Second, you need the resources to undertake the projects themselves, following approval at the Detailed Investigation Gate.

> **White space gives you the resources to effect change in the future. 'We are in a fast moving environment' is the common cry nowadays. If this is truly the case, then you need to ensure that you have 'white space' resources ready to meet the future needs.**

Compare the former to a company putting a bid together – if this is done by inappropriate people, the bid may be lost or the company may have committed itself to a financial disaster. Just because business projects are 'internal' it does not mean you need not apply the same rigour as you would with external matters. It's your organisation's future at stake in both cases.

Figure 16.1 represents 'white space' in graph form. The figure could apply to a complete organisation, a division, a function or whatever. However, unless you can build this picture you will be taking risks every time you need to set off another initiative.

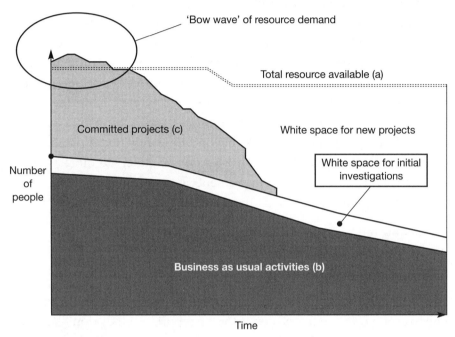

Figure 16.1 White space
White space is the gap between the resources you have (a) and those already committed (b + c). In the very short term this should be small. It will grow as you look further into the future. Notice the short-term bow wave which results from optimistic demands to the immediate needs.

How can I meet the three conditions?

The extent you need to employ formal systems to collate the past and future use of your resources depends on your organisation. At one extreme, you will need time recording to know what people have been working on, at the other you can rely on the line managers filling that gap.

Time recording

Those organisations which require time recording for other business critical needs will, like as not, already have it. Few organisations who don't, won't. It is an emotive system to implement. It can look and feel like bureaucracy gone mad. Some people are so against it they will leave a organisation rather than fill in a time sheet. It is often bound up in emotive words such as 'trust'. 'If you can't trust me to work on the right thing, I don't want to work for you.' Few finance or marketing functions are on time recording. However, it is very common in engineering and technical departments. Despite this, time recording can be the key to making a flat structure work. It allows people to be accountable for activities and projects which range far beyond their functional patch. It can enable job enrichment. It also enables you to delegate more without losing visibility and control. If implementing time recording, you need to balance the cost of doing it with the information gained. Consider:

- what the reports provided by the system will tell you;
- how they are structured;
- who has access to them.

Also consider the timing for implementing a time-recording system. The only reason you have the system is for the reports – if they don't help you meet your overall needs at the moment, don't do it yet. If the basic understanding and acceptance of their use is not in place you will have an uphill struggle to make them work. Preferably, you should wait until those within your organisation (project sponsors, project managers, functional resource managers) have identified the need themselves.

> *If you don't have some kind of time recording, you won't know how much your projects are costing. Consequently, you will rely on line management reports for controlling costs, which in turn keeps the balance of power firmly in the line management camp rather than shifting it toward the project view of life.*

Finally, remember that if you don't have some kind of time recording, you won't know how much your projects are costing. Consequently, you will rely on line management reports for controlling costs, which in turn keeps the balance of power firmly in the line management camp rather than shifting it toward the project view of life. Time recording, if properly implemented with appropriate reporting, will give you an extra degree of freedom to manage your business.

Manpower forecasting

Manpower forecasting is a natural follow-on from time recording. It is merely a prediction of how many hours will be booked by whom against a particular activity or project. Forecasts can be created by one of three different roles.

Forecast made by	Comment
Each individual forecasts his/her own time input based on what he/she has already been briefed on and is committed to doing	In most cases, individuals will not have sufficient visibility of the work needed. They will only forecast the work they have been told to do, not what their managers know needs to be done, but for which no briefing has as yet been given. Forecasts on this basis will be very short term and hence of limited use
The resource manager forecasts the people required to meet commitments already made	This lets the 'supply' side drive the forecast. This means that the estimates are likely to be good BUT unless well coordinated with every project manager, the timing may be very wrong. The total of such forecasts may show no deficit of resources, but the functions may have made choices regarding the project priorities, which are not rightfully their decisions to make
Each project manager forecasts the people who he/she expects and requires to work on the project based on the project plan (see Figure 16.2)	This lets the 'demand' side drive the forecast. Estimates will match the plan timescales and should be agreed with the individuals on the project team. The total of these forecasts may show that certain resources are allocated beyond their capacity. This is good to highlight, then a business decision can be made to decide how to deal with the conflicts (see Figure 16.3)

On the whole, the third method is more likely to serve the needs of the business than the other two. It allows the project managers who are driving the change to set their demands in accordance with their business objectives. It highlights any conflicts and enables a business decision to be made, rather than one being made by the limiting function. Further, it allows the project manager to increase or decrease the demand for resources openly.

In Chapter 15 the principle was: 'Having decided to do a project, do it. But stop if circumstances change.' In other words, the project manager continues to flex his forecast of resources to complete the project, based on current knowledge. If the manpower forecast is costed and tied into financial forecasts you can be sure that the project will be reviewed if its cost exceeds the sanctioned amount. The business managers (e.g. project review group) can then make an assessment of whether the project should continue. It is their decision, not that of the functions supplying resource.

A major pitfall of putting in systems to enable you to have visibility of your resources is that they can be made too complicated. Take the following scenario:

1 The project schedule and scope drive resource needs.
2 You can assign resources in project plans using project-planning software and obtain a profile of who is required and when.
3 This can be downloaded into a central database and analysed for the organisation as a whole.
4 Resource conflicts are spotted by the 'system', which, based on priority rules, automatically levels the conflicting resources by moving lower priority activities back in time.
5 The output from the global resource analysis is fed back to the individual project plans, which show the resultant slippage.

There is software that can handle all this in an integrated way, so, no doubt, there are organisations who manage it this way. However, this level of integration and automation is neither always necessary nor always desirable. For example, it would mean that every project would need to use the same, or closely compatible, planning software and be fully resourced at activity level. On its own, this has dubious value, when all you need is 'visibility' of resources such that you can make decisions on overall resource availability. Detail is not necessarily needed.

Provided that you use the same high level work breakdown structures and projects as the basis for the forecasts, the resources can be held in a separate, simpler database. You use this to analyse and report on those resources where demand looks as if it will exceed capacity – this in turn tells you which projects may come into conflict. The project managers and the resource managers of the contentious projects and resources can then discuss and agree how the conflict should be handled. If they cannot agree, the issue should be escalated to the project review group. There is no need for sophisticated analysis and resource levelling rules – managers can manage it.

When you add up the total of resources required you will often observe a 'bow wave'. That is to say, over the short term, the demand for resources exceeds availability (see Figure 16.1). In systems I have seen this always happens. Project managers are optimistic about the work they believe will be done in the next month and not enough account is taken of the reactive work that people have to do in addition to their project duties.

Placing a 'cap' on the maximum hours forecast per person is a simple and effective way of dealing with the 'bow wave'. Assume that a month has four weeks, each of 36 hours, i.e. 144 hours. It is highly unlikely that anyone will actually book 144 hours against a single project on his/her time sheet. It is even less likely that a large population would all book 144 hours; some would be sick, be assigned to urgent work elsewhere, go on training courses, attend a presentation to a key customer, or whatever. By making a simple rule that if a person is full time on a project, you forecast only 85 per cent of 144 hours (122 hours) and build in an allowance for this.

By depressing the maximum forecasting capacity, you allow a contingency (white space) which allows you to do other reactive work or overrun current work without compromising the plan. Experience with forecasting will tell you the right percentage for your organisation.

Figures 16.2 and 16.3 show a typical manpower forecast for a project and a typical report on resource demand for a function.

Project: YT2Z/Triton 2000
Detailed Investigation Stage

MANPOWER – ROLLING FORECAST (HOURLY)

Period: 4 wks to 28 Sept 2011

Note: *This is the guide to the maximum hours per month* — maximum hours row:

Oct	Nov	Dec 2010	Jan 2011	Feb	Mar	Apr	May	Jun	Jul	Aug	Sep	Q3	Q4	Q5	Q6
134	134	157	127	134	172	119	119	172	127	134	172	432	425	425	432

Resources	F'cast Month	ACTUAL TO DATE Month	ACTUAL TO DATE Year	ACTUAL TO DATE Life	Oct	Nov	Dec 2010	Jan 2011	Feb	Mar	Apr	F'cast Outturn
Category 1	70	70	280	560	56	70	70	70	84	112	28	1050
Category 2	75	75	300	600	60	75	75	75	90	120	30	1125
Category 3	30	30	120	240	24	30	30	30	36	48	12	450
Category 4	95	95	380	760	76	95	95	95	114	152	38	1425
Mann. J P	130	130	520	1040	104	130	130	130	156	208	52	1950
Fuller. W	100	100	400	800	80	100	100	100	120	160	40	1500
TOTAL HOURS	500	500	2000	4000	400	500	500	500	600	800	200	
CUMULATIVE	500	500	2000	4000	4400	4900	5400	5900	6500	7300	7500	7500

Cumulative continues across remaining forecast columns (May–Sep, Q3–Q6, Beyond): 7500, 7530, 7500, 7500, 7500, 7500, 7500, 7500, 7500, 7500.

Note: *This number of hours are forecast by the Project Manager to complete this stage.*

Note: *Forecast may be by resource category or by individual.*

Figure 16.2 Manpower – rolling forecast by project

This is a typical report on which manpower needs can be forecast. In this case, the figure shows the forecast for the detailed investigation stage of a project. It shows, on the left, the actual hours already booked to the stage and, on the right, the forecast hours and total. The guide for the maximum hours is shown below the date line. If this report is costed it provides the data required for the time cost line in the financial forecast (see Figure 21.4). (Adapted by kind permission of Professional Applications Ltd, UK.)

Development Function KLO
Function Manager: Perry, TM

MANPOWER - ROLLING FORECAST BY FUNCTION (HOURLY)

Period: 4 wks to 28 Sept 2011

Each person or employee category in the function is listed here

Hours committed

% availability

The total committed hours for the function is shown here. The availability is White Space

The projects the person is assigned to are shown against their name. The cost centre with management accountability is also given

Discipline

Grade

Name/Number	DETAILS Gd	Disc	ASSIGNED TO Project Code	Managed by:		Oct	Nov	Dec 2010	Jan 2011	Feb	Mar	Apr	May	Jun	Jul	Aug	Sep	Q3	Q4	Q5	Q6
						134	134	157	127	134	172	119	119	172	134	127	172	432	425	425	432
Brown, HJ/00345	B	KT	Y4RT	KLO		120	100	70	50	20	10	20	60	60	20	5					
			Y5FT	KLO		4	25	25	50	50	60	50	20	20							
			Zf5H	HNY		23	9	20	20	8	16	5									
			Total			147	134	115	120	78	86	75	80	80	20	5					
			% available			-10%	27%	6%	42%	50%	37%	33%	53%	85%	96%	100%	100%	100%	100%	100%	100%
Green, HJ/00346	C	KT	Y4RT	KLO		20	10		10	20	10	10	10	5							
			HJUI	HNY		110	80	20		10			5								
			Total			130	90	20	10	30	10	10	5								
			% available			3%	33%	87%	92%	78%	94%	92%	96%	100%	100%	100%	100%	100%	100%	100%	100%
Unassigned	D	KT	Y4RT	KLO		9	20	70	50	70	5	5	5	5							
			YTDD	FE		120	20	20	20	20	30	20									
			KRG	HNY		129	45														
			Total								35	25	5								
			% available			4%					80%	79%	96%	100%	100%	100%	100%	100%	100%	100%	100%
TOTAL HOURS COMMITTED						4603	4987	4976	3426	3467	3479	2156	1087	432	210	25					
TOTAL % AVAILABLE						-1%	-9%	7%	21%	24%	41%	47%	73%	93%	95%	99%	100%	100%	100%	100%	100%

Figure 16.3 Manpower – rolling forecast by function

Once all the project manpower forecasts have been collated, they can be sorted to give each line manager a listing of the people in his/her department or function, stating to which projects each is committed. (Adapted by kind permission of Professional Applications Ltd, UK.)

How detailed does resource forecasting need to be?

High level forecasting versus detail

The objective of resource management, in the context of portfolios of projects, is to have sufficient visibility of the use and availability of your resources to enable you to commit, with confidence, to starting new projects without compromising the completion of existing projects. It follows then that the forecast does not need to be fully detailed. In fact, as all forecasts are, crudely, a range of very good to very poor guesses, the likely deviations in elements which make up the forecast can be very significant while not affecting the total figure much at all.

Forecasts can be on two levels:

- high – this is equivalent in manufacturing of a master production schedule;
- detailed – this is equivalent in manufacturing to a shop schedule.

It is the high level forecast that you should be concerned with in managing portfolios of projects. The detailed forecast is the accountability of the line and project managers; they decide when the work is actually done and by whom. You should not try to combine the two! In the example I used to explain resource management, the organisation used the following for its high level forecasting:

- forecast, by person or skill group/grade in hours;
- per month, for the next 12 months;
- per quarter, for the following year;
- per year, for the next 3 years

This was in the context that at the start of any financial year this organisation had 50 per cent of its resources for the year already committed. The reason they used hours was simply because that is the basis on which they charged their clients and hence how their time sheets were completed and actuals were reported. Their forecasting frequency was monthly; weekly forecasts would have given little, if any, extra value. However, their manpower (or time sheet) frequency and reporting was weekly. Monthly was too infrequent as deviations from plans would be spotted too late for corrective action to be taken.

Sales pipelines are very difficult to estimate especially in industries where the buying pattern is a few large purchases rather than the mass market consumer pattern. An industrial engineering organisation had a pipeline of about 350 prospects, totalling potential revenue of £300m, which, after factoring in the probability of the customer wanting to proceed and the probability of the bid being won, totalled £50m. Despite this being made up of inputs from six different people, in six different divisions on three continents, one third of the prospects churning every quarter, and potential sales and win probabilities changing frequently, this pipeline stayed very consistent in total displaying little major shift month on month.

In contrast to this, another organisation, at the start of the financial year only had 25 per cent of its resources for the year already committed. They, therefore, used to forecast by person only, in days per week. They used 'days' as their measurement unit as, again, that was how they charged their clients and hence how their time-recording system captured and reported the data. Their frequency for forecasting was weekly for manpower and monthly for other costs.

Avoiding micro planning – a solution by applying constraints theory

The primary constraint for a project is usually the resource that can be applied. No resource equals no progress. We also know that micro planning every activity for every person on every one of maybe 50–500 projects is likely to be a fruitless exercise. Reality changes too fast and estimating is not that reliable. So how can we find a way through this such that our estimates and our commitments to undertake the work are realistic?

Every system, process, or organisation has a constraint which limits how much it can achieve (its throughput). In corporate, multiproject environments, there is a single department or work group which is the **constraint**. In very complex organisations it may be very difficult to identify who this is; however, most people intuitively feel where the problems lie. You hear it in their language, 'Oh, it's those people in IT', or 'we'd better design this so Technology don't need to be involved'. Some people actually argue that you could assume there is no resource constraint at all; we just spend our time flitting from task to task in a complex round, wasting energy. They say if we organised better, there would be plenty of resources to do what we really need to do. Others say there are many constraints, not just one, each one sheltering behind the other. Whatever your view, be you a purist 'there is only one constraint' person or a realist saying 'it's all a constraint!', the problem remains and needs to be addressed.

A solution lies in the practical application of the Theory of Constraints. If it is so difficult to find the bottleneck, simply choose a department to be the appointed constraint. Then plan the workflow through this single department to ensure maximum throughput. This means ensuring:

- they receive early warning of work;
- they receive the work as soon as it is ready (no hand-off delays);
- they work only on this (or a defined minimum number) and clear it as soon as possible (that is to say, they avoid bad multi-tasking).

We also need to ensure that delays on one project do not have a knock-on effect on all subsequent projects. We do this by ensuring that between each project, the resource has sufficient safety margin built in to absorb the routine, 'unexpected' delays. This is called a **capacity buffer**.

By protecting the constraint in this way, we stagger the flow of projects in the organisation. We only need to schedule this one resource fully. The constraint becomes in effect a drumbeat to which all other departments march. We can plan projects independently of each other but, by tying them to the 'drum', we are able to stagger them in a rational way. The safety (or buffers) provided around the drum resource also provide safety time for work in other departments. Figure 16.4 illustrates this.

- Planning is used to resolve as many problems as possible as early.
- Monitoring during execution is done by managing the buffers.
- There would need to be a strong hold on when projects are released for work; this would be the accountability of the project review group (see p. 188).

If applying this method, individual projects should also be planned in such a way as to increase the reliability of delivery. This is discussed in more detail in Chapter 21 and is the subject of Eli Goldratt's *Critical Chain* (North River Press, 1997).

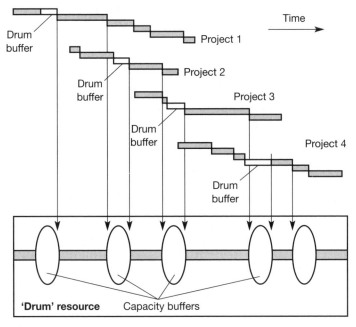

Figure 16.4 Building project timescales around the drum department
The projects are scheduled so that work required in the 'drum' department is done in logical sequence without bad multi-tasking. A drum buffer in each project protects the resource from delays within each project. A capacity buffer protects the knock-on effects of delays in one project on all downstream projects.

WHO IS RESPONSIBLE?

This critical chain solution is not simplistic and is not an easy one to put in place. It requires some fundamental changes in behaviour:

Senior executives will have to stagger the release of new projects and new project stages. (Most havoc in multiproject environments is wrought by top managers wanting 'just one more … NOW!')

Resource managers will have to reduce bad multi-tasking in their departments (perhaps no more favours!).

Team managers and members will have to undertake their work as fast as possible, ensuring a smooth handover.

… and organisations in cash-rich industries will find this more difficult because there is little financial imperative to change behaviour.

WHAT'S YOUR 'WHITE SPACE?'

This workout is for you to use as a discussion point or to identify the capacity your organisation has available to change itself. Assume that any projects to change your current way of working need to be managed and staffed from within your current head count. Try to construct a picture, as in Figure 16.1. As a start, look 12 months ahead only.

Hints

Break up the problem by function if this helps.

Use the list of projects you derived from Workout 3.2 – number each project.

Try to cluster similar groups of people together and build the picture in the following order:

1 total head count (a);

2 people (either grouped or as individuals) running the current operations (processes) (b);

3 people (either grouped or as individuals) working on projects which are currently in progress (c).

Your percentage of white space is (a – (b + c)) / a %;

Consider how fast your business and competitive environment is moving and in this context discuss the following points:

1 Will the amount of white space you have allow you to develop enough new products and sufficiently improve your operational and management systems and processes to maintain or enhance your position in the market?

2 How far into the future does white space become available? If you had a requirement NOW, how long would you have to wait before you could start working on it without displacing any of your current projects or activities?

3 Is there hidden capacity in your business? How do you know?

4 Do you have any people who can be deployed quickly onto new projects and who probably do not know what they will be doing next week (i.e. resources for initial investigations)?

5 Have you ever started off a set of change projects or initiatives which people say they are keen on but which fail to deliver because insufficient time is made available for them? If so, what does this tell you?

An Environment for Managing Your Portfolio

New structures for old

Support offices

The tools to help it work – systems

Lists – keeping tabs on your projects

Harnessing web technology

What would such a system look like?

Management accounting systems

Putting your systems together

Some organisations are well on their way to managing themselves 'out of their functional boxes'. Most are not.

'I've got a little list. I've got a little list.'

W S GILBERT

In this chapter I will look at the type of environment you need to have in place around your projects and throughout your organisation if a projects approach is to succeed. You should now have a feel for the way a project progresses through its life cycle (Part Two) and how the wider decision-making framework can be organised to help you choose the right projects and not overcommit your resources.

In Chapter 2 we saw how any process does not sit in isolation but in the context of the structures, culture and systems you choose to wrap it in. In this chapter we will look at structures very briefly and then at the systems.

New structures for old

The whole approach for projects is to enable you to deploy the people you need anywhere in the organisation where they can, due to their mix of skills and competences, add the greatest value. The objective is to break through functional and departmental barriers to the extent that the word 'cross-functional' becomes unnecessary. In effect, your functional structure – which was so important in the 'old days' – becomes secondary to the key business pro- grammes and projects which work across it. In such an environment, reorganisation, as a means of responding to problems, becomes less necessary (now what are the new execu- tives going to do to prove they've arrived?). See also cartoon on p. 41.

> **The power bases of the new organisations will be more associated with the roles of people and groups. Consequently, the important structures will be those associated with project sponsorship and decision-making bodies; these are the people and groups which will carve out the future shape of the organisation.**

The power base of the old functions was that they held the people, the budgets and any decisions within their domain. Often these were decisions which should have been taken on an organisation-wide basis. The power bases of the new organisations will be more associated with the roles of people and groups. Consequently, the important structures will be those associated with project sponsor- ship and decision-making bodies; these are the people and groups which will carve out the future shape of the organisation. They will be more associated with directing and coaching than managing. In fact, one could conceive of an organisation where the traditional 'director at the top of a function' is no longer deemed to be a sensible arrangement. When it comes to 'direction', we should be directing whole organisations and not just parts of it. Of course, every function needs a 'person at the top' to ensure that the work undertaken is of the highest standard, that people are happy and the 'architectures' are robust. However, just because someone is an exceptional people manager or gifted technical expert, it does not mean he/she has the breadth of knowledge, skills or competence to direct a corporation, or even that he/she wants to be a director! The corporate world is full of people promoted beyond their levels of competence, through no fault of their own.

Some organisations are well on their way to managing themselves 'out of their functional boxes'. Most are not. The decrease in importance of functional hierarchy is not going to happen by someone merely decreeing it. It has its place and its uses. Much of the day-to-day work in many organisations is ideally suited to departments, provided the hand-offs and process flows are efficient and uninterrupted. It's when it comes to change that the problems and limitations become apparent. Before you let go of the reins of traditional cost centre management, you need to build alternative communication channels, management frameworks and systems. You cannot 'fly blind'. Once in place, they will be so useful that the old hierarchies will naturally decay, fall into disuse and become less relevant.

An organisation ran itself on a full matrix. It knew all its costs both by cost centre and by project and activity. It had had a stabilised structure for many years but finally decided that the emergence of new disciplines and a more unified approach to the market required a reorganisation of departments. This took about three months to put in place. However, financial reporting and work continued as usual as mostly everyone was working to a set of roles relating to prescribed accountabilities. The fact that there were no departments for a while made little difference to day-to-day work or reporting. They were already used to crossing boundaries.

DISCUSSION: REORGANISATION

If you dismantle the functional structure of your organisation, in whole or in part, would you be able to maintain full management visibility, control and reporting during the change period?

17.1

Support offices

Leadership – from the top

If you are serious about enterprise-wide programme and project management you must realise that it doesn't run itself. It needs leadership to establish its profile and to enforce the accountabilities. The opportunity may have been recognised by a few middle-management enthusiasts in various parts of your business and they may even get as far as agreeing some common methods and practices (PRTM Level 2; see p. 482). However, that is not enough if you are to reap the full rewards. You will need to have the following:

- Someone with top level accountability for the adoption and direction of the full environment across the whole organisation, preferably reporting directly to the CEO, deputy CEO or COO. I will call this a **Programme Management Director** and provide a typical set of accountabilities below.
- Someone with specific accountability for the architecture (accountabilities, process, systems and culture) of project management. I often refer to this person as '**programme/project management design authority**' and provide a typical set of accountabilities below.
- An organisation to support these people in undertaking their roles. After all, you seldom find directors at this level doing all the detailed work themselves. I call these **support offices**.

The **Programme Management Director** is accountable to the chief executive officer for ensuring that all business change is planned, directed and managed in an effective and efficient way using appropriate programme and project management techniques.

Programme Management Director

- Championing good value business programme and project management and a benefits-driven culture.
- Introducing, maintaining and improving common programme management framework, process and methods, including for business planning, project selection and project authorisation.
- Creating an environment in which business programme and project managers and teams are developed and recognised for their skills.
- Recommending changes to senior management to improve the effectiveness and efficiency for delivering business change.
- Providing independent reviews of projects.

The **Programme Management Design Authority** is accountable to the Programme Management Director for acting as guardian for the organisation's 'best practice' methodology, processes, tools, systems and templates for authorising and undertaking programmes and projects.

Programme Management Design Authority

- Updating, supporting and obtaining user feedback (including lessons learned) on the project environment and future developments.
- Developing and communicating changes to the environment.
- Ensuring that the staged project management framework and associated project controls are in place and used throughout the organisation.
- Preparing and leading briefings on the frameworks and their use.
- Ensuring there is a consistent and complete range of project management training and development programmes available.
- Ensuring consistent recruitment and selection tools and processes are available for project management related appointments.
- Ensuring that the project processes interface at a high level with other core processes within the organisation.
  Providing consulting, coaching and facilitation to users of the project framework.

DESIGNING ACCOUNTABILITIES

When designing accountabilities, make sure they are mutually compatible. You cannot design any accountability in isolation; it must always be designed in relation to the other accountabilities with which it interfaces. Never design an accountability which undermines another. For example, notice the Programme Management Director is not accountable for benefit realisation as that sits with the Business Programme Sponsors (see p. 170). In the accountability sets in this book I have taken the view that accountability for delivery and benefit realisation pass through the Project/Business Programme route, but that the methods they use are owned, for the total organisation, by the Programme Management Director.

Support offices – who supports whom on what?

This brings us to the subject of 'project support offices'; what exactly should a 'support office' do to support programme and project management and how should this service be provided? Whilst many proprietary methods define a 'support office' role, you will find they often have different activities and styles associated with them. To make matters worse, many of them are not clear who they are supporting. As with many project management related topics, there is no single commonly agreed definition or approach; you have to create your own, drawing on whatever experience is available (including this book!).

I find the easiest way to approach this is to:

- assume a support office has no accountabilities of its own;
- decide which roles the office supports;
- look at which aspects of the supported roles can be undertaken by the support office.

You can then look at the discrete accountabilities associated with each supported role and decide which will benefit from a support service. This gives you a list of what the support office needs to do. Project Workout 17.2 provides you with a step-by-step approach. You may find the list is very short and focused. It may, however, be very wide ranging; if so, you should consider if a single office is the best way to provide the service. You may find it better to design a network of local support offices, each supporting different roles, but which in total provides the services you require.

How the offices undertake the support services very much depends on:

- whether the aspects of the roles supported are optional or mandatory;
- the overall culture of the organisation.

If the activities are optional, the support office will need to rely on 'pull' influencing styles in order to move forward. If the aspect being supported is mandated by policy, then assertion can be used (see p. 284 on influencing styles). If the organisation culture is very loose, allowing senior managers a high degree of freedom in how they carry out their accountabilities, the support office is unlikely to be accepted if it takes a very prescriptive approach. In which case, use your finance department as the tough guys!

Finally, you need to determine the staffing competencies and volume of work (throughput) the offices need to cope with, so that you can decide on the staffing levels. For instance, will a central office supply all services to everyone? Will it expect some services to be provided by 'local' offices, or expect some accountabilities to 'serve themselves' while using tools and methods which are centrally owned?

The key roles to be supported

In Chapter 14, I proposed a set of governance accountabilities for enterprise-wide programme management (see Figure 14.2). By adding project management and line management to these, we can draw up a process and accountability model for the entire organisation (Figure 17.1). Notice that I have also added the accountability for a Programme Management Director, which I introduced at the start of this section. Against each of these accountabilities you can list the types of support service which you feel should be provided in your organisation and the extent to which that service is supplied. By doing this, it soon becomes very obvious that the needs of the accountabilities are very distinct and hence the roles of the support offices different. For example, supporting a project manager in planning and risk management is totally different from supporting a Business Programme Manager on business planning.

Figure 17.1 The key roles which may require a support service
When deciding what support offices you need, think first of the roles which need to be supported. Then decide what aspects of the roles would benefit from a support service and the extent to which the service needs to be supplied. Look for combining offices where it makes sense, e.g. the Enterprise Programmes Office and Authorisation Support Office.

NAMING THE OFFICES

There is no set standard for naming the support offices. What the United States calls a 'Project Office', the UK calls 'Project Support', with 'Project Support Office' used for the corporate level office. In practice, you'll find every conceivable combination of the words 'programme', 'project', 'support', 'management' and 'organisation'. Where possible, name the offices after the entity, role or group it supports. Hence a 'Project Support Office' supports a 'project'. 'Projects Support Office' supports a number of projects and 'Business Programme Office' supports a Business Programme. If an office supports a particular project, then name the office after that project, e.g. 'Trident Project Support Office'. You will not believe how many phone calls I used to receive from 'the project office' with little clue as to which of about 40 were calling!

You will of course have to fight your way through the 'project' versus 'programme' debate when choosing names (see below). You should then ensure each office has a role description comprising a few lines of summary and the individual activities bulleted. The summary can then be used liberally in communications, so there is little doubt as to what the office supports.

Support offices – some examples

The permutations for designing a support office infrastructure are limitless and can be very daunting. Project Workout 17.2 provides you with a process to follow in creating your own, but in order to bring this to life the following illustrates a snapshot of a typical support office set-up, which you can use as a basis for developing your own. Do note, however, that the service level provided by the offices very much relates to the maturity of the organisation in respect of programme and project management. As the organisation matures, the range of services that the office provides will increase. Its focus, however, will shift. In the early days much time will be spent on the basics of administration, project control and understanding the staged framework. Once this is established, such support will be available either from local offices or colleagues on a less formal basis. The offices will have swung to implementing or improving other aspects of capability. The proactive nature of support offices in continuously pushing corporate capability forward is essential to moving up the maturity ladder.

The proactive nature of support offices in continuously pushing corporate capability forward is essential to moving up the maturity ladder.

The Enterprise Programmes Office, or, as some people presumptuously call it, the 'Centre of Excellence' (I do dislike that term!), is the hub for all things related to programme and project management. It supports the Programme Management Director, ensuring the organisation has a complete programme and project environment commensurate with its level of maturity. It sets the 'way we work' for the organisation in relation to all programmes and projects by providing methods and systems; a key role in this respect is the Programme Management Design Authority. The office also provides an overview of the aggregated performance of the organisation with respect to programme and project management, with a specific focus on benefits realisation.

Other services offered by the office can include the following:

- Undertaking independent reviews and audits of projects.
- Developing, procuring and selecting project management support tools and systems.
- Consolidating programme and project reporting.
- Monitoring resource usage across the organisation.
- Providing consulting and coaching and advising project sponsors and managers in carrying out their roles. This can range from simple 'response to phone calls' to providing a full facilitation and consulting service on specialist topics such as project set up, risk management, issue management, planning and project closure.
- Maintaining standards for recruitment and development of project management staff (often working with the HR department).
- Providing Project Support Office services (see below).
- Providing trained project management staff for assignment to projects.

In some cases it is beneficial to combine this office with that of the Business Planning Office and Authorisation Support Office (see below) to create an extremely powerful grouping which not only provides methods but also helps those accountable drive strategy through delivery to benefits realisation.

The Business Planning Office supports the Business Strategy and Planning Board in the development, update and monitoring of the Business Plan. It has a strategic focus.

The Business Programme Offices each support the respective Business Programme Sponsor and Manager and are at the heart of driving the part of the business strategy and plan within their scope. Key to this is developing the Blueprints (description of future state) and Business Programme Plans and then executing them through initiating and running programmes/projects together with managing benefits realisation. Whilst they should use the approaches developed by the Enterprise Programmes Office, they may create tailored variants to suit the particular types of project and work they do. For example, the product development process is a special form of the project framework. They may also have their own variants for project approval.

Other services offered by such offices include the following:

- Checking documents prior to submission through the project authorisation process.

- Managing the flow of documents for authorisation, whether locally authorised or by higher authority.
- Providing a secretariat service for the Business Programme Sponsor/ Manager and communicating the outcomes and decisions.
- Undertaking independent reviews and audits of projects.
- Providing consolidated programme and project reporting within the Business Programme.
- Assisting in identifying and engaging stakeholders.
- Resource usage monitoring for programmes and projects within the Business Programme.
- Consulting, coaching and advising project sponsors and managers in carrying out their roles.
- Providing Project Support Office services (see below).
- Providing trained project management staff for assignment to projects.

If the business programme supports external projects (those for clients/ customers), it may also include a sales and bid management capability.

The Authorisation Support Office supports the Project Review Group (see p. 188), ensuring flow of documentation to the correct decision makers (authorisation process) and providing a secretariat service for running decision-making meetings, communicating the outcomes, updating systems (e.g. releasing cost codes) and securely archiving the relevant documents. In addition, this office may provide a quality review service for the documentation which is submitted through the process, to ensure the decision makers have reasonable documents presented and to provide a commentary on aspects they should focus on or query. This role can be combined within the Enterprise Programmes Office.

The Project Support Office(s) supports project sponsors and, in particular, project managers in their accountabilities. This can range from ad hoc advice and guidance to providing a fully resourced service for tasks such as project planning, procurement or contract management, if not already provided by specialist central functions. The focus of these offices tends to be administrative support for the project manager. A number of models are used and the extent to which a service is provided may vary significantly, including:

- a single office providing services to a number of key projects;
- a single office providing a service to all projects, regardless of size;
- a number of offices each providing services to a number of key projects;
- a number of offices each providing a service to a portfolio of projects, regardless of size;

- each major project having its own project support office, staffed from centrally owned resources;
- each project organising its own arrangements for support.

Typical activities undertaken by the Project Support Office include the following:

- Administering Project Board meetings.
- Maintaining and operating the communications and stakeholder plans.
- Administering change control, risk logs, issues logs and action lists.
- Setting up and maintaining project files.
- Establishing and operating document control procedures.
- Maintaining plans (data collection and tools update for cost, schedule, scope and interdependencies).
- Administering the quality review process and standards.
- Reviewing key project documents (e.g. business cases).
- Administering document control and configuration management.
- Assisting with the compilation of reports.
- Administering contracted-in resources and facilities.
- Ensuring compliance and best use of corporate methods.
- Providing specialist knowledge, tools and techniques.
- Project assurance.

FIGHTING YOUR WAY THROUGH THE OFFICE FOG

This workout should be undertaken with the design authority and other key advocates of project and programme management. It should be carried out after you have established the key roles and accountabilities for your programme management framework. If these are not yet completed, use the roles and accountabilities provided in this book, but do remember to check back later to see if they are still valid for your organisation. If some support offices already exist, include the managers of them in your workout and determine where they sit with respect to the new roles and accountabilities. You should allow up to a day for this, not including the write-up and agreement after the workshop is completed.

17.2

1 Using a paper-covered wall, construct a table which includes the roles and accountabilities in your framework. (There is a model to get you started on the CD-ROM.)

2 Put a tick against each accountability/activity for which you believe support would be beneficial.

3 Against each accountability requiring support, decide what the support may comprise. Use three levels of support (high, medium and low), describe on a Post-It Note what that means in practical terms. Place the notes on the wall chart. Select which level of support you feel should be provided by marking the relevant Post-It note with a different coloured note (you may change your mind later). In writing these, consider the style and mandate you want the offices to have. Use active verbs to describe the service, being as specific as possible, e.g. assist; advise; guide; review; recommend; provide; own; enforce; decide; instruct. Be specific about who owns, develops or uses a process/method.

4 Name any existing support offices in the right-hand columns. For each existing support office, write on a Post-It Note what service it provides against the relevant accountabilities. If it provides a service for an unlisted accountability, add it to the bottom of the chart.

5 Based on the support requirements and the existing provision (if any), decide on an initial guess for different support offices. Name these in the right-hand columns.

6 Transfer the 'desired support service' Post-It from step 3 to the column for the support office which you think is best placed to provide the service.

7 Take a break! Clear your head.

8 As a group, run through the accountabilities of each office. Look for opportunities to consolidate services into fewer support offices.

9 For each office decide its primary location, being the best location from which to provide the service. Some offices may be 'virtual,' with staff residing in different locations.

10 Briefly outline the type of infrastructure the offices will need to operate. For example, shared intranets, document management systems and project support tools are usually essential for modern programme management.

11 For each office define the type of people required to staff it. Purely administrative activities need lower-qualified staff than activities requiring specialist knowledge and skills.

12 Based on your knowledge of the volume of projects and work involved, take a view on the numbers of people required. Decide if they all need to be full-time staff or if some roles (e.g. coaching) can be supplied by practising managers on a peer to peer basis.

You now have a detailed set of accountabilities for your offices, together with an outline of staffing, location and infrastructure needs. This is sufficient to include in a project plan for implementing your office structures.

The tools to help it work – systems

'The most useful thing I have is a list of what I'm meant to be working on,' said a senior manager from an information systems function.

He was pointing out that, previously, the people in his function were asked to work on the systems parts of numerous projects spanning marketing information, financial, billing and customer service processes among many others. He had learned that it was impossible for his function, on its own, to prioritise this workload and decide what needed to be done and when. The outputs they produced were valueless unless they were combined with the other component parts of the project. By having an agreed 'list' of projects, he is now very clear which projects the organisation wants done and that no others should be worked on. In addition, the staged framework ensures that any particular part of the project does not proceed ahead of the others and that full checks on resource availability have been carried out.

> The conclusion is that the key control tool to help you manage your project portfolio and ensure that work around the organisation is aligned is the publication and maintenance of a 'list of projects'.

The conclusion is that the key control tool to help you manage your project portfolio and ensure that work around the organisation is aligned is the publication and maintenance of a 'list of projects', sometimes called a 'project register'.

What does the project 'list' look like?

Once people start talking about lists, the words 'computers', spreadsheets' and 'databases' spring easily to mind. These are the tools that make managing the 'list' easier. All too often, however, these systems can be made too complicated and have a tendency to be taken over by the technical people who create them – they can be fun. You need to keep in perspective that they are only tools, which help the organisation achieve its objectives and so must be suited to the processes, systems and culture they serve. Reporting is a key part of the tools. It does not matter how good the data you put in are, if you can't get useful information out, they prove an empty shell at best and totally misleading at worst. (You will find that if you can't get the information out, people will not bother to put anything in, no matter how much you plague them!)

SYSTEMS AS REINFORCERS FOR CULTURAL SHIFT

Good systems can help support the drive to move culture in a particular direction. If, for example, you want to favour a projects environment where personal accountability is key, then having real people's names attached to accountabilities can be powerful. This is especially so if the system that holds that data is easily accessible to those named people and to those who depend on them.

Systems needs

Your 'list' system needs to be designed such that users, with differing requirements, can access the same data to obtain the information they need, in a format which is convenient for them. They need to be able to:

- **select** the data they want to view;
- **sort** the data in an order that suits them;
- **report** in a format or template which serves their needs.

Information systems for keeping track of portfolios of projects generally centre around three sets of data:

- resources;
- non-financial data;
- financial data.

I dealt with resources in Chapter 16. The other two sets are dealt with in the following sections. Finance functions tend to have specialist accounting systems dealing with the 'money matters'. These systems are not primarily designed for holding the non-financial data which you will find useful. Systems are available which can do both, but they are mostly in their infancy and not mature enough to deal with the wide range of ways people want to manage their businesses.

An investment approval process in a major organisation required that all the departmental managers impacted by the project had to sign the front sheet in ink. The result was a sheet with anything up to 25 signatures on it. Somewhere in that forest of names was a decision maker.

The new process still requires the impacted functions to review and commit to the project; however, no signatures are required. The only signatures are those of the decision makers:

- the project sponsor;
- the director of the department with overall project management accountability;
- the director with the budget which will fund the project.

It is quite clear who is accountable for the decision: the person who wants it, the person who does it and the person who pays for it.

> *'No snowflake in an avalanche ever feels responsible.'*
>
> STANISLAV LEE

Lists – keeping tabs on your projects

If you are to keep track of your projects you will need to have a definitive list of the requests for new proposals and the projects currently in progress. The following should give you a feel for the basic requirements.

Capturing the new proposals

A proposal needs to be logged with a unique reference number from the moment a sponsor wishes to declare its existence. This MUST be prior to the Initial Investigation Gate. It may be as early as when a strategy or plan document is created and flags up the need for a potential project and hence earmarking of funds. A proposal document need not be created before a request is logged; however, sufficient information must be available to describe the objectives and benefits of the potential project.

A proposal is converted, via the Initial Investigation Gate, to a project as an initial investigation and on into the staged framework.

It should be possible to track back from any project that is in progress to find where the original request/proposal came from. In addition, if a request/proposal is converted to a project, it should be possible to see whether the project was in fact completed or terminated early. 'Key word searches' are useful to analyse the population of activities based on any of the header or other data for each proposal (e.g. rejected, terminated, etc.).

Projects list

There is a need for a central 'database' which can be used as an information system/reporting tool for individual projects and portfolios of projects. This system(s) should contain all projects being undertaken in the organisation. The database should provide information in support of gate decision makers, resource managers, business planners and project sponsors.

The requirements are for you to have:

- project header data (name, accountabilities, etc.);
- interdependencies with other projects;
- milestone data;
- cost data;
- progress information;
- useful and targeted reporting.

Project header data

The following data should be held for each project:

- project number, project name, business objectives, project framework stage, project sponsor, project manager, managing business area; this will be in the business case (see p. 294);
- which 'Business Programme' the project belongs to (if any);
- which programme the project is part of (if any);
- its status (proposed, in progress, on hold, terminated or completed);
- whether the project is 'standard', 'simple' or 'emergency', as defined in Part Two;
- the platforms, systems, processes and products impacted by the project;
- specific header data which are relevant to specific categories or type of project, e.g. project review group.

Project interdependencies

The project definition of each project includes its interdependencies. A dependency is defined as a deliverable produced by one project which is needed by another project in order to achieve its targeted benefits (see also pp. 299, 353). It is essential that this is known, defined and maintained. It must be possible to enquire:

- which project(s) depend on this project;
- which project(s) this project depends on.

A simple listing of projects and those which it depends on may be sufficient for your needs, but if the database is to be used as a decision support tool to enable portfolios of projects to be analysed and the business impacts seen, you may need to include more detail. This could comprise the planned and forecast dates for the transfer of each key dependent deliverable from one project to the other.

If the database is to be used as a decision-support tool to enable portfolios of projects to be analysed and the business impacts seen, you may need to include more detail. This could comprise the planned and forecast dates for the transfer of each key dependent deliverable from one project to the other.

Milestone data

The system should hold milestone schedule data as original baseline (with date set), current baseline (with date set), achieved date (if completed) and forecast date (for uncompleted milestones) for the following:

- the gates in the staged framework (Detailed Investigation Gate, Development Gate, Trial Gate, Release Gate, Release, project completed);
- additional project manager-defined milestones in addition to those already stated.

Cost data

If project costs are held in a separate financial system, it is useful to import them into a central management information system to enable you to report on mixes of financial and non-financial information. The system should hold:

- actual costs to date for the project by project stage;
- forecast costs to completion by project stage;
- costs in two categories:
  - manpower (time costs);
  - external purchases.

See Figure 22.4 for an example.

Benefits forecasting data

The system should hold the 'benefits' forecast for each project both in 'plan' form (i.e. as per the authorised business case) and as a forecast (i.e. the estimated outcome at the current point in time). This may also be in the form of 'conditions of satisfaction' (see p. 332).

Progress information

The system should be able to be used as a corporate reporting repository, capable of producing a standard report (see p. 311) for each project, containing:

- key header data;
- business objectives;
- progress summary and outlook;
- financial summary;
- milestones;
- issues and risks;
- changes (via formal change management).

Reporting generally

The requirement is to provide a range of user roles with targeted, selected and sorted reports to meet their needs. Users will require either:

- detailed reports on individual projects, or
- summary reports for portfolios of projects as selected, sorted using any of the other data field criteria.

So users:

- **select** which projects they are interested in (based on the data stored in the information system;
- **sort** the data in the order they need (at least three levels of sort criteria);
- **choose a report** from a set of prescribed templates at a full, summary and/or analysis level. This can be either printed or exported to external applications.

The standard reports should be either:

- qualitative (i.e. non-numerical);
- or quantitative (cost-based, benefit based, timescale), with subtotals and totals.

Examples

1 A project sponsor may select a portfolio report showing all the projects he/she is sponsoring.

2 A director may select a portfolio report of all the projects being sponsored by him/herself and anyone else in the function.

3 Or he/she may select a report of all the projects which will benefit his/her function.

4 A line manager may select a portfolio report of all the projects which are being managed by his/her staff

---

ACTIVE AND PASSIVE REPORTING

You should always distinguish between active and passive reporting. If you want stakeholders to know something, you should tell them. You should not expect them to consult a database to find out if anything of interest has happened which is critical for them to know. Project databases are passive and you cannot assume that anyone will look at them.

Harnessing web technology

One of the biggest advances in project management over recent years is the provision of internet (or intranet)-based environments for displaying project and programme information. Everything we have talked about in the preceding sections has very much been for the benefit of those directing and managing portfolios of projects. Whilst essential for corporate management, to the project managers and teams who actually enter project data into databases (rather than use aggregated reports from the data bases) it is all too often seen as 'non-value-added bureaucracy'. In many cases such tools duplicate the project manager's own records and systems.

It is an obvious step to 'web enable' the project register. This has two advantages:

- roll out of the tools is simplified as the key interface is through the web browser (such as Internet Explorer or Firefox);
- the information can be made available to anyone who needs it. The more people who use it, the more likely those supplying the data are to keep it current.

The next step, however, is to turn the web environment into the actual tools the project manager and team can use on a day-to-day basis. For this to happen, a number of additional features are needed, such as document libraries, control logs, action lists and 'talk zones'. In this way, the basic data collection for central reporting and tracking is drawn from the *actual* data the project managers are using and most of the drudge associated with central reporting systems is eliminated; it becomes a secondary effect of 'doing the project properly'.

There are a number of criteria you need to consider if such web-enabled environments are to be effective:

- Someone must be accountable for the system and its features. These tools always attract a wonderful array of possible enhancements. Unless someone has a very good grasp of the architecture *and* how it fits the project methods in the organisation, destructive complexity and inconsistencies will soon be introduced.
- Someone has to be accountable for the data quality of portfolios of projects. Every project manager should be accountable for his or her own data but above that level, someone needs to check (say, at Business Programme level) overall integrity. The introduction of a 'quality score' is a good method for assessing this. The score should be designed to tell users of the data the extent to which they can 'trust' the project and portfolio reports which are generated.
- Anyone who needs access should be given access. If half the team are 'locked out' behind a firewall, any information they need will have to be duplicated elsewhere. It truly needs to be an enterprise-wide system and may often need to include suppliers and contractors;
- Manually duplicating data which is held in other systems should be avoided. If it can be imported or drawn on directly, then do so. Systems based on open architectures are particularly good for this.
- User response time has to be acceptable. If adding data or drawing off reports takes too long, people will not use it.

What would such a system look like?

There are an increasing number of web-based project and knowledge management environment systems on the market. They enable you to direct, manage and coordinate project teams and information, regardless of where they are based or which organisations people belong to.

Features, complexity and reporting

When deciding the features for your project management environment, you will find that the options are endless. The more features you have, the more complexity is likely to result, with all the difficulties that entails. Look for systems which are built on a core of base features, each of which enables a high degree of user configuration at both corporate (portfolio and programme) and project levels and each of which has an obvious use in real life. There may be some features you do not want yet (or at all); see if you can 'disable' these so they won't clog your screens with 'useless' clutter. Again this should be at both corporate and project level. Many software suppliers make their profit from 'customising' their offerings. On the face of it, this can look very customer-focused, but it can also be a very expensive and not necessarily fruitful pathway. The design of all systems is based on an assumed operating model. If your customisation conflicts with this model (for example, you have a totally different view on how to allocate access permissions), the impacts can be very unpredictable. However, one area that I feel customisation should be given free rein in is reporting. Systems are useless if they do not convert data into meaningful information through screen-based, printed and exported reports. Designing new reports and creating better ways to present information is non-intrusive to the system architecture but adds value for the user.

Apart from the usual project management features you may find the following capabilities useful:

- **Organisation** – the ability to assign roles and put people in teams (such as user groups, decision-making bodies).
- **News** – on-line newspaper to keep your team and wider stakeholder community up to date without boring them with the standard progress report!
- **Communications** – integrated e-mail, so the e-mails are stored with the project rather than on a corporate e-mail server 'somewhere', which no one can get at.
- **Meetings** – agenda, minutes linked to actions.
- **Notifications** – the system tells you when something you want to keep an eye on changes.
- **Talk** – on-line threaded discussions – great for capturing lessons learned and quality reviews.
- **Timesheets** – if you need to track time and there is no corporate system.
- **Search and report** – essential if a system is to be of any use. If you can't find something, it's useless!

An example of a system

For illustration, I will use e:PSO, one of the many tools currently on the market, but you should look for similar capabilities on whatever system you select. The e:PSO is based on the best practices and principles found in this book, but can be adapted to fit virtually any method.

The system recognises who you are through your 'login' details, which are entered on the main screen. From here, you are taken to your 'My Home Portal', which contains links to all elements of the system relating to you (including existing projects, outstanding issues, actions, etc.). (Figure 17.2). By using the menu options along the top of the screen you can move to different areas of the system; for example, you can view a flow chart of all projects within the system. This flow chart divides the projects between different stages of the project life cycle. Clicking on a stage will bring up a list of all projects currently at that stage, together with a high-level view of some of the details, such as location, cost and priority (Figure 17.3). Some of the details only show at certain levels – in the example, showing projects in the different life cycle stages, the overall

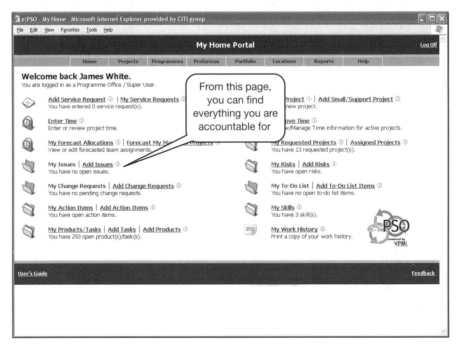

Figure 17.2 Keeping track of your accountabilities!
The power of systems is that you can find what you need quickly. In this case, I can see an overview of every item I am accountable for.

status of the project is also shown. Each project included on the list also has a set of 'Quick Links', which enable you to move to more detailed screens, such as milestones, risks and product/tasks.

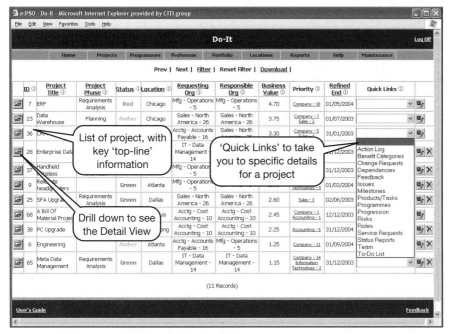

Figure 17.3 A typical project listing
This screen displays a list of projects satisfying the user's search criteria (in this case the life cycle stage). From this we can see some of the key 'headline' project data. We can also 'drill down' for more detail.

Selecting any one of the projects takes you into that project's 'Detail View' (Figure 17.4). This screen provides a high-level description of the project, together with a summary of the key data. From here you can then access all the detailed information about the project using the 'Quick Links' at the top of the screen.

This approach enables the project sponsor, project manager and team to keep track of risks, issues, milestones and many other aspects of the project. The example in Figure 17.5 shows a listing of the risks relating to a specific project. Selecting the 'Open Record' option enables you to see more detail about the specified risk.

For a demonstration of this tool, go to **www.live.projectworkout.com**.

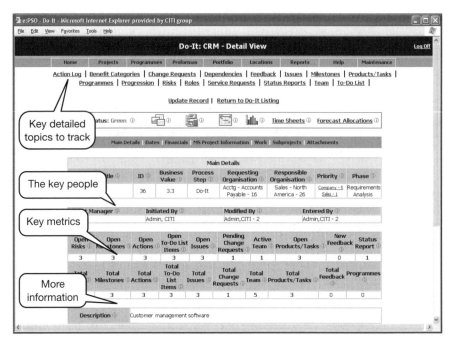

Figure 17.4 A project's 'Detail View'

Each project has a 'Details View' from which all the key information relating to the project can be found. The front page shows an overview of each area of the project and the links found at the top of the page can be used to navigate to even more detailed views.

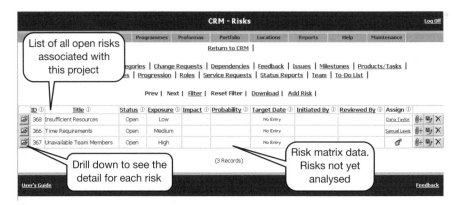

Figure 17.5 One of the control tools – the risk log

Specific information on a project can be accessed using the links at the top of each project's 'Details View'. In this case, the risk log is shown. You can view more details by selecting the 'Open Record' button next to your chosen risk.

RAG STATUS

If using critical chain project scheduling (see p. 373), the RAG status would indicate the degree to which the project buffer had been used.

Management accounting systems

The missing dimension

'What we do is more important than where we sit in the organisation.' This may be what we feel but it is not what many of our management accounting systems measure or report. Currently many organisations count money in only two dimensions:

- a cost centre code (against whose budget money is spent);
- an analysis code (what it is spent on).

They do not say *how* the money is applied, i.e. what is actually done with it.

Sometimes they try to do this in part by using a cost centre code or an analysis code to capture the essence of where money is applied. For example, a cost centre is opened to capture costs for a particular project. While this may be pragmatic, it does not serve the full management accounting needs of the organisation of the future.

A third dimension of accounting is needed to cover the use to which our funds are put, regardless of what they are spent on and which cost centres resource them. I call it an 'application code'.

In essence, this is a 'source and application of internal funds', which is useful at a grass roots management level as well as at senior management level.

So the three dimensions are:

- **cost centre code** – where money/resources come from;
- **analysis code** – what it is spent on;
- **application code** – why it is being spent.

The sum of each will always equal the same number as they are just different ways of looking at the money used in the organisation. It is essential this balance is made or we will encourage 'leakage' of funds or 'cheating'.

The application code

What does an 'application code' look like? There should be three mutually exclusive application code types:

- **P type** – this is about creating change; taking us from what we do now to what we do tomorrow, i.e. projects.
- **A type** – this is doing 'business as usual' processes. In the steady state, e.g. retaining and acquiring customers, doing management tasks (business processes).
- **X type** – this is down time such as sickness, leave, training.

Typically, the X type is about 20 per cent of total 'people' expenditure. Who really knows, however, how much we spend on running our existing business (A type) as opposed to changing it (P type)? Do we even have a feel for what this should be?

A P, A and X type of management accounting system would give us the knowledge to sharpen our focus and ensure that we only do those things which are important to our meeting our strategic objectives, rather than merely keeping track of who spends the money.

Consider the picture of the business when using the traditional cost centre code approach:

	Total spend
Cost centre 1	20
Cost centre 2	30
Cost centre 3	40
Cost centre 4	10
Total organisation	**100**

We know the costs in each cost centre (the shaded part) (cost centre 1 = 20, cost centre 2 = 30, etc.), but we have no idea how the money and people are applied. This is revealed when the third dimension is added, giving us a richer picture of our business:

	Down time	Process activities			Projects		Total
	X	A1	A2	A3	P1	P2	
Cost centre 1	4	10	4	–	2	–	20
Cost centre 2	7	5	10	–	3	5	30
Cost centre 3	10	10	–	–	20	–	40
Cost centre 4	2	–	–	8	–	–	10
Total organisation	**23**	**25**	**14**	**8**	**25**	**5**	**100**

For the first time we will be able to run our organisations based on 'what counts,' i.e. where we apply our efforts rather than 'what we can count', i.e. the cost centre.

In this environment, cost centres will become 'homes' where 'pay and rations' are sourced and experience and expertise fostered. Many cost centres will be focused on particular activities but that is not a prerequisite. The application code will say what they are doing:

- away on paid leave?
- being trained?
- performing as part of the 'business as usual' task?
- working on a project?

By introducing the third dimension on all of our costs (people included), we will know what we are applying ourselves to.

The advantage of this is that the balance of power will move away from cost centres as the 'fund-holding barons' of the old hierarchical organisation toward the flat structured 'what we do is important' new corporation. AND . . . our key management tool (the management accounting system) will support this.

Management by accountability will thrive, as accountabilities will be tied to application codes which operate across the whole organisation, regardless of the cost centre to which the person holding the accountability belongs. In this way, any person can sponsor or work on any project or activity anywhere in the organisation without you losing control of the finances or the head count. For example, Figure 17.6 shows a typical financial report for a project sponsor. It shows the person is sponsoring five projects, one of which is terminated, one on hold and three in progress. This person is accountable for over $1m spend across the organisation.

As the three dimensions must balance, there is little scope or benefit for 'cheating'. If a project is running over budget, there is no point in hiding its cost within another project or activity even if the owner would accept it! It would merely rob Peter to pay Paul and different performance indicators would move in opposite directions accordingly.

It would stop the racket of 'head count'. It would no longer matter how many people you had in a cost centre as you would be concentrating more on what they did. There need be no pushing people out of the 'home' cost centre to do a 'project' only to fill their position with another (net effect equals one more head).

This may sound a radical approach, but it is within the capability of many organisations. It would require 'time sheeting for all', but we all do it now (e.g. we all fill in sickness notes, paid leave forms, etc.). In addition, as the bulk of employees only do one A type application and some X types, time sheets could be generated by default with only the exceptions requiring input. This would give you the freedom to deploy anyone anywhere, not 'lose them', and know what their input is being applied to. Thus 'doing projects' will stop being dangerous; no longer will they be the fast track to redundancy!

> *We are in a rapidly moving business world. By adopting the management approach given here, reorganisations of departments will become less important and can be done at any time in the financial year.*

Further, we are in a rapidly moving business world. By adopting the management approach given here, reorganisations will become less important and can be done at any time in the financial year. P, A and X will be the way we will run our businesses!

The requirements for such a system, incorporating project costing, would be that each application code should:

- have a unique reference number;
- have costs captured against a work breakdown structure, representing, as a minimum, the stages of the project framework;
- have forecasts set;
- be viewed with or without absorbed overheads;
- have the staged authorisation of funds;
- have three status for transaction postings:
  - open for forecast only;
  - open for cost and forecast;
  - closed.

Reporting should be flexible to reflect the life of a project, the current financial year and the future, enabling interest groups (such as project sponsors) to see their own projects as a portfolio.

Figure 17.6 is an example, showing the costs associated with Phillipa Brixham's sponsorship portfolio. If your management accounting system is linked to your project database, these data could also appear at the foot of the report shown in Figure 17.4. Similar reports should be produced, selecting and sorting from any of the data which are held in the accounting system, with the ability to summarise at any level of the project work breakdown structure.

BOOKKEEPING!

You should distinguish between the management of costs from a management accounting perspective and from a financial perspective. The latter relates to 'bookkeeping' and where the transactions appear in the formal chart of accounts. In the management of projects, this is of little or no use. Managing the actual spend and cash flow provides far greater control.

Project Sponsor: Brixham, Phillipa

PROJECT SPONSOR PORTFOLIO REPORT

Period: 4 wks to 28 Sept 2011

$ 000s

No	PROJECTS	MONTH Actual (A)	Actual to Date (B)	Previous to Date (C)	LIFE F'cast Outturn (D)	LIFE Revised Budget (E)	LIFE Variance (F)	Commited (G)	Original Budget (H)	FINANCIAL YEAR Actual to Date (J)	FINANCIAL YEAR F'cast Outturn (K)	FORECAST TO COMPLETION This FY (L)	Next FY (M)	Beyond (N)	Total to Complete (P)
In progress															
755	Inventory free warehouse Phase 1	12	56	44	214	220	6	43	200	56	182	126	32		158
828	International acquisition B	14	72	58	167	150	-17	12	150	60	120	60	30	5	95
627	Logistics Management System IV	23	567	544	590	600	10	34	600	234	257	23			23
On hold															
832	Automated HR Appraisals		124	124	156	160	4		150	32	64	32			32
Terminated															
721	Improve Customer Support		12	12	24	24			110	12	24	12			12
	TOTAL PORTFOLIO	49	831	782	1151	1154	3	89	1210	394	647	253	62	5	320

The total line shows the sum of the projects that the person is sponsoring

Figure 17.6 Typical financial summary

This report shows the financial summary of Phillipa Brixham's sponsorship portfolio. This report shows that she is accountable for $1.15m authorised spend on five projects, one of which has been terminated and another put on hold. Only one of her projects, 828, is forecast to overspend.

Putting your systems together

In the previous sections, we looked at the three primary information needs (resources, non-financial and financial) and have seen how they could be handled in our information systems. We have also seen how resource management relates to project cost forecasting and how this in turn builds into the business plan. Each system is targeted at a particular need; however, they are all related. Figure 17.7 shows the relationship in diagrammatic form. Actual expenditure on your projects is captured by the accounting system (the shaded boxes). These costs can be handled on both a project-focused basis and on a more traditional, cost centre basis. Forecast of manpower (person hours) is costed and then combined with the forecast of purchases to produce an overall cost forecast for the projects.

At the point marked 'A' the manpower forecasts are taken off and collated to give an early view of resource needs for line managers and the organisation as a whole. Once the actual costs and forecast costs have been collected they can be combined to produce the project financial accounts and summary reports. They can also be fed into the project database and combined with other, non-financial data, to produce an overall reporting capability. Where you keep your data, and how the reports are produced, will depend very much on the systems you have in your organisation. Regardless of this, however, the overall logic and flow should be very similar to that examined here. It won't be easy to put in place, but if you have a vision of the future of your enterprise system's strategy, you will gradually be able to build the full set. You will also find that having simple, separate systems may be the most pragmatic way forward, even if it means some temporary duplication of data and the risks that entails. It is better than not having a view of your project portfolio at all.

Web technologies are ideally suited to providing quick, simple and effective reports from disparate systems. They also have the advantage that user training is minimal. Web technologies can also be used for data capture.

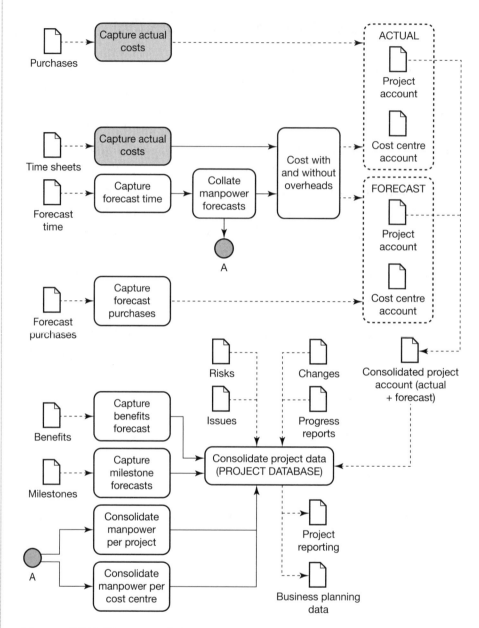

Figure 17.7 The complete system
The links between resources, costs, benefits and other project systems. The outputs include both project reporting and the necessary inputs required for business planning (see also Figure 14.3).

YOUR OWN SYSTEMS

17.3

1 Make an enlarged copy of Figure 17.7. Mark it up with highlighter pens, indicating the elements you currently have in place (shade in yellow) and those parts which you already plan to put in place (shade in another colour).

2 Are the elements you have shaded designed to be compatible with each other?

3 On a flip chart:

- list elements which are missing;

- list the data which would be contained within these elements;

- list the information you are lacking as a result.

4 Consider, based on what you have in place, what actions you could take to fill any gaps you have identified in the systems environment supporting your projects framework.

Don't think a systems solution is always the best solution

Part Four

MAKING PROJECTS WORK FOR YOU

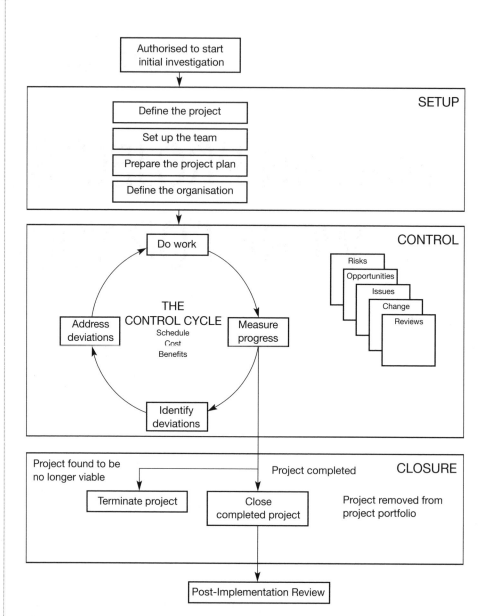

Figure 18.1 The full project control environment

The project control environment can be represented in three sections, starting with 'setup' and ending in 'closure'. Between these are the tools and techniques for monitoring and controlling the project. These controls apply throughout the life of the project.

'People love chopping wood. In this activity one immediately sees results.'

ALBERT EINSTEIN

In Part Two, I explained the management framework for a single project, taking it from being an idea through the various life cycle stages until benefits are being realised for your organisation.

In Part Three, I showed how you could manage a number of projects, which together make up the portfolio of initiatives which are changing your organisation to suit its future strategic direction.

In this part, I return to the single project and explain the tools and techniques you can apply to ensure that projects are kept under control and are likely to realise the promised benefits. Figure 18.1 shows the full project control environment, starting with 'setup' and ending in 'closure'. Between these are the techniques for monitoring progress and handling risks, issues, opportunities and reviews. At the heart is the project control cycle. These factors apply throughout the life of the project, regardless of which stage you are currently working within.

- **Encourage team work and commitment.**
- **Practice single point accountability.**
- **Break down functional barriers by using a cross-functional team.**
- **Manage your stakeholders' expectations.**
- **Build excellence in project management techniques and controls across your organisation.**
- **Ensure success by planning for it.**
- **Monitor and control against the agreed plan.**
- **Manage changes to the plan actively.**
- **Close the project formally.**

How to use Part Four

The chapters in Part Four are written as working guides for you either to apply directly or to adapt to include in your own control framework. Many of the chapters include workouts to help you apply the guides in practice.

Project Teams and Style

Culture – the way we do things around here

Project teams

Leadership and influence

I thought you were doing that! – accountability

An environment in which energy is expended on blame and fault finding, rather than looking for solutions to problems, will damage morale and hinder the performance of any team.

'I must follow them. I am their leader!'

ANDREW BONAR LAW

- **Encourage team work and commitment.**
- **Practice single point accountability.**
- **Break down functional barriers by using a cross-functional team.**

Culture – the way we do things around here

Culture has two fundamental elements:[1]

- the norms and behaviours of a group;
- unconscious programming of the mind leading to a set of similar collective habits, behaviours and mind sets.

While this book is not primarily aimed at culture, interpersonal skills and the often named 'soft' aspects of project management, it would be remiss not to summarise the key aspects which have been shown to encourage success in a projects environment.

As Obeng has pointed out, 'People create change and people constrain change', and culture is what people are about. Let us remind ourselves of the fundamental differences between working in a project, as opposed to in a line environment.

Line management is about maintaining the existing processes. It is performed in a relatively stable environment. It often abhors change as it affects the ever increasing drive for efficiency. People work in defined jobs and have defined work to carry out. It is often (but not always!) predictable.

Project management is about change. Projects are one-off activities, carried out over a finite time period. They often break new ground and step into the unknown. They require management that can adapt to conflicting pressures, changing requirements and unfamiliar situations. Projects are often staffed by groups of people from disparate functions and locations.

[1] *Source*: Eddie Obeng, *Putting Strategy to Work* (Pitman Publishing, 1996)

The managers of these environments do not necessarily share the same skills and competences, nevertheless, an organisational environment must be set up such that the two aspects of management (steady state and change) can coexist. This is at the heart of matrix management.

Project teams

In line management, the manager or the supervisor has the power and authority to instruct a person in his/her duties. In many organisations, however, the project managers have little authority of this nature. Ideally, they should have this authority, but that is not always the reality. They have to deliver the project using a less visible power base, which is more rooted in the shared commitment of the team than in directives. No matter how good a project proposal is or how thoroughly the investigative stages have been undertaken, the bottom line is that success is rarely achieved by a poorly led, ill-motivated group of individuals. (Notice that I have not used the word 'team'.) It is widely recognised that team work and team spirit in line roles leads to better results than sticks and sanctions. In projects, team working is even more crucial. A project team has a short time to form, normalise its behaviours and start performing. In addition:

Success is rarely achieved by a poorly led, ill-motivated group of individuals.

- a team may be dispersed geographically;
- its members may have other duties to attend to;
- the most appropriate people may not be available.

This can place demands on individuals, particularly those new to projects, as it can set the stage for conflicts of loyalties, which the project manager and others must recognise and try to avoid. The project manager must be the leading player in creating and fostering a team spirit and enrolling the commitment of those associated with the project. The project sponsor and line managers of the project team members have a similar responsibility. Their behaviour and actions can derail a project just as drastically, or even more so, than any by the project manager. Clear reporting lines, good information flow, realistic work plans and defined project roles will also help 'ease' the pathway.

Leadership style and team values are also important. An open, even-handed approach which encourages good communication and gives those in the project the confidence to raise potential problems tends to be the most effective. An environment in which energy is expended on blame and fault finding, rather than looking for solutions to problems, will damage morale and hinder the performance of any team. This approach must be present in fact as well as theory. For example, most project-scheduling software shows which activities were completed late. What's the point of reporting on them if you can't do anything about it? What is important is knowing which ones count (are critical) and which are likely to be late.

When dealing with your team, or indeed any other stakeholders, assume they will act to avoid pain and seek pleasure. Assume they won't really care about anything else. If you concentrate on inconsequential trivia and absolute adherence to process, so will they. Publicly reward the behaviours you want to encourage. Success depends on the commitment and willingness of each team member to succeed.

> **Publicly reward the behaviours you want to encourage.**

'He that complies against his will
Is of his own opinion still.'

SAMUEL BUTLER

Encouraging open communication

A team progress meeting had just finished and the participants were talking as they left the room. One was overheard by the project manager saying to a colleague that a deliverable he is accountable for was going to be nine months late. This had major implications on the project and yet had not been raised at the progress meeting. The project manager was understandably annoyed, not about the delay, but about the fact that it had not been reported. He took the view that he needed to know about delays in sufficient time to deal with them. He therefore made a point of encouraging the reporting of bad news, being careful not to harangue the messenger for delays or whatever. This did not mean he was soft on people not delivering to plan but rather showed his focus on recognising problems and achieving the objectives in spite of them.

Leadership and influence

There are probably more books and seminars on effective personal style than any other management topic, and yet time and time again projects go wrong for very human reasons. During the 1990s it was estimated that ten academic papers a day were published on the subject and nowadays virtually every organisation includes leadership as a topic within their management or executive development programmes, but few actually include 'project sponsorship' in those programmes. Project management roles are interesting in this respect as they challenge many of the traditional assumptions associated with power and leadership. Prime amongst these is the likelihood of the following:

- You may be leading or managing across the organisation, impacting people and capabilities outside your traditional line management remit and even from other organisations; further, these people may be from different disciplines with different ways of working, language and values.
- Traditional hierarchy and ranks may be side-stepped, with apparently senior line managers accountable to managers they perceive to be more junior.
- You may have no direct authority over the team you are accountable for as seen from a line management perspective. As such, the normal disciplinary sanctions for non-performance of individuals may not exist – you have no 'big stick.'

In such situations, certain aspects of 'pushy', 'blue' or 'hard' styles, such as assertion and persuasion, can be ineffective:

- **Persuasion** is only useful if the issue is open to rational debate and you are perceived as being competent in the topic under discussion. It is notoriously poor if used in a highly charged emotional environment.
- **Assertiveness** can be powerful if your needs are legitimate and you stand to lose if those needs are not met. The list of accountabilities associated with your role gives you your legitimacy but do check what incentives you can offer or sanctions you can impose to gain agreement or compliance with your wishes. If you can provide neither, assertion can be fruitless.

'Pull', 'green' or 'soft' styles such as bridging and attraction may be more effective:

- **Bridging** involves gaining others' commitment and is most valuable if it is seen that you are open to influence and value their opinions. Look at your key stakeholders and you will probably find this form of influence is appropriate for many situations involving them.
- **Attraction** or envisioning is all about generating enthusiasm and excitement, taking people beyond the everyday to higher plains and new possibilities. It is often seen as totally irrational, but is no less effective for that. If shared values and trust are what you need to achieve your aims, this is a good influencing style.

In summary, the 'best style' to use depends on the situation you find yourself in and the person you want to influence. However, on the whole, if you find yourself saying the following, think again:

- 'Don't come to me with problems, come with solutions.'
- 'I only accept "can do" as an option.'
- 'Don't come moaning to me; just do it.'
- 'I want action NOW!'

All these expressions may lead to over-optimistic reports of progress, the truth being hidden and blame being cast on others for failure to deliver. It is more powerful for a leader to surround him/herself with 'constructive dissenters' who are prepared to tell the truth or ask awkward questions than with 'yes men' who merely repeat what the leader wants to hear.

Remember, the benefits from whatever the project produces will only start to flow once those deliverables have been put into use in the operational environment. If those leading the project have not obtained the consent of the senior managers who will actually operate the 'new order', their efforts and that of the team will come to nothing. It would have been more cost effective to send the team and their families on holiday to Spain for three months than to create something which is never used.

I thought you were doing that! – accountability

How many times have you been in a meeting, with your colleagues and the following has happened:

Chairman: Right. That's agreed then. Bob and Dave, you sort that one out and let us know next week.

Next week . . .

Chairman: Bob, what happened?

Bob: I don't know. I thought Dave was doing something on this.

Dave: Oh! I was waiting for you to phone me.

Some clarity on who was actually accountable was needed. Bob and Dave might both have been necessary, as skilled, knowledgeable resources, to carry out the action, but only one of them should have been accountable. This is called 'single point accountability'.

The person who is accountable is not necessarily the person who does the work, but the one who sees that it is done. This is not only useful in a meeting environment but also in planning projects. We have already introduced the accountabilities of the project sponsor and project manager. The project manager is accountable for managing the work on a day-to-day basis, ensuring the deliverables are in place at the required time, quality and cost. He or she cannot do it all, or in many cases manage it all. We have also seen how a project is deconstructed into life cycle stages (see p. 58). This decomposition can be followed through with major packages of work being made the accountability of a particular, named, core team member. These work packages may be divided into smaller packages and ultimately into individual activities and tasks. This deconstruction is called a work breakdown structure (see p. 141).

> *In practice, single point accountability means every work package at any level in the work breakdown structure has a person named as accountable for it.*

In practice, single point accountability means every task, activity and work package at any level in the work breakdown structure has a person named as accountable for it. This has four advantages:

- It is clear what is expected of each person.
- Overlaps should be eliminated as no deliverable can be created within two different work packages.

- If a gap in accountability appears (due to loss of a team member, for example), the next person up the tree is accountable to fix it.
- If scope, cost or time proves to be inadequate to create the deliverables, it is clear who is accountable for raising these issues.

In practice, accountability is shown in the way that project plans (bar charts) are designed. The examples given in Chapter 21 clearly show accountability.

Accountability: what you can count on a person to do. That person and only that person can be called to account if something he/she has accountability for is not done.

Responsibility: what a person is, or feels, responsible for. It assumes commitment on the part of that person, beyond his/her own accountabilities, to act responsibly to ensure that the project objectives are met.

You may be *accountable* for ensuring a computer system functions correctly. I would be acting *responsibly* if I told you of any defects I observed.

In projects it is essential that accountabilities are clearly stated and are unambiguous so everyone knows who is called to account and who they are accountable to. Similarly, team commitment should be fostered, which promotes responsible and open behaviour by all team members.

> 'The business of everybody is the business of nobody.'
>
> LORD MCCAULAY

Encourage an open, even-handed style to encourage communications

Copyright © 1997 Robert Buttrick

Project Setup

How to go about it

Set up the project team

Prepare a project definition

Prepare the project plan

Define your project organisation

Engage your stakeholders

This chapter explains the steps you need to take during the Initial Investigation Stage to set up a project and ensure that control is established from the very start.

'Mix a little foolishness with your serious plans; it's lovely to be silly at the right moment.'

HORACE, 65–8 BC

- **Understand the driving business need.**
- **Define the scope and boundaries for the project.**
- **Use your team to define and plan the project.**
- **Harness your stakeholders' influence.**

This chapter explains the steps you need to take during the Initial Investigation Stage to set up a project and ensure that control is established from the very start. For clarity these steps are described sequentially, but in practice you will find that you need to do them in parallel, as each step may influence any of the other steps.

How to go about it

There are five key activities for you to undertake when setting up a project:

1 Set up the project team.
2 Prepare a project definition and business case.
3 Prepare a project plan.
4 Define your project organisation.
5 Engage your stakeholders.

The purpose of formally setting up the project is for you to state explicitly the *business drivers, scope* and *objectives* for the project, that is:

- *why* you are doing it;
- *what* you will produce;
- *when* you will produce it;
- *how* you will approach the project;
- *who* will be involved;
- *how* much it will cost and benefit you.

This information is gathered in a document set which, together with the associated plans, provides you with the starting point (baseline) on which all subsequent project decisions will be taken and against which you can measure project performance. Different organisations have different sets of documents to support this, the common ones being:

- Project Initiation Document (Prince2);
- Project Definition;
- Project Management Plan (APM, PMBoK);
- Business case.

All these mostly contain the same information, it is just the way they are assembled and named that changes. For example, the Project Management Plan often comprises a subsidiary set of documents defining how each aspect of the project is managed, for example risk management plan, schedule management plan. Some organisations combine the 'business case', which justifies why you are dong a project and proves its viability, with the 'definition', which defines the scope, schedule and costs. The reason for this is simply to ensure the two documents align as there is often a degree of duplication. In this book, I have assumed the business cases and the project definition are combined in a single document, called a 'business case'.

The headings under which you should define your project follow. I have chosen to structure the document in three parts, each serving a different interest group. It is important for you to avoid having to write up your project in many differing ways to meet differing needs. For example, it is not unusual for finance functions to want a 'special' document on which to base the authorisation of funds for the project (hence why some organisations have a separate business case document altogether). However, good design of a key document, such as that outlined here, can avoid such duplication and thus reduce your workload and the discrepancies which can appear if separate documents are required for different interest groups.

WHAT A WASTE OF TIME!

'But why do I need to write it all up? Isn't it just a waste of time?'

Writing up your project in a structured and thorough way helps you to ensure that all the important aspects are covered. The template is, in itself, a checklist for building quality into your projects.

Unless you are the only person involved in the project, you will need to communicate your intentions. *You* may know everything about the project, but if the others who need to be involved don't understand what you are trying to achieve, the project will fail. The document is your explicit form of communication.

Keep the document brief. Put in the minimum content to communicate the bare essentials. Ironically, the simpler the project, the more people tend to write, as they know so much about it. Larger, more complex projects are frequently ill defined and too brief.

Headings to define your project

The three parts of the business case are:

Part 1 – Finance, which is primarily aimed at the finance function. They will be interested in this section as a priority and then Section 2.1 to 2.4. The project sponsor will also be interested in this as it sets out the financial criteria to be met.

Part 2 – Project Definition is of interest to the project sponsor, stakeholders and project team. It is the meat of the document.

Part 3 – Project Organisation is of most interest to the project manager, team and line managers as it sets out how the project has been organised.

The business case comprises:

Section	Section heading	Question answered
1	FINANCE	
1.1	Financial appraisal	HOW MUCH?
1.2	Sensitivity analysis	HOW MUCH?
2	PROJECT DEFINITION	
2.1	Background	WHY?
2.2	Business objectives	WHY?
2.3	Benefits	WHY?
2.4	Output description	WHAT?
2.5	Scope, impacts and interdependencies	WHAT?
2.6	Deliverables	WHAT?
2.7	Timescales	WHEN?
2.8	Risks and opportunities	CONTEXT?
2.9	Prerequisites, assumptions and constraints	CONTEXT?
2.10	Project approach	HOW?
2.11	Analysis of options	HOW?
3	PROJECT ORGANISATION	
3.1	Review and appraisal points	HOW?
3.2	Change control	HOW?
3.3	Progress reporting	HOW?
3.4	Project team and stakeholders	WHO?

The content of Part 2 is described in detail later in this chapter.

Set up the project team

The typical 'project structure' was described in Chapter 4 and is shown again in Figure 19.1.

Project teams are:

- short term, being established only for the duration of the project;
- cross-functional, to provide the necessary skill mix;
- frequently part time, with team members fulfilling line and project tasks.

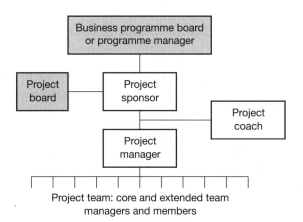

Figure 19.1 A typical project organisation structure
The project sponsor requires the benefits, possibly supported by a project board and reports to the project review group or to a programme manager. The project manager reports to the project sponsor and is accountable for the day-to-day running of the project. A project coach supports these key roles. All team managers and members report to the project manager. See also Chapter 4.

Bearing this in mind, it is essential that you agree the project roles from the start (e.g. project sponsor, project manager and project board membership) with the individuals concerned and their line managers (if appropriate). As many of the team members are likely to be part time and have other daily duties to attend to, it is essential that you agree with their line managers what their commitments are and how you should handle changes to this. The line managers may also have a quality assurance role to undertake, if so this must be agreed. If necessary, write and agree a role description, defining the individual's accountabilities. Even if these descriptions are never referred to again, the act of creating them with the individuals, and agreeing them, will clarify each person's role and ensure there are fewer misunderstandings. Finally, do ensure that accountability for any activity or work package on the project rests with a single person only. Shared accountabilties do not work; they lead to omission, duplication and confusion (see also p. 286). Summarise the key members' roles in Section 3.4 of the initial and full business case documents.

You should create, with the team, a set of values for the project to share and an agreed way of working together. Project Workout 19.1 provides some ideas for this. Fostering team spirit is the responsibility of all on the team, led by the project manager. The sooner the team can settle down to work together in an environment of openness and trust, the better it will be for the project. Project setup is the ideal time to do this. Even if *you* know what to do on the project, sparing the time for the team to contribute will lead to greater commitment and better results. Preferably the early days of the project should be spent as much as possible as a group working in a creative environment. Project planning is an ideal vehicle for forming the team as well as being of vital importance to achieving results. Projects that are designed solely by one person usually lack the vitality and level of involvement necessary for achieving extraordinary results.

> *Projects that are designed solely by one person usually lack the vitality and level of involvement necessary for achieving extraordinary results.*

WELCOMING NEW TEAM MEMBERS

It is all well and good ensuring the team is bonded and aligned from the start but do not forget that as the project moves through its life cycle, team membership will change. Welcome new team members and ensure they have bought into the team values and the project objectives. If there are a number of new members, for instance for a new project stage, treat it as if it is a new project. Project Workout 19.1 (The first team meeting) and those related to planning can easily be adapted for the start of each stage.

19.1

THE FIRST TEAM MEETING

This is best done in a relaxed atmosphere without any tables acting as barriers between people. The 'board room' arrangement is not recommended. Team meetings are best in rooms with space to move around and wall room for flip charts. Confined rooms confine thinking.

The first time team members gather is very important and can set the tone for the rest of the project. Some individuals may know each other (and you) well. Others may know no one. Some may have worked together before on other projects. Even if some have not met before, they may have preconceived ideas of others on the team based on gossip and rumor from other colleagues. It is you, as project manager, who must bond this disparate group into a committed team. One way of doing this is to:

● bring the group members to respect each other;

● create a set of team rules!

Respect each other

1 Ask all present to introduce themselves and say a little about their interests outside work. Ask them to tell the others something about themselves that none of the others knows.

2 Ask each person to say what his/her commitments are to the project, why he/she would like to see it succeed and what that person will do to help success become a reality.

3 When the individual has finished, each of the other team members should build on what that individual has said about him/herself by saying what skills and competencies they know or feel the person has which they respect. Keep to positive and strong points only.

On receiving this acknowledgment, the individual should not be embarrassed. 'Thank you' is all he or she needs to say.

4 Steps 1 to 3 should be gone through for every person in the group.

This may sound contrived, but it does work if treated seriously. It can remove or dispel rumour. It brings people onto a personal footing.

Team values

Creating a set of 'rules' that the team agrees to live by and uphold is also a powerful way of bonding:

1 Brainstorm a set of values or rules for the team to live by. Put these on a flip chart.

2 The team should then select those which it wants to live by.

3 Display the values prominently in the team's workroom and at every team meeting.

During the brainstorm, individuals will often shout out things that annoy them. For example, if someone really gets heated if meetings start late, he/she may want the rule/value 'All meetings start on time'. The brainstorm list, therefore, becomes a set of potential 'hot buttons', which can turn each person from a likeable, rational soul into an angry unreasonable one. It's good to know what these are at the start! Some of the most powerful values can also appear very shallow. One senior team had 'chocolate' as a value. At every meeting someone was accountable for bringing one or two bars of chocolate. It became a symbol of 'looking after each other' and something to joke about to lighten the tension when business issues were weighing heavily and the team could not agree a way forward.

Prepare a project definition

Part 2, the project definition section of the business case document, defines your project – why you are doing it, what you will produce and how you will go about it. The details for each section are as follows:

2 Project Definition

2.1 Background

Describe, briefly, the background to the project:

- Explain why the project has come about (e.g. as a result of a strategy study, as a result of findings from another project).
- Refer to any other associated projects or initiatives, business plans, or conclusions from previous studies.

2.2 Business objectives

You should describe why you are doing the project. Explain:

- the business objectives the project will satisfy;
- the needs the project fills;
- how the project supports your business strategy.

2.3 Benefits

You should describe the benefits you hope to achieve from the project (see also Chapter 20). These may be in two forms:

- *Financial* – these should be stated in 'money' terms (e.g. increased revenue, cost savings, etc.).
- *Non-financial* – changes in operational and key performance indicators should be quantified. If you are unable to quantify a particular benefit, describe it as best you can – just because you can't count it, doesn't mean to say it does not count.

Include a statement on what else the project will accomplish, for example say what new possibilities will be created operationally, commercially, or for new projects.

In addition you should outline:

- the minimum conditions of satisfaction required in order to declare the project a success (e.g. achievement of a specific market share, revenue, cost saving);

- the method for measuring and confirming the achievement of each benefit;
- any possible events which, if they occur, will lead you to consider terminating the project.

Answering the question 'Why?' is very important. There are four basic reasons why you should want a project:

- to earn more revenue;
- to save costs;
- to reduce working capital;
- to enable you to remain in business.

All programmes (related projects) will ultimately be aiming for one or more of these. In a programme, however, individual projects may focus on other benefits, for example improving performance or service quality. Other projects are created as vehicles to learn about new markets, technologies or approaches. Be honest when stating the business objective. If you pretend a 'learning' project is a revenue generator, don't be surprised if it is cut in favour of projects which generate greater revenue.

2.4 Output description

You should describe, in one paragraph, what the project is going to produce overall. This may be a new product, a new culture, process, manufacturing line, computer system, etc. Section 2.6 will list the key deliverables and these need not be stated here. The output description document will contain the detail.

2.5 Scope, impacts and interdependencies

Define the work necessary to meet the business objectives outlined in Section 2.2 and to create the output described in Section 2.4. Include:

- the areas impacted by the outcome of the project (boundaries of the project);
- any aspects which are specifically excluded from the project;
- key interdependencies with other projects (see p. 353).

You should also state, in broad terms:

- the impact the project will have on current operations and existing projects;
- the functions or departments in your organisation which will be affected.

Interdependency. If Project B requires a deliverable from Project A in order to achieve its objective, Project B is dependent on Project A, i.e. a deliverable is passed from one project to another.

For example, Project A builds a computer platform as one of its deliverables. Project B uses this platform to run software it has built as one of its deliverables. If Project A failed, Project B will fail as it is dependent on it.

A deliverable can be created by one project only. It may, however, be used by many subsequent projects.

SCOPE

The project scope must comprise everything which is needed to ensure that the benefits can be realised. There should be no assumptions that 'others' are providing a key part. If other projects are providing deliverables, this must be stated explicitly as a dependency, and not assumed.

2.6 Work packages and deliverables

List the work packages and major deliverables from your project, which are needed to create the output described in Section 2.4. Deliverables may take two forms:

- *Final deliverables* – which are to be handed over by the project team to the users at the end of the project (e.g. hardware, software systems, brochures, product specifications, tariffs, business processes, advertising campaigns).
- *Temporary deliverables* – which are to be produced during the course of the project for review and sign-off (e.g. feasibility report, business case).

For each deliverable, specify:

- the format and content in which it is to be produced (e.g. a written report, TV advertisement);

- the named individual accountable for its production;
- the named individual(s) accountable for reviewing and/or approving it.

If the list is extensive, you should detail them in an appendix and list only the key ones in the main body of the document.

2.7 Timescales

Outline the overall project timescales by stating the target completion dates for key milestones. Include all the staged framework milestones: Development Gate, Trial Gate, Release Gate, launch, project complete (see p. 60). Add any other significant milestones or events such as the letting of a major contract.

2.8 Risks and opportunities

This section should contain:
- a list of the significant risks and opportunities that may potentially jeopardise or enhance the success of the project;
- actions that will be taken at the outset to reduce the likelihood or impact of each risk identified;
- actions or contingency plans that may be implemented, should any risk or opportunity happen.

You may conveniently present this in the form of a risk and opportunities log. (See Chapter 23 for a full discussion of risks and opportunities.)

2.9 Prerequisites, assumptions and constraints

Include:

- any circumstances outside your control which must be in place if your project is to be successful;
- all assumptions that have been made about the environment (e.g. economic factors, competitors, systems, people) in which your project is to be conducted;
- any constraints which have been imposed on your project which may affect the outcome.

It is important that you list all assumptions and constraints, even if they appear obvious to you; they may not be so obvious to others associated with the project.

> *It is important that you list all assumptions and constraints, even if they appear obvious to you; they may not be so obvious to others associated with the project.*

2.10 Project approach

Describe how the project will be undertaken and explain why you have chosen this particular approach. Include:

- a work breakdown structure (e.g. phases, stages, subprojects, work packages) with justification;
- key interdependencies between subproject elements and with suppliers.

Where subprojects are complex, you should consider having each one formally defined by the sub project manager using Parts 2 and 3 of this document.

2.11 Analysis of options

Summarise the key points from the investigative studies, stating which options have been rejected and which have been carried forward for further analysis. Give your reasons for any choices made.

DEFINING A PROJECT

19.2

Take any new project that you are associated with. With the project sponsor, project manager and key team members, create, on flip charts in a workshop environment, the project definition part of the business case document. Base it on the template given above.

Ensure you answer every section fully – it all counts.

Note where there are gaps in the answers and be honest. You will fool no one but yourself in the long term.

Work with the team to fill the gaps identified in this workout:

- If you don't know *why* you are doing the project, consider terminating it.
- If you don't know *what* you are delivering, regard your costs and timescales as unstable and your risk high.
- If you don't know *when* it will be done, carry out more investigations until you do know.
- If you don't know *how* you will approach the project, regard risk as high and investigate further.

PROJECT DEFINITION CHECKLIST

Use this checklist to review any projects currently in progress.

Criteria

19.3

☐ Has a project definition been written, reviewed by the stakeholders and approved by the project sponsor?

☐ Do the scope and objectives of the project meet the needs of the business?

☐ Have the benefits been fully assessed and quantified wherever possible?

☐ Do the benefits match the needs?

☐ Have all significant risks been identified, categorised and taken into account in the plan and business case?

☐ Has a comprehensive and satisfactory work breakdown been developed?

☐ Does the work breakdown reflect the deliverables to be produced?

☐ Are all key logical relationships between projects and activities clear?

☐ Has the plan been developed to minimise or offset the risks?

The only way a project can be delivered is by its deliverables. For each deliverable check:

☐ Are the project deliverables relevant and are they feasible both to produce and use?

☐ Have quality criteria been established?

☐ Is it clear who is accountable for preparing each deliverable?

☐ Is it clear who will review the deliverable prior to signing off acceptance of each deliverable?

☐ Is it clear who will approve each deliverable?

☐ Has sufficient time been allowed for reviewing/amending each deliverable?

Project definitions

A major food manufacturer was undertaking a radical reorganisation of its processes and working methods. This involved warehousing, distribution, manufacturing, marketing, human resources and sales. In all, there were seven projects within the complex change programme. A considerable amount of study work had been completed and some of the projects had actually started. The managing director asked his management team, each member of which was sponsoring one or more projects, to write up each project in a form similar to that given in this book. When asked how long it would take, they all said a week. The managing director gave them two weeks.

Seven weeks later the last project definition arrived. 'What took you so long?' the managing director asked. One director said that as he was writing his, it dawned on him he wasn't really sure what he was doing. Further, when they read each others' documents they were surprised and often perturbed at what they were doing. The extra time was to work on the gaps and to check that they all formed a coherent programme.

TESTING IF PEOPLE ARE REALLY WORKING ON THEIR DEFINITIONS OR MERELY PAYING LIP SERVICE

With the projects in the case study, I designed a front cover with a space for the name and signature of the project sponsor and project manager, No one was asked to sign anything. Of the seven documents, four came back, unprompted, with both signatures and the other three with only that of the project manager.

Guess which projects proceeded more smoothly and with fewer misunderstandings!

I do not advocate inky signatures on every piece of paper. It looks too much like bureaucracy. However, it can be used as a device to test commitment in a culture where a signature has value.

Prepare the project plan

Preparing a project plan enables you to control the project by:

- **defining the scope** – specify the activities which need to be performed to complete the project scope and the target dates for their completion;
- **assigning accountability** – identify an owner for each activity who will be accountable for its completion;
- **monitoring progress** – provide the baseline against which progress will be measured.

The content and format of the schedule plan are described in the following sections. While these deal with schedule plans, the approach is also valid for the related resource and cost plans which should always use the same work breakdown structure.

Earlier in this chapter we discovered that 'Projects which are designed solely by one person usually lack the quality and level of involvement necessary for achieving extraordinary results'. I was illustrating the vital team-building benefits of working together at the start of the project. However, the benefits are far more practical and tangible than that. If a team develops an approach to the project and plans it together, there will be debate and argument based on the differing perspectives of each team member. As a result of such discussions, each member will come to understand the needs and viewpoints of the others. Building a good plan is hard work, however, and, once done, all the reasons for it being as it is are embedded in the minds of those who created it. Each individual is less likely to make independent decisions on his/her work scope which will have adverse effects on the work of others. Similarly, when things go wrong (as they probably will), the team will know more instinctively the correct way to handle it. Team members will be more likely to concur on the method of resolution: they will have already cleared away all the inter-functional blockages in their minds when they created the original plan.

If you have no plan, all roads lead there

The project was one which comprised a number of related software changes to four interrelated systems. The owners of each system had planned their parts of the project, BUT no one had as yet put them all together. They spent two full days locked in a room listing what each needed from the others and eventually built a plan which showed how the whole project fitted together. They had it on large sheets of paper with Post-It Notes joined by arrows. It was hard work. They didn't understand each other. Everyone else was unreasonable. They didn't know why the 'others' had to do their work in such an inconvenient way (a way inconvenient to them).

Once completed, the plan looked obvious. The approach was clear and the team members were happy with each other. They had even agreed who would be accountable for end-to-end testing across the systems (previously missing from the plan). When the inevitable happened and one team member's part went wrong, there was no blame apportioned, only solutions offered. They didn't even need to consult the plan; they knew it well enough as it was theirs.

The project was completed successfully.

'Planning is everything – the plan is nothing.'

EISENHOWER

Content of the project plan

A good project plan should include consistent plans for benefits, schedule, cost and resources and would include:

- **Stages** – these represent the natural high level break points in the project life cycle (e.g. initial investigation, detailed investigation, develop and test, trial, release).
- **Work packages** – these represent the clusters of work within each stage, usually focused on a key deliverable.
- **Activities** – these are the individual components of work within the work packages that must be undertaken to complete the project. Each activity should be defined in terms of its start and end dates and the name of the individual accountable for its completion.
- **Milestones** – these are the significant events (often representing the start of a stage) which should be used to monitor progress at a summary level.
- **Deliverables** – each of the key deliverables defined in the project definition should be shown in the plan. Use milestones to represent their completion.

- **Reviews** – include reviews at key points throughout the project when progress and performance will be critically evaluated.
- **Interdependencies** – define all inputs from (and outputs to) other projects. These should include all those defined in the project definition.

You will very rarely be able to plan a project in full at the very start but you should always be able to plan the next stage in detail, with an outline plan for the remainder.

Format of the project plan

Cost and resource plans are best shown in tabular format, perhaps summarised in a graphical format (S-curve) or histogram. See Chapter 21 for a fuller treatment of this topic.

Project schedule plans are most conveniently presented as bar charts, two forms of which are illustrated on the following pages:

- In detail – (Figure 19.2) a progress bar chart, used by the project manager and the team members to control their day-to-day work. This contains all the elements defined in the previous section.
- In summary – (Figure 19.3) a management summary used to present overall progress of the project to the project sponsor, project board and other interested parties. This should show the stages, milestones and other important activities necessary to give an overview of the project. (See Chapter 20 for a fuller treatment of schedule planning.)

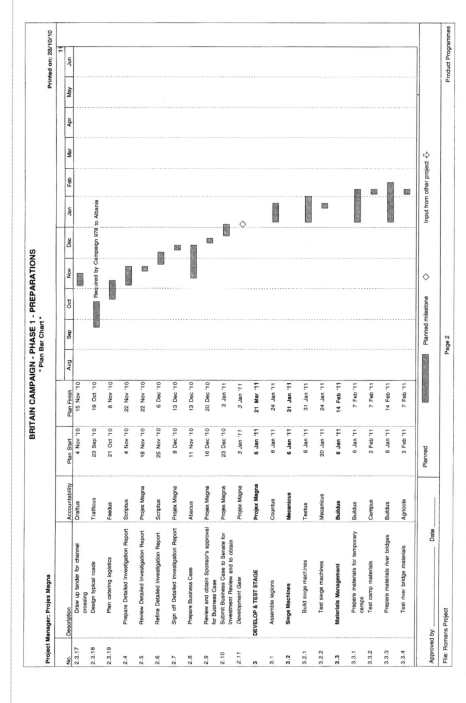

The table within the figure contains the following data:

BRITAIN CAMPAIGN - PHASE 1 - PREPARATIONS
Plan Bar Chart

Project Manager: Projex Magna

Printed on: 28/10/10

No.	Description	Accountability	Plan Start	Plan Finish
2.3.17	Draw up tender for channel crossing	Draftus	4 Nov '10	15 Nov '10
2.3.18	Design typical roads	Trafficus	23 Sep '10	18 Oct '10
2.3.19	Plan catering logistics	Feedus	21 Oct '10	8 Nov '10
2.4	Prepare Detailed Investigation Report	Scriptus	4 Nov '10	22 Nov '10
2.5	Review Detailed Investigation Report	Projex Magna	18 Nov '10	22 Nov '10
2.6	Refine Detailed Investigation Report	Scriptus	25 Nov '10	6 Dec '10
2.7	Sign off Detailed Investigation Report	Projex Magna	9 Dec '10	13 Dec '10
2.8	Prepare Business Case	Abacus	11 Nov '10	13 Dec '10
2.9	Review and obtain Sponsor's approval for Business Case	Projex Magna	16 Dec '10	20 Dec '10
2.10	Submit Business Case to Senate for Investment Review and to obtain Development Gate	Projex Magna	23 Dec '10	3 Jan '11
2.11	*Development Gate*	*Projex Magna*	*3 Jan '11*	*3 Jan '11*
3	**DEVELOP & TEST STAGE**	**Projex Magna**	**6 Jan '11**	**21 Mar '11**
3.1	Assemble legions	Countus	6 Jan '11	24 Jan '11
3.2	**Siege Machines**	**Mecanicus**	**6 Jan '11**	**31 Jan '11**
3.2.1	Build siege machines	Testus	6 Jan '11	31 Jan '11
3.2.2	Test siege machines	Mecanicus	20 Jan '11	24 Jan '11
3.3	**Materials Management**	**Buildus**	**6 Jan '11**	**14 Feb '11**
3.3.1	Prepare materials for temporary camps	Buildus	6 Jan '11	7 Feb '11
3.3.2	Test camp materials	Campus	3 Feb '11	7 Feb '11
3.3.3	Prepare materials river bridges	Buildus	6 Jan '11	14 Feb '11
3.3.4	Test river bridge materials	Agricola	3 Feb '11	7 Feb '11

Timeline columns: Aug, Sep, Oct, Nov, Dec, Jan, Feb, Mar, Apr, May, Jun

Annotation: Required by Campaign 978 to Albania

Legend: Planned ■ | Planned milestone ◇ | Input from other project ⇨

Approved by: _____ Date _____

File: Romans Project

Page 2

Product Programmes

Figure 19.2 A typical detailed project schedule plan

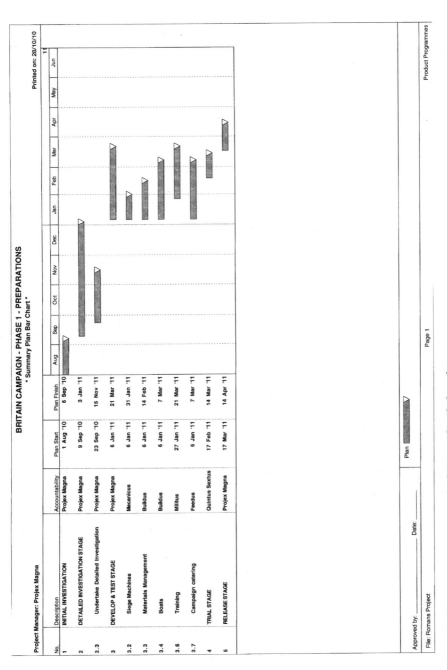

Figure 19.3 A typical summary project schedule plan

Define your project organisation

Once you have your project defined and planned out you should make sure that other organisational aspects of the project are addressed, including defining:

- project administration needs (filing);
- project progress reporting needs;
- who can authorise changes to the project;
- what formal review points are required.

The last three points are documented in Sections 3.1 to 3.3 of the initial business case.

Project administration

Projects can generate a considerable volume of information, correspondence and reports, most of which needs to be accessible and some of which needs to be archived. It is essential that the project manager sets up the administration of the project as soon as practical and that he/she makes sure that all team members and support staff understand what is required and available. The format and media for storing such documentation can vary from being paper based to a full electronic 'groupware' platform accessed via an intranet. In many cases, different sections will be held in different formats thus harnessing the capabilities of any support tools and avoiding duplication. Regardless of how you choose to store the information, its content will be similar. The following comprises a checklist on which to base your own project administration requirements. Benchmarking shows that many organisations have a prescribed structure, such as the following, to ensure that records are kept in a consistent way, enabling newcomers to the project to know where to start looking for the information they require.

Contents of a project file

1 Project summary details
This should comprise a short description of the project and the names of those holding the key accountabilities. The summary, as held on a project-tracking system, should fulfil the needs of this section (see p. 263).

2 Contact list
A list of all the team members, their roles and how they can be contacted.

3 Project log

A chronological record, owned by the project manager, of significant meetings, events and commitments. This should refer to detail in other sections of the file where appropriate.

4 Business case and change log

This section contains the fundamental definition of and case for your project. The change log is an amendment record, listing any changes to the business case which are under consideration or which have already been approved or authorised. By having a change log as a supplement to the Business Case, you avoid the need for updating the main document for every change. You need only reissue it when the number of changes becomes too unwieldy to keep in separate documents.

5 Progress reports

All regular and special progress reports should be retained. If a number of different reports are to be prepared for particular audiences, this section should be subdivided accordingly.

6 Project logs

- Issues log.
- Risk and opportunity logs.
- Lessons learned.

7 Schedule

This section contains a copy of the most recent schedule showing achievement and forecast against the agreed plan.

8 Finances

This section contains a copy of the most recent cost and benefit position showing achievement and forecast against the agreed plan.

9 Meetings

All meetings should either be minuted or notes should be produced to promote clear communication. This should include:

- agreements: record any agreements made (even agreements to disagree!);
- actions: be clear who has the accountability for any actions, when they have to be done by and who the recipients are for outputs from those actions.

10 Key deliverables

This section comprises a listing of the key deliverables (with accountabilities for preparation, review and approval). Copies of the documents themselves must be held for team use and archive purposes.

For Gate Decisions	Other deliverables
Proposal Ready for Trial Report Ready for Service Report Project Closure Report Post-Implementation Review Report	Output Description Feasibility Report Test Plan Test Results Trial Plan Trial Results

PLUS any others that are required, as defined in the project, such as detailed specifications, requirements, documents, tender documents, etc.

11 Correspondence
Record of all incoming and outgoing correspondence.

12 Reviews
Copies of any additional project reviews, other than the mandatory gate reviews (held in Section 10), should be kept.

For complex projects, individual subprojects and work packages should follow a similar structure to that held for the overall project.

Progress reporting

If you are the project manager, you are accountable for controlling the project and taking the necessary actions to ensure that it delivers the expected outputs. You therefore need to be clear what is actually happening.

You should gather your team together on a regular basis (preferably physically) and check what progress has been made and what progress is forecast. You should also assess the issues which have arisen and the risks which are looming on the horison.

Progress should be recorded by updating the project benefits, schedule and cost forecasts to show:

- activities completed and milestones achieved;
- forecasts of completion dates for activities in progress (or not yet started) where these are known to differ from the agreed plan (e.g. slippage);
- costs spent to date;
- forecasts of costs to complete the current stage of the project and for completing the project in full.

Additionally you should prepare, for the project sponsor and other key stakeholders, a concise written progress report which includes the following information:

1 **Business objectives.**
2 **Progress summary and outlook.**
3 **Financials.**
4 **Milestones.**
5 **Issues.**
6 **Risks and opportunities.**
7 **Changes.**

A description of the content of each of these sections follows. Progress reporting should be active, with you telling the stakeholders what they need to know in as concise a form as possible. If your organisation has a single defined format for the report then that is excellent. It helps make sure the reports are full and complete and aids the reader by providing a familiar, consistent format. So, if you have a reporting system, use the same headings.

Make sure your reports:

● are forward looking, focusing on the likelihood of the benefits being realised and objectives achieved;
● are honest and open, without undermining confidence;
● are focused on key issues;
● balance the good and the bad news;
● acknowledge the achievements of the team members.

Contents of progress report

1 Business objectives
As many stakeholders will not be familiar with your project from its number or title, you should summarise:

● the business objectives the project will satisfy;
● how the project supports your business strategy.

This is taken from Section 2.2 of the business case (see p. 298).

2 Progress summary and outlook
Briefly describe the progress of the project both in terms of achievements to date and expected future performance. Will it achieve its objectives? For any significant schedule slippage or cost variance give the reason, its impact and any corrective action being taken.

£000	Actual spend this month	Actual to date	Previous to date	Estimate to completion	Forecast at completion	Budget
Time costs	20	920	900	370	1290	1180
Purchases	20	480	460	150	630	520
Scope reserve				0	0	100
Contingency				70	70	200
TOTAL	40	1400	1360	590	1990	2000

3 Financials

Provide a summary of the project finances in terms of expected benefits, spend to date and total expected spend compared to that planned.

4 Milestones

List the major milestones. These should at least be the gate milestones as defined in Part Two. For each give:

- original and current baseline date;
- forecast date or actual date achieved;
- confidence indicator (your confidence in achieving the forecast date).

	Original date	Current baseline	Current forecast date	Date achieved date	Confidence H/M/L
Initial Investigation Gate	31 Jul 2010	31 Jul 2010	31 Jul 2010	31 Jul 2010	
Detailed Investigation Gate	01 Sep 2010	01 Sep 2010	01 Sep 2010	01 Sep 2010	
Development Gate	01 Oct 2010	01 Oct 2010	01 Oct 2010	01 Oct 2010	
Trial Gate	24 Oct 2010	24 Oct 2010	24 Oct 2010	24 Oct 2010	
Release Gate	31 Oct 2010	31 Oct 2010	31 Oct 2010	31 Oct 2010	
Launch	01 Dec 2010	01 Dec 2010	18 Dec 2010		High
Project completed	02 Jan 2011	15 Jan 2011	08 Feb 2011		High

5 Key issues

Describe the key issues which require escalating for resolution. For each give:

- the nature and impact of the issue;
- action being taken to resolve the issue and who is accountable.

6 Key risks and opportunities

Summarise the high risks and major opportunities which have arisen. For each give:

- the nature and impact of the risk or opportunity;
- action being taken to manage the risk or opportunity and who is accountable.

7 Changes

List all outstanding changes which are beyond the project manager's authority to authorise. For each give:

- the reason for the change;
- impact of the change;
- who is accountable for authorising the change.

8 Attachments

It may be convenient to attach, for detailed reference:

- cost report;
- progress bar chart;
- issues log;
- risks log;
- opportunities log;
- change log.

UNDER A BUSHEL

Don't be modest; if you don't acknowledge the achievements made by you and your team on the project, don't be surprised if the stakeholders don't either. It has been said that the definition of an easy project is one which is successful. If it wasn't easy, it would have failed. The project managers and teams of successful projects are, therefore, in danger of becoming 'invisible' or having their achievements undervalued even if it was their own hard work, excellent planning and adherence to best practice which got them there. DON'T BE INVISIBLE!

Change control

Once the project has been authorised, its scope, cost, benefits and timescale are baselined and used as the basis on which to monitor progress. Under certain circumstances it is, however, legitimate (and often desirable and/or unavoidable) to change these baselines. Who authorises such changes depends very much on the impact. It is, therefore, essential that the extent of the authority given to the project manager and project sponsor is defined. (Chapter 25 describes this more fully.)

Document who has accountability for authorising changes in Section 3.2 of the business case.

Review points

The management framework comprises a staged approach to projects with the 'gates' defining the key points when a formal project review is undertaken. However, the time lapse in some stages can be very long, particularly in the Develop and Test Stage. It is, therefore, essential that a sufficient number of additional review points are built into the plan to check that:

- the project still meets a real business need and is achievable;
- the quality of the deliverables is adequate;
- the plans are in place;
- the project organisation is working.

As a guide, a project should have a formal review every three months or when a major commitment is to be made. The occurrence of such reviews should be formally documented, as they comprise an essential part in managing the risks.

As a guide, a project should have a formal review every three months or when a major commitment is to be made. The occurrence of such reviews should be formally documented, as they comprise an essential part in managing the risks.

Reviews are often regarded as taking up valuable time and hampering progress on the project. However, it is in the project sponsor's interest that reviews take place with accountability to make sure they happen. (Chapter 26 discusses reviews more fully.)

Document the additional reviews in Section 3.1 of the Business Case.

PROJECT ORGANISATION CHECKLIST

Use this checklist to audit any projects currently in progress.

Criteria

19.4

☐ Have progress reporting formats been set up?

☐ Have progress reporting lines been set up?

☐ Has a system for capturing and managing risks and opportunities been set up?

☐ Has a system for capturing and managing issues been set up?

☐ Has a system for recording and approving changes been set up?

Engage your stakeholders

Ignore stakeholders at your peril

Every project will create some change in the organisation; otherwise there is no point in undertaking it! However, some changes are 'easier' to effect than others as they align with the status quo and do not cross any politically sensitive boundaries. In essence, most of the people carry on as they always have done. Other changes, however, are fundamental and will result in shifts in power bases internal to the organisation or even external, such as unions, suppliers or customers.

Stakeholders are those affected by the project. All those involved in the project are, therefore, stakeholders. However, there are also those who take no direct part in the project as team members, but whose activities will in some way be changed as a result. These could be users of new systems, people in new departments resulting from reorganisations (or those made redundant), those taking roles in new processes as managers, supervisors and workers. Often the project is of little importance to them but they are of great consequence to the project if their consent is critical to success. It is essential to identify them because it is critical to enroll them at an early stage in the project to ensure their power does not cause the project to fail later. Never underestimate stakeholders' ability to ruin your best laid plans!

> *Never underestimate stakeholders' ability to ruin your best laid plans!*

It is both the project manager's and project sponsor's role to ensure that all stakeholders are adequately briefed on the project. Too much communication will drown them – they won't read it. Not enough will mean your project will be lower down their priority list than you want it to be.

Engaging stakeholders and keeping them enrolled is a taxing but essential task. It is accomplished both by a formal communication plan and by 'enrolling behaviour' on behalf of all the project team on both a planned and opportunistic basis.

Sources of power

All organisations are 'political' to some extent and the greater your project's scope to change the status quo, the more you will need to be tuned in. You will need to identify the power bases you and others are operating from. These include:

- **Position**, which results from rank and formal authority. This can be actual or 'reflected' (when a person uses the position of their boss to enhance their own standing).
- **Status**, which results from how people perceive an individual, often related to their charisma and leadership qualities and may bear no relationship to facts of any particular project.
- **Resource**, where a person has direct authority over resources and can therefore smooth the way for, or block, any initiative requiring those resources. This can be directors, managers or unions.
- **Expertise**, where the knowledge or skill of an individual is such that others listen to and follow them.
- **Legal and regulatory**, where a group or body has authority over the 'rules of engagement' for your industry.
- **Customer**, where individuals or groups can influence you through persuading your customers to buy or not buy from you.

STAKEHOLDER INFLUENCE MAPPING

To be done in project team mode.

19.5

1 Brainstorm who your stakeholders are. Write each on a Post-It Note and stick them onto a white board or flip chart. Stakeholders may be individuals or groups.

2 Cluster the stakeholders into groups based on similar need or impact from the project. Rationalise the stakeholder list if possible, but don't worry if you can't.

3 Define the role of each stakeholder (Figure 19.4). Stakeholder roles are defined as:

- **Decision maker** – this stakeholder is required to make a decision regarding the project.

- **Influencer** – this stakeholder has influence over the project and/or over the decision makers.

- **Player** – this stakeholder is required to play a part in the project, perhaps providing resources, facilities or review time.

- **Consent** – the consent of this stakeholder is required if the project is to be a success (e.g. computer system users, customers).

4 Take each stakeholder in turn and, using one flip chart per stakeholder, answer the following questions:

- What is this person or group's stake in the project?

  - What is their role in the organisation?

  - What will they gain as a result of the project?

  - What will they lose as a result of the project?

  - What do they control, which the project needs?

  - What is their source of power now (see above)?

  - What will be their source of power after the project (see above)?

  - What is their attitude to the project?
    (strong/weak/positive/neutral/negative)?

  - How are they likely to be influenced (e.g. emotion or logic)?

It may be convenient to capture this information in a template for future reference (See CD-ROM for an example).

D = Decision maker
I = Influencer
C = Consent
P = Player
+/++ = positive / strongly positive
O = neutral
-/ -- = negative / strongly negative
? = unknown attitude

? D Chief Executive
? D Strategy Director
⊖ I Services Director
+ + D Project Sponsor
+ D Chief Financial Officer
+ + I Consultant
? C Head of distribution
+ + I PHIL
ME
? I Head of Engineering
+ C Distribution employees
+ I Head of support service
?
+ C Services employees
? C Engineering employees
? I Union committee

ACTION PLAN		Confidential
Ref Action	Name	Date
1 Meet CFo to discuss	Dave	1/2/10
2 Sound out CFO manager	Phil	15/1/10
3 Get contact number for GH	Jane	12/2/10
4 Sort out Geoff at CTT event	Bob	21/2/10
5 Meet Jim		
6 Contact		
7 Sound ou		
8 Arrange		
9 Leak the		
10 Pretend		

STAKEHOLDER ANALYSIS						Confidential
Name	Role	Gain?	Lose?	Controls	Power	Attitude
Theresc	fdwefcfeef	efcaef	efcfcfc	ccawc ca ca	xcwdawdcx	wcawawdcaw
Wqxx x	\cx cwcwwq	cccwc	\c\c\c\	cdcdc\ c c\d	\dc\ c\ cd\	\a\ \c\d\\\c\
A a\\\\\	d\dccccc	abhny	\cdcfcff	vfvg bg gfdgf	dc vdfvd v f	dfdfv b g bgb
E g cec	ff vd faw l	rty 7	tvrtbyy	bbr br tyb rty	tty b t nyynty	rtydrtybdrty
Theresc	fdwefcfeef	efcaef	efcfcfc	ccawc ca ca	xcwdawdcx	wcawawdcaw
Wqxx x	\cx cwcwwq	cccwc	\c\c\c\	cdcdc\ c c\d	\dc\ c\ cd\	\a\ \c\d\\\c\
A a\\\\\	d\dccccc	abhny	\cdcfcff	vfvg bg gfdgf	dc vdfvd v f	dfdfv b g bgb
Theresc	fdwefcfeef	efcaef	efcfcfc	ccawc ca ca	xcwdawdcx	wcawawdcaw
Wqxx x	\cx cwcwwq	cccwc	\c\c\c\	cdcdc\ c c\d	\dc\ c\ cd\	\a\ \c\d\\\c\
A a\\\\\	d\dccccc	abhny	\cdcfcff	vfvg bg gfdgf	dc vdfvd v f	dfdfv b g bgb
E g cec	ff vd faw l	rty 7	tvrtbyy	bbr br tyb rty	tty b t nyynty	rtydrtybdrty

Figure 19.4 A typical stakeholder influence map

The typical output from stakeholder analysis. Key individuals have been identified and a list of their characteristics drawn up. Relationships are shown by lines between the individuals – thick lines represent strong relationships. A number of key individuals have unknown attitudes to the project. Use existing relationships or develop new relationships to address these. Don't rely on the hierarchy. Finally, agree an action plan and be very careful who you allow to see these documents!

5 Write 'ME' in a bubble in the centre of a white board. Write those stakeholders you have direct access to around 'ME' and join them to 'ME' with a line. Use a thin line for a weak link and a thick line for a strong link. Use +, – or 0, to indicate if they are positive, negative or neutral to the project. Use ? if you don't know. This map indicates the stakeholders you have direct access to.

6 Write the remainder of the stakeholders in boxes around the edges of the white board. Using + , – or 0, to indicate if they are positive, negative or neutral to the project. Use ? if you don't know.

7 Write on the white board the names of others you have access to but who also have access to one or more of your stakeholders. You now have a 'stakeholder influence diagram'. You can use this to decide your action plan to enrol a particular stakeholder. You may do it yourself or it may be more effective to have others do it on your behalf.

- Regarding stakeholders who are negative or neutral. You need to address them.
- For those stakeholders where the line of influence is missing or very long. You must aim to shorten it to gain access to that person.
- As for those whose attitudes are unknown, you must find out what they are.
- Monitor the neutral ones, to ensure they do not become antagonistic.

STAKEHOLDER COMMUNICATION PLANNING AND TRACKING

Work with your project team using the output from Project Workout 19.5.

19.6

Planning

1 On a flip chart, brainstorm the following for each stakeholder:

- the messages you need them to receive;

- possible methods/media or people you could use to communicate with them;

- frequency of communication.

2 Consider, if you were them, what you would want to know and when? Aim to see things from their perspective. If possible, ask them!

3 On a large sheet of paper or a white board, list each stakeholder along the top.

4 Decide who should receive the standard regular progress report. Put an asterisk over the relevant stakeholder to indicate this.

5 Brainstorm the possible communications which you may wish to send out to the stakeholders. Write each on a Post-It Note. Place these on the chart on the left-hand side, in chronological order.

6 On smaller Post-It Notes, add a tick to show which stakeholder(s) is/are 'hit' with each particular communication.

7 Review how frequently each stakeholder will receive a message. Is it too often? Is it not frequently enough? Rearrange the Post-It Notes until you create a plan that the team is comfortable with (Figure 19.5).

	Date	Sponsor	Chief executive	Strategy director	Finance director	Heads of units
Start-up brief	1/3/11	✓	✓	✓		
Team brief	12/3/11	✓				
Memo A	14/3/11		✓	✓	✓	✓
Memo B	21/4/11		✓	✓		
Presentation	4/4/11	✓				✓

Figure 19.5 Stakeholder communications
An example of a chart to keep track of communications to key stakeholders.

8 Transfer the key communications to your schedule plan and 'fix' the plan onto your white board by rewriting directly onto it rather than onto Post-It Notes.

Do not be concerned that you cannot see very far into the future. The objective is to make sure you consider who you need to communicate with, when and how.

Tracking

Using the same white board output, simply write the communication made and the date on the left hand side, ticking the relevant stakeholder columns.

You will thus build a listing from which you will easily see who you have missed. You can then work both from your formal plan and add extra communications when you see these as desirable. You will also be confident that they look rational and consecutive to the recipients.

Managing Benefits

Benefits and drivers

Forecasting benefits

Timing of benefits

In short, benefits are about making more money, about using existing resources and assets more efficiently, and about staying in business.

'What is a man profited, if he shall gain the whole world and lose his own soul?'

MATTHEW 16:26

- Always measure benefits against a known baseline.
- Make benefits tangible, where ever possible.
- Place benefits in the wider business context.
- Look out for unwanted side effects from your project.

Benefits and drivers

Legitimate projects

Realising benefits is the sole reason for undertaking a project. If there are no benefits, there should be no project. It is for this reason that the role of project sponsor is vital. He or she is the person in the organisation who requires the benefits to fill a particular need, in pursuit of a stated business objective.

To be 'legitimate,' a project must satisfy at least one of the following conditions:

1 maintain or increase profitable revenue to the business, now or in the future;
2 maintain or reduce the operating costs of the business, now or in the future;
3 maintain or reduce the amount of money tied up within the business, now or in the future;
4 support or provide a solution to a necessary or externally imposed constraint (e.g. a legal or regulatory requirement).

In short, benefits are about making more money, about using existing resources and assets more efficiently and about staying in business. Drivers are frequently defined by words such as 'growth', 'efficiency', 'protection' or 'demand', which reflect an organisation's focus at any point in time.

The first three conditions relate to the net cash flow into the organisation. Money is the organisation's key measure of commercial performance in the private sector and value for money in the public sector. It includes measurement of revenue, investments and the costs of running the organisation.

The fourth condition is often referred to as a 'must do' project. It is nevertheless essential that such projects are fully costed in order to determine the least cost, highest value approach to fulfilling the need. This cost can then be placed in the context of the organisation as a whole in order to determine whether the organisation, or the impacted part of the organisation, can afford the change and remain viable.

Value drivers – what they are and why they are useful

If you have worked in mergers and acquisitions you may be familiar with how due diligence is carried out to assess the value and the liabilities of the target company. Acquiring companies look at those things about the target company that drive its costs, its revenues and its asset value. The approach, however, is also useful when driving out greater efficiency and effectiveness in your own organisation. The objective is to identify the set of value drivers that are specific to the organisation, which can be checked off against the organisation's chart of accounts (if it is simple enough – one organisation I know of has more than 11,000 account headings!). Example value drivers are:

1 **Reduced personnel costs**
   - Reduced head count
   - Reduced/avoided recruitment
   - Reduced employment overheads
2 **Reduced cost of ownership of assets**
   - Reduced maintenance costs
   - Reduced security costs (inc. losses)
3 **Reduced cost of rectification**
   - Reduced effort per error on investigation and recovery
   - Reduced volume of re-supply per error
4 **Profitable acquisition**
   - Profitable acquisition of valuable estate
   - Profitable acquisition of valuable IT systems
   - Profitable acquisition of valuable production assets/plant
5 **Improved profitable sales infrastructure**
   - Enhancement of profitable new sales personnel skills and relationships
   - Acquisition of profitable improvements to sales processes
   - Acquisition of new company data and knowledge that are put to profitable use in sales

If you know what drives your organisation's costs down and what drives its revenues and asset values up, you can compare these against the business changes your project is enabling and start to see exactly how your project is driving benefits realisation. This technique is the part of Isochron's Dimension Four® method (see p. 330), which enables a project sponsor to identify extended benefits, just as projects normally identify their extended costs. These benefits usually go far beyond those that people think of when they are working within imposed, budget-cutting targets. Dimension Four® recognises six categories of benefits, which expand the four 'legitimate projects' mentioned earlier:

1 bottom-line savings in the cost of what we are spending now, in this Profit-and-Loss year;
2 avoided costs of future committed spend;
3 future revenue increases;
4 new valuable assets;
5 'real options' – assets the project will build which creates options to generate more cash benefits in the future;
6 value-for-money – benefits that have no cash value to the organisation but are things that stakeholders want and have been promised.

One of the useful spin-offs of using value drivers is that it often increases the project team's (and sometimes the business's!) understanding of where their organisation's money comes from.

BEWARE OF EFFICIENCY 'SAVINGS'

When looking for efficiencies, be very careful not to waste time and energy suboptimising aspects of your business. What counts is the **throughput** of your business, not the individual efficiencies or asset utilisation of the different parts. Partially finished goods are not the aim, finished goods are. The trap people fall into is assuming that by increasing the efficiency of every part of a business, the whole business will become more efficient. This is not the case, as efficiencies are not additive. This can be very simply demonstrated.

Consider a factory with a five-step process, machines A, B, C, D and E, with a required throughput of 100 units/day. In an ideal world each machine would be sized for 100 units/day. But we live in a world of breakdowns and unexpected events. If each machine operated with 90 per cent reliability, the chances of you actually obtaining 100 units/day are only 60 per cent. You therefore need to oversize your machines to protect your throughput and you deal with breakdowns by ensuring that each machine has a stockpile in front of it to protect against a breakdown further up the chain. However, much of the time individual machines won't break down and if you are aiming for each machine to operate as near as possible to its limit (i.e. peak efficiency) you will find that stockpiles of partially finished goods will swamp the downstream machines. The net effect will be **decreased** efficiency downstream because it simply cannot cope with the corresponding increase in throughput.

Eli Goldratt likens this to a chain in his Theory of Constraints. A chain's strength is determined by the weakest link and you cannot strengthen the chain by adding weight to any other link. In fact, you only weaken the chain, as the weak link now has an even greater load to bear.

Business objectives and benefits

Whilst the conditions in the previous sections may make a project 'legitimate', they are not, on their own, sufficient to define the business objectives for the project, nor indeed the wide range of benefits which may result. Business objectives need to include not only the financial figures, but also statements on market positioning, service/product mix, target markets, service quality and such like. Organisations which focus purely on 'making the numbers' often end up by 'making the numbers up'. A finance plan is not a business plan; it is a subset of a business plan. You must always ensure the benefits from each project really are moving the organisation toward its business objectives.

Organisations which focus purely on 'making the numbers' often end up by 'making the numbers up'.

Some project sponsors have no trouble envisaging the end state of the business after the transformational changes. Ask them what their objectives are and their eyes will light up and they will talk with certainty and precision about how the organisation will function in the future and what they see happening. Others will also become animated but will talk in terms of the future being 'exciting', 'exhilarating' or 'challenging', with little or no information as to how the future organisation will function.

Another group will look blank and talk only about what is not going right and what the risks are. Sometimes they can be very despairing about the present and fearful of the future. Isochron has developed a technique for this 'doomsday' eventuality. It is called 'Transfiguration' because it enables groups of people to move from a position where everything appears impossible to a position where everything has proved possible and looks perfect. The approach taken is to list all the complaints and grievances in a workshop and then look for outcomes which would negate these. This is done by rephrasing the complaint in a positive way. This is described more fully in Project Workout 20.3.

Tangible and intangible benefits

Benefits can be:

- **tangible** – those which can be stated in quantitative terms;
- **intangible** – those which should be described as far as is possible.

Wherever possible, benefits should be tangible and clearly articulated. Tangible benefits may be measured either in financial or non-financial terms. **Financial benefits** describe the business objectives in terms of:

- revenue;
- contribution;
- profit enhancement;
- savings in operating costs or working capital.

Non-financial benefits describe the value added to a business that is directly attributable to the project but which cannot be described in financial terms. Again, these benefits should be tangible and measurable, such as:

- operational performance measures;
- process performance measures;
- customer satisfactions measures;
- key performance indicators (KPI).

Care should be taken, however, to query why we should spend money addressing any particular measure or indicator; if it doesn't eventually help you achieve any of the four conditions given at the start of this chapter, you should seriously consider terminating the project. You may argue that increasing service quality could help you to retain customers, or attract new customers, in which case a financial benefit should result; increasing service quality may enable you to remain in business. You should be able to justify any such assumptions even if the calculation of financial effect is somewhat tenuous.

Intangible benefits are frequently the most problematic to deal with. Whilst it is difficult to link tangible benefits back to a project output, the problem is far more difficult when dealing with benefits which are almost impossible to describe and measure numerically. Some people take the view that *all* benefits should be meaureable and that if a project has none, it should not be undertaken. This is an extreme approach and not one I agree with. Take for instance a project to implement an accounting system. We all know that any but the smallest organisation needs one and that, intuitively, justifying its cost through financial measures alone is 'missing the point'. I suggest you treat this as a 'must do' project in the first instance, determine the most efficient and effective way of meeting the need and see, in the context of your overall business plan, whether you *can* afford this and *want* to afford it, bearing in mind everything else you are doing or want to do. Portfolio management techniques are extremely useful in this context (see p. 199). Examples of intangible benefits you will often see in business cases are strategic positioning, competitive positioning (proactive and reactive) and the provision of management information.

ISOCHRON

Isochron® is a specialist 'think tank' and consulting organisation, which has developed a set of techniques and tools for benefit realisation which are grouped in a methodology called Dimension Four®. Put together, they reduce the uncertainty of the outcome of a project, but the techniques can be used separately to deal with awkward project difficulties. The method doesn't have to replace other approaches and complements the approaches taken in this book. Parts of it can be used to together with the Managing Successful Programmes (MSP) and Prince2 methodologies, it also endorses and backs up Lean approaches and Goldratt's Theory of Constraints.

Like this book, Isochron takes a business-centric view of projects, proposing that projects should be done 'by the business for the business'. It asserts that, short of external or market changes, any alteration in the cash flows of an organisation can only come about by changes in how the organisation operates and that therefore all benefits must be connected to observable changes in how the organisation works. In the private sector it proposes that every change must be connected to a cash benefit, even mandatory and regulatory ones, and it has a means to do this. It calls the observable changes 'Recognition Events®' and the start of observable changes in cash flow 'Value Flashpoints®'.

The name of the methodology – Dimension Four – is a hint that time is regarded as fundamental in the operation of an organisation. The main processes in the method work right to left – from the future back to the present, from the intended benefit to the cause. Uncertainty is transferred from the outcome to the process – the benefits are treated as non-negotiable but the project plan and solutions are seen as agile and highly negotiable.

Needs, benefits, and project deliverables

All too often the needs which initiated a project can become divorced from the outputs a project produces. It is essential for you to be able to maintain the linkage. When push comes to shove and you need to trim the project back due to overspends or budget cuts, having a clear view on this will ensure you trim the right things. Always remember benefits do not come from projects, they come from using the deliverables which the project produces. Key questions are:

● What are the over-riding business objectives for the organisation?
● What are the needs (or opportunity) to be filled if these objectives are to be met?
● What benefits will result through filling these needs?
● What deliverables do you need to realise those benefits?
● In what way will those deliverables help meet the need?

There is a technique called the functional analysis systems technique (FAST) that has been used for a long time in value engineering, but its inherent simplicity also lends itself to rigorously questioning the benefits a project is being set up to achieve, i.e. the business objectives. You start by stating what you are trying to achieve and then, by asking a series of **how** questions, you deconstruct this into increasingly specific statements which show the impact of doing one thing on the next one in line. The technique helps you ensure that only necessary elements for meeting the objectives are included in the project. The technique is often called 'How–Why' charting, and as such can be used not only in creative thinking (working left to right – **how**) but also to analyse a current situation (working right to left – **why**). See Project Workout 20.2 for how to use this method.

Difficulties with measurement

The quantitative benefits above can be measured at corporate level; however, they cannot always be measured directly for an individual project. You may need to take alternative approaches as illustrated in the following examples.

Example 1 – using a surrogate measure, it is not always possible to measure profit for products. In such cases, an alternative measure should be chosen which can be measured and which has a known relationship to profit. Revenue and margin may be such measures. You may also use measures such as numbers of customers, churn, percentage utilisation.

Example 2 – measuring at a higher level, it is not always possible to relate an increase in demand for a service directly to a recent enhancement to that service; it might be the result of other dynamics in the market. In such cases, the project should be tied to a higher level programme or business programme, where the benefits can be measured. For example, an enhancement to a service may be bundled with the overall service which is tracked at product level rather than by the individual projects and initiatives which make up the product plan.

Conditions of satisfaction

Despite difficulties with measurement, every project should have a recognisable method for knowing whether it has been a success. Conditions of satisfaction (introduced in Chapter 19) are used to supplement benefits measurements. They are the conditions which, if met, enable you to declare the project a success. They need to be chosen such

> **Conditions of satisfaction are the conditions which, if met, enable you to declare the project a success.**

that they are indicative of realising the benefits and may relate to a reduction in faults, increase in customers, observable change in behaviour and so on, measured or noted at a particular, defined point in time.

CRITICAL SUCCESS FACTORS (CSFs)

In organisations you will see reference to 'Critical Success Factors'. These are factors that will ensure achievement of the success criteria for the project – they are *not* the success criteria. The idea is that if you identify and focus on these success factors, you will directly influence success. The logic is theoretically sound *but*, in my experience, CSFs are seldom described effectively. Often they are mere platitudes and statements of the obvious, e.g. '... that IT provide resources' or 'Regular written communications to stakeholders are vital.' There is little point in repeating such generalities in project documents. In practice, they often represent risks (and as such should appear on the risk log) or are used to define what are better defined as 'dependencies' (deliverables required from other projects). My advice is not to use them, but if you do, make them *very specific* to the project. Concentrate instead on the conditions of satisfaction (see text above) and use your other controls to capture the factors.

NET BENEFITS

When talking of benefit always think in terms of **net benefits**, that is to say, what's left after you've counted the cost.

Isochron's recognition events and value flashpoints are special types of 'condition of satisfaction'. Since the value flashpoints each have an estimated monetary value (together with the sources, assumptions and calculations used), they enable finance and business managers to see how much each business change is worth and where its impact can be looked for in the cash flows. The problem of measurement at a higher level resolves itself because both the recognition events and value flashpoints are almost always found to be duplicated across projects – they all belong to one business level and viewpoint, that of the project sponsor. De-duplication often results in simplification and re-scoping of the projects around the project sponsor's business needs, as opposed to around the chosen solutions. We maintain a direct link from 'action' to 'benefit'.

If you use Isochron's approach the project sponsor and stakeholders will have defined, from the outset, precisely what their conditions of satisfaction are – the recognition events that will tell them when their expectations have been met. In the same methodology, the completion of the value streams triggered by the value flashpoints will be the conditions of satisfaction for the financial benefit goals enabled by the project. Isochron solves the 'measurement problem' in their methodology by using three spreadsheets:

- One lists the business change outcomes that the sponsor will recognise – the 'Recognition Events®'.
- The next lists the specific changes to cash flows that the recognition events will cause – the 'Value Flashpoints®'.
- The third connects the recognition events to the value flashpoints, to show indicatively how much the achievement of each change in the business will contribute to each value flashpoint.

Forecasting benefits

An initial estimate of the benefits and costs must be prepared during the Initial Investigation Stage. During the Detailed Investigation Stage the estimates must be turned into firm forecasts and be agreed by the project sponsor.
  Forecasts serve two purposes:

- first, they enable evaluation of the project;
- second, they provide information against which the post launch performance of the project can be measured.

There are four guiding principles for forecasting revenues and benefits:

1 Forecasts must be realistic.
2 Benefits must be matched by the costs of achieving the benefits.
3 Benefits (prices, sales volume, etc.) and costs must be based on the same assumptions.
4 Costs and benefits must be forecast for the worst, best and most likely outcome (scenarios).

Profit (or contribution) forecasting needs to take account of three factors:

1 Volume/demand.
2 Pricing.
3 Costs.

The overall financial contribution to an organisation is the product of demand and price less costs. This is the basis for justifying any number of projects whether they are for a new product, a campaign or for increasing efficiency. It is important to keep the total picture in mind to make sure that projects are

not created which merely suboptimise a part of the business, creating little overall benefit. For example, there is little point in installing a highly efficient new platform for a service for which demand is decreasing and the volumes required to achieve the efficiency will never be realised.

Timing of benefits

When looking at benefits always consider the timing. The earlier you can obtain benefits, the better it is for your business and the quicker you will recover your investment. Discounted cash flow calculations are designed to ensure that the time value of money is taken into consideration when comparing different projects and when deciding whether to invest. This is also why you need to look for opportunities to design your projects to ensure early benefits delivery.

Just as early benefits are a good thing, so delayed benefits are bad. The cost of delays can far outweigh any investment costs and turn a viable project into a financial embarrassment.

Figure 20.1 shows the cash flow for a project over a four-year period. The organisation is looking for a 30 per cent return on investment and this meets it adequately. If this project were to slip two quarters, the benefits would also slip, reducing the present value of the project by about 30 per cent. It would actually be worth overspending by 50 per cent in order to prevent this delay in benefits and regain some of the potential loss. This is not to say that project overspends should be encouraged, especially in a situation when you cannot be sure that injecting money will actually improve anything. It all comes down to risk. What is important is to understand how sensitive a particular project is to slippage and plan accordingly. (Sensitivity analysis is dealt with in Chapter 23.)

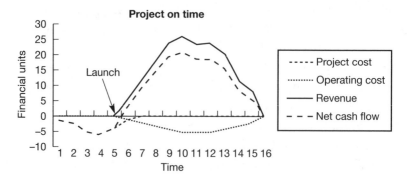

Project on time

Financial units (y-axis: −10, −5, 0, 5, 10, 15, 20, 25, 30)

Launch

Time (x-axis: 1 2 3 4 5 6 7 8 9 10 11 12 13 14 15 16)

----- Project cost
.... Operating cost
——— Revenue
- - - Net cash flow

Figure 20.1 Cash flow for a project 'on time'
A two-quarter delay to this project would turn it from being a good investment to a financial embarrassment.

20.1

WHY ARE YOU DOING THIS PROJECT NOW?

Write your list of projects from Project Workout 3.2 on a flip chart. Against each write:

● why you are undertaking the project;

● why it is being done now, rather than later.

Link your answers back to your business plan or business strategy. For internal projects, consider whether you have the right portfolio. For external projects (i.e. those for customers/clients), test whether that work is targeted at a chosen market segment.

Timing is often critical to success

Copyright © 1997 Robert Buttrick

LINKING OBJECTIVES AND NEEDS TO DELIVERABLES

This workout is best done early in the project with the project sponsor, project manager and a selection of key stakeholders comprising those likely to benefit and those who will produce the deliverables. You will need a large paper-covered wall and a supply of Post-It Notes. At the top left write the word 'How', with an arrow pointing right. At the top right, write the word 'Why', with an arrow pointing left.

1 Write the need/opportunity to be filled on a Post-It Note. Place it toward the left of the wall. If there is more than one need, record each of these on separate notes.

2 Test these initial needs statements by asking 'Why do this?' against each. Write your answer on a Post-It and place it to the left of the original note, linking it with an arrow.

3 Continue this until you are satisfied with the resultant core needs. They should match your overall organisation's business objectives.

4 Go back to your original Post-Its and then for each one ask the question 'How do we do this?' Write your answer on a note, place it to the right and link it with an arrow. Keep doing this until you have derived a set of 'create deliverable' notes, which are sufficient to define the scope of the project.

Notes

- Describe each note using an 'active verb + noun' combination. Ensure the verbs are as direct and descriptive as possible, describing an 'effect' (e.g. 'provide' is not a good word, be more precise). Ultimately the nouns on the right of the chart will be the deliverables.

- Take time to resolve any disagreements over descriptions and placing of notes. These discussions are critical in reaching a common understanding.

- This technique can be used, as above, for overall needs analysis but can also be used on discrete parts of the project as part of detailed design for specific deliverables.

- A variant of the approach is to put the 'noun' in the Post-It Note box and the 'active verb' on the arrow.

TRANSFIGURATION

This workout should be undertaken by a prospective project sponsor with the key stakeholders prior to formally starting a project. It is aimed at determining the business objectives for the project in a 'turn-round' situation. By capturing people's fears and grievances you demonstrate you have listened to them and then you concentrate on solving those issues. This approach can be supplemented by Project Workout 24.1, Resolving issues – from breakdown to breakthrough.

1 Bring together the people who are unhappy about the current position or antagonistic to what is about to happen. Ask them to tell you all their problems and concerns; write them down on a flip chart. On no account disagree with them – use 'brainstorming rules'! Take an active interest and help them to remember all the bad things they can.

2 When they have had a good moan, ask them to pick the worst half-dozen of the complaints.

3 Write the chosen complaints in the top half of a new flip chart – one sheet per complaint.

4 For each complaint develop a positive statement which is the opposite of the complaint. Write this on the lower half of each respective sheet.

5 Hide away the complaints, by folding over the sheets to show them just the positive outcomes. Ask them:

● when they'd like the world to be like that,

● whether they think it is possible. See what answers you get.

6 Ask them what they will hear/see/feel happening that will show them that the world has changed. Their answers help to frame their objectives and help build your conditions of satisfaction.

Caution – objectives gained in this way are only the mirror images of current failures. You should still try to find objectives from visionary people. Published Company Accounts, publicised vision documents and manifesto promises are also good sources for business objectives.

Managing the Schedule

The project schedule

Summary and detailed schedule plan

Tracking progress toward your objectives

Schedule reports

Reports used when drafting a plan

Report used to update the forecast

Reports used for progress reporting

So why are we nearly always late?

The management of the project schedule is one of the most important and fundamental of project management techniques; so much so that many people (wrongly) think that schedule management is project management.

'There can't be a crisis next week. My schedule is full.'

HENRY KISSINGER

- **Plan in outline for the full project.**
- **Break the project down into manageable pieces (work packages).**
- **Plan in detail before you start any work.**
- **Once a plan is agreed, baseline it.**
- **Measure progress against the baseline.**
- **Keep your eye on the future – forecast, forecast, forecast.**

The project schedule

You will find the management of the project schedule is one of the most important and fundamental of project management techniques; so much so that many people (wrongly) think that schedule management is project management. At a simple level, the schedule tells you how long the project, or any part of it, will take. In addition to giving dates, a well-produced project schedule also tells you:

- who is accountable for every aspect of the project;
- the approach being undertaken;
- the major deliverables from the project;
- the timing of key review points.

SCHEDULE OR PROGRAMME?

I have used the word 'schedule' to mean the management of project timescales. I use this word rather than the common alternative 'programme' as the latter has come to mean many different things including:

- a very large project;
- a set of interrelated projects;
- a sequence of phased projects;
- a portfolio of projects bundled for management reporting;
- a portfolio of projects bundled by management accountability.

In this book 'programme' is defined as a tightly aligned and tightly coupled set of projects (see also p. 62).

The schedule is also the basis on which cost and resource plans are constructed. However, unlike costs and resources, which are seen by only a few people observing a project, key dates are very visible. A well-publicised delivery date for a project is, when missed, very hard to hide. While 'time' may not be the most important aspect for you on some of your projects, an observer may develop their own perception of 'success' or 'failure' purely from the performance of your project against the publicised target dates.

The ability to build and manage the schedule plan is one of the essential skills that all project managers should have. Planning is far too important for you to delegate to junior team members, especially in the early stages of the project when the overall strategy and approach are being developed. The plan sets the course for the remainder of the project. Once agreed and set (at the Development Gate) it is very difficult to change or improve on. All the decisions which have the most leverage on time, costs and benefits will have already been made.

> *Planning is far too important for you to delegate to junior team members, especially in the early stages of the project when the overall strategy and approach are being developed.*

Done effectively, the project plan will benefit you and the team by providing:

- a baseline against which to measure progress (without a plan, words such as 'early' or 'late' have no meaning);
- a common understanding of the approach you are taking to achieve your objectives;
- a breakdown of the project workload into manageable pieces (work packages) based on the deliverables/outputs wherever possible;
- a clear way of showing interdependencies between activities and work packages within the project and to/from other external projects;
- a listing of accountabilities for different activities and work packages;
- a tool for evaluating when corrective action is needed.

Further, as already discussed in Chapter 19, the actual activity of creating a project plan by using the full team serves to forge a team spirit and a high level of common commitment.

All projects are undertaken within an environment of risk. Good planning is done in the full knowledge of those risks. You should therefore:

- avoid avoidable risks by planning the project in a different way;
- have a plan contingency for the unavoidable risks.

'The only way to be sure of catching a train is to miss the one before it.'

G K CHESTERTON

Summary and detailed schedule plan

You need to consider your plan on two levels:

- summary (or outline);
- detail.

The former is used to map out the entire project, while the latter is used to show the detail for the current stage. For work packages done by others (for example, by a contractor), the person or group doing the work will prepare the detail. However, you need to be satisfied that the plan is workable and includes sufficient checkpoints for you to monitor progress. Developing a schedule plan is an evolutionary process which starts with a statement of key objectives, deliverables and scope, followed by the preparation of a summary plan (Figure 21.1). This will comprise:

- the approach to be adopted (or alternatives from which the preferred option will be chosen during the detailed investigation);
- the breakdown of the project into stages and work packages relating to project deliverables (note these same packages should also be used for resource and cost management);
- the key dates, milestones and time constraints relating to the project;
- review or decision points;
- interdependencies with other projects.

From this you should be able to estimate:

- the resources required;
- the cost of the project.

Before you start work on any stage of the project, you should ensure that detailed plans are prepared. The criteria for all the entry gates in the staged framework from the Detailed Investigation Gate onward include a detailed plan as a prerequisite. Detailed planning will involve work undertaken within your own organisation and checking that third parties (such as contractors and suppliers) have planned in sufficient detail with adequate checkpoints for control purposes. The detailed planning process is similar to the outline process except that you will be be working in more detail, on perhaps one aspect of the project at a time. This includes:

- breaking down each work package into activities to represent the work content for each project deliverable;
- identifying dependencies between activities;
- agreeing completion dates for each activity with those accountable;
- checking that key milestones and the overall project completion date can still be achieved;
- ensuring that there are appropriate check and review points;
- ensuring that time and resources are allocated for planning the next stage.

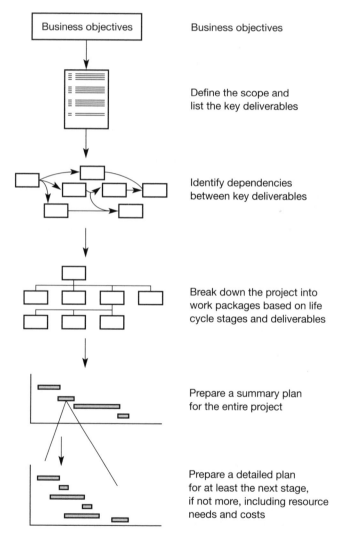

Business objectives

Define the scope and list the key deliverables

Identify dependencies between key deliverables

Break down the project into work packages based on life cycle stages and deliverables

Prepare a summary plan for the entire project

Prepare a detailed plan for at least the next stage, if not more, including resource needs and costs

Figure 21.1 Project planning
Project planning starts with the business objectives and ends with detail plans, including schedules, resources and costs. (See Project Workout 21.1.)

STARTING THE PLAN OFF

Introducing Post-It Note planning from the future – backcasting!

I said earlier that planning is too important to delegate to junior team members. 'But,' argue many people, 'I do not know how to use these sophisticated planning packages we have on our PCs,' or 'I haven't any planning software on my PC,' or even 'I haven't got a PC!'

Such excuses do not make sense. Projects have been with us for centuries and certainly since well before computers became commonplace. All you need to start planning is:

● your brain;

● your team;

● a set of Post-It Notes;

● flip chart markers;

● a very big wall covered in paper or a large white board onto which to stick your Post-It Notes.

You should do this exercise as soon as possible. In the early stages of a project it is more important to start getting the feel of the task ahead of you than to worry about 'correctness' and detail.

Take the project definition output from Project Workout 19.2 and with the same team in workshop format, using flip charts, white boards and Post-It Notes:

1 Display the flip charts from Project Workout 19.1 on the walls so that the team can see the project's objectives and conditions of satisfaction. If you are familiar with Isochron's techniques (from Chapter 20) you can use the recognition events to depict the objectives/outcomes.

2 List each outcome on a Post-It Note and place these at the right of the wall.

3 Pointing at the one of the outcomes, ask the question: 'What smart moves did we make to create this success?' This should lead you to identify milestones and deliverables; add them to the board to the left of the outcome, with an arrow leading to the outcome. For example:

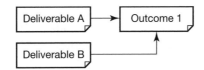

4 Take each deliverable in turn and ask the same question: 'What smart moves did we make to create this?' This will be either:

- more deliverables;

- activities you need to do which you want to capture.

If you 'invent' an activity, label it with 'A' in the top left. Add Post-It Notes to the board to the left of xyz deliverable with an arrow leading to it. For example:

5 Continue as per step 4, on the deliverables, milestones and activities, until you are satisfied that you have identified the starting point for the project. Don't be worried if you do not know what order some deliverables are put in or do not know the exact sequence of activities in all areas. If you did know this, your project would be relatively simple. Make a note of the 'problem areas', as they are issues which must be planned into your work schedule as problems to investigate and solve. Once you have finished, stand back and look at the pattern. Relocate some stickers to simplify if necessary. You may also notice that some deliverable or actions lead to a number of outcomes. This is good news as it reflects a fundamental of life, that one solution can remove many problems. (Look at Chapter 24 on issues, where you will notice the same effect.) It also indicates which of your activities and deliverables are really valuable and important to invest in. Finally, it may indicate that your project may be somewhat simpler than you first realised. Concentrating on planning towards outcomes, rather by defining departmental 'workstreams' always leads to simpler projects!

6 Look at the plan again and make broad estimates of how long each activity will take. Don't worry if you are wrong. Note down those for which you have very little confidence in your estimate on your list of 'problems to solve later'.

7 You should notice several tranches of notes, each of which leads to an particular outcome. These are clues to your work breakdown structure (WBS) and the key packages of work within each stage of your project. Where possible choose your WBS with as few interdependencies between work packages as possible.

Relocate some of the Post-It Notes to simplify the appearance if necessary. Rationalise any long sequences if it does not seem that showing them adds value to the overall plan. (Remember this is a summary plan only.)

8 Consider alternative ways of approaching the project, perhaps by brainstorming or discussion. Start again using an alternative approach.

9 Repeat the above for each outcome.

10 You should have created one or two summary plans. You will have discussed differing options, identified areas of uncertainty or ignorance and have started coming to a common understanding. You should also have been able to add some flesh to the bones of your project definition and be well on the way to creating a realistic, achievable plan. This may be sufficient at this stage or you may need more sessions. Assuming you have made as much progress as you can, the work packages should be allocated to key team members to start working on as part of the initial investigation. By starting 'in the future' and working back to the present, you ensure that only those deliverables and activities necessary to achieve the outcome are within the plan. This means you have no excessive, non-value-added work in the plan. This 'from the future' planning approach is often called 'backcast' planning, or simply 'backcasting'.

USE OF PROJECT MANAGEMENT PLANNING SOFTWARE PACKAGES

There are many commercially available software packages for schedule management, all of which also have the capability for handling resources and costs. Using planning packages can be of great assistance to project managers in their work, particularly for projects with more than 50 to 100 activities. The point at which using a software package is effective depends on how well a person can use it. More experienced users will find project-planning packages more beneficial for smaller projects than those who are less able. The examples shown in this book were prepared using Microsoft Project but similar layouts and reports can be prepared using other software packages (e.g. Primavera, PlanView, Asta, etc.).

Remember, planning software is a tool for you to use and not an end in its own right. It is not magic and will only give you a short cut to calculating and reporting on schedules. It cannot tell you if your fundamental approach is wrong or a major task is missing.

One danger of planning software is that a 'planner' works in isolation to construct a plan for the team. Computer screens are small and do not make good work sheets for teams. In addition, most work counter intuitively by assuming that you start planning by concentrating on activities, rather than deliverables. The Post-It Notes method in Project Workout 21.1 will test your basic approach and will ensure your team are agreed and aligned. When that has been done, by all means 'computerise it'.

I was given the task of looking at a project plan which had been created for a complex change project for a manufacturing organisation. I was told that there were six projects and about 400 activities. The complexity was due to over 50 interdependencies between the projects.

I printed out a network chart of the project (the equivalent of the Post-It Note plan) and laid it out on the factory floor like a carpet. A half day of study and marking up resulted in a much simpler programme. There were still six projects, but now only five interdependencies. The original project scopes had been defined largely on departmental lines. By focusing on deliverables, I was able create relatively independent projects so that each project manager had greater degrees of freedom to plan and manage his or her projects without the need to involve the others.

Good planning pays dividends

Copyright © 1997 Robert Buttrick

Tracking progress toward your objectives

'Nothing is inevitable until it happens.'

A J P TAYLOR

Tracking progress toward your objective is essential. If you don't do it you simply won't know when you are going to arrive. The control cycle is shown in Figure 21.2: once a plan has been agreed, it is necessary to measure progress against the plan, reforecast to the end, note any variances and take steps to bring the project back on schedule if need be.

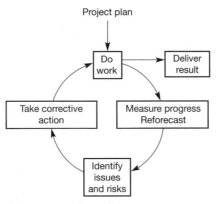

Figure 21.2 Schedule control cycle

There are many ways to measure progress, the commonest being:

- assessing percentage complete;
- assessing the remaining duration for an activity;
- estimating the date when a task will be completed.

Many people use the 'percentage complete' method. However, this method has potential problems if a realistic estimate of percentage complete cannot be determined (such as measuring hours worked); it is not unusual to find an activity is 90 per cent complete for 90 per cent of its duration! A simpler method is to estimate the date when a task will be completed.

> *It is not unusual to find an activity is 90 per cent complete for 90 per cent of its duration!*

An activity is either:

- completed (i.e. 100 per cent complete);
- not started (i.e. 0 per cent complete);
- or started, but not complete (treat as 0 per cent complete).

Activities which are started, but not finished, are assumed to be 0 per cent complete, but a current best estimate of the expected finish date is made. A special form (see Figure 21.8) can be designed to record this information.

The schedule should be updated at least monthly, but for faster moving projects, weekly or fortnightly would be more appropriate. This update cycle should tie in with the regular progress reporting on the project as it is the most concise method of showing what has been achieved and what is to happen next. Summary reports should be used for reporting upward and detailed reports should be used for reporting to the project team.

Do not concentrate only on what has been completed. Look at what is coming up next. Consider, based on your experience to date, whether the timescales allocated are adequate; if they aren't, you may need to take corrective action. Anticipating problems is good practice and gives you more time to find solutions. If problems are ignored they don't go away, they grow. Keep in mind your main focus: to reach the RFS Gate, when benefits start to flow. You do not need to have every activity completed on time.

> *Keep in mind your main focus: to reach the RFS Gate, when benefits start to flow. You do not need to have every activity completed on time.*

Every duration in your plan is basically a guess. Some will be good, some will be appalling, others will be the unfortunate victims of Murphy's Law. As project manager, too much concentration on the wrong detail will divert your attention from the real issues.

Reforecasting the schedule is not a change to the plan. It is an assessment of how the project is proceeding compared to the plan.

PLAN INSTABILITY

Quite often you will find that when starting work and monitoring against a plan you have difficulty assessing progress. This may happen because the work is in fact being undertaken in a different way from that planned. In most cases this is not a problem if the key milestones, dates and interdependencies are not affected. It can be symptomatic of 'microplanning', i.e. planning done at too detailed a level.

At other times it is simply because the plan has not been fully thought through. In which case it needs to be changed to reflect the actual work to be done (using the change management guidelines, of course). Changes of this nature often occur in the early part of a project as a result of uncertainty. The plan should become stabilised quite soon if you apply yourself and your team to it. You may also find that a particular work package is unstable. This could indicate that the manager in question has not planned it properly and is not in control, or that it is inherently risky. Both reasons need your management attention.

Schedule reports

Consistent format and layout

You must have a clear and consistent legend for the family of reports you will produce. Figure 21.3 is a typical example.

Bar charts can be confusing to the uninitiated and difficult to read. Therefore, it is good practice to use consistent formats and styles. The following points should be noted:

- The numbering used for activities clearly shows their level in the project hierarchy. The list is ordered such that each activity is shown within its relevant work package within the relevant life cycle stage.
- Activities are best described using an active verb, e.g. 'Prepare data'. Milestones or targets are activities of zero duration and are best described using a passive verb, e.g. 'Phase 1 completed'. The dates on the activity list should be updated to reflect progress and current expectations of finish dates.
- The accountability column has the name of the single point of accountability for every activity at every level.
- Show both the plan and the actual/forecast on the graphical section of the chart. In this way progress is very obvious.

When reading any of the project reports, it must be clear where the report came from and what it refers to. It is, therefore, good practice to have 'quality' headers and footers on each page so that the reader is absolutely certain of the source and status of the report being read.

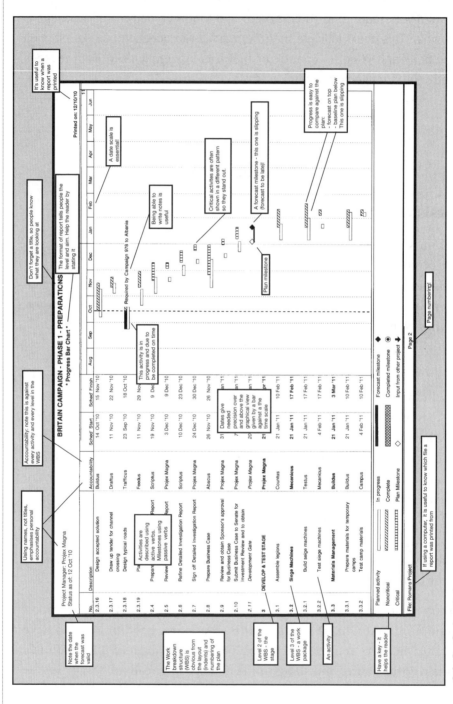

Figure 21.3 Schedule report

Inter-project dependencies

Many projects require deliverables from other projects as a prerequisite to completion. For example, a software project may require another project to deliver a particular hardware configuration before it can be tested.

It is very important to ensure that the scope of each project is well defined, particularly when different departments in an organisation are involved. If the full scope of each project is not clear, then accountability for delivery becomes vague and this will threaten project success. It will often be found that senior management and line management who are not intimately involved in a project or series of projects will have different perceptions of the scope of a project and may even view a package within a project as a 'project' in its own right.

The breakdown of a project into discrete work packages related to specific deliverables is essential if confusion is to be avoided. The plan for a project should show only those activities for which the project manager is accountable. Activities done by others in other projects should not be shown in detail. Such linkages should, however, be explicit and the example reports shown later in this chapter have been designed with this in mind. The reports show a **down arrow** on the date when the deliverable is due to be completed and is ready for use by the receiving project.

The plan for a project should show only those activities for which the project manager is accountable. Activities done by others in other projects should not be shown in detail. Such linkages should, however, be explicit.

When considering dependencies between projects, the following question should be asked: *'What do I (in Project A) require from other projects in order that I may complete the defined scope of work?'*

This may result in a list of one or more specific deliverables which should be identified in the other project plan(s). The project manager(s) of the other project(s) should be aware of what you require and by when. Two projects cannot be accountable for delivering the same deliverable!

Two projects cannot be accountable for delivering the same deliverable!

Report formats

The following section contain examples of schedule reports and are presented in the order in which they will normally be used (Figure 21.4).

The examples were prepared using Microsoft Project, but similar layouts can be prepared using other packages. They are all derived from the same basic data; they are simply different ways of viewing those data.

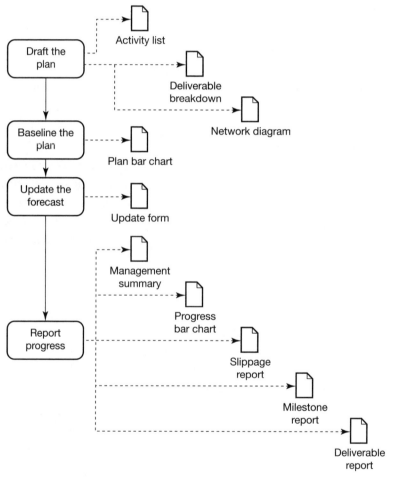

Figure 21.4 Schedule report formats
Different reports are used for different purposes. You will not find one to suit all your needs.

Reports used when drafting a plan

Deliverable/product breakdown structure

Purpose

The deliverable (or product) breakdown structure provides a summary listing of each deliverable created by the project team.

When to use it

The breakdown structure is used to show a structured view of all the deliverables from the project (or stage of a project). As such it is created whilst planning.

Completion

The breakdown structure is derived whilst planning, often in tandem with the network diagram (sometimes called a product flow diagram). By concentrating on the physical deliverables, those doing the planning are able to visualise the output of the project, starting with a few key deliverables and then breaking each of these in turn into smaller and smaller components. This helps ensure the outputs from the project will be sufficient to meet the business objectives. Strictly, this should be shown as a tree diagram; however, it is far more convenient and useful to use a tabular format, with the breakdown represented by the numbering system and indentation of progressively lower levels of the breakdown.

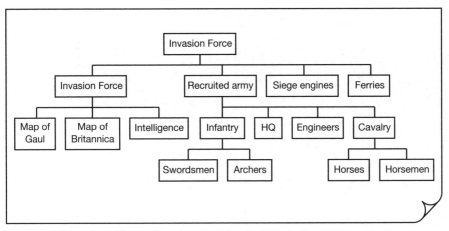

Figure 21.5 A deliverable (or product) breakdown structure

BRITAIN CAMPAIGN

WBS	Description	Accountable	Dur'	Plan start	Plan finish	Sched' Start	Sched' Finish	Number	Preceded by?	Summary?	Comment	Sign-off?
1	INITIAL INVESTIGATION	Projex Magna	27d	1 Aug '10	6 Sep '10	1 Aug '10	6 Sep '10	1		Yes		
2	DETAILED INVESTIGATION STAGE	Projex Magna	96d	9 Sep '10	3 Jan '11	9 Sep '10	20 Jan '11	12	11	Yes		
2.1	Assemble Team	Projex Magna	10d	9 Sep '10	20 Sep '10	9 Sep '10	20 Sep '10	13		No		Sponsus
2.2	Prepare Development Definition	Publius	16d	23 Sep '10	25 Oct '10	14 Oct '10	14 Oct '10	14	13	No		
2.3	Undertake Detailed Investigation	Projex Magna	51d	23 Sep '10	15 Nov '10	20 Sep '10	29 Nov '10	15	13	No		
2.3.1	Locate mapping of Gaul	Surveyus	10d	4 Oct '10	4 Oct '10	23 Sep '10	4 Oct '10	16		No		
2.3.2	Maps of Gaul available	Surveyus	0d	4 Oct '10	4 Oct '10	4 Oct '10	4 Oct '10	17	16	Yes		Cartus
2.3.3	Do reconnaissance	Surveyus	20d	23 Sep '10	18 Oct '10	14 Oct '10	8 Nov '10	18	16FS-10d	No		
2.3.4	Estimate enemy troop numbers	Countus	15d	7 Oct '10	25 Oct '10	28 Oct '10	15 Nov '10	19	18FS-10d	No		
2.3.5	Define number of legions required	Countus	10d	14 Oct '10	25 Oct '10	4 Nov '10	15 Nov '10	20	19FS-10d	No		
2.3.6	Prepare recruitment plan	Countus	5d	28 Oct '10	1 Nov '10	18 Nov '10	22 Nov '10	21	20	No		Claudius
2.3.7	Investigate possible routes	Surveyus	20d	7 Oct '10	1 Nov '10	7 Oct '10	1 Nov '10	22	16	No		
2.3.8	Design siege machines	Mechanicus	30d	23 Sep '10	1 Nov '10	20 Sep '10	31 Oct '10	23	20	No		Marcus
2.3.9	Draw up tender for siege machines	Draftus	10d	4 Nov '10	15 Nov '10	1 Nov '10	14 Nov '10	24	23	No		
2.3.10	Design temporary camps	Buildus	30d	23 Sep '10	1 Nov '10	26 Nov '10	15 Nov '10	25		No		Hadrian
2.3.11	Draw up tender for siege machines	Draftus	10d	4 Nov '10	15 Nov '10	7 Nov '10	20 Nov '10	26	25	No		
2.3.12	Design river bridges	Buildus	25d	4 Nov '10	15 Nov '10	18 Nov '10	15 Nov '10	27		No		Neptune
2.3.13	Draw up tender for river bridge parts	Draftus	10d	4 Nov '10	15 Nov '10	29 Nov '10	29 Nov '10	28	27	No		
2.3.14	Receive funnel designs	Buildus	0d	23 Sep '10	23 Sep '10	14 Oct '10	14 Oct '10	29		Yes	From Campaign 321 - Gibraltar	Orpheus
2.3.15	Decide how to cross English Channel	Buildus	10d	7 Oct '10	4 Oct '10	14 Oct '10	4 Oct '10	30		No		
2.3.16	Design accepted solution	Buildus	25d	4 Nov '10	8 Nov '10	14 Oct '10	15 Nov '10	31	30	No		
2.3.17	Draw up tender for channel crossing	Draftus	10d	4 Nov '10	15 Nov '10	11 Nov '10	22 Nov '10	32	31FS-5d	No		
2.3.18	Design typical roads	Trafficus	20d	23 Sep '10	18 Oct '10	1 Nov '10	18 Oct '10	33		No		
2.3.19	Plan catering logistics	Feedus	15d	21 Oct '10	8 Nov '10	1 Nov '10	29 Nov '10	34	18	No	Required by Campaign 978 to Abd Mercury	
2.4	Prepare Detailed Investigation Report	Scriptus	15d	4 Nov '10	22 Nov '10	19 Nov '10	9 Dec '10	35	15FS-10d	No		
2.5	Review Detailed Investigation Report	Projex Magna	5d	18 Nov '10	22 Nov '10	3 Dec '10	9 Dec '10	36	35FS-5d	No		
2.6	Refine Detailed Investigation Report	Scriptus	10d	25 Nov '10	6 Dec '10	10 Dec '10	23 Dec '10	37	36	No		
2.7	Sign off Detailed Investigation Report	Projex Magna	5d	9 Dec '10	13 Dec '10	24 Dec '10	30 Dec '10	38	37	No		
2.8	Prepare Business Case	Abacus	25d	11 Nov '10	13 Dec '10	26 Nov '10	30 Dec '10	39	35FS-10d	No		Sponsus
2.9	Review and obtain Sponsor's approval for	Projex Magna	5d	16 Dec '10	20 Dec '10	31 Dec '10	6 Jan '11	40	39,38	No		
2.1	Submit Business Case to Senate for Inves	Projex Magna	10d	23 Dec '10	3 Jan '11	7 Jan '11	20 Jan '11	41	40	No		Sponsus
2.11	Development Gate	Projex Magna	0d	3 Jan '11	3 Jan '11	20 Jan '11	20 Jan '11	42	41	Yes		

Figure 21.6 A typical activity list

Activity list

Purpose

The activity list records all activities associated with the project, i.e. what needs to be done, who is accountable, how long it will take and by when it should be completed. The list is used to identify activities and milestones and to give information on outline plans (Figure 21.6).

When to use

The activity list is best used when drawing up a plan, to aid thinking through the key activities, milestones and their dependencies. It is a simple and useful way of communicating a plan if bar charts or other graphic presentations cannot be prepared.

Completion

This report is for those people who love lists! It is simply a list of the activities and milestones together with the name of the accountable person, duration and dates.

BRITAIN CAMPAIGN - PHASE 1 - PREPARATIONS
* Bar Chart *

Project Manager: Projex Magna
Status as of: 12 Oct '10

Printed on: 12/10/10

No.	Description	Accountability	Start	Finish
1	INITIAL INVESTIGATION	Projex Magna	1 Aug '10	6 Sep '10
2	DETAILED INVESTIGATION STAGE	Projex Magna	9 Sep '10	20 Jan '11
2.1	Assemble Team	Projex Magna	9 Sep '10	20 Sep '10
2.2	Prepare Development Definition	Publius	23 Sep '10	25 Oct '10
2.3	Undertake Detailed Investigation	Projex Magna	20 Sep '10	29 Nov '10
2.3.1	Locate mapping of Gaul	Surveyus	23 Sep '10	4 Oct '10
2.3.2	Maps of Gaul available	Surveyus	4 Oct '10	4 Oct '10
2.3.3	Do reconnaisance	Surveyus	14 Oct '10	8 Nov '10
2.3.4	Estimate enemy troop numbers	Countus	28 Oct '10	15 Nov '10
2.3.5	Define number of legions required	Countus	4 Nov '10	15 Nov '10
2.3.6	Prepare recruitment plan	Countus	18 Nov '10	22 Nov '10
2.3.7	Investigate possible routes	Surveyus	7 Oct '10	1 Nov '10
2.3.8	Design siege machines	Mechanicus	20 Sep '10	31 Oct '10
2.3.9	Draw up tender for siege machines	Draftus	1 Nov '10	14 Nov '10
2.3.10	Design temporary camps	Buildus	26 Sep '10	6 Nov '10
2.3.11	Draw up tender for siege machines	Draftus	7 Nov '10	20 Nov '10
2.3.12	Design river bridges	Buildus	14 Oct '10	15 Nov '10
2.3.13	Draw up tender for river bridge parts	Draftus	18 Nov '10	29 Nov '10
2.3.14	Receive tunnel designs	Buildus	14 Oct '10	14 Oct '10
2.3.15	Decide how to cross English Channel	Buildus	23 Sep '10	4 Oct '10

Months: Aug Sep Oct Nov Dec Jan Feb Mar Apr May

From Campaign 321 - Gibralter

Activity | Actual | Milestone | Completed milestone | Input

File: Romans Project   Page 1   Product Programmes

Figure 21.7 A typical bar chart

Bar chart

Purpose

The bar chart (or Gantt chart) is a representation of the schedule plan in graph form. It shows the duration of activities against a timescale. It also defines who is accountable for each activity and work package and the place of each activity in the work breakdown structure (Figure 21.7).

When to use

The bar chart is probably the most effective way of communicating a schedule. For this reason it is highly recommended for inclusion in the project plan and for use in communicating plans whenever possible.

Completion

Bar charts can be produced manually or by using computer software, at summary and detailed levels. They are produced from the activity list once the start and end dates of each activity have been calculated. The left-hand portion contains a reference number, description, duration, the name of the person accountable, and the start and finish dates. The right-hand part shows a bar against a timescale which spans from the start to the finish of the activity. Milestones (dates for key events) are shown as diamonds. Dependencies from outside the project are shown as down arrows.

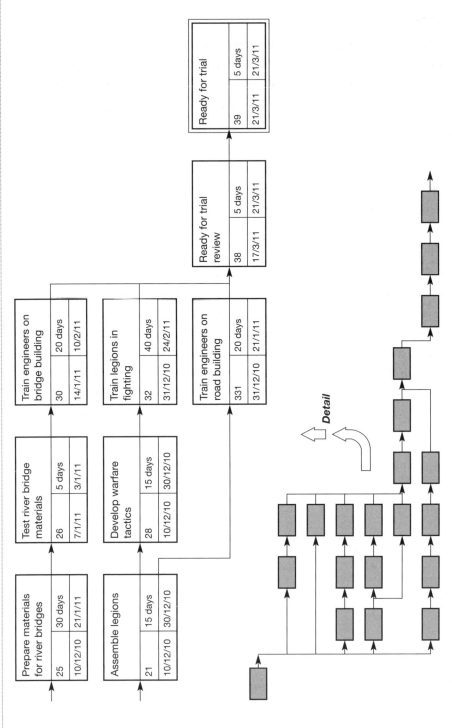

Figure 21.8 A typical network diagram

The boxes in the network diagram contain:

Prepare materials for river bridges			Test river bridge materials			Train engineers on bridge building		
25	30 days		26	5 days		30	20 days	
10/12/10	21/1/11		7/1/11	3/1/11		14/1/11	10/2/11	

Assemble legions			Develop warfare tactics			Train legions in fighting		
21	15 days		28	15 days		32	40 days	
10/12/10	30/12/10		10/12/10	30/12/10		31/12/10	24/2/11	

Train engineers on road building		
331	20 days	
31/12/10	21/1/11	

Ready for trial review			Ready for trial		
38	5 days		39	5 days	
17/3/11	21/3/11		21/3/11	21/3/11	

Detail

Network diagram

Purpose

The network diagram is probably the most useful but least used way of depicting a project. It is used to show the logical relationship (dependencies) between different deliverables, activities and work. Network diagrams can be used for identifying natural checkpoints in the project as the network will show where various strands come together. They are invaluable for calculating project float and determining the critical path (Figure 21.8).

> *The network diagram is probably the most useful but least used way of depicting a project.*

When to use

A network should be used whenever a complex sequence of events needs to be shown clearly. This is particularly useful when first drawing up a plan, as it is not always obvious what the logical dependencies are. It is also a useful format to use at planning workshops, for determining dependencies between activities, before any idea of timescale/duration has been gained.

Completion

The plan is developed by mapping out those activities which can be performed in parallel and those which must be carried out sequentially. Activities or milestones are represented in boxes and their relationships with preceding and succeeding activities are shown using arrows. An activity may not start until its predecessor has been finished. This is called a 'precedence network' and is the most versatile method for depicting the logical sequence within a project. For complex projects they are best prepared using project planning software.

For planning workshops the activities, milestones and deliverables may be written on Post-It Notes. Then, starting at the end of the project with the final deliverable, you need to ask yourself: 'What would I need to have in place in order to achieve this?' This sequence is repeated until the start point in the project is reached (see Project Workout 21.1 on p. 345).

BRITAIN CAMPAIGN - PHASE 1 - PREPARATIONS
* Update Form *

Project Manager: Projex Magna
Status as of: 12 Oct '10

Printed on: 12/10/10

No.	Description	Accountability	C or S	Dur	Actual Start	Actual Finish	Expected Finish	Fcast Start	Fcast Finish	Plan Finish	Comments
2	DETAILED INVESTIGATION STAGE	Projex Magna									
2.3	Undertake Detailed Investigation	Project Magna		96d	9 Sep '10	NA	NA	9 Sep '10	20 Jan '11	3 Jan '11	
2.3.3	Do reconnaissance	Surveyus		51d	20 Sep '10	NA	NA	20 Sep '10	29 Nov '10	15 Nov '10	
2.3.4	Estimate enemy troop numbers	Countus		20d	NA	NA	NA	14 Oct '10	8 Nov '10	18 Oct '10	
2.3.5	Define number of legions required	Countus		15d	NA	NA	NA	28 Oct '10	15 Nov '10	25 Oct '10	
2.3.7	Investigate possible routes	Surveyus		10d	NA	NA	NA	4 Nov '10	15 Nov '10	1 Nov '10	
2.3.8	Design siege machines	Mechanicus	S	20d	7 Oct '10	NA	NA	7 Oct '10	1 Nov '10	1 Nov '10	
2.3.9	Draw up tender for siege machines	Draftus		30d	20 Sep '10	NA	NA	20 Sep '10	31 Oct '10	16 Nov '10	
2.3.10	Design temporary camps	Buildus	S	10d	NA	NA	NA	1 Nov '10	14 Nov '10	1 Nov '10	
2.3.11	Draw up tender for siege machines	Draftus		30d	26 Sep '10	NA	NA	26 Sep '10	6 Nov '10	15 Nov '10	
2.3.12	Design river bridges	Buildus		25d	NA	NA	NA	7 Nov '10	20 Nov '10	1 Nov '10	
2.3.14	Receive tunnel designs	Buildus		0d	NA	NA	NA	14 Oct '10	14 Oct '10	23 Sep '10	From Campaign 321 - Gibralter
2.3.16	Design accepted solution	Buildus		25d	NA	NA	NA	14 Oct '10	15 Nov '10	8 Nov '10	
2.3.17	Draw up tender for channel crossing	Draftus		10d	NA	NA	NA	11 Nov '10	22 Nov '10	15 Nov '10	
2.3.18	Design typical roads	Trafficus	S	20d	23 Sep '10	NA	NA	23 Sep '10	18 Oct '10	18 Oct '10	Required by Campaign 976 to Albania
2.3.19	Plan catering logistics	Feedus		15d	NA	NA	NA	11 Nov '10	29 Nov '10	8 Nov '10	

File: Romans Project   Page 1   Product Programmes

Figure 21.9 A typical update form

Report used to update the forecast

Update form

Purpose

The update form is used to collect data for tracking progress on the project (Figure 21.9).

When to use

The form is used every time the project manager wishes to check on progress. This should be at least monthly, at month-end, but for many projects it is desirable to update the project weekly or fortnightly.

Completion

The form comprises a filtered selection of unstarted and incomplete activities within a given date range. It has the following columns:

- the reference number of each activity;
- activity description;
- C column (complete) and S column (started);
- the actual start and finish dates;
- the expected finish date (for started activities);
- the forecast start and finish dates calculated the last time the project was updated;
- the baseline planned finish date (as a reminder);
- a comment column to record pertinent notes.

The person responsible for reporting progress:

- enters S for all started activities in the 'S' column and the actual start date and expected finish date in the relevant columns;
- enters C for all completed activities in the 'C' column, giving actual start and actual finish dates.

If it is apparent that forecast dates for future activities are wrong, sufficient information should be given to enable these to be replanned. Those activities which should have started, but have not, should be slipped forward to start on the update date – their finish date will also slip unless the duration is changed.

Figure 21.10 A typical management summary

Reports used for progress reporting

Management summary

Purpose

The management summary is a concise presentation of the progress bar chart (Figure 21.10) aimed at providing a summary report on project progress.

When to use

This format is best used for reporting to project boards, project sponsors and other stakeholders.

Completion

The report contains only the specific lines of information (summary, detail or milestone) that you wish to present. The report should be kept as short as possible, concentrating on the project life cycle stages, key work packages and milestones.

BRITAIN CAMPAIGN - PHASE 1 - PREPARATIONS
* Progress Bar Chart *

Project Manager: Prolex Magna
Status as of: 12 Oct '10

Printed on: 12/10/10

No.	Description	Accountability	Sched' Start	Sched' Finish
2.3.16	Design accepted solution	Buildus	14 Oct '10	15 Nov '10
2.3.17	Draw up tender for channel crossing	Draftus	11 Nov '10	22 Nov '10
2.3.18	Design typical roads	Trafficus	23 Sep '10	18 Oct '10
2.3.19	Plan catering logistics	Feedus	11 Nov '10	29 Nov '10
2.4	Prepare Detailed Investigation Report	Scriptus	19 Nov '10	9 Dec '10
2.5	Review Detailed Investigation Report	Projex Magna	3 Dec '10	9 Dec '10
2.6	Refine Detailed Investigation Report	Scriptus	10 Dec '10	23 Dec '10
2.7	Sign off Detailed Investigation Report	Projex Magna	24 Dec '10	30 Dec '10
2.8	Prepare Business Case	Abacus	26 Nov '10	30 Dec '10
2.9	Review and obtain Sponsor's approval for Business Case	Projex Magna	31 Dec '10	6 Jan '11
2.10	Submit Business Case to Senate for Investment Review and to obtain	Projex Magna	7 Jan '11	20 Jan '11
2.11	*Development Gate*	*Projex Magna*	20 Jan '11	20 Jan '11
3	**DEVELOP & TEST STAGE**	**Projex Magna**	**21 Jan '11**	**7 Apr '11**
3.1	Assemble legions	Countus	21 Jan '11	10 Feb '11
3.2	**Siege Machines**	**Mecanicus**	**21 Jan '11**	**17 Feb '11**
3.2.1	Build siege machines	Testus	21 Jan '11	17 Feb '11
3.2.2	Test siege machines	Mecanicus	4 Feb '11	10 Feb '11
3.3	**Materials Management**	**Buildus**	**21 Jan '11**	**3 Mar '11**
3.3.1	Prepare materials for temporary camps	Buildus	21 Jan '11	10 Feb '11
3.3.2	Test camp materials	Campus	4 Feb '11	10 Feb '11

Required by Campaign 978 to Albania

	Planned activity	In progress		Forecast milestone
Noncritical		Complete		Completed milestone
Critical		Plan Milestone		Input from other project

File: Romans Project

Page 2

Product Programmes

Figure 21.11 A typical progress bar chart

Progress bar chart

Purpose

The progress bar chart is a more complex version of Figure 21.8 which is used to compare forecasts against the agreed plan and hence highlight variances (Figure 21.11).

The progress bar chart shows the current forecast dates for each activity and milestone compared with the baseline plan. The dates given are the actual or current forecast dates. Comments from the progress 'update form' (see Figure 21.9) may be included against any item.

When to use

The bar chart is probably the most effective way of communicating a schedule. Progress reports may be made more concise if a bar chart is used to detail progress rather than progress being described in text.

Completion

Bar charts can be produced manually or by using computer software at summary/outline and detailed levels. They are produced from the activity list once the start and end times of each activity have been calculated. The left-hand portion contains a reference number, description, duration, the initials of the person accountable, and the start and finish dates. The right-hand part shows a bar against a timescale which spans from the start to the finish of the activity. Milestones (dates for key events) are shown as diamonds. The plan dates are shown as a line below the current forecast so that a visual appreciation of slippage is readily apparent. Figure 21.3 describes how to read the bar chart.

More complex but informative versions of the progress bar chart can be developed which show the 'float' available for each activity and dependencies between activities.

Slippage report

Purpose

This report is used to focus attention on activities which are likely to be late. This enables the project manager to take whatever action is necessary to bring the project back on schedule. The objective is not to use the report as a tool to 'punish' those accountable for slippage, but rather to focus attention on putting things right. With this in mind, the slippage report details only incomplete activities (Figure 21.12).

When to use

This report is useful for identifying those current and future activities which are forecast as slipping and hence focus attention on remedying the situation. It is best used for plans of more than 50 activities when a software package can extract the 'offending' activities automatically. If you are using critical chain schedule management this report will be replaced by a buffer report (see Figure 21.17).

Completion

The report is compiled by extracting the late (and unfinished) activities from the updated activity list. Most computer project-planning packages have routines for preparing this type of report.

BRITAIN CAMPAIGN - PHASE 1 - PREPARATIONS

Project Manager: Projex Magna * Slippage Report *

Status as of: 12 Oct '10 Report printed on: 12/10/10

WBS	Description	Accountability	Planned Finish	Scheduled Finish	Slippage (days)
2	DETAILED INVESTIGATION STAGE	Projex Magna	3 Jan '11	20 Jan '11	11d
2.3	Undertake Detailed Investigation	Projex Magna	15 Nov '10	29 Nov '10	10d
2.3.3	Do reconnaisance	Surveyus	18 Oct '10	8 Nov '10	15d
2.3.4	Estimate enemy troop numbers	Countus	25 Oct '10	15 Nov '10	15d
2.3.5	Define number of legions required	Countus	25 Oct '10	15 Nov '10	15d
2.3.6	Prepare recruitment plan	Countus	1 Nov '10	22 Nov '10	15d
2.3.10	Design temporary camps	Buildus	1 Nov '10	6 Nov '10	3d
2.3.11	Draw up tender for siege machines	Draftus	15 Nov '10	20 Nov '10	3d
2.3.12	Design river bridges	Buildus	1 Nov '10	15 Nov '10	10d
2.3.13	Draw up tender for river bridge parts	Draftus	15 Nov '10	29 Nov '10	10d
2.3.14	Receive tunnel designs	Buildus	23 Sep '10	14 Oct '10	15d
2.3.16	Design accepted solution	Buildus	8 Nov '10	15 Nov '10	5d
2.3.17	Draw up tender for channel crossing	Draftus	15 Nov '10	22 Nov '10	5d
2.3.19	Plan catering logistics	Feedus	8 Nov '10	29 Nov '10	15d

File: Romans Project	Page 1	Product Programmes

Figure 21.12 A typical slippage report

Milestone report

Purpose

The milestone report shows progress against the key targets for the project. These are items which should be specifically mentioned in the project documentation (Figure 21.13).

When to use

This format is an excellent, non-graphical way for communicating progress and expectations on the timing of key milestones such as the delivery dates for products, or interface dates with other projects.

Completion

The report is presented in tabular form showing the milestone description, the planned date, the current forecast of the date and the actual date achieved. The final column indicates the slippage (how late) of a milestone compared to the plan. The report is made up of all those activities of zero duration from the activity list which the project manager wishes to highlight. Most computer project-planning packages have routines for preparing this type of report.

BRITAIN CAMPAIGN - PHASE 1 - PREPARATIONS

Project Manager: Projex Magna   * Milestone Report *

Status as of: 12 Oct '10   Printed on: 12/10/10

WBS	Description	Planned Finish	Forecast Finish	Actual Finish	Slippage	Comment
2	DETAILED INVESTIGATION STAGE	3 Jan '11	20 Jan '11	NA	11d	
2.3	Undertake Detailed Investigation	15 Nov '10	29 Nov '10	NA	10d	
2.3.2	Maps of Gaul available	4 Oct '10	4 Oct '10	4 Oct '10	0d	
2.3.14	Receive tunnel designs	23 Sep '10	14 Oct '10	NA	15d	From Campaign 321 - Gibraltar
2.11	Development Gate	3 Jan '11	20 Jan '11	NA	11d	
3	DEVELOP & TEST STAGE	21 Mar '11	7 Apr '11	NA	11d	
3.3	Materials Management	14 Feb '11	3 Mar '11	NA	11d	
3.3.5	Material test certificates ready	7 Feb '11	24 Feb '11	NA	11d	
3.7	Campaign catering	7 Mar '11	7 Mar '11	NA	0d	
3.7.3	Place contract for food supplies	17 Jan '11	3 Feb '11	NA	11d	
3.10	Ready for Trial	14 Feb '11	3 Mar '11	NA	11d	
4	TRIAL STAGE	14 Mar '11	31 Mar '11	NA	11d	
4.3	Ready for Service	14 Mar '11	31 Mar '11	NA	11d	
5	RELEASE STAGE	14 Apr '11	29 Apr '11	NA	11d	
5.2	Quick March!	21 Mar '11	7 Apr '11	NA	11d	
5.5	Project Completed	14 Apr '11	29 Apr '11	NA	11d	

File: Romans Project	Page 1	Product Programmes

Figure 21.13 A typical milestone report

Project Manager: Projex Magna
Status as of: 12 Oct '10

* Deliverable Report *

Printed on: 12/10/10

WBS	Description	Accountable	Planned Finish	Forecast Finish	Review by:	Sign off by:	Comment
2	**DETAILED INVESTIGATION STAGE**	**Projex Magna**	3 Jan '11	20 Jan '11			
2.2	Prepare Development Definition	Publius	25 Oct '10	14 Oct '10	Project Team	Sponsus	
2.3	**Undertake Detailed Investigation**	**Projex Magna**	15 Nov '10	29 Nov '10			
2.3.2	Maps of Gaul available	Surveyus	4 Oct '10	4 Oct '10	Vercingetorix, Flavius, Antonio	Cartus	
2.3.6	Prepare recruitment plan	Countus	1 Nov '10	22 Nov '10	Lucretia, Vespasian	Claudius	
2.3.8	Design siege machines	Mechanicus	1 Nov '10	31 Oct '10	Hannibal Minor, Romulus	Marcus	
2.3.10	Design temporary camps	Buildus	1 Nov '10	6 Nov '10	Flavia, Sextus	Hadrian	
2.3.12	Design river bridges	Buildus	1 Nov '10	15 Nov '10	Hannibal Minor, Romulus	Neptune	
2.3.14	Receive tunnel designs	Buildus	23 Sep '10	14 Oct '10	Vercingetorix, Flavius, Antonio	Orpheus	From Campaign 321 - Gibraltar
2.3.18	Design typical roads	Trafficus	18 Oct '10	18 Oct '10	Vercingetorix, Flavius, Antonio	Mercury	Required by Campaign 978 to Albania
2.7	Sign off Detailed Investigation Report	**Projex Magna**	13 Dec '10	30 Dec '10	Project Team	Sponsus	
2.9	Review and obtain Sponsor's approval for Business Case	**Projex Magna**	20 Dec '10	6 Jan '11	Project Team, the Senate, Abacus	Sponsus	
3	**DEVELOP & TEST STAGE**	**Projex Magna**					
3.2	**Siege Machines**	Mecanicus	21 Mar '11	7 Apr '11			
3.2.1	Build siege machines	Testus	31 Jan '11	17 Feb '11	Hannibal Minor, Romulus	Marcus	
3.3	**Materials Management**	Buildus	14 Feb '11	3 Mar '11	Hannibal Minor, Romulus		
3.3.5	Material test certificates ready	Buildus	7 Feb '11	24 Feb '11	Hannibal Minor, Romulus	Neptune	
3.4	**Boats**	Buildus	7 Mar '11	24 Mar '11			
3.4.1	Build boats	Floata	7 Mar '11	24 Mar '11	Hannibal Minor, Romulus	Neptune	
3.5	Develop warfare tactics	Tacitus	24 Jan '11	10 Feb '11	Mark Anthony, Octavian	Julius Caesar (retired)	
3.7	**Campaign catering**	Feedus	7 Mar '11	7 Mar '11			
3.7.4	Obtain for food for troops	Feedus	7 Mar '11	7 Mar '11	Hannibal, Quintus, Septimus	Remus	
3.9	Ready for Trial Review	**Projex Magna**	14 Feb '11	3 Mar '11	Project Team	Sponsus	
4	**TRIAL STAGE**	**Quintus Sextus**	14 Mar '11	31 Mar '11			

Figure 21.14 A typical deliverable report

Deliverable report

Purpose

The deliverable report lists all the key deliverables from the project stating who is accountable for preparing them reviewing them and finally signing them off. These are items which should be specifically mentioned in the project documentation (Figure 21.14).

When to use

This format is used when the project manager wants to focus on the deliverables and be explicit about who is accountable for the quality aspects for each.

Unless we know who is to review a deliverable and sign it off, we cannot be certain that what is being produced is really fit for purpose.

Completion

The report is an extract from the full project plan with those activities and milestones relating to deliverables filtered out to produce a listing. Most computer software packages can be customised to do this.

So why are we nearly always late?

'How does a project get to be late? … one day at a time.'

F BROOKS

Despite decades of project management experience, backed up by ever more sophisticated technology, projects are still late. Unless, of course, the timescales set were so generous that even a donkey could have brought it in on time. That, however, is hardly a situation most business managers will find themselves in. When really questioned about project timescales most people will admit that speed is not necessarily the most important aspect but *predictability* is. If you are developing a new product, most marketing and sales people would rather have it in four months' time, if promised in four months' time (and working) than have it in three months' time when promised it in two. Once you have achieved predictability, you can concentrate on reducing the overall time taken.

We have seen that a project's duration is basically the sum of the guesses of the durations of those activities on the critical path. This is the definition of critical path. We decide the project approach using network planning and guess (some guesses are very sophisticated) how long each activity will take, bearing in mind the resources needed to work on it. It's all very logical. From here on, human behaviour takes over. If I am a project team member, which of the following should I ask the project manager to put in the plan:

- a short duration I am unlikely to meet;
- a medium duration I might meet if I'm lucky;
- a prudent (longer) duration I'll probably meet?

Most people will choose the last of these – they like to be considered reliable. What then happens is they:

- start work on the activity as late as possible as more 'urgent work' is needed first (it's just as well they put in a prudent estimate);
- work on other projects at the same time, juggling between the frantic exhortations of the different project managers and their line manager;
- have a meeting cancelled and so actually start work and finish it EARLY. But they don't tell anyone, just in case they are expected to be so fortunate next time, i.e. late handovers.

In short this one activity is protected by a safety margin which the team member's experience shows is needed. In fact, all activities have their in-built safety. The major drawback is, from an organisation's viewpoint, it doesn't matter whether a particular activity is late or not. What matters is when the project as a whole delivers and bene-fits start to flow. Conceivably a project could be 95 per cent on time and grossly late. Safety is not additive if it is wasted. Statistically, projects plans built this way are more likely to be late than on time. They will hardly ever be early!

> *It doesn't matter whether a particular activity is late or not. What matters is when the project as a whole delivers and benefits start to flow.*

The critical chain – a solution?

In his book *Critical Chain*, Eli Goldratt proposes a solution to this problem. Rather than add safety into each activity, as described here, add it in a single lump at the end of the project (Figure 21.15). In practical terms he says:

- cut the durations given by the team in half;
- at the end of the project, add a safety time equal to half the sum of the safety times you trimmed.

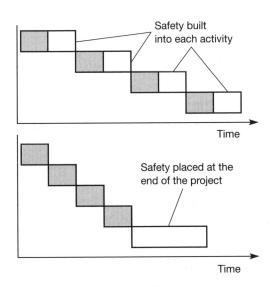

Figure 21.15 Putting safety where it counts

Removing the safety from each activity and placing it at the end of the project enables you to use it when you need to rather than have it wasted by the student syndrome (i.e. doing work at last minute), multi-tasking or late handovers.

In this way you can place the safety in a position where it really counts, at the end of the project, where you can use it.

In this way you can place the safety in a position where it really counts, at the end of the project, where you can use it.

However, you will have a number of challenges:

- Why should anyone accept you trimming their time estimates? Be very clear that you are adding half of it back at the end of the project.
- You'll need to be very used to activities being 'late'. In fact, 'late' may no longer be a useful word and this may have implications on reporting.
- You will need to become used to tracking projects by measuring how much safety is consumed rather than by activity completion alone.
- You will need to resist senior managers cutting the safety from the end and thus dooming you to certain failure.

You will also need to encourage three behaviours:

- Stop the student syndrome (i.e. doing work at the last minute).
- End multi-tasking.
- Encourage handover as soon as the activity is finished.

END OF THE PROJECT?

The safety should not actually be put at the end of the project. It should be placed prior to the point in the project when you start earning benefits. For most projects following the project framework in Part Two, this is at the Release Gate. The work beyond this, while essential, is not critical to immediate benefit realisation.

This method relies on you producing a good network diagram and resourcing the schedule in a similar way to traditional critical path methods. It differs, however, in:

- choosing a critical route through the project which includes activities which are either on the critical path or which form a constraint due to resource contention;
- the choice made for activity duration and where any safety is placed.

As we have seen, safety is placed towards the end of the project. This is called a **project buffer**. However, if a project has a network with several feeders, you will need to protect the critical chain from delays in incoming activities. **Feeder buffers** are used for this. A project buffer protects the entire project from any delay in the critical chain activities. The feeder buffers protect the critical chain from delays on non-critical chain activities (Figure 21.16). The project manager uses a buffer report as the key monitoring tool (Figure 21.17).

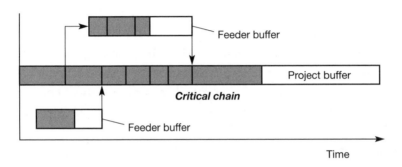

Figure 21.16 Project and feeder buffers

A project buffer protects the entire project from any delay in the critical chain activities. The feeder buffers protect the critical chain from delays on non-critical chain activities.

Ref	Buffer name	Buffer end	Buffer length	% Buffer used	RAG
56	FB| Training agreed	2 Feb 2010	6 days	100%	Red
62	FB| Unit test 5	27 Feb 2010	8 days	73%	Red
109	PB| Ready for Service	21 May 2010	22 days	36%	Amber
87	FB| Acceptance	24 Apr 2010	12 days	31%	Green
48	FB| Roll out hardware	15 Jan 2010	6 days	0%	Green
91	FB| Integration test	13 Mar 2010	10 days	0%	Green

Figure 21.17 A typical report using critical chain schedule management

Rather than concentrate on activity dates, the report shows each buffer by type (FB = feeder buffer; PB = project buffer), its length and how much has been used. From this, the project manager can pinpoint the parts of the schedule which require attention. A simple RAG status helps summarise the status, e.g. Green more than 66% of buffer remaining; Red less than 33% of buffer remaining; Amber 33–66% remaining.

Steps in the critical chain

1 Identify the constraint

The critical chain is the sequence of dependent events that prevent the project from being completed in a shorter interval, given finite resources. For a project, the critical chain is the constraint. Plan the network, resource the network, ensure that the activities have safety built in. Schedule the network with everything as late as possible.

2 Exploit the constraint

You need to ensure those activities on the critical chain have the most effort applied to them and that people hand off their work to the next person as soon as they are finished. Also, those taking over need to be warned and so be ready to accept the handover (this is called a resource buffer or flag). You also need to protect the entire critical chain with a safety margin (the project buffer) towards the end of the project.

3 Subordinate every other activity

Where other activities join the critical chain, protect them from delays by introducing feeder buffers.

4 Elevate the constraint

Apply more of the right resources so that key activities within the critical chain can be undertaken in parallel or in a shorter time.

5 Begin again?

Having elevated the constraint, it is probable that the critical chain will have moved. You could therefore start the process again. However, in practice this will not usually create significant gains for you unless you have created a very significant change. Generally, it is better to stick to the plan, the inefficiencies in realigning the project team to understand the new plan will far outweigh most other gains. The exception to this is when approaching the RED zone in your project buffer – you will need to take action and this could be one option to investigate.

The steps outlined are a central part of applying the Theory of Constraints (TOC). A full explanation of critical chain schedule management in both single and multiproject environments is to be found in *The Critical Chain* by Eli Goldratt (North River Press, 1997).

Managing the Finances

Just as a schedule plan is used as the baseline for measuring progress in terms of 'time', the financial plan is the basis for measuring costs and financial benefits.

'We haven't the money, so we've got to think.'

LORD RUTHERFORD, 1871–1937

- **Plan in summary for the full project.**
- **Base your costs on the same work breakdown as your schedule.**
- **Estimate in detail before you start work on the next stage.**
- **Once a budget is agreed, baseline it.**
- **Keep your eye on the future – forecast benefits and costs regularly.**

The financial plan

After managing time, management of the finances is the next most important and fundamental aspect of project management. Without a good schedule plan it is impossible to have a reliable financial plan. However, while the schedule is the aspect of a project most visible to outsiders, cost is often the most visible to insiders, such as the management team – sometimes it is the only aspect they see (or want to see!).

At a simple level, a financial plan will tell you:

- what each stage and work package in the project costs;
- who is accountable for those costs;
- the financial benefits deriving from the project;
- who is accountable for the realisation of those benefits;
- financial commitments made;
- cash flow;
- financial authorisation given.

In addition, some organisations also derive the net effect of the project on their balance sheet and profit and loss account.

Just as the schedule plan is used as the baseline for measuring progress in terms of 'time', the financial plan is the basis for measuring costs and financial benefits. Many of the other principles I have already explained on schedule management are also applicable to the management of finances. Schedule and cost plans should share the same work breakdown structure (WBS) (see p. 141). By doing this you ensure that:

- accountability for both the schedule and cost resides with the same person;
- there is no overlap, hence double counting of costs;
- there is no 'gap', i.e. missing costs.

In practice, you will develop the financial plan to a lesser level of work breakdown than you would the schedule plan.

The financial plan, like the schedule plan, is developed in summary for the full project and in detail for the next stage. There is little point in developing an 'accurate' and detailed financial plan on the back of an unstable schedule plan. No matter to what level of granularity you take the calculations, they will be fundamentally inaccurate. You should take the level of accuracy and confidence forward with the schedule and related costs matching.

The costs are influenced by the following, which you must take into account when drawing up your plan:

- the scope of the project;
- the approach you take to the project;
- the timescale to complete the project;
- the risks associated with the project.

Financial management controls

Financial management of a project comprises:

- estimating the costs and benefits (preparing the financial plan);
- obtaining authorisation to spend funds;
- recording actual costs, committed costs;
- forecasting future costs and cash flow;
- reporting.

This is illustrated in Figure 22.1 and done in the context of the project control cycle. Tracking progress toward your objective is essential. If you don't do it you simply won't know how much the project will cost. The control cycle is exactly the same as that used for schedule management and is shown in Figure 22.2: once a financial plan has been agreed, it is necessary to measure progress against the plan, reforecast to the end, note any variances and take steps to bring the project back within budget if need be.

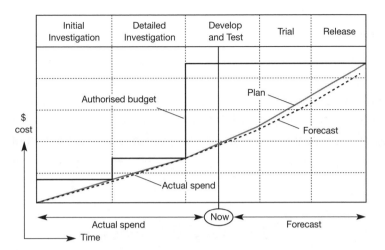

Figure 22.1 Project costs

This figure shows cumulative spend for a typical project, which includes the sum actually spent plus the forecast to completion. This can be compared against the plan (or budget). In the example, the project is forecast to be completed slightly below budget. Also shown is the authorised budget. This goes up in steps. At first a small amount of funding is given to undertake the initial investigation only. This is then increased, based on the results of the initial investigation, to cover the cost of the detailed investigation. Finally, a full business case provides the basis to authorise the remaining funds to complete the Development and Test, Trial and Release Stages.

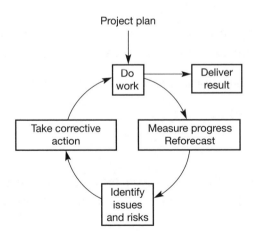

Figure 22.2 Project control cycle

The project control cycle comprises doing the work as set out in your plan, identifying any risks, opportunities or issues and taking corrective action to keep the project on track. From time to time, results, in the form of deliverables, are generated.
(Copyright © PA Consulting Group, London.)

BOOKKEEPING!

You should distinguish between the management of costs from a management accounting perspective and from a financial perspective The latter relates to 'bookkeeping' and where the transactions appear in the formal accounts. In the management of projects, this is of little or no use. Managing the actual spend and cash flow provides far greater control.

Estimating the costs

'A little inaccuracy sometimes saves tons of explanation.'

SAKI

Your cost estimates should be based on the work scope and schedule plan defined in the project definition. You should use the same work breakdown structure as the schedule plan and estimate to the same level of accuracy (summary versus detail).

Your estimate should be made up of:

- the cost of using your own employees;
- the cost of external purchases made as a result of the project.

The overall cost plan should be built up from three elements:

- the base estimate;
- scope reserve;
- contingency.

The base estimate is the total of costs for all the activities you have identified, including the cost of your own employees' time and all external purchases.

The scope reserve is an estimate of what else your experience and common sense tells you needs to be done, but has not yet been explicitly identified. This can be very large: for example, the scope reserve required in software projects can be as high as 50 per cent of the base estimate.

The authority to use 'scope reserve' is normally delegated to the project manager who should use formal change control to move funds from 'scope reserve' to 'base estimate'.

Contingency is included in the estimate to take account of the unexpected, i.e. risks. It is *not* there to compensate for poor estimating. If a risk does not occur, the money put aside as contingency should not be spent. For this reason, the authorisation for spending contingency rests with the project sponsor. Again, formal change control should be used to move the costs from 'contingency' to 'base estimate'.

The proportion of your estimate divided between these elements will alter as the project moves through its life cycle stages. You should expect a higher proportion of scope reserve and contingency in the early stages than in the later stages. The accuracy of estimates also alters depending on the life cycle stage of the project. Figure 22.3 shows that in the earlier stages you expect the bulk of the cost to be 'soft' except for the next stage. The next stage should be a 'hard' estimate. This matches the principle of summary and detail planning. Summary plans tend to be soft, detail plans hard.

A soft estimate is one to which only a low level of confidence can be placed.

A hard estimate is one in which you have high confidence.

Regardless of whether your estimates are soft or hard it is important that you state any assumptions, constraints, or qualifications you have. These should be recorded in Part 1 of your business case (see p. 294).

Don't be driven solely by bookkeeping

Copyright © 1997 Robert Buttrick

	Initial Investigation	Detailed Investigation	Develop and Test	Trial	Release
At Initial Investigation Gate	Soft	None	None	None	None
At Detailed Investigation Gate	ACTUAL	Hard	Soft	Soft	Soft
At Development Gate	ACTUAL	ACTUAL	Hard	Hard	Hard
At Trial Gate	ACTUAL	ACTUAL	ACTUAL	Hard	Hard
At Ready for Service Gate	ACTUAL	ACTUAL	ACTUAL	ACTUAL	Hard

Contingency

Scope Reserve

Base Estimate

ACTUAL COST

Figure 22.3 Estimating accuracy
In the earlier stages you should expect the bulk of the cost to be 'soft' except for the next stage. The next stage should always be a 'hard' estimate.

Authorisation to spend funds

All organisations have rules which prescribe who has the authority to spend money. If you are a subsidiary, such rules may be imposed on you by your parent organisation. Such processes can be onerous and time consuming if not matched to the project process you are using. As a minimum you should ensure that the timing of financial authorisation, as laid out in your finance processes, matches the gates in your project framework.

Each of the gates in the project framework offers the opportunity to allocate funds to the project. You should allocate a limited amount of money at the very start of the project (Initial Investigation Gate) to investigate the proposal so that an informed decision on whether to proceed can be made later at the Detailed Investigation Gate. Subsequently, further funds can be allocated on a stage-by-stage basis until the project is completed.

Alternatively, it may be more convenient to allocate funds for more than one stage, thus avoiding the need to obtain authorisation a number of times and saving time on your projects. If this is done it is still part of the project sponsor's and project manager's accountabilities to undertake the gate reviews to check on the on-going viability of the project. Just because you've been given the money, it doesn't mean that you continue blindly.

For long stages it may be prudent to hold back full authorisation and introduce intermediate review points, when the project is

> *Just because you've been given the money, it doesn't mean that you continue blindly.*

reassessed prior to further funding being authorised. Such points may conveniently be prior to major commitments, such as letting a contract.

The project framework will work for whichever way you choose to arrange fund authorisation. The key is to ensure that such authorisation processes:

- are consistent with the principles of the project framework;
- concentrate only on substantive issues;
- are not too lengthy;
- do not duplicate other reviews or approvals.

The decision-making approach outlined in Chapter 3 (p. 57) poses three questions:

- Is the project on its own viable?
- What is its priority relative to other projects?
- Is funding available?

The control document (Business Case) used at the Detailed Investigation Gate and at the Development Gate is the same one for each question – you do not need to provide a different document for each question. This has two advantages:

- You do not need to write a number of different but similar documents.
- You can be sure that the answer to each question is based on compatible (the same!) information.

In certain circumstances you will be able to delegate all the decisions to the same person or group. This all depends on how you are organised. However, distinguishing between the key questions being addressed will help you concentrate on making the decision. For example, there is no point in prioritising a project (question 2) which cannot stand up in its own right (question 1).

Throughout this book I have distinguished between the terms **approval** and **authorisation**. **Approval** is used when an individual accepts a deliverable as fit for purpose such that the project can continue. **Authorisation** is used for allocating the funding and resources needed to carry on the project and giving the project sponsor and project manager the authority to direct and manage the project.

Approval in some form is always required before any funding is authorised. However, the converse is not true; just because authorisation of funding has been given, it does not mean that *approval* has been given to complete the project. For example, you may have been given, at the Detailed Investigation Gate, full funding to complete a simple project. Work during any of the subsequent stages may uncover issues which cannot be resolved. In which case approval at subsequent gates may not be forthcoming and the project should be terminated. In such circumstances the unused project funds should be returned to their source.

Authorisation of funds is usually based on some form of investment appraisal. I do not intend to go into this in any detail. There are many books which deal with the plethora of methods which can be used. While each organisation will have its preferred approach, the following key points should be considered:

- Investment appraisal should be based on cash flow.
- Discounted cash flow techniques are the most favoured.
- Use least cost development (lowest net present value, NPV) if you must do the project.
- Use internal rate of return for other projects.
- Concentrate on substantive elements only. If a figure is wrong and has no significant impact on the appraisal, don't waste time changing it.
- Use sensitivity analyses liberally – they give you more feel for the project than spurious accuracy in estimates.
- Use scenario analysis to check possible outcomes.

And finally:

- Do not consider financial criteria as sacrosanct. Many projects are worth doing for non-financial reasons because they support your basic strategic direction.
- Some things can't be reduced to financial terms. Just because you can't count them doesn't mean they don't count!

> **Some things can't be reduced to financial terms. Just because you can't count them doesn't mean they don't count!**

Recording actual costs and committed costs

If you are to have any visibility over the cost of your project, you will need to have a system of capturing the costs, from wherever they originate in your organisation and allocating them to the project. Similarly, you will need to have a method of capturing commitments relating to each project (see also p. 265). (Commitments are orders placed and hence the money, although not yet spent, is committed as part of an agreed contract.) If this is to have any meaning costs should be split into:

- money that stays within the organisation (e.g. cost of labour, drawing on internal stores);
- money that leaves the organisation (e.g. paid to contractors, consultants, suppliers).

In cash flow terms this distinction is critical as the former have already been 'bought', but you have not yet decided what project or activity to apply them to. The latter are not spent at all if the project does not proceed.

In addition, it is essential to have the costs captured for each stage of the project so that you can confidently manage actual spend against authorised budget on a stage-by-stage basis. Most mature organisations also capture costs at a lower level in the work breakdown structure than that.

WHAT IF I CANNOT MEASURE COSTS AS YOU SUGGEST?

Having a good project or matrix accounting system is vital if you are to reap the full benefits from business-driven project management. If you are unable to account for costs on a project-by-project basis you will have to rely on conventional cost centre-based accounting or manual processes to maintain control: you have no alternative. This will mean that the balance of power remains firmly with the functions that own those cost centres and away from the project (see Figure 2.11).

It is still well worth using the tools, techniques and guidance given in this book but you will be limited in the depth to which they can be applied and ingrained in your culture. No matter what you as managers say concerning the importance of projects, line managers will pay more attention to their cost centre accounts simply because they are visible.

In Chapter 2, I pointed out that any process sits within a balance of systems, culture and structure. You will therefore need to adapt how you apply the process to meet your system limitations while you drive towards the flexible culture you seek.

Financial reporting

The future is more important than the past. Any money you have already spent is lost and cannot be recovered. For this reason you must not only log what you have actually spent, but also forecast what is yet to be spent. The important figure to concentrate on is 'what the project will have cost when it is completed'.

To arrive at this figure you simply add any costs incurred to date to any cost you have yet to incur. The forecast is simply an estimate of what figures are going to appear on your project account during any particular period. So your forecasts must:

- use the same costing methods as actuals are measured;
- be forecast on at least a stage-by-stage basis;
- be timed to match the actuals (usually a monthly cut-off is used).

Figure 22.4 shows a typical report for building up the forecast.

Organisations, by means of their accounting and operational systems, collect a considerable volume of data. Unless these data are converted into meaningful information, they are useless. Any reports you produce must be aimed at providing useful information which will act as a prompt for action. This implies the reports should be targeted at specific roles within your organisation. As the reports seek to promote action they should be:

- timely;
- as accurate as possible within those time constraints;
- forward looking.

Further, unless individuals involved in collecting the data gain some benefits themselves from them, the quality of the data will erode and the reporting will become useless.

Figure 22.5 is a typical financial report and tells you, in financial terms:

- what has been spent to date;
- the expected outcome for the project;
- the impact on the current financial year;
- the cost of work yet to be done.

In addition, you should have detailed reports which:

- list every transaction/purchase made on the project;
- detail time booked to the project.

Project: YT2Z/Triton 2000
Project Sponsor: Kelly, PJ
Project Manager: Jeffries J

PROJECT – ROLLING COST FORECAST   Period: 4 wks to 28 Oct 2011

$000s	ACTUAL TO DATE F'cast Month	Month	Year	Life	COST FORECAST Oct 11	Nov	Dec	Jan 12	Feb	Mar	Apr	May	Jun	Jul	Aug	Sep	Q3 O-D 12	Q4 J-M 13	Q5 A-J 13	Q6 J-S 13	Beyond	F'cast Outturn
Initial Investigation			53	53																		53
Time costs			50	50																		50
Purchases			3	3																		3
Detailed Investigation	6	7	30	55	6	7	5	5	18	10	4											110
Time costs	5	5	20	40	4	5	5	5	6	8	2											75
Purchases	1	2	10	15	2	2			12	2	2											35
Develop/Test												15	26	33	6	6	13					99
Time costs												5	25	32	5	5	12					84
Purchases												10	1	1	1	1	1					15
Trial																	13	11	2			26
Time costs																	12	10	2			24
Purchases																	1	1				2
Release																			22			22
Time costs																			18			18
Purchases																			4			4
TOTAL COST	6	7	83	108	6	7	5	5	18	10	4	15	26	33	6	6	26	11	24			310
Time cost	5	5	70	90	4	5	5	5	6	8	2	5	25	32	5	5	24	10	20			251
Purchases	1	2	13	18	2	2			12	2	2	10	1	1	1	1	2	1	4			59
CUMULATIVE COST					114	121	126	131	149	159	163	178	204	237	243	249	275	286	310	310	310	310

Annotations:
- *Labour (time) costs are calculated from the 'hours' forecast*
- *For each stage you can see the labour and non-labour costs*
- *Total cost for the project*
- *Total cost for the project*

Figure 22.4 A typical report for building the forecast

This report gives a stage-by-stage summary of the total costs for a project and is ideally suited for building the forecast. For example, the time cost line could be derived from a manpower forecast such as that given in Figure 16.2.

Figure 22.5 The financial report

A report such as this gives you, on a stage-by-stage basis, all the key financial information you should require: actual costs, forecast costs, commitments for the project as a whole and by financial year; it is derived directly from the data in Figure 22.3.

Earned value

Integrating cost and time reporting

One of the difficulties with measuring project costs against planned costs is that, on its own, you can gain very little information from a fact such as: 'At this point in the project we planned to have spent £340,000 but have only spent £250,000.' What does this apparent £90,000 underspend mean?

- Have we underspent and the project is going very well?
- Are we running late, but spending at the correct rate?
- Are we overspending and running late?

From the basic facts I have given you, you cannot tell. Earned value analysis (now called earned value management) was created by the US Department of Defense in the 1960s to help solve this problem and bring greater clarity to measuring the performance of their contractors. The use of this approach is often mandated by government agencies and some multinational organisations when letting contracts and it is in this context you are most likely to find it. It is less apparent in other situations and rarely (if at all) seen practised on an enterprise-wide basis.

The Project Management Institute's glossary defines earned value management (EVM) as: 'A method for integrating scope, schedule and resources and for measuring project performance. It compares the amount of work which was planned with what was actually earned with what was actually spent to determine if cost and schedule performance are as planned.'

I doubt there are many people who can understand that in one reading! Perhaps this inherent complexity is what makes its use so rare except in mandated circumstances and what has led the PMI to replace a plethora of abbreviations (such as BCWS, BCWP, ACWP) with simpler equivalents.

The S-curves

For many organisations, the simple two-line 'S-curve' ('planned cost' and 'actual cost + forecast') shown in Figure 22.1, supplemented by milestone tracking, is sufficient for project tracking purposes. Nevertheless, as more organisations automate their project management environments it is possible that earned value techniques could become more common. Whilst Figure 22.1 uses only two lines for cost tracking, EVM adds a third line, which shows the earned value of work completed to date. The earned value line is costed using the same basis as used in the plan. Thus if work package A is planned to cost $25,000, once it is completed, the earned value is $25,000 *regardless of how much it actually cost*. It's rather like standard pricing. It follows that if a project produces all its deliverables at the point in time they were planned to be delivered, the earned value and planned lines would be coincident. Figure 22.6 shows this in the form of S-curves.

You can calculate two specific variances from these three lines:

Cost variance	earned value – actual cost	The difference between what has been delivered (based on planned cost) and what it actually cost	+ve = underspent −ve = overspent
Schedule variance	earned value – planned value	The difference between what has been delivered (based on planned cost) and what it was planned to have cost	+ve = early −ve = late

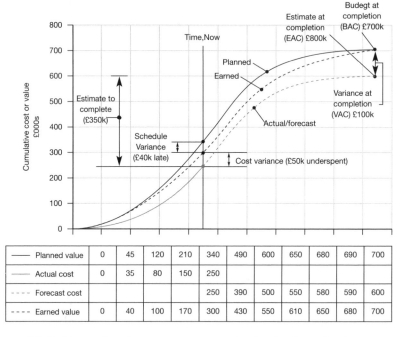

—— Planned value	0	45	120	210	340	490	600	650	680	690	700
—— Actual cost	0	35	80	150	250						
- - - - Forecast cost					250	390	500	550	580	590	600
- - - - Earned value	0	40	100	170	300	430	550	610	650	680	700

Figure 22.6 Earned value management – typical project
The three lines used in the method are shown – Planned, Earned and Actual – each of which shows the typical S-curve shape. If the project ran exactly as planned, these lines would be coincident.

Looking at Figure 22.6, we can now see the answer to the question I posed at the start of this section. Progress on the project is mixed: it is underspent but running late. So far, what has been completed has been delivered £50,000 cheaper than planned (cost variance = +50) but £40,000 less work has been completed than should have been (schedule variance = −40). On the other hand, the project is forecast to be completed £100,000 under plan and almost one period early. You may wonder what is behind such an optimistic forecast; perhaps all the difficult work has been done up-front, thereby forming a better basis for undertaking the remainder of the project.

Performance indices

Estimating the cost of the project at completion is where one of the more controversial calculations for the method comes in. A factor called the cost performance index (CPI) is widely used to forecast total cost of the project at completion. If a work package within a project is in progress and is over-budget, the calculation assumes that the final cost will exceed the planned cost by the same margin. This assumption implies that things will neither improve nor deteriorate further. In our example, the method would indicate a cost at completion of £583,000, somewhat less than the £600,000 forecast by the project manager.

CPI	Cost performance index	earned value/actual cost	120%	>100% = underspent
SPI	Schedule performance index	earned value/planned cost	88%	<100% = late
EAC	Estimate at completion (Project manager estimate)	Total estimated cost for the project	600k	
BAC	Budget at completion the project	Total planned cost for	700k	
VAC	Variance at completion	EAC − BAC	100k	+ = underspent

Experts in the use of this method will spot the problem immediately. In the example, the project has been treated as a single entity, whereas proper use of the method requires the project to be divided into a large number of work packages, with the earned value analysis performed discretely on each. They are then summed to provide the overall status for the project.

How useful is the method?

The usefulness of earned value management as a method is controversial. The greatest critics see it as a waste of time, whilst there are enthusiastic advocates claiming it is 'the only way'. In the middle are people who see that the information gained is potentially useful but are sceptical as to whether the effort needed to collate the data is worth it. As stated earlier, the method was primarily designed for the contracting environment and as such is more applicable to the post-investigative stages (Develop and Test, Trial, Release). The uncertainty around the investigative stages makes it very difficult for the method to add any additional information for the data collection and analysis effort required.

Its usefulness is dependent on having:

- a detailed plan, with appropriate WBS;
- accurate cost information;
- realistic progress reporting;
- project managers skilled in the method.

If any one of these is deficient, the benefit of the results will be significantly devalued. For enterprise-wide project management, it is not likely to prove useful simply because of the wide range of project management competencies such an environment encompasses. Simplicity and ease of data collation is the key if the method is to gain a strong foothold outside its traditional 'large contract' environment. In such cases, however, the results can provide management with an early indication as to the performance of a project, provoking action to resolve problems sooner rather than later.

PROJECT FINANCES

1 Take the list of projects that your business is currently undertaking or, alternatively, the output from Project Workout 3.2.

22.1

2 Choose any five projects which are in the Develop and Test Stage or beyond.

3 Ask each of the following people questions (a) to (e):

- the finance manager;

- project sponsor;

- project manager.

(a) For both time costs and purchases, provide, for the project as a whole, as at the close of the last month's accounting period:

    – costs spent to date;

    – costs spent this financial year;

    – estimated cost at completion;

    – agreed budget, when the project was authorised.

(b) Answer question (a) for the current work stage.

(c) How are 'time costs' calculated?

(d) Where were these data obtained from?

(e) State how easy or how difficult the information was to obtain.

4 Consider the replies. How long did it take for them to be compiled? Do they give the same information? What parts are missing? Were the same sources for the data used? If there is great consistency, fine. If not, look behind the replies. For example, if it takes a long while to compile the information or some is missing, can you reasonably expect your project managers to work within their budgets? Is it acceptable to make them 'fly blind' without adequate instruments?

WHEN VALUE DOESN'T MEAN VALUE!

The term 'value' has much wider uses than that described in this section. You therefore need to be clear what this method doesn't give you. Earned value does not tell you:

- the residual 'value' of the project at a point in time if it were to be terminated;
- the benefit gained from the project to date;
- the value of any assets produced by the project.

Nor does it have anything to do with another discipline – value management – which is aimed at choosing the most effective way to meet a particular business need. This is a technique which is primarily used during the investigative stages of a project.

Managing What Might Go Wrong (Or Right):
Risks and Opportunities

Considering possible risks and opportunities

Addressing risk at the start of the project

Addressing opportunities at the start of the project

Monitoring once the project is in progress

Tips on using the risk and opportunity log

More sophisticated risk evaluation techniques

Taking active steps to reduce the possible effects of risks is not indicative of pessimism, but is a positive indication of good project management.

'It is certain because it is impossible.'

TERTULLIAN, c. AD 160–225

- **Risk management starts when the project starts.**
- **Reduce the likelihood of threats materialising.**
- **Contingency plan in the event that threats do materialise.**
- **Focus on the 'big ones', but don't lose sight of the others.**
- **Look for opportunities to increase benefits, but not at the cost of increasing risk.**
- **Plan for the most likely opportunities.**

Considering possible risks and opportunities

Risk is any potential uncertainty, threat or occurrence which may prevent you from achieving your defined business objectives and benefits. It may affect timescale, cost, quality or benefits. All projects are exposed to risk in some form but the extent of this will vary considerably.

Opportunity is the possibility that your project may go better than you planned.

Figure 23.1 shows how risk and opportunity sit within the context of other project controls; a risk will become an issue if the event occurs. Issues can be resolved either within the scope of the project as currently defined or via a change to the project. An opportunity is similar to a risk but has a potentially beneficial impact rather than a negative impact. Like risk, an opportunity will become an issue if the event occurs. Figure 23.2 also shows that, once the project is well under way, the risk, or 'down side', is usually bigger than any 'up side' opportunities.

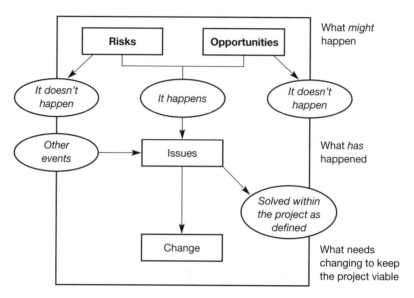

Figure 23.1 Risks, opportunities, issues and change

A **risk** or **opportunity** will become an **issue** if the event occurs. Issues can be resolved either within the scope of the project as currently defined or via a **change** to project.

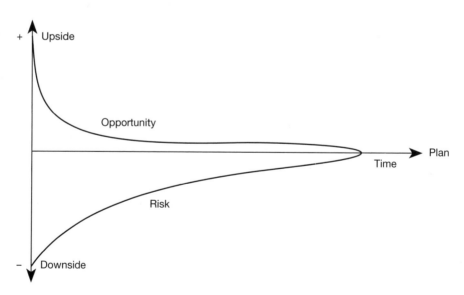

Figure 23.2 Upside and downsides to a project

Once the project is well under way, the risk, or 'downside', is usually bigger than any upside opportunities. This is because people are usually optimistic.

The purpose of risk and opportunity management is to ensure that:

- risks and opportunities on projects are identified and evaluated in a consistent way;
- risks to the project's success are recognised and addressed and significant opportunities are exploited without undue delay.

You cannot use risk management to eliminate risk altogether, but by careful planning you may be able to avoid it in some instances or minimise the disruption in others. But what if identified risks do not materialise? What if a new approach (opportunity!) comes about which will further your business objectives better than planned? You have two options:

- You can keep to the original plan, as something quite unexpected may still go wrong and eat into the time and money you've saved.
- You can build the new found opportunity into the project and 'mine it' for all it's worth.

Traditionally, the former approach is the more prudent but that does not mean it makes the most business sense in all cases.

Addressing risk at the start of the project

You should address risk when the project is first being set up during the Initial Investigation Stage. Risk is an important section within the project definition; when a project sponsor approves a project he/she does so in full knowledge of the stated risks, accepting the consequences should things go wrong. It is important that the project sponsor accepts the risks as the person undertaking this role is the primary risk taker.

> **When a project sponsor approves a project he/she does so in full knowledge of the stated risks, accepting the consequences should things go wrong.**

Often people are very good at identifying what might go wrong in terms of creating the deliverables, but less so at assessing what may go wrong in terms of benefits realisation. If your projects are truly business led, both are important. To ensure you do not forget this, think of your risks in terms of *project risks* and *business risks*. Project risks are those which impact delivery during the project, whereas business risks are those which will impact benefits realisation. Naturally a project risk, e.g. significant delay to the project, may also have an adverse effect on benefits. Don't be too purist! The key is to recognise that there are some risks (often uncertainties), such as changes in exchange rate or competitor action, which are clearly not associated with project delivery, but with benefits (i.e. a business risk).

The steps are:

- Brainstorm all the risks that may jeopardise the success of the project. Remember to include those which are under the control of the project team (e.g. completeness of project scope, quality of technical solutions, competence of project team) as well as those which are largely outside the control of the team (e.g. legislative changes, competitor activity, economic climate). Use checklists to supplement the list after the brainstorm is complete.
- Review each risk in turn:
  - assess the likelihood of the risk occurring;
  - assess the severity of the impact on the project if it occurs.
- Use a risk matrix such as the one that follows to determine the 'risk category' (high, medium, low).
- For high risks, consider ways of preventing or avoiding the event, reducing the impact, or transferring the risk to someone else. Contingency planning is a last resort but, as the risk is high, consider making your 'contingency plan' the mainstream plan.
- For medium risks, take preventative, reduction or transfer measures. Failing that, prepare a contingency plan.
- For low risks, continue to monitor them as they may become more significant. Decide whether other action should be taken based on individual circumstances.

Taking active steps to reduce the possible effects of risks is not indicative of pessimism, but is a positive indication of good project management.

Many possible options exist for addressing risk, including:

 Prevention – where countermeasures are put in place either to stop the threat or problem occurring or prevent its having any impact (avoidance).

 Reduction – where the actions either reduce the likelihood of the risk occurring or limit the impact on the project to acceptable levels.

Risk matrix	Likelihood of event occurring			
Severity of impact	*Very unlikely* <5%	*Unlikely*	*Likely* >50%	*Very likely* >75%
1 Minor impact on project schedule or cost. No impact on benefits	Low	Low	Medium	Medium
2 Major impact on project schedule or cost. Minor impact on benefits	Medium	Medium	Medium	High
3 Major impact on project schedule or cost. Major impact on benefits	Medium	Medium	High	High

Transference – a specialist form of risk reduction where the impact of the risk is transferred to a third party such as a contractor or insurance organisation. Another form is where the risk is elevated to a higher level in the organisation, which effectively acts as an 'insurer' for a large number of projects. This approach is beneficial as it should lead to a reduction in the total amount of funds held in contingency.

Contingency – where actions are planned or organised which will come into force as and when the risk occurs.

Acceptance – where the organisation decides to go ahead and accept the possibility that the risk might occur and is willing to accept the consequences. (Not recommended, but all too often done!)

Consider also:

- bringing risky activities forward in the schedule to reduce the impact on the project outcome if they cause delays;
- modifying the project requirement to reduce aspects with inherently high risk, e.g. new, leading edge technologies;
- allowing appropriate time and cost contingencies;
- using prototypes and pilots to test the viability of new approaches.

> **Once past the Development Gate, a project should not usually contain any high risks. If it does, the project plan should be reconsidered to lower the overall risk.**

Once past the Development Gate (see p. 66), a project should not usually contain any high risks. If it does, the project plan should be reconsidered to lower the overall risk by using an alternative approach or by introducing ways of reducing the likely impact.

A convenient way of recording risk is in the form of a 'log' shown in Figure 23.3.

BEWARE THE DIFFICULTIES OF 'RISK CONVERSATIONS'

To raise the subject of risk is not admitting failure. If the culture in your organisation is to see the discussion of risk as a failure, you must change it fast. Driving risk 'underground' is not the way to deal with it. If you are truly in control, there is every benefit in sharing risks and understanding the measures you can take to manage them. Research shows that addressing risk with your 'eyes wide open' is a significant factor in ensuring a successful project outcome.

Things still go wrong. Risk management is not infallible. Something may still happen which will destroy your project. For instance, irrational behaviour by individuals in your organisation, from competitors or from government cannot be predicted. Emotional actions and behaviours are often the most difficult to deal with.

Risk Log

Ref No	Description of Risk	Date Raised	Probability of occurrence	Severity	Risk Category	Risk Management: Action	by/date
1	Seigathon may launch a new product at the same target market.	2/3/10	Unlikely	3	Medium	Monitor Seigathon market activity	G Smith 1/5/10
2	The product launch relies on Project X being delivered. There is a risk that this will be delayed.	13/4/10	Unlikely	2	Medium	Monitor Project X progress	F Kent 1/7/10
3	The contractor for the project is unable to deliver on time due to lack of resources and other commercial commitments.	20/6/10	Very Likely	2	Medium	Build relationship with contractor Find alternative supplier Build contingency time into schedule	G Smith 1/8/10
4	The warehouse management system release will be delayed beyond the planned start of testing.	29/6/10	Certain	2	High	Provide paper based system and procedures during initial testing (see issue log)	J Arnold 1/7/10
5	The credit control system release will be delayed beyond the planned start of testing.	29/6/10	Very likely	2	High	Build 3 months' contingency into the schedule	F Kent 1/8/10

Figure 23.3 A typical risk log

A risk log is used to record the risk, the date it was recognised, its category and risk management action (with accountability).

IDENTIFYING RISKS – 1

23.1

'If a man begin with certainties, he shall end in doubt; but if he will be content to begin with doubts, he shall end in certainties.'

FRANCIS BACON, 1561–1626

This workout should be done with the project team.

1 Use brainstorming or other creative methods to generate as many possible risks as you can. You should include anything that anyone wishes to raise. By involving the team you will start to develop an idea of where their concerns lie and what confidence they have in other team members or departments. In addition, group members will hear one another's concerns and this also helps to form the team. Do not let anyone criticise or comment on any risk raised – just capture thoughts. Hint: look at any assumptions made and at any constraints (as listed in the project definition).

2 Write each risk on a Post-It Note as it is called out; ask for clarification if the risk is not understood but otherwise do not allow comments.

3 Put each Post-It Note on a board where everyone can see them. Carry on generating risks until the team have no more to offer.

4 By inspection, cluster the risks into similar groups. This may be around technologies, people, legal, employee relations, funding, etc. Choose any clusters that 'fit' the situation.

5 Rationalise the risks, combining some, clarifying or restating others; number each risk sequentially.

6 Evaluate each risk using the matrix on p. 403 and plot all medium and high risks onto a flip chart.

7 Take time for the team to review the output so far. Are there any themes noticeable in the risks or in the way they are clustered. Are there any particular aspects of the project which appear to be problematic?

8 Begin with the high risks: start generating possible ways of dealing with them. Allow all options to be raised. Do not evaluate, just capture the possible risk management actions for later evaluation.

9 Evaluate and agree which risk-management option should be followed and who is accountable for managing each particular risk.

Task – strive to eliminate any high risks.

- Avoid those risks you can, by using a different approach to the project for example.

- Build investigative work into your plan to drive out risks which result from having insufficient information.

- Capture your risks in a log (similar to Figure 23.3).

IDENTIFYING RISKS – 2

This workout should be done with the project team.

1 Take the output from Project Workout 21.2 (the Post-It Notes network diagram) and display it on a wall.

2 Start at the first Post-It Note and ask:

- What can go wrong with this?

- How likely is that to happen?

- What effect will that have on the timescale?

3 Use the risk matrix to evaluate the risk category. Using a different coloured Post-It Note, mark up the risk and its category adjacent to the relevant part of the network.

4 Repeat this until every Post-It Note in the network has been evaluated.

5 Take time for the team to review the output so far. Are there any themes or noticeable streams of the project which appear to be problematic?

6 Begin with the high risks: start generating possible ways of dealing with them. Allow all options to be raised. Do not evaluate, just capture the possible risk management actions for later evaluation.

7 Evaluate and agree which risk-management options should be followed and who is accountable for managing each particular risk.

Task – strive to eliminate any high risks.

- Look for alternative way of approaching the work which avoids sequences of risks, creates contingency time, or brings risky elements forward.

- Replan the project around these risks putting your contingency (safety) where it counts.

- Capture your risks in a risk log (similar to Figure 23.3).

23.2

Addressing opportunities at the start of the project

Like 'risk', opportunities may influence your whole project strategy and plan.

You should address opportunities when the project is first being set up during the Initial Investigation Stage. Like 'risk', opportunities may influence your whole project strategy and plan. You should:

- Brainstorm all the opportunities that may potentially enhance the success of the project (some of these will be the converse of risks you have already identified).
- Review each opportunity in turn:
  - assess the likelihood of each occurring;
  - assess the impact on the project if it occurs.
- Use an opportunity matrix, such as the one that follows, to determine the 'opportunity category' (major, medium, minor).

Opportunity matrix	Likelihood of event occurring			
Impact	*Very unlikely* <5%	*Unlikely*	*Likely* >50%	*Very likely* >75%
1 Minor impact on project schedule or cost. No impact on benefits	Minor	Minor	Medium	Medium
2 Major impact on project schedule or cost. Minor impact on benefits	Medium	Medium	Medium	Major
3 Major impact on project schedule or cost. Major impact on benefits	Medium	Medium	Major	Major

- For major opportunities, consider amending your baseline plan to build the opportunity in from the start.
- For medium opportunities, prepare an outline contingency plan you could use should it happen.
- For minor opportunities, take no immediate action; stay with your current plan.

There are many possible options for you to exploit, examples include:

- modifying the project timescale such that it is possible to bring the release date and hence benefits, forward should a risky aspect of the project proceed without undue problems;
- using time and money saved to incorporate outputs which originally had to be discarded (but make sure these really add benefit rather than are 'nice to have').

A convenient way of presenting opportunities is in the form of a 'log', similar to the risk log shown in Figure 23.3. This is very similar to the risk log and in practice you may choose to use the same log for both, marking them as a risk or opportunity, as appropriate.

OPPORTUNITY – 1

'Probable impossibilities are to be preferred to improbable possibilities.'

ARISTOTLE, 384–322 BC

23.3

This workout should be done with the project team. Perhaps do this after the risk workout (Project Workout 23.1) to put a more positive light on the project.

Follow the instructions for Project Workout 23.1, but instead of concentrating on risks, look for opportunities.

Task – build all major opportunities into the base plan.

- Set yourself up to exploit opportunities by designing the project strategy and approach accordingly without compromising your risk-management strategy!
- Build into your plan investigative work to convert medium opportunities into major ones.
- Capture your opportunities in a log (similar to Figure 23.3).

OPPORTUNITY – 2

23.4

This workout should be done with the project team. Follow the instructions for Project Workout 23.2, but instead of concentrating on risks, look for opportunities.

Task – strive to exploit major opportunities.

- Look for alternative sequencing of the work which allows you exploit opportunities, should they arise, without compromising your risk-management strategy!
- Replan the project around these opportunities.
- Capture your opportunities in a log (similar to Figure 23.3).

An organisation had to upgrade some security features of its internal data network. This involved the upgrading of the software on two major associated computer systems as well as changes to a number of nodes within the network itself. Unfortunately, the upgrading of one computer system was seen as very risky due to its inherent instability and the number of other changes being made to it at the same time. The schedule showed a seven-month duration for the remainder of the project with the critical path passing through the problem software upgrade. No work on the network nodes could be started until this upgrade was done.

By following a sequence such as in Project Workouts 23.1 and 23.2 the project team identified that they could delink the network node work from the problematic software upgrade and allow it to proceed immediately (this involved a change to the upgrade specification in the second computer system). This simple change in the project approach resulted in the schedule plan of seven months having three months float in it; ample time to investigate and solve any problems on the computer system or to implement a manual alternative.

This exercise showed how team working produced a better result than any individual could – there was no one person who had the technical knowledge to devise the adopted solution. Further, the team formed a bond of understanding that stayed with them throughout the remainder of the project.

Monitoring once the project is in progress

Once the project has started, you should:

- Maintain a log of the risks and opportunities similar to the example given in Figure 23.3.
- Regularly monitor them with the team and reassess the likelihood of occurrence and seriousness of impact.
- Log, categorise and report new risks and opportunities together with the action being taken to deal with them.
- Report new, high risks in the regular project progress report (see Chapter 19) and highlight potential, significant opportunities.

During the course of a project, either of the following can happen:

1 A risk or opportunity 'event' occurs – this should be noted in the 'action' column and a corresponding entry made on the issues log.
2 A risk or opportunity event is passed, i.e. the project proceeds and the event does not occur. The category should be recorded as 'none'.

In both cases, the log entry is 'closed' and the line in the log should be shaded to show that the event no longer requires management attention.

Expect some things to go better than you expected

A major change project undertaken by an organisation relied on completing a contract with a third party for out-sourcing a part of their operations. The risk of being unable to sign a mutually beneficial contract was considered highly unlikely but it was considered that negotiations could be very long, at least four to six months.

The preparatory work for handover to the out-source organisation was expected to take two months and could take place in parallel with negotiations. Rather than delay starting this preparatory work, it was decided to proceed with it immediately so in the event of the contract being signed early the organisation would be in a position to bring forward the implementation date (Figure 23.4).

Figure 23.4 The effect of planning to create your own luck

In the original plan, (a), work would not start on preparation until the latest possible time in order to meet the required date. However, there was a possibility that the contract could be signed early and there was little risk of failing to sign. In plan (b) the preparatory work started as soon as possible. In fact, the situation that happened is represented by (c). The contract was signed early and the organisation was in a position to reap the rewards earlier.

Tips on using the risk and opportunity log

- Phrase each to fit the sentence 'There is a risk (or opportunity) on this project that … caused by … resulting in …'
- Make sure your risks are truly 'risks' and not merely 'worries'.
- Only have one risk or opportunity per 'line' – grouping can make managing them difficult.
- Do not add to existing entries, except to provide clarification.
- Cross-reference to the issues log when an event 'happens'.
- Keep all risks and opportunities visible, even those which have been passed or have happened. This acts as a check in case others' perception is different. Shading passed risks and opportunities makes it clear which are live and which are not.

RISK? OPPORTUNITIES? ISSUES? BUT WHAT DO I DO FIRST?

In managing a project you will always have to make choices about where to apply your time. Frequently there is not enough time or resources to manage every aspect of the project as fully or as rigorously as the 'theory' or the benefit of hindsight demands.

Having a framework within which you can deal with these aspects of project management helps ensure that they all have visibility and are not forgotten. When under time pressure you should concentrate on the 'issues' as they are now 'facts on the ground' and have to be dealt with. Delegate as many as you can, leaving the most critical for your own attention.

Next apply yourself to the risks. Your mission is to deliver the project according to the plan and keeping your eye on the future. Preempting future issues is part of that. Remember some risks are potentially more dangerous than issues. They are definitely more dangerous than opportunities.

Finally, look for the opportunities.

If, as part of the Initial and Detailed Investigation Stages, you have promoted a dialogue on risks and opportunities within your team (for example, by doing the workout exercises), the team itself will intuitively scan the environment for risks and opportunities on your behalf, thus sharing the workload. After all, what is a team for!

More sophisticated risk evaluation techniques

The basic approach to risk described so far in this chapter can be used by any person on any project. It requires no special tools, technical or statistical knowledge. In many cases it is the most powerful and effective approach, relying on the creativity and common sense of the team.

Nevertheless, there are occasions where other tools and techniques are very valuable for supplementing intuitive analyses.

Sensitivity and scenario analysis

So far we have looked at risk as a black and white occurrence. Either it happens or it doesn't. In practice, however, there may be a range of outcomes, with impacts ranging from the disastrously negative to the unbelievably positive. You can identify such items easily; these are your assumptions. All assumptions are risks and should be treated as such. Examples are market rates, customer usage, plant efficiency, inflation, customer demand, cost forecasts and timing. For most projects, uncertainty will have a greater impact on the benefits than on project cost and schedule.

Sensitivity analysis is used to review the impact on the project of the possible range of values for each assumption made. In this way, you will be able to decide which assumptions are substantive to the case and need to be addressed further. The steps are:

1 identify your assumptions;
2 decide on a range of values for each assumption;
3 rework your calculations (business model), using these values to see the effect on project viability on variations to that particular assumption;
4 identify those assumptions which have most impact and log them as risks;
5 decide on your response to these risks.

For example, in the following table, we see the project viability is more sensitive to percentage moves in tariff than costs.

Scenario analysis takes sensitivity analysis a step further by looking at alternative futures. A scenario comprises a set of **compatible** assumptions, chosen from the risk and sensitivity analysis, which describes the future. This often requires a model to be built so that the different assumptions can be used consistently, e.g. fewer customers may lead not only to less revenue, but also less cost of sales, while fixed costs may remain the same. Three scenarios should be investigated:

1 optimistic;
2 most likely;
3 pessimistic.

Assumption		−20%	−10%	+10%	+20%
Change in cost	NPV ($)	215k	416k	764k	978k
	IRR	14%	32%	52%	67%
Change in tariff	NPV ($)	10k	234k	865k	1234k
	IRR	9%	17%	16%	102%

Thus for a pessimistic scenario you may assume a late project completion date with a cost overrun with slower customer take-up and usage, with more severe downward price pressures than anticipated. This can be tabulated, for example:

Parameter	Pessimistic	Most likely	Optimistic
Timing of RFS	2 months late	On time	2 weeks early
IT cost	$450k	$340k	$320k
Customer take-up	+5%	+12%	+15%
Usage	35 minutes/day	50 minutes/day	65 minutes/day
Tariff erosion	−15% annual	−5% annual	−5% annual
IRR %	−6%	40%	87%
NPV ($k)	−1767	2990	3875
Payback	No payback	3 years	2 years

As for sensitivity analysis, the aim is to provide decision makers with an objective view of what may be the consequences of continuing the project thus enabling them to balance the possible opportunities (up side) with the associated risks (down side).

Risk simulation

Risk simulation can be used to help analyse a project with respect to its most sensitive parameters and likely scenarios. It relies on the application of a range of durations, costs and benefits associated with a particular element in a project. This is input as:

- the lowest likely value;
- the most likely value;
- the highest probable value.

The simulation software will then analyse the network and calculate a range of likely costs and durations with a set of probabilities. The results are plotted on a chart such as that shown in Figure 23.5.

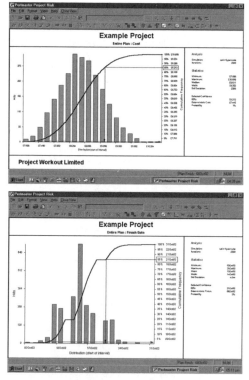

Figure 23.5 A typical output from a Monte Carlo analysis

The figure (created using Pertmaster Project Risk®) shows typical outputs you can expect from a Monte Carlo analysis. At the top is a histogram for costs, so you can place a percentage confidence measure on completing the project within a stated cost. The bottom screen is the same project, but shows the variation in schedule for a range of confidence percentages. In this example, we can be 85% confident the project will be completed by 21 October and for less than £9,200.

Software for critical chain scheduling (see p. 000) also includes risk and probability distributions to enable a rigorous plan to be built, tested and rolled out.

At the end of the 1990s a famous American hamburger restaurant chain decided to celebrate its birthday by providing cut-price offers on its leading product. The PR behind the event was superb. Not only did the advertising reach its target but also many news and magazine channels on radio and television as well as the press covered the forthcoming event. As it happened the consumer demand far outstripped supply to such an extent that many restaurants closed early and thousands of people had to be turned away. The event was dubbed by the press as 'McBungle'. Was this a success? True, the advertising was effective, but what was the real cost to the organisation as its supply chain failed and its customers became angry? What of the financial cost in having to provide about four times as many cut-price meals as expected? What of the cost in lost revenue as the irate customers chose to use a competitor in future?

- How do you think the marketing executives viewed this campaign?
- How do you think the operations executives viewed the campaign?
- How did the hourly paid shop staff feel having worked harder and then had their day (and pay) cut short?
- What actions could have been taken to avoid the situation?

And remember, before you look at this with the benefit of hindsight, maybe they did do all the right things but Murphy's Law proved too strong an adversary!

Ignore risks at your peril!

Copyright © 1997 Robert Buttrick

Managing What Has Gone Wrong (or Right!):
Issues

What do we mean by 'issues'?

When an issue is identified

Tips on using the issues log

*An issue is something that **has** happened and either threatens or enhances the success of the project. Compare this to a risk or opportunity, which are things that **might** happen.*

'There are no hopeless situations: there are only men who have grown hopeless about them.'

CLARE BOOTH LUCE

- **Be open about issues within your team – declare them.**
- **Never 'sit' on an issue – escalate it if you can't deal with it.**
- **Use the team to resolve the tricky issues.**

What do we mean by 'issues'?

Issues management is the process for recording and handling any event or problem which either threatens the success of a project or represents an opportunity to be exploited. Figure 24.1 shows the context: an issue occurs either as a result of an identified risk or opportunity event occurring or as a result of some unexpected event. An issue can either be dealt with within the project, as defined, or will require a change in order to keep the project viable. Examples of issues are:

Problem issues:

- the late delivery of a critical deliverable;
- a reported lack of confidence by users;
- a lack of resources to carry out the work;
- the late approval of a critical document or deliverable;
- a reported deviation of a deliverable from its specification;
- a request for additional functionality;
- a recognised omission from the project scope.

Opportunity issues:

- a contract negotiation is concluded early;
- a breakthrough on a new technology cuts months off the development time;
- a new, cheaper source of raw materials is located;
- the enrolment of key stakeholders happens sooner than planned;
- a contract tender comes in significantly less than the pre-tender estimate.

An issue is something that *has* happened and either threatens or enhances the success of the project. Compare this to a risk or opportunity, which are things that *might* happen.

When talking to people be careful, as 'issue' can also mean a 'topic' or an 'important point': unless you are both tuned to the same definition you may find your conversations confusing!

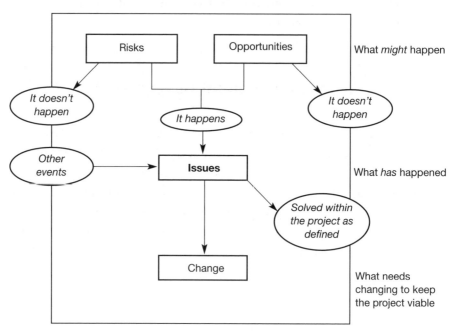

Figure 24.1 Risks, opportunity, issues and change
An **issue** occurs either as a result of an identified **risk** or **opportunity** event occurring, or as a result of some other unexpected event. An issue can either be dealt with within the project, as defined, or will require a change in order to keep the project viable.

When an issue is identified

When an issue is identified, you should:

- Record in the issues log any issue which has been drawn to your attention for resolution. (An example issues log is shown in Figure 24.2.) You should:
  - describe the issue;
  - record who brought it up and when (date);
  - rate the issue priority (1 (critical) to 4 (minor impact)).

- Decide and agree who will be accountable for managing the issue's resolution. If the issue cannot be dealt with by the project team you should refer outside the team to a person who has the necessary level of knowledge and/or authority to deal with it (to the project sponsor or project board for example). You should record, in the log:
  - the name of the person accountable for managing the resolution of the issue;
  - the date by which resolution of the issue is expected.
- Regularly update the progress commentary on the log.
- Once the issue has been resolved, record the method and date of resolution in the log. The line can then be shaded to show that the issue no longer requires attention. If the issue resolution requires an amendment to the project scope (deliverables), cost, timescales or benefits, it should be handled through the change control process (Chapter 25).
- Report new, significant issues in the regular project progress report (see Chapter 19).

You should expect a large number of issues to be raised at the start of the project or at the start of a new stage within the project. These will mainly be from people seeking clarification that aspects of the project they are concerned with have been covered. This is a rich source of feedback on stakeholder concerns as well as a check on completeness of the project plan.

> *Make sure you record issues, even if you have no time to address them or cannot yet find a person to manage the resolution. Just making them visible is sometimes enough to start resolving them.*

Make sure you record issues, even if you have no time to address them or cannot yet find a person to manage the resolution. Just making them visible is sometimes enough to start resolving them (see case study). Many issues cannot be resolved on their own simply because they do not reach the core problem; they are merely symptoms. Once other 'symptoms' appear as issues it is possible to start making connections which can help identify the core problem. Once this is solved a number of issues can be struck off in one go.

Issues Log

1997   1 July

Ref	Description of issue	Date raised	Raised by (name)	Issue owner	Resolution date	Priority (1,2,3,4)	Comment: progress: resolution
1	The mobilisation of the 24th Legion has been delayed and it will not be ready for the start of the campaign. How can we ensure the campaign progresses on time and victory is not delayed?	1/4/10	Marcus	Lucius	2/6/10	2	From Risk 4: delay demobilisation of the 19th Legion veterans
2	No time has been allocated for training recruits. How can we ensure the campaign is launched and there are sufficient legionnaires trained to take part?	5/4/10	Flavius	Keaso	15/7/10	1	
3	There is a general lack of awareness of what this campaign will do for the Roman Empire. How can we address this?	5/4/10	Trajan	Lucius	15/4/10	3	Provide an 'update' in the Senate and bribe senators to vote additional funds to the campaign
4							

Priority   1: Critical – needs escalation
           2: Major impact – can be handled by team
           3: Medium impact
           4: Minor impact

Figure 24.2 Typical issues log

The issues log contains the list of all the 'happenings' which either threaten the success of the project or which may lead to an opportunity. It comprises a description of the issue, the date it was raised, who it was raised by, the name of the person accountable for resolving it and a target date for resolution. The final column contains notes to help the reader understand the current situation or record how the issue was resolved.

A project manager was heard to say to another, after running an issues log for some months:

'This is my magic list. All I do is list the problems on it, share them with my team and . . . magic! They get resolved!'

'I don't believe you; it looks like a load of bureaucratic nonsense to me.'

'Honestly. I have to work on some of the key ones quite hard myself, but many others are sorted out by the team without me. They see them written there and just act on them if they can. It's all a matter of creating your own luck.'

The power of the issues log is related to its accessibility. If it is kept secret, no one will know what the problems are and hence will not be able to help. This openness does, however, carry its own risks. If seen by an uninformed stakeholder, an issues log can look like a negative and damning document for the project. You should, therefore, be very careful how you write up the issues and how you circulate or communicate them. Avoid being personal and concentrate on problems: the old saying 'be tough on the problem, not on the people' is very pertinent here.

> *This openness does, however, carry its own risks. When seen by an uninformed stakeholder, an issues log can look like a negative and damning document for the project. You should, therefore, be very careful how you write up the issues and how you circulate or communicate it.*

'I know that's a secret for it's whispered everywhere.'
WILLIAM CONGREVE, 1670–1729

Murphy will strike, so learn how to handle it!

Copyright © 1999 Robert Buttrick

Tips on using the issues log

- Phrase the issue as a question; this is more powerful in helping to focus on a solution.
- Have only one issue per 'line'. Grouping a number of issues together (even if related) makes identification of a solution difficult.
- Do not add to existing issues or they will never be resolved; record a new issue if a different facet becomes apparent.
- Make cross-references between issues or refer back to the risk or opportunity logs (by a note in the 'comment' column) if this is helpful.
- Keep all issues visible, even those which have been resolved, as this shows achievement in overcoming problems and exploiting opportunities. It also acts as a check in case the same issue resurfaces later. Shading completed issues makes it clear which are live and which are resolved.
- If the resolution of the issue requires a project 'change', put a cross reference to the change log in the resolution column.
- Be open with your issues log; share it with the project team and others on whom the project will have an impact.

A manufacturing organisation was relocating its works. It was intended that the existing plant would be moved and operated in the new location. After the site was acquired and construction was almost completed an issue was raised under European legislation that the old plant would not be allowed to run in the new location. It was deemed to be a new site and hence all plant had to conform to new emission restrictions immediately.

An issue was logged and immediately escalated to the project sponsor as the project manager had no knowledge or power to deal with this. The project sponsor quickly circulated the problem among various contacts within the organisation. Very soon a specialist unit was identified in the head office that was able to review the issue. It found that the issue was a misinterpretation of the legislation and was not valid. The issue was potentially a show stopper for the project. By identifying it and describing it accurately, however, the issue was able to be circulated and resolved (or in this case dissolved). A potentially very expensive change to the project was thus avoided.

POINT OF INTEREST

Remember, an issue can be raised at any time by anyone and is the means of making a problem visible and having it escalated to the level where it can be resolved.

RESOLVING ISSUES – FROM BREAKDOWN TO BREAKTHROUGH

The following process, if used in full, is a very effective and powerful driver for resolving issues. Followed rigorously it will enable you to 'breakthrough' an issue which is blocking your project or programme. The toughest part is to declare that you do in fact have a problem. Doing this puts you in a position of responsibility which will enable you to proceed. Be careful, however; the natural tendency will be for you to dwell on what's wrong: what's wrong with you, or with the project, or with 'them'. Steps 3 to 8 should be done with those who have a stake in the issue in a facilitated, workshop setting, recording the input from the group on flip charts. Do all the steps and do them in the right order. Do not jump ahead.

1 Declare that you have an issue!

Tell everyone who could possibly have an impact on resolving the issue, particularly those you do not want to know about it. Don't hide the issue. Merely putting it on your issues log is not enough. Actively tell people!

2 Stop the action

Call everything around the issue to a halt. Don't react. Don't try to fix it. Relax.

3 What, precisely is the issue?

Exactly what did or didn't happen? When? Distinguish between facts and rumours. Then describe the issue in one sentence. This is the sentence you should write in the issues log.

4 What commitments are being thwarted?

Which of your commitments is being thwarted, stopped or hindered by the issue? Remind yourself of the reasons for the project in the first place and the drivers for action.

24.1

5 What would a breakthrough make possible?

What would the resolution of the issue, under these circumstances, look like? What would it make possible? Are you really committed to resolving this and furthering these possibilities? If so, continue.

6 What's missing? What's present and in the way?

Take stock of the entire project. What's the situation now (stick to facts!)? What's missing, which, if present, would allow the action to move forward quickly and effectively? What's present and standing in the way of progress?

7 What possible actions could you take to further your commitments?

Leave the facts of the current situation and what is missing in the background. Stand in the future, a breakthrough having been accomplished, and create an array of possible actions. Look outside your paradigm. Think laterally.

8 What actions will you take?

Next, narrow down the possibilities to those with the greatest opportunity and leverage. Not necessarily the safest and most predictable! Then choose a direction and get back into action. Make requests of people and agree the actions needed. Hold them to account on those actions.

(Adapted, with kind permission of the London Peret Roche Group, from their 'Breakdown to Breakthrough' technology. Copyright © 1992, N J.)

Let's Do it Differently!:
Change Control

Controlling change

The change control process

Accountabilities for change decisions

The change request form

Changes are an inevitable fact of project life.
Unless you manage these changes effectively you
will soon lose sight of the objectives and scope
and thereafter lose total control of the project.

'Change is certain. Progress is not.'

E H CARR

- **Change is inevitable – manage it.**
- **Have a clear, simple process for introducing changes.**
- **Assess the impact of proposed changes.**
- **Only include beneficial changes.**

Controlling change

Changes are an inevitable fact of project life (Figure 25.1). Seldom does a project go exactly to plan. Unless you manage these changes effectively you will soon lose sight of the objectives and scope and thereafter lose total control of the project.

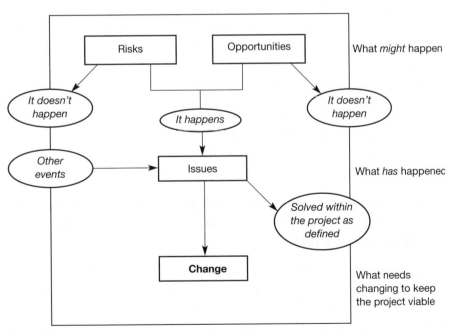

Figure 25.1 Risks, opportunity, issues and change

A **risk** or **opportunity** will become an **issue** if the event occurs. Issues can be resolved either within the scope of the project as currently defined or via a **change** to the project. If this 'issue' is to be resolved by a change to the defined project, the impact of this change should be assessed, particularly with respect to the expected benefits.

Controlling change does not mean preventing change, but rather allowing only beneficial changes to be adopted and included in the project.

Change control is related to risk, opportunity and issue management; a risk or opportunity will become an issue if the event occurs. Issues can be dealt with either within the scope of the project as currently defined or via a change to the project. If this 'issue' is to be resolved by a change to the defined project, the impact of this change should be assessed, particularly with respect to the expected benefits (see Figure 25.1).

Change may result from a number of sources:

- changes in business needs/requirements driven by the project sponsor or other stakeholders;
- changes in the business environment (e.g. economics, social factors, competitor action);
- problems or opportunities which occur during the course of the project;
- modifications or enhancements identified by the project team (beware of these!);
- faults detected by the project team or users (these must be addressed).

Change, in the context of a project, is any modification to the benefit, scope, time, or cost targets that have previously been approved. This means that there can only be a 'change' if there is an approved 'baseline'. The baseline is provided by the project definition (included in the initial and full business case) which defines the:

- benefits to be realised by the project;
- scope of work and detail for each deliverable;
- project timescale and intermediate milestone dates;
- project cost.

Change control is the process through which changes to a project (to cost, schedule, scope or benefits) are introduced and evaluated prior to their adoption or rejection.

'Scope creep' is a phenomenon where a project overruns its agreed timescale and budget due to many extra (often minor) 'requirements' being added in an uncontrolled manner. For this reason it is often easier to bundle a number of small changes together and assess them as a whole, choosing to implement only those which will further the objectives of the project. At the other end of the scale it is wise to consider delaying the addition of a major change until after the project is completed and introduce it as a second phase project.

Remember, the primary aim of a project is to fulfil a stated business need. As long as this need is satisfied, fine tuning, enhancing or embellishing the outputs is a potential waste of resource and time.

Inevitably, a time will come when an issue will arise on a project which cannot be resolved while still keeping the project viable. Either a time window will be missed or costs will be so high that even a marginal cost analysis leads to the conclusion that it is not worth continuing. In these cases, the impact assessment will result in a recommendation to terminate the project. Such an outcome should be treated as a success, as there is little point in continuing with a project which is not viable in business terms (for more on termination, see pp. 448, 463).

> *'Scope creep' is a phenomenon where a project overruns its agreed timescale and budget due to many extra (often minor) 'requirements' being added in an uncontrolled manner. For this reason it is often easier to bundle a number of small changes together and assess them as a whole, choosing to implement only those which will further the objectives of the project.*

Don't make decisions on changing the project without assessing the impact

Copyright © 1997 Robert Buttrick

The change control process

Because of the potential for changes to reduce projects to chaos, it is preferable to adopt a formal approach to assessing and authorising change right from the start (Figure 25.2):

- Note the proposed change in the change log (see Figure 25.3, for an example).
- Assess the impact of the change on the project and any interdependent projects. (See Figure 25.4 for a summary impact assessment form.)
- If within the project manager's authority, reject or accept the change proposal.
- If it is outside the project manager's authority, refer the decision (with a recommendation) to the appropriate level for a review and decision.

The change proposal may be:

- accepted for immediate implementation;
- accepted, subject to certain conditions being met;
- accepted but implementation is deferred to a later date;
- rejected (with/without recommendation to include in a later project).

Once the decision has been made, the project manager should:

- obtain further financial authorisation (if needed);
- record the outcome in the change log.
- If the change was accepted:
  - implement the change;
  - update the project documentation;
  - inform all interested parties about the change;
- inform the originator of the outcome and, if rejected, give the reason for the decision.

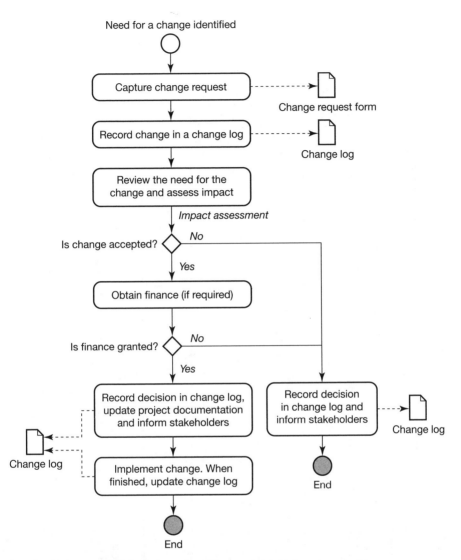

Figure 25.2 The change control process
The change control process comprises capturing the proposed changes, assessing the impact on time, costs, benefits and scope, making a decision on whether to approve the change and obtaining further funding, if required.

Project change log

Ref No	Description	Originator	Date raised	Impact assessment by (name)	Approval by	Approved Yes/No	Date approved	Date authorised	Comments
1	Extend scope of tracking system to include all customers	J Philips	3/8/10	LR Reagan	G Large	Yes	3/10/10	5/10/10	No impact on timescale Extra $12K required Funded from contingency
2	Change process for communicating to customers	S Stone	1/10/10	TD Hepper	K Mason (Project manager)	Not required			Required as a result of legal and regulatory issues which were not taken into account at the start of the project Extra $2K cost Funded from scope reserve
3									

Figure 25.3 A typical change log

The change log supplements the initial or full business case by recording all potential and approved changes to the project.

Accountabilities for change decisions

All proposed changes need to be reviewed and their impact assessed before they are accepted or rejected. A project may have several levels for the review and authorisation of changes, depending on how serious or far reaching the impact of the change will be. The following table suggests such levels.

Notice that the first two levels of authority lie within the project itself as the impacts do not affect other projects. Once other projects are affected, it is necessary to have the change reviewed and authorised by a higher authority that can balance the conflicting needs of different projects and sponsors.

The impact levels should be defined and agreed when the project is authorised. (Often an organisation has a standard set as part of its project authorisation process.) This should be documented in the Initial or Full Business Case.

Impact of change	Approval required by
No impact on overall schedule, cost or benefits Allocation of scope reserve	Project manager (record in change log)
Minor impact. Change affecting schedule or costs which can be accommodated without affecting other projects and are within the authority (tolerance) delegated to the project sponsor Allocation of contingency	Project sponsor (use change request form and record in change log)
Major impact. Change affecting scope, objectives, benefits, schedule or costs which cannot be accommodated within the authority (tolerance) delegated to the project sponsor or which affects other projects	Project review group (use change request form and record in change log) In some cases a business programme board may have delegated authority which would normally be at project review group level

The change request form

If a change is minor in nature and can be approved by the project manager, this may be noted directly in the change log. If approval is required by higher authority it is recommended that a change request form is used to ensure the relevant information is captured prior to completing the log.

A change request form is used to:

- document requested changes;
- summarise the impact of the change;
- formally record the decision regarding the change.

An example is given in Figure 25.4. While this is a 'paper-based' example, the logic lends itself to electronic-based workflow systems.

The project manager should:

- enter the relevant data into the change log (change reference number, description, originator, date raised, impact assessment by, assessment due);
- complete Part A of the change request form;
- assess (with the help of others) the impact of the change and complete Part B (impact) of the form;
- pass the form (with any supporting information) to the higher authority as appropriate (see p. 437) for approval. Any necessary financial authorisation documents should also be prepared.

The 'approver' should:

- review the proposed change and complete Part C as appropriate;
- return the form to the project manager.

The project manager should complete the entry in the change log.

Change Request Form		
Project title:		
Project number:		
Change number:		

PART A Proposed change (to be completed by the Project Manager)

Description of change requested

Reason for/benefits of the proposed change

Approval required from:		**By (date)**	

PART C Decision (to be completed by the 'Approver')

* ☐ The change is approved	**Name**
☐ The change is approved subject to the comments noted below:	
☐ The change is rejected	
*Delete as appropriate	**Date**

Action required / Comments

Figure 25.4 A change request form (page 1)
This sheet describes the change, the reason for it and records approval.

PART B Summary of impact
(to be completed by the Project Manager)

Quantifiable benefits	
Estimated incremental cost of change	
Effect on schedules	
Additional resources required	
Effect on other projects/activities	
Additional risks	
Recommendation	Change should be accepted / Change should be rejected
Assessment done by	
Date	

Figure 25.4 A change request form (page 2)
This sheet summarises the impact of the change on the project.

DO YOU CONTROL CHANGE ON YOUR PROJECTS?

1 Take any one of your longer running projects which is in the Develop and Test Stage or beyond. From the documentation which authorised the project extract the following data:

25.1

- the total budgeted cost;

- the baseline completion date (or other identifiable milestone);

- the scope;

- the expected benefits.

2 From the most recent project progress report extract the following data:

- total forecast cost;

- forecast completion date (or other identifiable milestone);

- the current scope;

- the current expected benefits.

3 Compare your answers from 1 and 2. If there are differences, are they due to time slippage or cost overruns? Or are they due to a deliberate decision to change one of the four key control aspects of a project? If the latter, how do you know?

HARNESSING INFORMATION TECHNOLOGY (IT) FOR RISK, ISSUES AND CHANGE

Now that many organisations have IT capabilities on virtually every desktop, the opportunity now exists to streamline the project control logs. Many organisations are now building database tools which integrate the risk, opportunity, issue and change logs into a single tool. In addition meeting notes, action and lessons learned are also often included. Such tools can greatly simplify administration. However, always remember you do need to communicate these logs/reports and therefore unless all your team members and stakeholders are equipped, you risk 'cutting them off'.

Reviews and More Reviews

443

You should always welcome reviews as they are the opportunity to correct any shortcomings or improve those things which are going well to make them even better.

> *'One sees great things from the valley; only small things from the peak.'*
>
> G K CHESTERTON

- **You, as project sponsor, should initiate the reviews.**
- **Focus on the business objectives and benefits.**
- **If the project is no longer viable – terminate it!**
- **Don't assume performance to date is an indicator of future performance.**
- **Be forward looking; don't dwell on past problems and failures.**
- **Agree an action plan and see it through.**

Keeping sight of the objectives

Your project is underway and may have been running for a long time. The team will be immersed in the day-to-day work of building and delivering the required outputs. This is when you are in danger of losing focus on the real business objectives which initiated the project in the first place. It is vital that you lift yourself above the day-to-day workload and **review** whether:

> *The team will be immersed in the day-to-day work of building and delivering the required outputs. This is when you are in danger of losing focus on the real business objectives which initiated the project in the first place.*

- the project still serves your business objectives;
- the conditions of satisfaction are clearly understood and are being pursued;
- continuation of your project is still justified before further costs are committed to (e.g. signing a major contract);
- your project is being effectively managed and the team is confident that the project will be completed.

Such reviews are an indispensable part of good project management, reassuring you, if you are the project sponsor, that the benefits you require will in fact be realised and, if you are the project manager, giving you an independent view on the effectiveness with which you are running the project. You should always welcome reviews as they are the opportunity to correct any shortcomings or improve those things which are going well to make them even better.

If a review is to be welcomed in this way it must be conducted in an open and honest way with 'fault' and 'blame' being rarely, if ever, used. Witch hunts during the course of a project rarely benefit anyone – be tough on the problem, not on the people. If you can foster this atmosphere of trust an open and honest review will:

- give you the confidence that your money is being well spent to provide clear business benefits and that these will be achieved (or conversely that a project which is no longer viable is terminated);
- give the project manager and team confidence that what is being done is really supported by the business.

Conversely, a review conducted in an atmosphere of retribution, fear and blame will not uncover a reliable picture of the status of the project.

It is important to distinguish between a 'review', a 'decision', and a 'progress check'. A **review** is when advice and comment, external to the project, is requested. Such advice may or may not be followed. A **decision** follows a review and is a choice between possible futures. Such a decision may draw on the collective 'wisdom' of the reviewers, but ultimately rests with the person making the choice. The role of the reviewers is to ensure that decision makers make informed choices. A **progress check** differs from a review in that it is conducted by the project manager and focusses on the execution of the project (what, when, how much) rather than its overall objective (why). In summary a review gives you the opportunity to:

- recall **why** you are doing the project;
- check that **what** you are doing is still appropriate;
- assess **how** you are going about it;
- confirm **when** it is going to be completed;
- confirm **how much** it will cost you;
- and . . . whether you still need it!

When should you have a review?

You should hold a review prior to making any key decisions affecting the future of the project. Typically these will be:

- at the Initial Investigation Gate when a proposal has been submitted;
- at the Detailed Investigation Gate when the initial business case is approved and the project is committed into your project portfolio;
- during the course of the project:
  - at the gates prior to starting key stages of the project:
    - Development Gate;
    - Trial Gate;
    - Ready for Service Gate;
  - when major contracts are to be let;
  - when major deliverables are to be accepted;
  - during stages which are inherently risky;
  - when a 'show-stopping' issue has been identified;
  - when the risks become unacceptably high;
- at the 'close' of the project (whether completed or terminated);
- at an appropriate time after the project completion so that achievement of the benefits can be assessed (Post-Implementation Review).

Notice that all these reviews are event driven and occur when a particular point in the project has been reached. They are not driven by calendar lapse time. You should plan the reviews into the project schedule in advance except for those which are driven by unplanned events (risks and issues).

Who is accountable for ensuring a review happens?

The project sponsor is accountable for the business benefits and it is, therefore, in his/her interest that reviews take place. There is little point in the project manager completing a project on time, within budget and to the expected standard, only to find it is no longer needed. Consequently, it is the project sponsor (or higher authority, e.g. business programme sponsor) who is accountable for ensuring that all reviews take place.

> *There is little point in the project manager completing a project on time, within budget and to the expected standard, only to find it is no longer needed. Consequently, it is the project sponsor who is accountable for that ensuring all reviews take place.*

You must be clear on the purpose of each review and know:

- the scope of each review (total project, subpart, etc.);
- driver for the review (the event which triggers the review);
- the names of the review manager and team members;
- evaluation criteria to be used (checklists, etc.).

Except for names and actual dates, these are all predefined in the staged framework for the gate reviews, closure review and Post-Implementation Review.

Generally, all reviews assess the deliverables, documentation and performance of the project to date. This is coupled with interviews with the project team, users, customers, third parties, suppliers and functional managers so that you can gain different perspectives on and perceptions of the project from the different stakeholders. Do also include the project manager. If the review comes up with recommendations concerning the running of the project it is important that the project manager is enrolled to implement them.

Unless included in formal gate deliverables, the review manager should record and communicate his or her findings in a brief report covering:

- the key findings from the review;
- recommendations for improvements/changes needed together with who should be actioned to implement them;
- areas where the project has performed well.

This report should be sent to the project sponsor (and project board if there is one) who should agree with the project manager which recommendations should be incorporated into the project, by when and by whom. If there are lessons which could usefully benefit other projects or which provide useful feedback on the project processes, these should be recorded and sent to the relevant people.

TERMINATING PROJECTS IS NOT INDICATIVE OF FAILURE

In some circumstances it is apparent that the project is no longer likely to meet its stated objectives and should be stopped. This may be because:

- the business need no longer exists;
- an issue has arisen which cannot be resolved;
- risks are unacceptably high;
- any prescribed criteria noted in the business case have been encountered.

Such circumstances should always be considered within any review and stopping projects as a result should not be treated as a 'failure'.

Review when a proposal is raised

The staged framework prescribes that any proposal for a new project is formally written up, sponsored and registered at the Initial Investigation Gate. The key question facing you at this point is 'Is this proposal worth consuming resources and money on undertaking an initial investigation?' Is the objective compelling? While information on costs, timescale and impact may be very sketchy, it should be possible to decide if the proposal fits within the current strategy. If this is not possible, the proposal should proceed no further.

Review at the Detailed Investigation Gate

One of the key lessons of project management is that if high emphasis is placed on the early stages of a project, the likelihood of project success is increased considerably. A thorough review at the time the project is formally committed into the project portfolio (at the Detailed Investigation Gate) is, therefore, essential as it is at this point that the proposal of 'what we **want** to do' becomes a project, i.e. 'what we are **going** to do'. The project sponsor is, in effect, stating he/she can be held accountable for all subsequent costs and benefits associated with the project no matter where they are spent or earned within the organisation.

The review is intended to ensure that all interested parties understand the objectives of the project, what they are accountable for during its execution and how it will affect them once it is implemented. The review should confirm that the correct project is being started at the right time; if the review finds otherwise, then the project should be terminated or postponed. (See p. 20.)

THE HEALTH CHECK

Project Workout 26.1 comprises a 'health check' which may be used to aid any review. This tool is designed to give an overall assessment of the supporting environment, within which the project exists together with an associated 'risk' rating.

Reviews during the project

Reviews during the execution of the project provide additional check points where the objectives and general 'state of health' of the project can be assessed.

Reviews related to stages and gates

Within the staged framework these are at the gates prior to starting new stages, for example, at the Development Gate, the Trial Gate and the Release Gate. In such cases, the review should focus on the decision to proceed with the project (or not) and, if so, check the adequacy of preparation for the next part or stage of the project.

> *For long stages, intermediate reviews should be planned into the project schedule. These should usually be event driven (i.e. a particular milestone has been reached such as signing a major contract) rather than time driven.*

For long stages, intermediate reviews should be planned into the project schedule. These should be event driven (i.e. a particular milestone has been reached such as signing a major contract) rather than time driven. It is good practice to plan reviews such that one is due approximately every three months. Notwithstanding this, it may also be appropriate to review a project prior to the regular quarterly business refracts. These reviews should confirm that the costs, timescales and project targets remain achievable and that the expected benefits will be delivered to the business.

Finally, the project management practices should always be assessed to confirm that they are being implemented effectively. The 'health check' tool included in Project Workout 26.1, later in this chapter, can be used to assist in this.

Reviews related to deliverables

When project deliverables are produced, they need to be reviewed and approved against predetermined criteria. The criteria may be documented in any convenient form; however, I have found the 'product description' to be a useful fall-back in the absence of anything else. A product description defines the following:

- the title or name of the deliverable;
- the purpose of the deliverable – what it is used for;
- composition – what are the components of the product? For example, if the product is a document, this would be a list of the expected chapters or sections. For a low-level component, this section will be a description of the product;
- derivation – what are the source products from which this product is derived?
- format and presentation;
- users of the deliverable;
- quality/acceptance criteria – what quality specification must the product be produced to and what quality measurements will be applied by those inspecting the finished product?
- type of quality check required – what kind of test, inspection or review is to be used to check the quality or functionality?
- quality skills/domain knowledge requirement – what quality skills/ domain knowledge is required to inspect or review and acceptance of the product?
- approval and review panels – identify the appropriate approval and review panels.

It may be appropriate to link a review of the entire project to a key project deliverable.

Reviews related to risks or issues

You cannot predict when these are needed. They are the most difficult to set up and manage as there is the persistent hope that all will come right in the end, especially if you don't have to waste time doing a review! Realism, honesty and openness are what are called for. The project manager needs to recognise when circumstances are conspiring against the project and the project sponsor needs to be made aware. The project sponsor also needs to recognise that the benefits he/she seeks may not be realised through this project. In such cases it is important to focus on **why** the project was started and look at what else could be done to meet those same objectives.

> *There is the persistent hope that all will come right in the end, especially if you don't have to waste time doing a review!*

Project closure review

A project can be closed either when it has been completed or if it is terminated. (Any review may lead to termination!) It is important that a project is closed down in a controlled way and that all accountabilities relating to it are discharged and lessons learned. The **closure review** aims to fulfil this and is described more fully in Chapters 10 and 27. It should:

- review the efficiency of the project in terms of meeting the original time, cost and resource targets;
- confirm that the benefits have been built into the business forecast;
- record and communicate any lessons which can be beneficial to future projects.

As far as the project sponsor is concerned, either the project has been completed and he/she can now expect to benefit from it, or the project has been terminated. In the latter case, this may be because the original business need no longer exists, but, if it does, the project sponsor will need to take action to address the unresolved business need which initiated the project in the first place.

Post-Implementation Review

Between three to six months after the project has been completed, you should undertake a formal review to assess whether the project has, in fact, met its stated business objectives or is on course to achieve them. This is called a **Post-Implementation Review** (see also Chapter 11). It should:

- assess the benefits which have already been achieved and compare them with those originally planned;
- assess how well the outputs for the project are working in practice;
- make recommendations for corrective actions (if any);
- record and communicate any lessons which may be useful for future projects.

It is important that the review is considered from the differing viewpoints of the various stakeholders involved, for example:

- project sponsor;
- benefiting functions and units;

- operational users;
- third parties;
- customers.

They will all have their own opinions as to whether the project was successful or not.

'Almost complete' is often not enough

Copyright © 1997 Robert Buttrick

Recording agreement – quality reviews

Obtaining agreement to key deliverables during the project is essential. However, it can often prove to be a difficult task to:

- identify those who need to be involved;
- engage them in taking time to address the review;
- be certain that a review has, in fact, been done.

For these reasons, it is often useful to follow a formal process for checking, agreeing and documenting the review and acceptance of project deliverables. This is key for final deliverables, but applies just as much to intermediate deliverables (i.e. those developed during the project) which set the 'agenda' for the next stage of work to be formally reviewed and signed off. Unless this is done, there is a danger that work may proceed on a premise which does not have the support of the users or other stakeholders.

The following is a recommended procedure where alternative formal 'quality processes' have not been adopted.

Standard record for reviews and approvals

A standard form (such as given in Figure 26.1) may be used instead of an e-mail, memo or letter as it provides a concise and recognisable document which clearly states what is required of the recipient. For example, some individuals may receive a deliverable for comment on particular points only, while others will receive a 'final' deliverable and will be required to accept (approve) it.

The project documentation should list the key deliverables from the project, stating who has responsibility for reviewing and accepting them. If a deliverable is not readily portable, alternative methods of review (demonstrations, tests, etc.) should be arranged.

Procedure

1 The originator of the deliverable (or project manager) sends the deliverable under cover of a request form (with Part A completed) to the reviewer.
2 The reviewer carries out the action noted under 'review and sign-off criteria', completes Part B of the form and returns it to the originator. It is not usually necessary to have a real signature, as e-mail or electronic signatures are generally adequate in most organisations.

Review and Approval Record	
Project title:	
Project number:	

PART A Request (to be completed by the person making the request)

Reviewer (name):		Review requested by: (name):	
Issued to Reviewer on (date):		To be returned to by (date):	

Deliverable to be reviewed

Review criteria

PART B Response (to be completed by the Reviewer)

I have reviewed the above deliverable on behalf of

* ☐   The deliverable is accepted/approved

☐   The deliverable is accepted/approved subject to inclusion of the comments noted below

☐   The deliverable is rejected for the reasons noted below

Tick appropriate box

Comments

Name		Function	
Signature		Date	

Figure 26.1 An example of an approval form

PROJECT HEALTH CHECK

26.1

This tool is a useful analytical device to assess the current 'health' of a project. It looks at the full project environment and using a set of key questions results in an assessment of the overall risk associated with the project. As such it fulfils two roles:

● as a checklist;

● as a tool to indicate where a project manager's efforts should be directed.

It is recommended that the 'health check' is carried out as a part of every project review and at least quarterly. Expect a higher level of risk at the start of the project. An Excel version of this tool is on the CD-ROM.

Instructions

1 Score each statement with a grading –4 to +4:

–4	=	strongly disagree or don't know
–2	=	disagree
0	=	neutral
+2	=	agree
+4	=	strongly agree

2 Enter the total score from each section in the summary section.

3 Add the scores together.

4 Use the key to assess the overall health of your project and hence the risk associated with it.

Project plan	☐	P score
Resources	☐	R score
Ownership	☐	O score
Justifiable case	☐	J score
Expertise	☐	E score
Clear solution	☐	C score
Targeted control	☐	T score
Total score	☐	

Key: degree of risk

☐ +14 to +7 = low   ☐ + 7 to 0 = medium

☐ 0 to –7 = high   ☐ –7 to –14 = impossible

(Adapted with the kind permission of the Strategic Management Group, based on the Project Implementation Profile by Jeffrey K Pinto and Dennis P Slavin.)

PROJECT PLAN

There is an outline plan for the full project (cost, schedule, etc.).

□

There is a detailed plan for the current stage of work
(costs, schedule, etc.).

□

The team's roles and accountabilities are defined and understood.

□

Slack time and transferable/flexible resource have been identified.

□

Known risks have been taken into account in the plan.

□

Total

□

P score = total/10

□

RESOURCES

Sufficient manpower exists to complete the project.

□

The project team have the facilities to undertake their work effectively.

□

Project tools and systems are suitable and are fully supported.

□

I am confident resource managers will release people to work
on the project.

□

All team members understand their roles.

□

Total

□

R score = total/10

□

OWNERSHIP

The project sponsor is fully committed to the project's success.

□

The project sponsor has the authority to undertake the role effectively.

□

The project sponsor is responsive to escalations and requests for advice.

□

Key stakeholders are demonstrably positive towards the project.

□

Stakeholders understand the benefits the project will enable.

□

Total

□

O score = total/10

□

JUSTIFIABLE CASE

The project fits the organisation's strategy.

☐

The project is financially viable and the source of funding is reliable.

☐

The option chosen for the solution represents the best approach.

☐

All suppliers offer value for money.

☐

I am confident the project objectives are achievable.

☐

Total

☐

J score = total/10

☐

EXPERTISE

People engaged on the project have the right skills.

☐

Specialist advice is available to team members from experts, when needed.

☐

The method for individual performance evaluation is effective and understood.

☐

All suppliers are fully capable of delivering to their contracts.

☐

Adequate training is available and timetabled within the project plan.

☐

Total

☐

E score = total/10

☐

CLEAR SOLUTION

The solution/output from the project is fit to meet the stated objectives.

☐

Ongoing operational aspects have been included in the project solution.

☐

The solution/output is fully defined, documented and configuration controlled.

☐

Future users of the solution are confident it will meet their needs.

☐

Transformation plans reflect the complexity of the change needed.

☐

Total

☐

C score = total/10

☐

TARGETED CONTROL

Risks and issues are being managed to bring them within acceptable limits. ☐

Defects are being captured, managed and resolved effectively. ☐

Changes to defined baseline are being effectively controlled. ☐

Reporting to necessary stakeholders is accurate, timely and effective. ☐

The right number and types of reviews are planned and taking place. ☐

Total ☐

T score = total/10 ☐

Closing the Project

Project closure

The closure report

The closure meeting

Closure actions

It is the project sponsor's role to approve the closure of a project. However, if a project is to be closed part way through and other projects are affected (the project definition will define interproject interdependencies), approval may need to be given by a higher authority or agreed with other affected parties.

'Yes, in the old days that was so, but we have changed all that.'

MOLIÈRE 1622–1673

- **Closure is the project sponsor's decision.**
- **Check interdependent projects before terminating yours.**
- **Make project closure explicit.**
- **Communicate closure to the stakeholders.**
- **Learn the lessons and share them.**

Project closure

The objective of project closure is to ensure that:

- a project is closed down in a controlled and organised way;
- all accountabilities relating to it have been discharged or handed over to the line or to another project.

Closure is the formal 'end-point' of a project: this is either because it is **completed** or because it has been **terminated**. Termination may occur because the project is no longer viable or because the risks associated with it have become unacceptably high. The closure review should:

- review the efficiency of the project in terms of meeting the original time, cost and scope;
- confirm that the benefits have been built into the business forecast;
- record and communicate any lessons which can be beneficial to future projects.

As far as the project sponsor is concerned, either the project has been completed and he/she can now expect to benefit from it, or the project has been terminated. In the latter case, this may be because the original business need no longer exists, but, if it does, the project sponsor will need to take action to address the unresolved business need which initiated the project in the first place.

There are three key steps to closing a project:

1 Prepare the closure report.
2 Formally close the project.
3 Close down and communicate.

The closure report

It is the project sponsor's role to approve the closure of a project. However, if a project is to be closed part way through and other projects are affected (the project definition will define any project interdependencies) approval may need to be given by a higher authority or agreed with other affected parties.

When a project is to be closed, you, as project manager, should:

- Check the status and completeness of the Business Case (including the project definition), the change and issues logs, the most recent progress report and any papers referring to early cancellation of project. (Do this using Project Workout 27.1.)
- Prepare a draft project closure report with the team, including the terms of reference for the Post-Implementation Review (PIR).

The purpose of the closure report is to record the reason for closure, the benefits the project is expected to achieve and any outstanding accountabilities which need to be handed over. It also documents any lessons learned regarding how the project was conducted and the efficacy of the supporting processes.

The project closure report should include the following sections:

1 Business objectives.
2 Closure statement.
3 Benefits measurement.
4 Outstanding issues and deliverables.
5 Project efficiency.
6 Lessons learned.
7 Acknowledgments.

An appendix should give the terms of reference for the Post-Implementation Review, if one is required.

Contents of a project closure report

1 Business objectives
Restate the business objectives as given in the Business Case, including any changes that have been approved since it was authorised (see p. 298). If there have been any major changes, state the reasons.

2 Closure statement

State the circumstances under which the project is being closed as one of the following:

- the project has been successfully completed;
- the project has been terminated prior to completion.

If the latter is the case, describe the reasons for termination and indicate the current likelihood of resurrection.

3 Benefits measurement

Restate the tangible benefits (given in the Business Case; see p. 298) which the project will provide and how these will be measured, together with who will be accountable for measuring them. In addition:

- state whether the current business plan/forecast reflects the project benefits;
- include defined review points for measurements of benefits.

4 Outstanding risks, issues and deliverables

List any issues or key deliverables not yet accepted. For each give:

- the nature of the risk and/or issue or reason for non-acceptance;
- who has agreed to be accountable;
- the proposed resolution (including date).

5 Project efficiency

State the actual cost and resources consumed as well as the actual schedule achieved compared with the plan.

Cost (£,000)	Resource (person days)	Trial Gate date	Release Gate	Launch date	Project completed date
Original baseline					
Current baseline					
Actual					
Variance					

6 Lessons learned

Referring to project efficiency and the project team's experiences, (e.g. major issues encountered, changes of strategy) state what could have been done better:

- Identify areas where time, money, or resource could have been better used.
- Recommend courses of action for future projects to help eliminate any inefficiencies found.
- Identify what worked well and recommend methods, processes, procedures and tools which other projects may find of use in the future.

7 Acknowledgments

Acknowledge all individuals who have made special contributions to the project.

Appendix A: terms of reference for PIR

The Post-Implementation Review (PIR) is designed to measure the benefits realised by the project against the conditions of satisfaction given in the Business Case (see also p. 298).

If a Post-Implementation Review is required, state:

- who is accountable for organising and chairing it;
- when it will occur;
- which functional areas and stakeholders are required to participate.

The closure meeting

You should invite key individuals to a meeting at which the project is formally approved for closure by the project sponsor. By drawing the group together, the project manager has an opportunity to:

> *The quality and sharing of feedback is always greater when done in a group than when conducted in isolation.*

- ensure feedback reflects the differing viewpoints of those involved;
- assign accountabilities for outstanding issues;
- acknowledge the team and celebrate.

The quality and sharing of feedback is always greater when done in a group than when conducted in isolation.

A suggested agenda for a closure meeting follows and is detailed in Figure 27.1:

1 Deliverables.
2 Outstanding issues.
3 Benefits and business plan.
4 Post-Implementation Review.
5 Acknowledgments.
6 Formal closure.
7 Lessons learned.

The draft project closure report, which should be circulated prior to the meeting, provides the briefing for the attendees. This will be amended based on the discussions and feedback received at the meeting.

Small projects

If the project is small or if the project sponsor and project manager do not believe a meeting will add value, formal closure should be agreed by the project sponsor after a review of the closure report by the relevant individuals.

Large projects

It may be advisable to hold two meetings for large projects; the first to cover items 1 to 6 and the second to cover item 7. This is particularly of value when it is known that the project can contribute greatly to the organisation's corporate learning.

PROJECT CLOSURE MEETING
AGENDA

1 Deliverables

Confirm that all final deliverables have been approved and accepted by their owners.

2 Outstanding issues

Review outstanding issues; for each issue, obtain agreement from a named person in the line or in another project that they will 'own' the issue and its resolution.

3 Benefits and business plan

Confirm that the benefits have already been built into the business plan or are due to be included in the next forecast.

Accountability for the monitoring of benefits should be agreed together with a timetable of defined review points.

4 Post-Implementation Review

If a PIR is required, the terms of reference should be agreed together with a timetable and named participants. The accountability for the review must be agreed.

5 Acknowledgments

Acknowledge all contributions to the project.

6 Formal closure

Assuming all the preceding business has been conducted, the project sponsor should 'sign-off' closure of the project.

7 Lessons learned

What worked well on the project? What did not? Were all the controls effective and useful? What would we use again? What would we do differently next time?

Suggested attendees:

- Project sponsor.
- Project manager.
- Project board members.
- Key team members.
- Functional line/process managers accountable for signing off key deliverables.
- Functional line/process managers who will accept accountability for outstanding issues.
- Project manager from any related projects who will accept account ability for any outstanding issues.

Figure 27.1 A suggested agenda for a project closure meeting

Closure actions

Following approval to close the project from the project sponsor, the project manager should:

- finalise the project closure report;
- prepare a communication, enclosing the approved project closure report to the project sponsor, project team and stakeholders, confirming the decision to close the project;
- complete any outstanding closure actions;
- feed back any suggested process improvements to the relevant project offices and/or process support group.

A full checklist is included in Project Workout 27.1.

WHAT HAPPENS TO THE LESSONS?

Collecting the lessons learnt from each project and focusing on them at project closure will ensure those involved in the project are less likely to fall into the same traps twice. It will not, however, ensure no one else does! If your organisation as a whole is to benefit, you need to be able to make these lessons more widely available. In large organisations this can be problematic as the volume of information can be daunting. Don't fall into the trap of just listing each lesson in a long document; no one will find anything. You must invest some time in making the lessons accessible and relevant. Think of a cookery book. It is not merely a set of recipes that the author has cooked over the past year. It is carefully divided up and indexed to make it as easy as possible for the reader to find what is needed. Your lessons learnt should be the same. Intranet capabilities are invaluable in helping you distribute the lessons.

Make sure you tell them it's over

Copyright © 1997 Robert Buttrick

CLOSURE CHECKLIST

1 Deliverables

27.1

☐ Have all project deliverables been approved and handed over to on-going 'owners'?

☐ Has accountability for outstanding deliverables been agreed?

2 Issues

☐ Have all issues been resolved?

☐ Has ownership of each outstanding issue been accepted by a named person in the line or in another project ?

3 Business forecast

☐ Have the functions and business units updated their plans to take into account the operational resources, costs and benefits relating to the project?

☐ Has the business forecast been updated or will it be?

☐ Has a person accepted accountability for monitoring the benefits?

☐ Have review points for measuring the benefits been defined?

4 Post-Implementation Review (PIR)

☐ Has a decision been made to have a PIR?

☐ Have the timing and terms of reference for the PIR been agreed?

☐ Has it been agreed who is accountable for ensuring the PIR takes place?

5 Team and stakeholders

☐ Have all who need to know about the closure of the project been informed?

☐ Have all team members been reassigned to other activities?

☐ Have project team appraisals relating to the project been completed?

☐ Have those who deserve special acknowledgment been acknowledged?

6 Project documentation

☐ Has all documentation pertaining to this project been filed, archived and referenced?

7 Facilities

☐ Have all project facilities (desks, computers, office space, etc.) been released?

☐ Have all facilities reserved for the project outputs or contracts raised been cancelled?

8 Project accounting and other systems

☐ Has the project account been closed such that no further expenditure can be attributed to the project?

☐ Have other corporate or functional project tracking systems and registers been updated?

Part Five

IMPLEMENTING THE FRAMEWORK

Implementing the
Framework

Advice from other organisations

Corporate maturity

Finding help in implementing a project's approach

Justifiably different – tailoring

A strategy for implementation

The implementation task is very large but not so large that you should give up now! Implementing a project's approach is not a single project.

'If there are obstacles, the shortest line between two points may be a crooked one.'

BERTOLT BRECHT

You've read and understood the book, bought into the principles, and now you want to apply them to your organisation. You've some projects going on but you are not quite sure how many. You do not know what stage in the project framework they are. You might not know who wants the benefits or even who is managing them. You now want to do something about it – but what?

Advice from other organisations

I asked a number of organisations what their advice would be to anyone embarking on the introduction of a projects approach to business in their organisation, be it for the organisation as a whole or for one particular cross-functional activity such as product development. All the advice given matched that which you would find in any good book on the management of change. However, despite this body of common sense much of this advice had been ignored by many of the companies to their cost!

'It is the true nature of mankind to learn from mistakes, not from example.'

FRED HOYLE

'Top management' support was always stated as essential, particularly as the 'project approach' relies on them as decision makers. This is one of the few business processes where they are required to 'live' the process rather than monitor it. Where they are not the fire-fighting problem solvers but a key link in the chain. If they don't perform by making good, timely decisions, it will slow projects down at best or set off the wrong projects at worst. One chief executive of a major engineering group held back his implementation for six months until he was convinced that his board was really committed. This was in an organisation where cross-functional working and project management were already well established.

COMMITMENT OR INVOLVEMENT?

Consider the great British breakfast of bacon and eggs. The hen is involved but the pig is committed.

Other valuable advice included:

- Don't underestimate the training and coaching effort needed.
- Don't underestimate the resources needed to support your implementation.
- Use champions embedded in the business to promote the process.
- Roll it out in parts – you can't do all of it at once.

Finally, keep any supporting documentation simple. One organisation had the basic process written on just ten sheets of paper. This was supported by a number of more detailed guides to aid the users with particular aspects.

Of course, you have to direct and manage your business regardless of whether you have a project process to aid you or not. Many organisations have operated as functional hierarchies for years and not even heard words such as 'cross-functional' or 'project'. By the same token, there are organisations today where the use of the word 'cross-functional' is no longer needed. They always work in teams, drawing on the most appropriate people from across the organisation to work together in pursuit of objectives. They can't conceive of any other way to work effectively. I know which sort of organisation I'd rather work in!

A projects approach will give you the capability to know:

- what you are doing to change your business in pursuit of your strategy;
- the interdependencies between your programmes and projects;
- the benefits and risks you are signed up to.

It does this by making projects, and hence the implementation of strategy, very visible. It does not reduce or affect your discretion to direct and manage your business as you see fit. In fact, it gives you the knowledge to enable you to make better informed decisions. It also enables you to delegate more than you ever have before. You can assign programmes or projects to your colleagues and subordinates but, because they are visible and defined, you do not lose sight of them.

Implementing a projects approach entails introducing complex changes encompassing processes, systems, accountabilities and culture. This book gives you an insight into the processes, the systems, accountabilities and cultures that have been shown to work best but it is impossible to be prescriptive about how it will look in your own organisation. The easier parts to implement are the processes and systems. These are tangible, they can be written down and created. However, structure and culture are another matter. As soon as you start changing the structures, for example, relating to decision making, the defence mechanisms of those who feel threatened will rise. Similarly, just because you have a process, it doesn't mean that some will do anything but pay lip service to it. You have to grow a culture which wants to play the game and engages all your people from top to bottom. Earlier in this book I talked about the organisation which always looked to 'people problems' when their process broke down. They had learned that this was usually the root cause of break-

> *You have to grow a culture which wants to play the game and enrols all your people from top to bottom.*

downs rather than the process itself. We also discovered that project management is one of the few business processes which senior management take a part in rather than watch from afar. It is therefore vital that your implementation includes full briefing of the roles that those key people are to take. Remember, this is not just about processes and project managers but is about project management in totality.

Corporate maturity

One of the greatest obstacles to the effective implementation of enterprise-wide project management is the corporate culture with respect to cross-functional accountabilities from top to bottom. There are a number of maturity models being published, the most prominent being CMMI, from the Software Engineering Institute. All have a set number of 'maturity levels', with defined criteria and best practices. CMMI, according to the official website, is described as follows:

> *Capability Maturity Model® Integration (CMMI) is a process improvement approach that provides organisations with the essential elements of effective processes. It can be*

used to guide process improvement across a project, a division, or an entire organisation. CMMI helps integrate traditionally separate organisational functions, set process improvement goals and priorities, provide guidance for quality processes, and provide a point of reference for appraising current processes.

www.sei.cmu.edu/cmmi

In other words, it seeks to be a set of best practices, which, if followed, will lead to business advantage. It has four levels of 'maturity', ranging from totally 'immature' to 'optimising':

- **Level 1** is where most people are: ad hoc project management. In fact, by definition everyone who isn't at level 2 or above is at level 1!
- **Level 2** means you can do one project at a time, but maybe all your projects are done differently.
- **Level 3** means you have a common way of undertaking all your projects. This is the minimum level I advocate, as evidenced by this book.
- **Level 4** means you are truly metrics driven and are an organisation which is optimising its performance.

The CMMI handbook is not a gripping read. It is the only book I've read which I needed to go on a course to know what it really means to say! That said, once you get through the style and the jargon there is a lot of sense in it. Used properly and supported by the right consultants, CMMI can make a difference to organisations in the system and software engineering sectors. The main driver, however, seems to be that many government departments are starting to require it as a prerequisite to bidding. That can be its success and its downfall as many organisations are likely take CMMI on in order to 'get the badge' rather than to really make a difference to their business operations.

I have used CMMI and can reconcile it with my own ideas in *The Project Workout*. However, like the Project Management Institute (PMI) (see **www.pmi.org**) it shows its IT contractor industry roots and perhaps that is why it is so difficult to understand.

Another maturity model has been developed by PRTM (a management consultancy specialising in high technology businesses, see **www.prtm.com**). It has a five-level progression model from not doing projects at all, to being able to undertake not only one project but whole herds of them. I like the model as it acknowledges the 'ignorant' who have no realisation of the benefits business-led project management can provide and also acknowledges the importance of organisations working together (partnering), which is increasingly common today. Figure 28.1 summarises the model.

Questions

- Which level of maturity are you at now?
- Which level are you aiming for in your implementation and what timescale?
- Are you clear on the business reasons for wanting to improve?

Finding help in implementing a project's approach

Finding help in putting the principles and practice outlined in this book into effect can be a daunting first step. The options include:

- asking a consultant to advise you;
- asking your in-house experts;
- finding out how others solve this problem (benchmarking).

Employing an outside consultant is an obvious and frequently used choice. However, their solutions may be resisted from within the organisation. 'We're different', 'That's too theoretical' and 'You don't understand how complicated our business is' are commonly heard. Unfortunately, much good experience, advice and money are wasted if an organisation lacks trust and belief in what its consultants are saying. Before you ignore the complaints of your people, however, consider whether the consultants you have chosen (or propose to use) really know what they are doing. Check a number of consultancies and check their former clients for references. Making a wrong move at the start could be catastrophic. Having made the selection, the benefits the consultant will bring include expertise and experience. In addition, they are able to challenge and coach your senior team to an extent that internal staff are often reticent to do.

PRTM maturity model		Comment
Level 0	Informal	Informal practices based on individual experience	**The Ignorant** – these organisations do not realise the importance and the power a staged project framework gives them. They spend little time on the early investigative stages and waste much effort in the later development stages. Their 'project' success rate is low. These organisations are inefficient and ineffective at implementing business projects
Level 1	Functional	Excellence within functions, but not across functions	
Level 2	Project excellence	Functions aligned for effective execution from concept to market	**The Enlightened** – these organisations realise that a project framework is powerful. They spend a significant amount of time on the investigative stages. Their project success rate is high. However, these organisations are operating below 'optimum' efficiency but are far more effective at implementing business projects than Level 0/1 organisations
Level 3	Portfolio excellence (Business Programmes)	Processes in place to achieve aligned product and corporate strategy, platform and technology leverage, portfolio balance and excellence in project selection and execution	**The Leaders** – these organisations can run not only individual projects but also portfolios of projects. They have a firm grasp on their strategy and what implementation looks like. Consequently, the proportion of time spent on investigative stages as a whole decreases as they are able to screen their proposals more effectively. (Note: the proportion of time spent on investigative stages on individual projects is still high.) They are able to select projects for their portfolio, taking into account constraints such as resources, funding and risk. Their project success rate is high. These organisations are both efficient and effective at implementing business projects
Level 4	Co-development excellence	Core processes linked across to internal and external business partners for maximum leverage in partnering	**The Leaders PLUS** – these organisations can run not only lots of their own projects, but are also effective at working with other organisations.

Figure 28.1 Maturity levels

PRTM's research shows it is not effective to move up a level until you have sufficient mastery of the preceding levels. They also show that productivity can increase by up to 50 per cent for those on Level 4 as opposed to Level 1, with commensurate improvements in growth, profit and time to delivery. Levels 0 to 2 can, to a greater or lesser extent, be driven by forward-thinking middle managers, whereas Levels 3 and 4 are impossible to attain unless senior management want it. Excellence at this level really does come down to a question of: 'How do we want to direct our organisation?' If you are a business leader, that's your choice.

Many organisations use their own people. They are cheaper than consultants and may even have been recruited from consulting firms in the first place. However, if they are seen as a 'prophet in their own country who is not believed', the result may be that they have less credibility than an external consultant. If you propose to use your own people, check them out as thoroughly as you would an external consultant. Look for evidence that they really know what they are talking about *and* that they can deliver the goods.

Nowadays the use of 'benchmarking' is becoming commonplace and is invaluable both to the commercial and the non-commercial sectors in improving performance and finding better ways of structuring and running organisations. Looking at other organisations enables you to look beyond your own immediate local problems and see how others really work.

That said, I have found that using a combination of consultants, internal staff and benchmarking is often the most productive route into the implementation maze if trust in the proposed solutions is to be generated:

- Consultants can give a dispassionate view based on their own specialist knowledge and bring to bear considerable experience in a particular field.
- In-house experts will know their own organisation, its culture and style; they will also have to live with any solutions which are adopted.
- Benchmarking gives you a wider perspective ('other organisations really do it that way!').

Often benchmarking may merely confirm that the approach being taken is correct but always has the additional benefit that it may suggest alternative and illuminating approaches and experiences. Both are very valuable and it is as comforting to know you are on the right track as it is to be put on the right track.

> **It is as comforting to know you are on the right track as it is to be put on the right track.**

Remember, if benchmarking is to work, you must be receptive to new ideas and even old ones you may have previously discarded. Benchmarking findings may otherwise be lost in a fog of mistrust, as may the wisdom of consultants and in-house experts.

Justifiably different – tailoring

You may have wondered, as you read this book, whether the implied 'one size fits all' approach is really practical. Can you really direct and manage a small internal project using the same processes as you would for a major multi-million pound endeavour? Common sense tells you this cannot be right . . . and usually common sense is right! All organisations are different and all have an emphasis on different types of project. The principles and building blocks in the book are applicable to all of them. However, the detail may differ. In Chapter 12, we looked at how we could adapt a standard project framework to suit different circumstances. We were 'tailoring' the approach for specific needs and documenting this in the business case. Similarly we can tailor any aspect of any topic in the book. For example, you will decide, based you your circumstances, what your project framework will be, how your risk log will look, how your business case will be constructed. Having defined these, you need to ask yourself:

- What differences will I permit?
- What parts are mandatory?

These are your 'tailoring limits'. They enable the users of your processes to make their own decisions, to alter some aspects of the process, to meet their needs. Projects are self-defining, in that the business case and its constituent project definition (Chapter 19) define not only why you are undertaking a project but also **how** you are undertaking it. In other words, it will state what tailoring you have applied. Approval of the document should imply approval of any tailoring.

'Difference' is a fact of life and you should use tailoring to enable people to take a legitimately different approach, where the circumstances require it. Formal tailoring creates the control over the 'differences' and stops it becoming a 'free-for-all'.

A strategy for implementation

Boil the ocean and eat an elephant

The implementation task is very large but not so large that you should give up now! Implementing a projects approach is not a single project. You cannot do it all at once, the scale of the changes needed are too extensive. You, therefore, need to split the project up into smaller parts, each of which will satisfy a particular need

> *Use the tools, techniques, lessons and principles in this book. What better test is there for a projects framework than to use it in its own creation!*

and give you some definite benefit. Each of these parts should be run as a project, using all the discipline that a projects approach entails. You can then ease your way forward a step at a time and start reaping the rewards early. As a start you could use the tools, techniques, lessons and principles in this book. What better test is there for a project framework than to use it in its own creation!

One word of warning: you will need to be very firm on maintaining the principles that a projects approach relies on. As the framework starts to bed in it will throw other processes and procedures within your organisation into sharp relief. Sometimes it will show them up to be inadequate. This is not necessarily the fault of the new projects process – the other procedures may always have been inadequate, it's just that they were hidden. Alternatively, it may be that the side effects of the new project process had been missed during your trial stage. The temptation is always to stop and fix every 'new problem'. Resist this. Keep on implementing the parts you decide to implement. If the 'new' problems have been with you for a number years lying unnoticed, a few more months will do no great harm. If you stop what you are doing to fix everything you find, you will end up being diverted to do more and more until you will indeed be trying to eat the elephant.

> *One word of warning: you will need to be very firm on maintaining the principles that a projects approach relies on. As the framework starts to bed in it will throw other processes and procedures within your organisation into sharp relief. Sometimes it will show them up to be inadequate.*

Building your implementation strategy

When undertaking complex change or business process reengineering we are often advised that it should be done in tranches, moving from one 'temporary mode of operation' or 'island of certainty' to another. Put some change in place, let it settle, put some more in place. This assumes a linear and sequential transition from one state to another. It also assumes that you can plan the overall implementation order and configurations at for each tranche, in advance (see Figure 28.2(a)).

Without trust in the solutions, the solutions will not work

A board of senior managers was listening to a presentation on the findings from a benchmarking study (Part One of this book!). A few of them were shaking their heads, commenting that 'The approaches being presented are not used in the 'real world'. The chief executive stopped the presentation stating: 'You may think these approaches don't work but the organisations we talked to are highly respected and successful and they do use them. This is the real world: forget about what you think we could or could not do in this organisation and listen.'

The design of the basic staged project framework was completed. It was agreed. It was ready to be introduced. However, one small question was raised:

Executive: 'The gates require us to make decisions – how do we do that? Could you design a decision-making process? We need that before we go any further. We need to know how to prioritise.'

Project champion: 'Why do you need that now? All I've done is design a management framework for projects. I haven't touched decision making. You make decisions on these things now, so continue the same way until we work out a better way.'

What had in fact happened, was that by rationalising one part, the fundamental aspect of decision making was shown to be lacking. You can't 'process' decision making, only process the points when they need to be made. You can, however, provide a capability to provide information to enable you to make informed decisions – but that relies on having a basic framework within which to manage in the first place. Delaying the implementation of the staged process until decision making is in place would not necessarily solve the problem and would probably lead to implementation being delayed until *all* process components (resources, business planning, fund management, etc.) were defined and approved. In practice, this probably means that nothing is ever implemented.

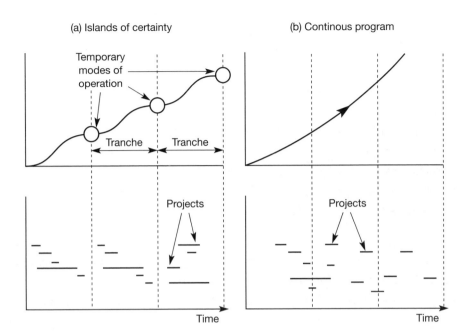

Figure 28.2 Islands of certainty and progressive change
Often the advice on implementing complex change is undertake a first tranche of changes, pause to allow the new changes to bed in (island of certainty or temporary mode of operation) and then move on with the next set of changes. In contrast, using a strategy of continuous change, moving from configuration to configuration, will give you the freedom to choose whether to carry on without limiting yourself to what may be arbitrary islands.

The advice to split the implementation up into projects and hence manage them as a programme is sound. However, the concept of progressing from one planned state to another can be unrealistic. The implementation will not be a 'painting by numbers' programme. Overall, it will start off as a fog and you will need to feel your way forward. Further, even if you did create a road map detailing your islands of certainty, you may impose constraints on your freedom to capitalise on implementation opportunities as they arise. Using a strategy of continuous change, moving from configuration to configuration, will give you the freedom to choose whether to push forward or pause every time a new project is set off (see Figure 28.2(b)). Such decisions must be taken in the knowledge of the prevailing workload in the organisation and level of acceptance you have achieved so far.

> *The advice to split the implementation up into projects and hence manage them as a programme is sound. However, the concept of progressing from one planned state to another can be unrealistic.*

Assume that you have decided to split your implementation up into projects as follows:

- high level design of the final state;
- staged framework and project management;
- decision making;
- strategic alignment;
- fund management;
- release management;
- resource management;
- business planning and forecasting.

Depending on where your organisation is now, you will have a certain amount of confidence in your current operational capabilities for each area of implementation covered by these projects. For you, some of the projects listed here will be painting by numbers, some will be quests and others may even be fogs.

If you start with the painting by numbers projects, you will have more confidence in delivery and hence in securing some benefits. As for the others, you will not know how long they will take or the order in which they can be completed. Neither will you really be sure on the timing, as much of the change relies on the development of a projects culture. So you cannot predict any further islands of certainty – you are in uncharted territory. Your starting point has affected your implementation strategy from the very first day. Don't despair, however, concentrate on what changes you want to see happen. Define these in terms of 'conditions of satisfaction' or Recognition Events™ and then work out, through back-cast planning, how you achieved these.

A possible implementation strategy would be:

Project set 1. Build a high level picture of what you ultimately want to achieve and define a programme of possible projects – classify them as painting by numbers, fog or quest. This picture is often called a 'blueprint' and should never be confused with a project definition.

Project set 2. Implement the staged framework and project management method.

Project set 3. Implement any other painting by numbers projects you have identified. You must look for early benefits if the programme is to be seen as credible.

Project set 4. Work on the remaining quests and fog projects as soon as you can make resource available, implementing them as soon as they become clear and the conditions in the organisation are right.

The overall design (Project set 1) is critical to sound implementation. This book is a reference to help you identify and design the elements of the framework for your organisation. You will also need to know how you are currently dealing with all the activities which will be a part of your future project framework (your present mode of operation). Do not spend too long on this. You need only know sufficient to make sure that your new framework fits into the organisation and that there are no gaps. Designing the new framework can be dealt with on an iterative basis. You will not design it correctly the first time; you are bound to make a few mistakes. Accept this and plan for it. A very effective way of designing and validating the framework is to take a part of it and trial it on a number of projects. Use the learning from these to refine the approach before moving into wider implementation.

> 'A man who makes no mistakes does not usually make anything.'
>
> EDWARD JOHN PHELPS, 12 JANUARY 1899

After completing your overall design you should implement the staged framework itself (Project set 2). The benefit of putting this in place first is that it provides the foundation block and hooks that all the associated processes need to lock onto. The teams undertaking the other projects will have a known reference point to join onto (look back at Figure 14.3). They cannot help but align to each other as they are all referenced to the same anchor (represented by the gates). The work scope for this set should include basic guides outlining the framework, together with foundation training for project sponsors, project managers, line managers and team members. You should also have project coaches available to guide newcomers through the framework – training, on its own, is seldom sufficient.

> *After completing your overall design you should implement the staged framework itself. The benefit of putting this in place first is that it provides the fundamental foundation block and hooks that all the associated processes need to lock onto.*

The choice of the next implementation projects is critical (Project set 3). They must be those you know how to do and what to do *and* which will remain stable once in place. They should be ones which, when coupled with those that follow, will ensure you progress up the benefits chain. In this way, you build a launch pad very quickly from which you can progress the remainder of the implementation. Decision making and establishing a project list should be a high priority.

You may then undertake your remaining projects (Project set 4) in any order, at any time, creating continual change toward your objective rather than moving from island to island in any predesigned order. This does not mean to say that there will be no critical dependencies between projects nor any overall programme plan. On the contrary, in order to have this flexibility you must be sure of your high level design and of the possible configurations you may pass through on the way. It may also be that the particular systems or related processes in your organisation will require some elements to be completed before others. You need to consider this in the investigative stages of each project and design your operational configurations accordingly. To do this, you may need to implement temporary systems, structures and processes along the way. For example, you will need to have a project portfolio list very soon after putting the staged framework in place, if you're to maintain control. That does not mean you must have the finished database, fully networked and operating on everyone's desk. A simple spreadsheet may be sufficient to start you off. It could even be beneficial as a prototype to help you decide the design requirements for the final system.

You should also try to ensure that one of the early projects provides management information and reporting which will be useful to the decision makers and others involved in the process. Reporting makes the process visible and serves as a driver of behaviour. Again, this helps set the scene for a cultural shift. Provided you use the new-found knowledge responsibly, the shift will be in the right direction. If you use the new information to expose 'wrong doers' and punish them, do not be surprised if people become less enthusiastic about the process and work to undermine it.

> *If you use the new information to expose 'wrong doers' and punish them, do not be surprised if people become less enthusiastic about the process and work to undermine it.*

When undertaking any of the projects, do not assume you need do them throughout your whole organisation at the same time. It is usually better to implement the new way of working on a particular portfolio of cross-functional projects, for example product development. Use this as the vehicle to refine and bed in the new processes, systems and structures and to start growing the new culture. Remember that business projects are usually by nature cross-functional, therefore, you will not be able to implement the framework on a phased basis, function by function. Do take into account, however, that if you implement in a phased way, you will probably come across some boundary issues where people will insist that certain projects are 'outside the new process'. Expect and accept this. Many people will take the opinion that they can move their projects forward quicker outside the project framework and a few of them may be right, in the short term at least. As the disciplines become better established the advantages of working within a known framework will become obvious – projects will meet their objectives.

As the disciplines become better established the advantages of working within a known framework will become obvious – projects will meet their objectives.

As some of your process infrastructure may be broken before you even start, it does not matter in which order the remaining projects are introduced. You choose the order which suits your own circumstances and the timing of when the quest and fog projects come to fruition (Figure 28.3). At the start you will notice inefficiencies but these will reduce as more of the 'final configuration' comes into being. People may even start to solve some problem areas outside the formal programme. As they will be aligned to the core staged framework there will be little danger of conflict. In this way, certain parts of the organisation can adopt certain elements before others if it suits their needs at that point in time. The fact that people do this is evidence that the approach is naturally gaining acceptance and that part of the cultural shift is happening.

Figure 28.3 Implementation of a projects approach

Think of the implementation of a jigsaw. The work from Project set 1 will give you a view of the final picture, although some parts may be fuzzy. Fill in the new pieces as projects are completed. The picture will become clearer as more of the pieces are in place. Do not think of it as building a wall. In a wall it is not possible to put the coping stone on until the bricks below are in place. With a jigsaw, you can put any pieces in place as and when you see fit.

WHAT DO I DO WITH THE EXISTING PROJECT PROCESSES? A CONVERGENT STRATEGY

You will most probably have some parts of your organisation already using a projects approach. They may also be backed up by excellent good practice tools and guides. Should you ask them to throw these away in favour of an organisation-wide approach which is as yet unproven? If you try this you will meet resistance. Your aim is ensure that change in your business is managed well and properly directed. Your aim is not to force people into a straitjacket process. Make sure you involve the key players who are champions of their local project processes. Have them design the detail of the new process adding whatever they can from their own toolkits. Don't insist they follow the new process from day one. Start off by saying it is for those people in the organisation who have nothing and it is for the senior managers who will act as project sponsors or project board members. You can then ask them to show how their local processes align to the new one. Where possible, ask them to adopt any new terminology (especially stages, gates and key roles) and any templates. Over time, the local processes will converge into a single 'best way'.

How long will this take?

The time taken to establish a viable project framework depends very much on your starting point. If you are an organisation that is used to cross-functional working and puts more emphasis on role than formal job description, much of the culture will already have been established. If, however, your organisation is a very functional-led hierarchy where rank is highly prized, the change will be a shock. If you have stable leadership, the speed with which you can move forward will be greater than if your leadership suffers frequent change. In fact, if your organisation is one where change is relentless, make sure that you implement in bite-sized chunks so that at least part of the jigsaw is established prior to a change at the top. Many implementations have failed as they never quite got there before the old top team went. Nevertheless, a period of two to three years for fully establishing a project framework, fully integrated into the business (shown on pp. 173–175) would not be uncommon.

A staged process together with its associated documentation and training can be launched within three to six months of a decision to move forward. After that aim to have another major piece of the jigsaw in place every three to six months. Remember that one factor which will influence your rate of change is the state of the business processes and culture in aspects which influence projects. The better they are, the quicker you can move forward.

BEING HELD ACCOUNTABLE

If you are an invisible project sponsor or manager on an invisible project which few people know exists, let alone what it is for, you may take your accountabilities less seriously than if your name is published to the organisation in a list against the project with key milestones appended. In the former case failure can be hidden, objectives can be recast to suit performance. However, in the latter you are being asked to deliver on a 'promise' and being held accountable. This may sound hard, but remember that the project has been approved in full knowledge of the risks and that stopping the project, if circumstances dictate it, is a success – you are not expected to be Superman or Wonder Woman.

A final thought ...

Books are not enough. They educate. They inform. They enlighten. But ...

'People create change ... people constrain change.'
EDDIE OBENG'S THIRD LAW OF CHANGE

Doing it by the book is never enough

Appendix A: Glossary

All cross-references are shown in *italics*.

Accountability What you can count on a person doing. That person and only that person can be called to account if something they have accountability for is not done.

Activity Individual components of work that must be undertaken to complete the stages of the project. Each activity should be defined in terms of its start and end dates and the name of the person accountable for its completion.

Approval The term used when an individual accepts a deliverable as fit for purpose such that the project can continue.

Assumption An assumption is made when an unknown is taken to be a fact. Assumptions can be tested using sensitivity analysis and often pose a *risk* to a project.

Authorisation The decision which triggers the allocation of the resources and funding needed to carry on the project and provide the project sponsor and project manager with the authority to undertake the project or the part of the project which has been authorised.

Backcasting Using the desired end result of a project as the principle basis and starting point for planning so that planning is initially conducted working backwards from project completion.

Bar chart Graphical representation of activities within a project over time. Each activity's duration is shown as a bar, the ends of which correspond to the start and end dates. A bar chart is also known as a Gantt chart.

Baseline The project plan you use to track progress against during a project. The baseline plan includes, start and finish dates of activities, resources, scope and costs. The baseline cost is often called a *project budget*.

Benefits Quantified increases in revenue, decreases in costs, reductions in working capital and/or increase in performance which occur directly as a result of a project.

Blueprint A description of the 'future business or organisation,' its working practices and processes, the information it requires and the technology that will be used. This term is usually used in the context of (business) programme management.

Brainstorming A technique for generating ideas in a group.

Budget Planned, approved cost for the project. See also *baseline*.

Business case A document providing the justification for undertaking (or for continuing) a project, defining the financial and other benefits which the project is expected to deliver together with the schedule and other constraints within which the project is to be undertaken. This is usually prepared in two stages. The first is the initial business case which is prepared for the Detailed Investigation Gate review. The second is the full business case which is prepared for the Development Gate review.

Business Programme A Business Programme comprises current benefit generating business activities together with a loosely coupled but tightly aligned *portfolio* of programmes and projects, aimed at realising the benefits of part of a business plan or strategy.

Business programme office A *support office*, which supports the roles of the Business Programme Sponsor and Manager.

Business programme plan A part of the organisation's business plan which focuses on the targets (benefits) and resources of a particular *business programme*.

Capabilities Building blocks of systems, process and competence which are combined with other capabilities to provide an organisation with operational potential.

Capacity buffer A *critical chain* term. Protective time placed between projects within the drum resource.

Change control The formal process through which changes to the *project plan* are introduced and approved. Changes are recorded on a change log. (Do not confuse with the *management of change*.)

Closure Formal 'end point' of a project either because it is completed or because it has been *terminated* early. Closure is formally documented in a closure report.

Conditions of satisfaction Conditions, which if met, enable one to objectively declare a project a success. These should be indicative of *benefits* realisation. *Recognition Events*® and *Value Flashpoints*® are special types of condition, used in the Isochron methodology.

Configuration management A discipline, normally supported by software tools, which gives management precise control over the *deliverables* of a project (or components of an operational environment) and ensures that the correct version of each part of a system is known and documented.

Constraint Defined restriction or limitation imposed on a project or operational work.

Contingency plan An alternative plan of action which should be followed in the event of a risk occurring.

Cost plan Document detailing items of cost associated with a project, in categories (work packages) relating to the schedule plan. See also *budget* and *baseline*.

Critical chain The critical chain of a single project is the sequence of dependent events that prevents the project from being completed in a shorter interval, given finite resources.

Critical path The path through a series of activities, taking into account dependencies, in which late completion of activities will have an impact on the project end date, or delay a key *milestone*.

Critical success factors Factors that will ensure achievement of success criteria. Note: success criteria are criteria to be used for judging if the project is successful (see *conditions of satisfaction*).

Culture Culture comprises two elements:

1 The norms and behaviours of a group (the way we do things here!).

2 Unconscious programming of the mind leading to a set of similar collective habits, behaviours and mindsets.

Deliverable Output produced by the project in the process of achieving the business objectives, e.g. a report, system or product. Each key deliverable should be defined in the *project definition* section of the *business case* document and represented by a *milestone* on the project plan. Alternative words are 'product', 'work product' and 'output'.

Dependency A constraint on the sequence and timing of activities in a project. Activities may be dependent on other activities within the same project (internal dependency) or on activities/deliverables from other projects (*interdependency*).

Detailed Investigation Stage The second stage within the project framework when a feasibility study is undertaken to choose the best solution and when that solution is defined in sufficient detail for delivery to start.

Detailed plan Developed throughout the project, from the *summary plan*, breaking down the forthcoming stage into manageable work packages and activities.

Duration The amount of time required to complete an *activity*. It is calculated as the finish date – the start date.

Earned value (1) A management technique which analyses project progress by comparing the actual money or hours (or other measure) planned with the value of the work achieved (measured on the same basis) and the amount actually spent. Mostly used on contractor-based projects.

Earned value (2) A method for integrating scope, schedule and resources and for measuring project performance. It compares the amount of work which was planned with what was actually earned with what was actually spent to determine if cost and schedule performance are as planned (PMI).

Effective Successful at realising an objective.

Efficient Providing progress or performance with minimal waste of resources.

Emergency project A project which is required as a result of a business issue which will severely damage the organisation if not addressed without delay. These projects may cause previously committed projects to be allocated a lower priority or to be *terminated* in order to release resources.

Escalation To increase the awareness and ownership of a problem or *issue* to a level in the organisation where the required resources, expertise and/or authority can be applied in order to resolve that issue.

Feeder buffer A feeder buffer protects the start of a *critical chain* activity from a delay of an upstream dependent non-critical chain activity. A project can have many feeder buffers.

Fog project (walking in a fog) Formally known as an open project, this type of project occurs when you are unsure of both what is to be done and how.

Gate The point, preceding each stage, at which all new information converges and which serves for:

- quality control checks;
- prioritisation;
- a point from which to plan forward;
- a go/no go decision point.

Health check A tool used in project reviews to assess the overall risk associated with the project.

Idea A possibility for a new or enhanced capability, system, service or product. This is written up as a *proposal*.

Impact The influence one thing has on another, with respect to how changes in one bring about changes in the other.

Impact assessment A study undertaken to determine the effect of an *issue* on the project. An impact assessment is required as part of *change control*.

Interdependency If Project B requires a *deliverable* from Project A in order to achieve its objective, project B is dependent on project A. Dependency is when a deliverable is passed from one project to another.

Internal Rate of Return (IRR) The discount rate at which the value of the opportunity will be zero. Note that in concept, the principle is that the higher the IRR, the 'better' the opportunity. However, this guideline should be used with caution.

Issue A circumstance (event, lack of knowledge, etc.) that has occurred and which will affect the success of a project. They are recorded on an issues log. An issue can either be resolved within the project as defined or a change may be required to accommodate it.

Late activity An *activity* which is forecast to end later than the *baseline* plan finish date. This is reported on a late activities report.

Life cycle A sequence of defined *stages* over the full duration of a project, i.e. initial investigation, detailed investigation, develop and test, trial, release.

Link A relationship between *dependent* activities.

Management of change A name often used to describe the process of transforming and organisation from one state to another. Not to be confused with *change control*, which is a technique used on projects to ensure that alterations to the project time, scope, *benefits* and cost are introduced in a regularised way.

Milestone A major event (often representing the start of a *stage*) which is used to monitor progress at a summary level. Milestones are activities of zero duration.

Movie project (making a movie) Formally a semi-open project, where the means are known but not the output.

Net Present Value (NPV) The value calculated by projecting the future cash flow and discounting the value of future years' cash at the discount rate to give its notional value today.

Network chart A diagram which shows dependencies between project *activities*. Activities are represented as boxes or nodes and the activity relationship is shown by arrows connecting the nodes. Often called a PERT chart.

Open project See *fog project*.

Opportunity The opposite of a *risk*. An opportunity is a possibility to enhance the project *benefits*. Opportunities are recorded on an opportunity log.

Originator The person who conceives an *'idea'* or need for a new development or enhancement and publishes it in the form of a *proposal*. This person can come from any function or level in the organisation.

Output definition document The fundamental sourcebook describing the project output in terms of 'feel', technology, commercial and customer/user needs. It is the document which integrates all the individual system, process and platform requirements and specifies how they will work together.

Phase A phase is a single project within a phased programme of projects (hence phase 1 project, phase 2 project, etc.). Note the PMI definition of 'phase' equates to the Project Workout definition for *'stage'*.

Pilot A pilot is the ultimate form of testing a new development and its implementation plan prior to committing to the full release. It is undertaken using a sample of potential customers and users. This would normally take place in the *trial stage* although may, in some cases, be treated as a limited release.

Portfolio A grouping or bundle of programmes and/or projects which are collected together for management convenience.

Portfolio management This is a process that aligns a portfolio of projects to the strategy of the organisation. As such, it is an integral part of business planning. It should enable an organisation to select those projects which will create the greatest value for the organisation, taking into account risk, strategic balance and constraints.

Post-Implementation Review (PIR) A review, three to six months after the end of the project, to assess whether the expected *benefits* and performance measures are being achieved. This checks the effectiveness of a project as opposed its efficiency which is reviewed as part of project *closure*.

Programme Programmes are a tightly coupled and tightly aligned grouping of projects.

Progress bar chart A bar chart which shows the actual and forecast dates for each *activity* compared with the *baseline* plan dates.

Progress report Regular report from the project manager to the project sponsor and other stakeholders summarising the progress of a project including key events, milestones not achieved and issues.

Product A term used in some project methods in place of *deliverable*. Hence the terms 'product breakdown structure', which identifies, in a hierarchical way, the deliverable/products which are required, and 'product flow diagram', which identifies each deliverable's derivation and the dependencies between them.

Project A project, in a business environment, is:

- a finite piece of work (i.e. it has a beginning and an end)
- undertaken in stages;
- within defined cost and time constraints;
- directed at achieving a stated business benefit.

Project board Body established to monitor the project and to assist the project sponsor in realising the benefits. Sometimes called a steering group or steering board.

Project buffer The project buffer protects the project end date from viability in the duration of the tasks in the *critical chain*. For a single project the size of the buffer depends on the number and duration of the critical chain activities and on the degree of risk associated with each. See also *feeder buffers*.

Project definition A section within the Initial and full *business case* which defines a project, i.e. what will be done, how it will be delivered and what business need the project supports.

Project manager Person accountable for managing a project on a day-to-day basis, from start to finish, to ensure successful implementation within agreed cost, schedule and quality targets.

Project plan The supporting detail to the *project definition* which details the schedule, resource and costs for the project. It can be in outline or detail.

Project portfolio A grouping or bundle of projects which are collected together for management convenience, e.g. the collection of projects sponsored by an individual is his or her sponsorship portfolio; those project managed by a person is a management portfolio; the full set of projects within a organisation is the organisation portfolio.

Project review group The term used in this book for the body accountable for the project authorisation process. There is no industry standard for this.

Project sponsor The person who sees a commercial possibility in an idea and who agrees to take ownership of the proposal. Once a project is approved, the project sponsor is accountable for realising the benefits to the business. Typically, he/she will:

- chair the project board;
- appoint the project manager;
- represent the business and users in key project decisions;
- approve key deliverables;
- resolve issues which are outside the project manager's control;
- ensure that the delivered solution matches the business needs;
- be the primary risk taker.

Project Support Office (PSO) A group set up to provide certain administrative and other services to the project manager and team. Sometimes a PSO provides its services to many projects in parallel. See also *support office*.

Proposal A short document prepared, by the *originator*, for the initial investigation gate review, which outlines the proposed project, its fit with current strategy and, if known, the impact on the organisation, broad estimates of benefits and cost, and expected time to completion.

Quality The totality of features and characteristics of a *deliverable* that bear on its ability to satisfy stated and implied needs. Also defined as 'fitness for purpose' or 'conforms to requirements'. Hence 'quality criteria' are the conditions which a deliverable must meet in order to be accepted as fit for purpose.

Quality Plan A document defining the quality policies that will be applied on a project. Hence 'quality planning' is determining which quality standards are necessary and how to apply them.

Quality Review A review of a *deliverable* against an established set of quality criteria.

Quest project (going on a quest) Quest projects are formally known as semi-closed projects. You are clear what is to be done but have no idea about how to do it.

RAG (Red–Amber–Green) A simple status reporting method,

enabling the reader of a report to grasp very quickly whether a project is likely to achieve its objectives. RAG stands for Red–Amber–Green.

- Red means there are significant issues with the project that the project team and project sponsor are unable to address.
- Amber means there are problems with the project but the team has them under control.
- Green means that the project is going well with no significant issues, although it may be late or forecast to overspend.

The RAG status is usually based on the project manager's own assessment of the situation and is useful for highlighting those projects which may have difficulties. Some organisations also have RAG status set automatically by systems, e.g. when a project is forecast to overspend.

Ready for Service (RFS) The *milestone* prior to the *release stage*, by when all prerequisite project work, testing and trials have been completed and full operational support is in place.

Recognition Event® A real-life happening that when it occurs tells a sponsor and other stakeholders that one particular expectation of the project plan has been met. This is a term used in the Isochron method. See also *conditions of satisfaction*.

Release Generic term used to denote when an output from a project is put into service, e.g. a product can be used by a customer under standard terms and conditions (i.e. not trial agreement), handover of a customised service for the customer to start using, a system started to be used, new process operational. It must not be confused with *ready for service* which is the point when all capabilities are ready to use but have not yet been put to use.

Release stage The final stage in the staged project framework during which the final output is launched and put into service.

Resource buffer A resource buffer is used in critical chain schedule management to provide early warning, from one *critical chain* activity to another critical chain activity, for an activity to start.

Resource manager A person in each unit and function who is accountable for knowing the future assignment of resources to processes and projects.

Responsibility What a person is or feels, responsible for. It assumes they have a commitment, beyond their own *accountabilities*, to act responsibly to ensure the project objectives are met.

Review A process used as a check point at which a deliverable or the project in full, can be evaluated against its business objectives. *Gates* are a special review point. Reviewers are contributors to a decision and do not actually make the decisions. See *approval*.

Risk Potential occurrence or uncertainty that would jeopardise the success of a project. These can be split into business risks, which impact benefits realisation, and project risks, which impact project delivery. Risks should be recorded on a risk log, continuously assessed and mitigation action taken.

Semi-closed project See *quest project*.

Semi-open project See *movie project*.

Simple project A project where the end point can be seen clearly from the detailed investigation gate. Typically, simple projects consume little resource or have their own separate resources which cannot be allocated to other projects.

Single point accountability The concept that any *activity*, or *work package*, at any level in the *work breakdown structure* has only one, named person accountable for it.

Slippage See *late activities*.

Sponsor See *project sponsor*.

Stage The natural high level breakpoints in the project *life cycle* (e.g. initial investigation, detailed investigation, develop and test, trial and release).

Stakeholder Any person or group who has an interest in the project or its outcome. Typically some support it, some are neutral and other are antagonists.

Stakeholder Influence Map A diagram used to depict the influence that individual stakeholders have on others. The objective is to identify the routes by which key influencers and decision makers can be enrolled in the project's objectives.

Subproject A tightly aligned and tightly coupled part of a project. Subprojects are usually run to their own staged *life cycle*.

Success A successful project is one which achieves its business objectives and realises the expected benefits. It may be that it is also delivered within the defined time, cost and quality constraints, but in the 'real world' that is not always essential. Success is formally measured using *conditions of satisfaction*; however, different *stakeholders* will have their own views on whether a project is successful, regardless of this.

Summary plan Initial part of the evolution of the schedule, resource and cost plan, developed at the start of the project, defining the overall targets and key dates.

Support office A group of people providing administrative and/or specialist services to defined roles in the project management environment. Hence *project support office* and *business programme office*.

Termination The premature *closure* of a project due to an issue which cannot be addressed or because the risks have become too high.

Theory of Constraints The theory expounded by Eli Goldratt which led to the development of *critical chain* schedule management.

Trial stage A trial of a capability in same environment as the customer or user will use it. Often denoted as a beta trial under special trial agreements.

Value driver The things which increase revenue, decrease cost or increase asset value in the organisation.

Value Flashpoint® A *recognition event* at which a particular project cash benefit starts to be realised. In the Isochron method, value flashpoints are used to map financial implications of the project to the organisation's accounts and ties all project activity and investment to the points where benefits start. See also *conditions of satisfaction*.

Value management A technique and process used in the investigative stages of a project for ensuring that deliverables are clearly defined and matched to business needs and that solutions represent value for money whilst remaining fit for their intended purpose. Do not confuse this with *earned value*.

White space Unassigned resources which are available to work on future projects. White space is required at short notice for initial investigations and at medium notice to resource future projects after the detailed investigation gate. Without white space, organisations are unable to change themselves without taking resource from previously authorised and committed work.

Work Breakdown Structure (WBS) A structured hierarchy of *work packages*.

Work Package Generic term used to describe a grouping of *activities*, *stages*, etc. each of which has a defined scope, timescale, cost and a single person accountable for it.

Appendix B:
A project process framework

'Life is one long process of getting tired.'

SAMUEL BUTLER (1612–1680)

Teach me to cheat

How to document and organise your processes can pose a number of problems. In one company I visited, they proudly showed me their process documentation (all to ISO 9001:2008 standards), in lever arch files covering about 5 yards of shelves. I was not impressed and, in fact, they were hoping I wouldn't be. This collection of files was their process before they reorganised it. After a pause, they pulled from the shelf a single, slim volume which was now the process documentation for the entire company. I asked how they managed this remarkable reduction. They told me they 'cheated' and would show me how to do the same. Their documentation was divided into three basic types:

1 Processes.

2 Guides.

3 Templates.

The processes were very simple tabulations stating the activity, who is accountable, the deliverable and who it goes to. In addition, they have a further column which referred to any relevant templates or guides. Flow charts were only used, if necessary, for clarification. The documents were kept very brief and factual with no explanation, education or guidance.

The guides were the 'education' documents. They contained the principles, the methods, best practice and checklists.

The templates were the actual documents. They not only contained the titles of each document but also described what each section was for, rather like I have on p. 298. Each template was supplemented by a product description, describing its purpose, the content, the quality criteria and who should review and approve it.

The slim document I was shown was in fact the processes only. The remaining documents were the guides and templates. These were all very necessary documents but not needed all the time. Most users could work from the process alone; if they needed more, the cross-reference was supplied. Another advantage is that the system requires very little administration and also lends itself to intranet publication with the process at the core and the guides and templates hyperlinked in the appropriate places.

Process *framework* – some methodological context!

A suggested process framework and its component parts are included in Figure B.1, which shows the main processes and the information which passes between them. In the suggested approach, each process is based on the separate roles, introduced throughout the book (see Chapter 4 for project roles and Chapter 14 for business programme roles). For example, the executive team would undertake the 'Direct and review business programmes' process; the project manager would undertake 'Control a project'. The separation of process by role, for management processes, ensures that the processes can be targeted at the appropriate users, without burying them in detail which has to be undertaken by others. Do note, however, that whilst writing processes in this form works well for management processes, which are essentially very iterative, it is not so good for more traditional, sequentially based processes, where there is less iteration. The UK's Prince2 method takes a similar role based approach for the management aspects. Oddly enough, the UK's Managing Successful Programmmes method (MSP) is rather muddled on this point, with the Senior Responsible Owner and Programme Manager roles combined in single processes, thereby losing the very clarity the roles are meant to promote. The PMI's process set is more difficult to use in an enterprise approach, as the strong distinction between 'sponsoring' roles and 'managing roles' is missing. For example, in PMI's PMBoK, the processes are all aligned around the project manager, with no processes for the project sponsor role. Further, the method makes little distinction between 'phase' and 'project', making it weak in the areas of starting projects, starting stages (gating) and closing phases and projects. You will also find the distinction between 'portfolio' and 'programme' emerging in many methods currently being written. The logic is that a portfolio may comprise both projects and programmes. In practice I have not always found this approach helpful. Taking it to an extreme, any programme which has sub-programmes immediately becomes a 'portfolio' and so, presumably, if this happened during the undertaking of a programme, the leadership team would suddenly take on a new set of 'roles' (e.g. portfolio manager) and use a different process. The distinction becomes rather academic and I have found the 'business programme', as used in this book, serves both the portfolio and programme use. Business programmes can have 'sub-programmes', and projects can have 'sub-projects' or be grouped into 'project portfolios' under a single business case. Too much definition and too many processes will restrict you. Keep things simple and open. Programme and project management are simply effective ways to manage certain types of work and should not be a dogma to straitjacket organisations in the face of common sense.

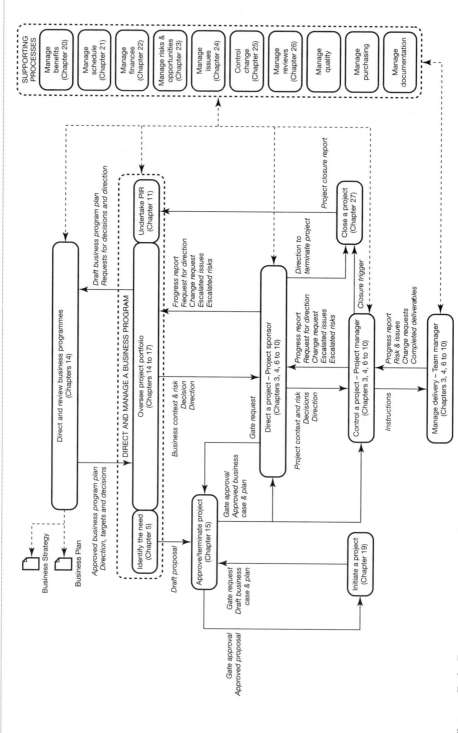

Figure B.1 Process components

The overall process architecture shows, in a single diagram, the key processes and interactions for a complete benefits-driven programme and project approach.

Process *framework* – the component parts

The processes are described as follows.

Direct and review business programmes

The purpose of this process is to ensure the organisation has a defined strategy and business plan, so that the business plan is segmented into discrete and manageable business programmes and appropriate targets are set. The business programmes should have as few interdependencies as possible; however, where such interdependencies exists, they should be managed through this process. This is often call 'portfolio management ' and is the accountability of the executive team.

Direct and manage a business programme

The purpose of this process is to ensure the targets for the delegated part of the business plan are met. This includes overseeing the full scope of work for the programme, including the project portfolio and any non-project work, to ensure the required benefits are realised. The roles of business programme sponsor and business programme manager are key in this process. Two important elements, which relate to project management are:

- identify the need, which is the means by which new projects are initiated (see Chapter 5);
- undertake post implementation review, which is the means by which the effectiveness of a project is assessed (see Chapter 11).

Approve/terminate a project

The purpose of this process is to ensure each stage of the project is started in the knowledge that the project is still required, has a viable plan and the risks are acceptable. In addition, the process is used to suspend (place on hold) a project over which there are doubts as to its viability and, if necessary, terminate it (see Chapter 15). I have not presumed who the decision makers at the gates should be. In practice, most organisations create a table with a list of criteria and who has the delegated authority to make the decisions. This is very organisation specific.

Direct and manage a project

The purpose of this process is to ensure the business objectives of the project are met through the efficient and effective creation of the project outputs and deliverables. It comprises a number of elements:

- Directing a project, which is undertaken by the project sponsor to ensure the business interests of the organisation undertaking the project are paramount.
- Initiating a project, which is undertaken by the project manager, supported by the team, to ensure the project is properly set up and planned (see Chapter 19).
- Controlling a project, which is undertaken by the project manager, supported by the team, to ensure each stage of the project is managed throughout its life.
- Closing a project, which is undertaken by the project manager, supported by the team, to ensure the project is closed, whether because it has been completed or because it has been terminated early (see Chapter 27).

Managing delivery

The purpose of this process is to ensure the deliverables from the project are developed to the right quality, within the cost and time constraints. This process is undertaken by the team manager, supported by the project team members. Specialist processes would be used for undertaking the work itself.

Project frameworks

In Chapter 3, I proposed that a single project framework is used across the whole organisation and that this is tailored to reflect the different types of project undertaken. The advantage is that, top-down, all projects will look similar to senior management, who will invariably have to sponsor many different types of project. It also simplifies the roll-up and collation of portfolio reporting (Chapter 17). However, I have come across organisations that have a number of different project frameworks, with different names and stage numbers. These tend to cluster different types of project around the different project frameworks and as such have a number of different reporting systems and process sets. Usually they arrive in this situation because that was where they started; different parts of the organisation had their own methods and did not want to lose their 'independence'. I have never seen an organisation arrive at this approach 'by design'. That does not mean the approach is wrong, it is simply different and can be highly effective as long as the organisation accepts the additional overhead that multiple systems and processes leads to. However, do keep in mind that projects are there for a purpose and do not slice project frameworks up on disciplinary lines: I still see this with 'IT projects ' under an IT Director and 'business projects ' under 'business directors'. When will they learn?

Supporting processes

In addition to the above management processes, there are a number of supporting processes, which I have shown on the right of Figure B.1. If I was running an organisation, I would not want each separate area within it using a different approach to risk management, for example. The supporting processes are there to ensure that all the techniques which are essential for effective programme and project management are used by all role holders at all levels. This simplifies reporting and communication dramatically. It also enables you to have a more cost effective tools strategy. Most of the topics essential to project management are contained in this book; however, you may wish to add others, to reflect the needs of your organisation. As examples, I have included 'manage quality', 'manage purchasing' and 'manage documentation ' in the list. Others you may consider are 'manage defects', 'manage transition', 'manage stakeholders and communications', 'manage reporting' and 'manage planning'.

Tailoring is the key

Not all organisations will want exactly the same set of processes and it is possible to assemble these in a number of different ways in order to emphasise different approaches or reflect an organisation's culture. For example, in Figure B.1, I have shown the gate requests going from 'Direct a project' as I have taken the view that as it is the project sponsor's project, he/she is the person who should make the request. This approach emphasises the role of the project sponsor as a leader, rather than letting them abdicate the role to the project manager. Other approaches may show the gate request going from the project manager, after verifying it with the project sponsor. Neither approach is better than the other; they are 'differently right' and a matter of choice. However, one thing you must make sure of is that you maintain consistency across your process set. If you were to take the MSP and Prince2 methods 'as is' you will find there are some different concepts and language used for the same things – they are not mutually consistent. You need to make them consistent by tailoring them and adapting your process flow and language accordingly. In this respect, the UK's Association for Project Management's (APM) Body of Knowledge has an extensive glossary of terms, many with commonly used alternatives. You will find the same happens if you base your approach on PMI's portfolio, project and project set; taken raw, they will lead you to create a process set of extraordinary complexity!

Useful references

The following are the most prominent project management organisations in the world:

APM – Association for Project Management

www.apm.org.uk
The APM is the UK's professional body for project management. Whilst it started with the traditional heavy engineering style projects it has made great strides to widen its appeal to all industry sectors, including general business projects. Its latest Body of Knowledge (5th edition) is an excellent reference of project management terms.

IPMA – International Project Management Association

www.ipma.ch
This is an international body representing about 45 national associations. It is very active in certification, training and conferences and has a very enthusiastic following.

Office of Government Commerce

www.ogc.gov.uk
Home of the United Kingdom's Office of Government Commerce (OGC), which has some 2000 pages of resources for you to pick through, review and adopt!

MSP – Managing Successful Programmes

http://www.ogc.gov.uk/guidance_managing_successful_projects.asp

Managing Successful Programmes (MSP) is the OGC's structured and flexible framework for managing programmes. Unlike many approaches it makes a clear distinction between programmes and projects. MSP's 'programme' is very close to Project Workout's 'business programme'.

PRINCE2

www.ogc.gov.uk/methods_prince_2.asp

The official website for the UK's most prominent standard methodology. If you are in the UK and working with the public sector, you cannot ignore this.

Project Management Institute (PMI)

www.pmi.org

This is the USA's association for professional project managers and the source for the USA's standard. It is well established with chapters all over the world. The USA has a different approach to project management than that which is emerging in the UK and Europe, there being very little emphasis on the importance of sponsorship.

Index